BATMAN BLACK and WHITE

VOLUME TWO

For Archie Goodwin, of course

D E D I C A T I O N

MARK CHIARELLO EDITOR-ORIGINAL SERIES **NICK J. NAPOLITANO** EDITOR-COLLECTED EDITION
VALERIE D'ORAZIO ASSISTANT EDITOR-ORIGINAL SERIES **SCOTT NYBAKKEN** ASSOCIATE EDITOR-COLLECTED EDITION
ROBBIN BROSTERMAN DESIGN DIRECTOR – BOOKS
DIANE NELSON PRESIDENT **DAN DIDIO** AND **JIM LEE** CO-PUBLISHERS **GEOFF JOHNS** CHIEF CREATIVE OFFICER
JOHN ROOD EXECUTIVE VP – SALES, MARKETING & BUSINESS DEVELOPMENT
AMY GENKINS SENIOR VP – BUSINESS & LEGAL AFFAIRS **NAIRI GARDINER** SENIOR VP – FINANCE
JEFF BOISON VP – PUBLISHING PLANNING **MARK CHIARELLO** VP – ART DIRECTION & DESIGN
JOHN CUNNINGHAM VP – MARKETING **TERRI CUNNINGHAM** VP – EDITORIAL ADMINISTRATION
ALISON GILL SENIOR VP – MANUFACTURING & OPERATIONS **HANK KANALZ** SENIOR VP – VERTIGO & INTEGRATED PUBLISHING
JAY KOGAN VP – BUSINESS & LEGAL AFFAIRS, PUBLISHING **JACK MAHAN** VP – BUSINESS AFFAIRS, TALENT
NICK NAPOLITANO VP – MANUFACTURING ADMINISTRATION **SUE POHJA** VP – BOOK SALES
COURTNEY SIMMONS SENIOR VP – PUBLICITY **BOB WAYNE** SENIOR VP – SALES

Cover illustration by Mike Mignola.

B A T M A N   B L A C K   A N D   W H I T E
V O L U M E   T W O

Published by DC Comics. Cover, introduction and compilation Copyright © 2008 DC Comics. All Rights Reserved.

Originally published in single magazine form in GOTHAM KNIGHTS 1–16. Copyright © 2000, 2001 DC Comics.
All Rights Reserved. All characters, the distinctive likenesses thereof and related elements featured
in this publication are trademarks of DC Comics.
The stories, characters and incidents featured in this publication are entirely fictional.
DC Comics does not read or accept unsolicited submissions of ideas, stories or artwork.

DC Comics, 1700 Broadway, New York, NY 10019
A Warner Bros. Entertainment Company
Printed by RR Donnelley, Owensville, MO. 11/8/13. Third Printing.
ISBN: 978-1-56389-917-1

SUSTAINABLE FORESTRY INITIATIVE

Certified Chain of Custody
At Least 20% Certified Forest Content
www.sfiprogram.org
SFI-01042
APPLIES TO TEXT STOCK ONLY

CONTENTS

C O N T E N T S

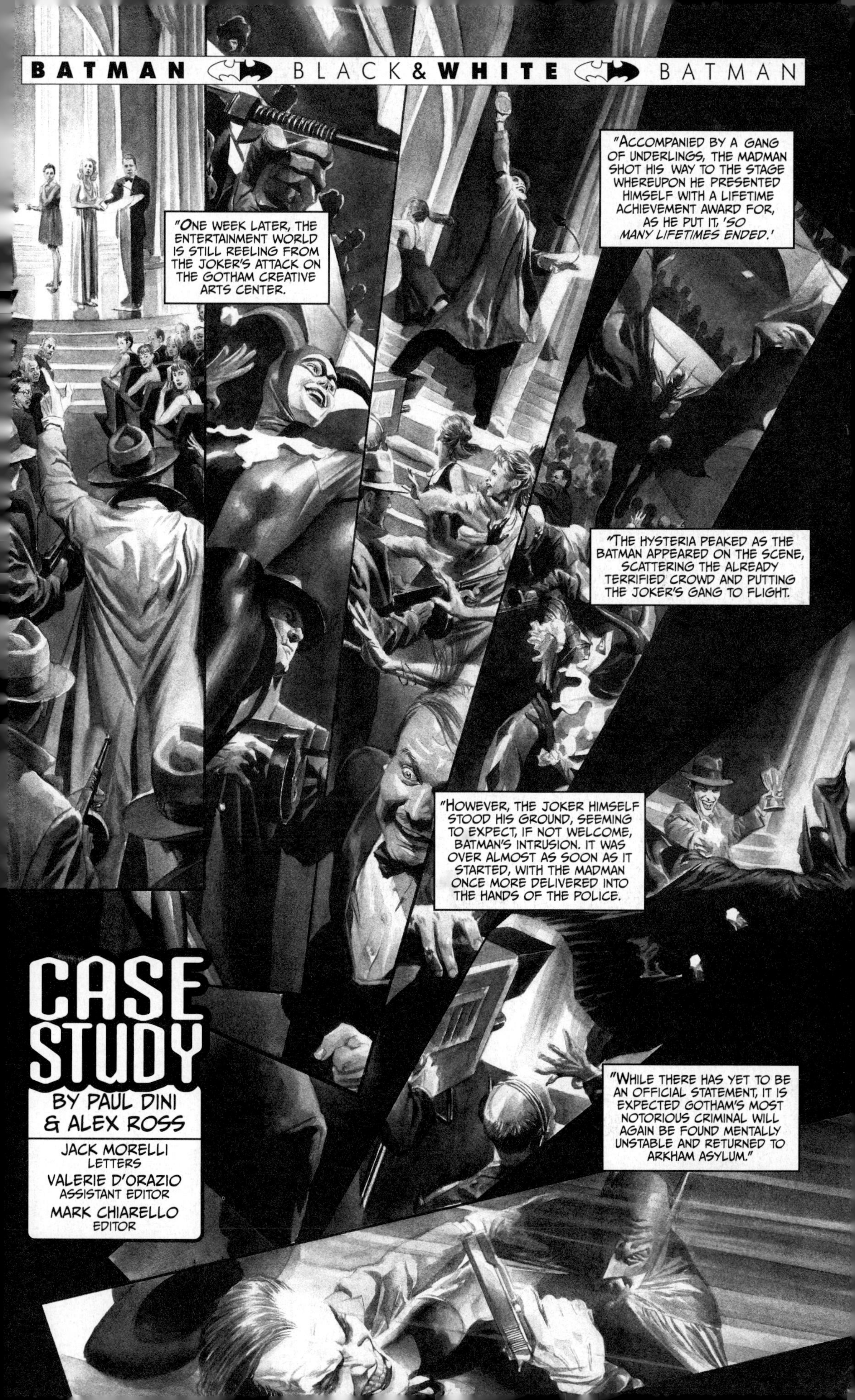
BATMAN BLACK & WHITE BATMAN
"ONE WEEK LATER, THE ENTERTAINMENT WORLD IS STILL REELING FROM THE JOKER'S ATTACK ON THE GOTHAM CREATIVE ARTS CENTER.
"ACCOMPANIED BY A GANG OF UNDERLINGS, THE MADMAN SHOT HIS WAY TO THE STAGE WHEREUPON HE PRESENTED HIMSELF WITH A LIFETIME ACHIEVEMENT AWARD FOR, AS HE PUT IT, 'SO MANY LIFETIMES ENDED.'
"THE HYSTERIA PEAKED AS THE BATMAN APPEARED ON THE SCENE, SCATTERING THE ALREADY TERRIFIED CROWD AND PUTTING THE JOKER'S GANG TO FLIGHT.
"HOWEVER, THE JOKER HIMSELF STOOD HIS GROUND, SEEMING TO EXPECT, IF NOT WELCOME, BATMAN'S INTRUSION. IT WAS OVER ALMOST AS SOON AS IT STARTED, WITH THE MADMAN ONCE MORE DELIVERED INTO THE HANDS OF THE POLICE.
CASE STUDY
BY PAUL DINI & ALEX ROSS
JACK MORELLI LETTERS
VALERIE D'ORAZIO ASSISTANT EDITOR
MARK CHIARELLO EDITOR
"WHILE THERE HAS YET TO BE AN OFFICIAL STATEMENT, IT IS EXPECTED GOTHAM'S MOST NOTORIOUS CRIMINAL WILL AGAIN BE FOUND MENTALLY UNSTABLE AND RETURNED TO ARKHAM ASYLUM."

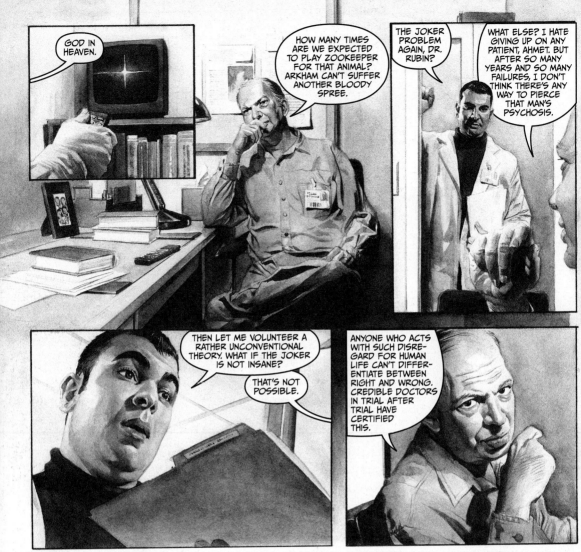

GOD IN HEAVEN.

HOW MANY TIMES ARE WE EXPECTED TO PLAY ZOOKEEPER FOR THAT ANIMAL? ARKHAM CAN'T SUFFER ANOTHER BLOODY SPREE.

THE JOKER PROBLEM AGAIN, DR. RUBIN?

WHAT ELSE? I HATE GIVING UP ON ANY PATIENT, AHMET. BUT AFTER SO MANY YEARS AND SO MANY FAILURES, I DON'T THINK THERE'S ANY WAY TO PIERCE THAT MAN'S PSYCHOSIS.

THEN LET ME VOLUNTEER A RATHER UNCONVENTIONAL THEORY. WHAT IF THE JOKER IS NOT INSANE?

THAT'S NOT POSSIBLE.

ANYONE WHO ACTS WITH SUCH DISRE-GARD FOR HUMAN LIFE CAN'T DIFFER-ENTIATE BETWEEN RIGHT AND WRONG. CREDIBLE DOCTORS IN TRIAL AFTER TRIAL HAVE CERTIFIED THIS.

I UNDERSTAND THAT, SIR. BUT WHILE GOING THROUGH OLD FILES ON THE JOKER, I'VE RECOVERED PARTS OF A REPORT THAT SUGGEST OTHER-WISE.

WHO'S THE RECORDING DOCTOR?

THERE'S NO NAME ON THE REPORT AS IT WAS NEVER OFFICIALLY FILED. BUT THE NOTES REVEAL OBSER-VATIONS GATHERED NOT ONLY THROUGH A STUDY OF THE JOKER HIMSELF, BUT ALSO THROUGH INTERVIEWS WITH OTHER CRIMINALS WHO REMEMBER THE MAN BEFORE HIS, SHALL WE SAY, TRANSFORMATION.

THAT'S HIM IN THE MIDDLE. THE MAN ON THE RIGHT IS EDDIE MARCONE, AN OLD-TIME HOOD WHO AGREED TO BE INTERVIEWED FOR THE REPORT.

"SURE, I REMEMBER JOKER.

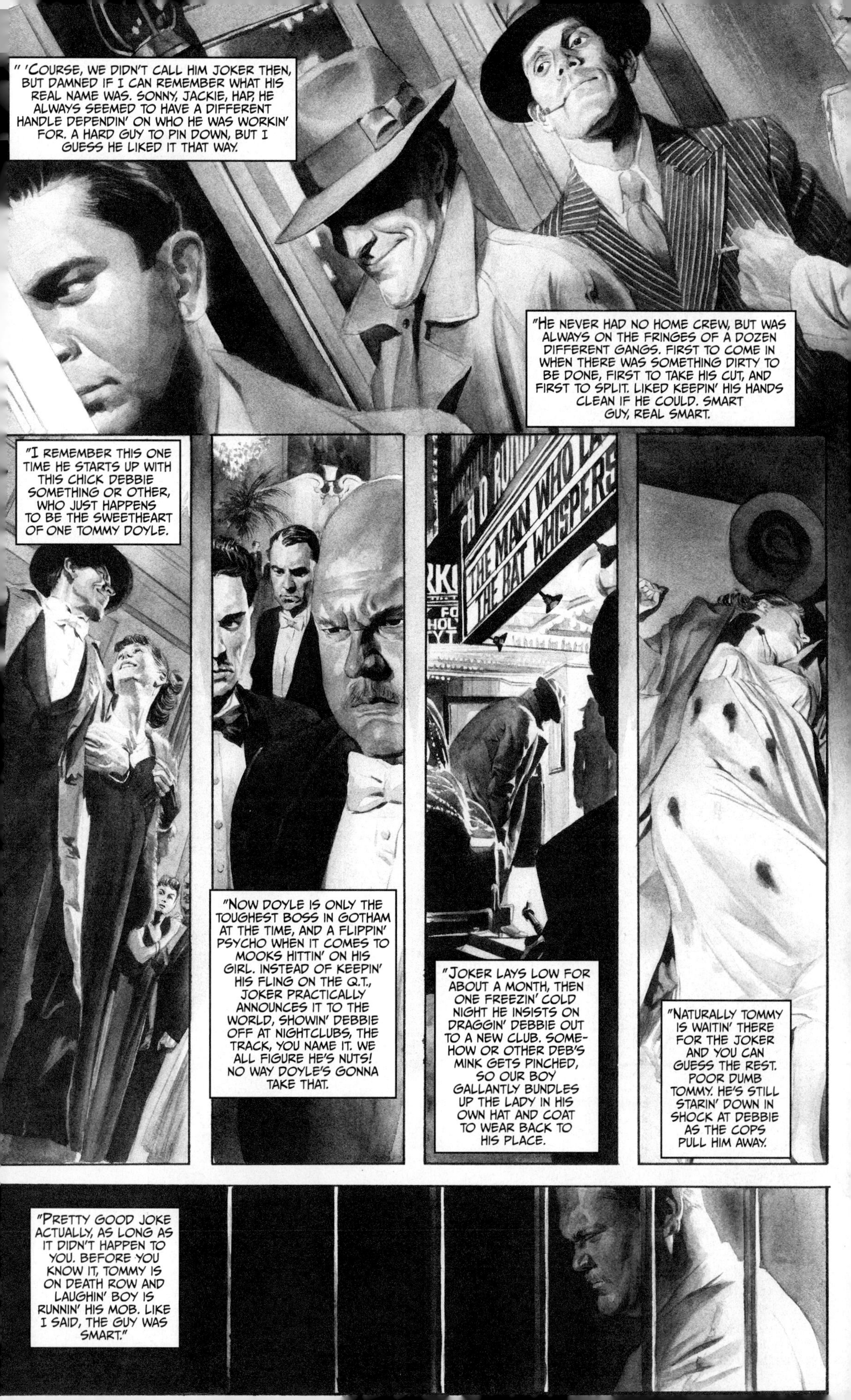
" 'COURSE, WE DIDN'T CALL HIM JOKER THEN, BUT DAMNED IF I CAN REMEMBER WHAT HIS REAL NAME WAS. SONNY, JACKIE, HAP, HE ALWAYS SEEMED TO HAVE A DIFFERENT HANDLE DEPENDIN' ON WHO HE WAS WORKIN' FOR. A HARD GUY TO PIN DOWN, BUT I GUESS HE LIKED IT THAT WAY.
"HE NEVER HAD NO HOME CREW, BUT WAS ALWAYS ON THE FRINGES OF A DOZEN DIFFERENT GANGS. FIRST TO COME IN WHEN THERE WAS SOMETHING DIRTY TO BE DONE, FIRST TO TAKE HIS CUT, AND FIRST TO SPLIT. LIKED KEEPIN' HIS HANDS CLEAN IF HE COULD. SMART GUY, REAL SMART.
"I REMEMBER THIS ONE TIME HE STARTS UP WITH THIS CHICK DEBBIE SOMETHING OR OTHER, WHO JUST HAPPENS TO BE THE SWEETHEART OF ONE TOMMY DOYLE.
"NOW DOYLE IS ONLY THE TOUGHEST BOSS IN GOTHAM AT THE TIME, AND A FLIPPIN' PSYCHO WHEN IT COMES TO MOOKS HITTIN' ON HIS GIRL. INSTEAD OF KEEPIN' HIS FLING ON THE Q.T., JOKER PRACTICALLY ANNOUNCES IT TO THE WORLD, SHOWIN' DEBBIE OFF AT NIGHTCLUBS, THE TRACK, YOU NAME IT. WE ALL FIGURE HE'S NUTS! NO WAY DOYLE'S GONNA TAKE THAT.
THE BAT WHISPERS
"JOKER LAYS LOW FOR ABOUT A MONTH, THEN ONE FREEZIN' COLD NIGHT HE INSISTS ON DRAGGIN' DEBBIE OUT TO A NEW CLUB. SOME-HOW OR OTHER DEB'S MINK GETS PINCHED, SO OUR BOY GALLANTLY BUNDLES UP THE LADY IN HIS OWN HAT AND COAT TO WEAR BACK TO HIS PLACE.
"NATURALLY TOMMY IS WAITIN' THERE FOR THE JOKER AND YOU CAN GUESS THE REST. POOR DUMB TOMMY. HE'S STILL STARIN' DOWN IN SHOCK AT DEBBIE AS THE COPS PULL HIM AWAY.
"PRETTY GOOD JOKE ACTUALLY, AS LONG AS IT DIDN'T HAPPEN TO YOU. BEFORE YOU KNOW IT, TOMMY IS ON DEATH ROW AND LAUGHIN' BOY IS RUNNIN' HIS MOB. LIKE I SAID, THE GUY WAS SMART."

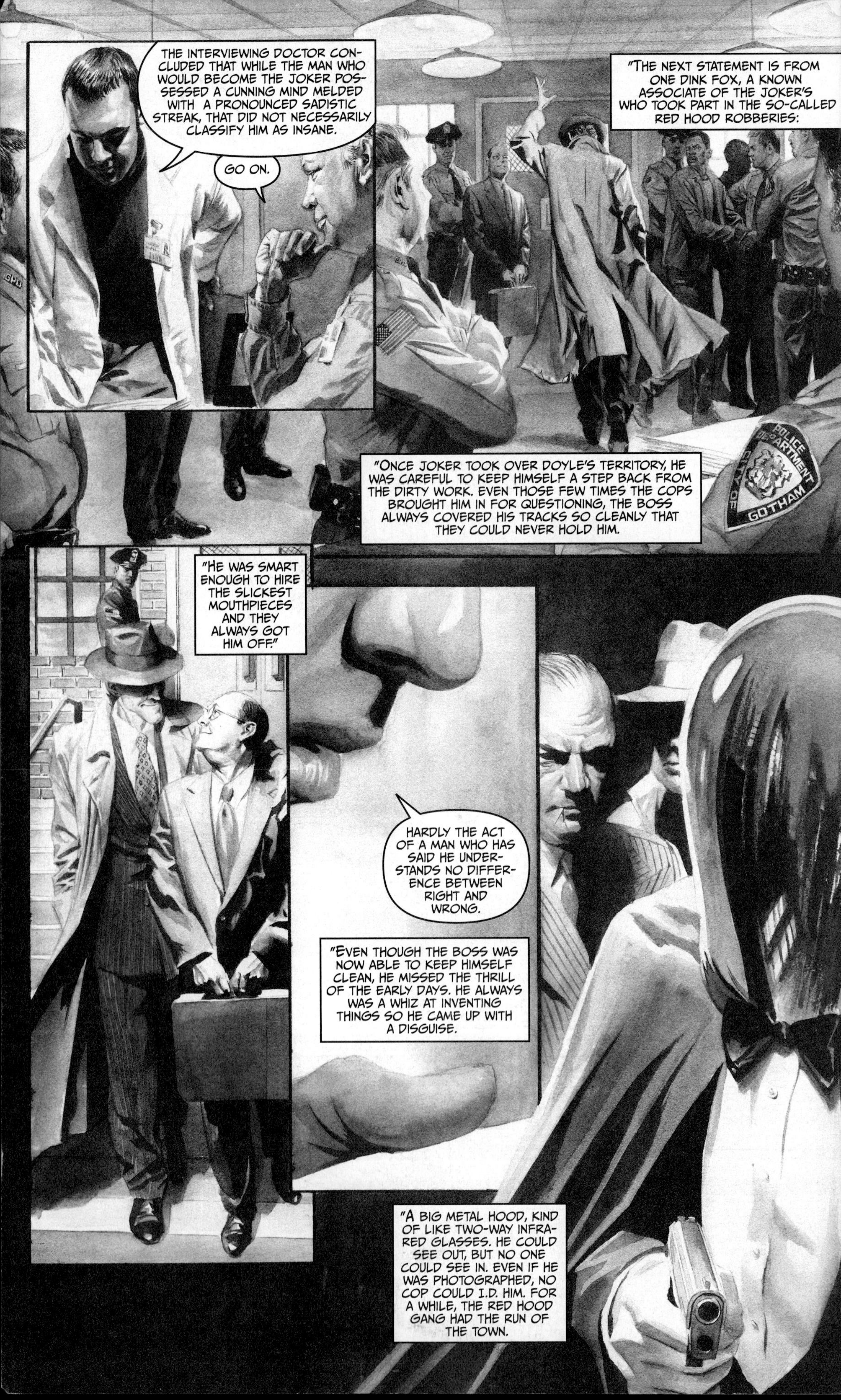
THE INTERVIEWING DOCTOR CONCLUDED THAT WHILE THE MAN WHO WOULD BECOME THE JOKER POSSESSED A CUNNING MIND MELDED WITH A PRONOUNCED SADISTIC STREAK, THAT DID NOT NECESSARILY CLASSIFY HIM AS INSANE.
GO ON.
"THE NEXT STATEMENT IS FROM ONE DINK FOX, A KNOWN ASSOCIATE OF THE JOKER'S WHO TOOK PART IN THE SO-CALLED RED HOOD ROBBERIES:
"ONCE JOKER TOOK OVER DOYLE'S TERRITORY, HE WAS CAREFUL TO KEEP HIMSELF A STEP BACK FROM THE DIRTY WORK. EVEN THOSE FEW TIMES THE COPS BROUGHT HIM IN FOR QUESTIONING, THE BOSS ALWAYS COVERED HIS TRACKS SO CLEANLY THAT THEY COULD NEVER HOLD HIM.
POLICE DEPARTMENT CITY OF GOTHAM
"HE WAS SMART ENOUGH TO HIRE THE SLICKEST MOUTHPIECES AND THEY ALWAYS GOT HIM OFF."
HARDLY THE ACT OF A MAN WHO HAS SAID HE UNDERSTANDS NO DIFFERENCE BETWEEN RIGHT AND WRONG.
"EVEN THOUGH THE BOSS WAS NOW ABLE TO KEEP HIMSELF CLEAN, HE MISSED THE THRILL OF THE EARLY DAYS. HE ALWAYS WAS A WHIZ AT INVENTING THINGS SO HE CAME UP WITH A DISGUISE.
"A BIG METAL HOOD, KIND OF LIKE TWO-WAY INFRARED GLASSES. HE COULD SEE OUT, BUT NO ONE COULD SEE IN. EVEN IF HE WAS PHOTOGRAPHED, NO COP COULD I.D. HIM. FOR A WHILE, THE RED HOOD GANG HAD THE RUN OF THE TOWN.

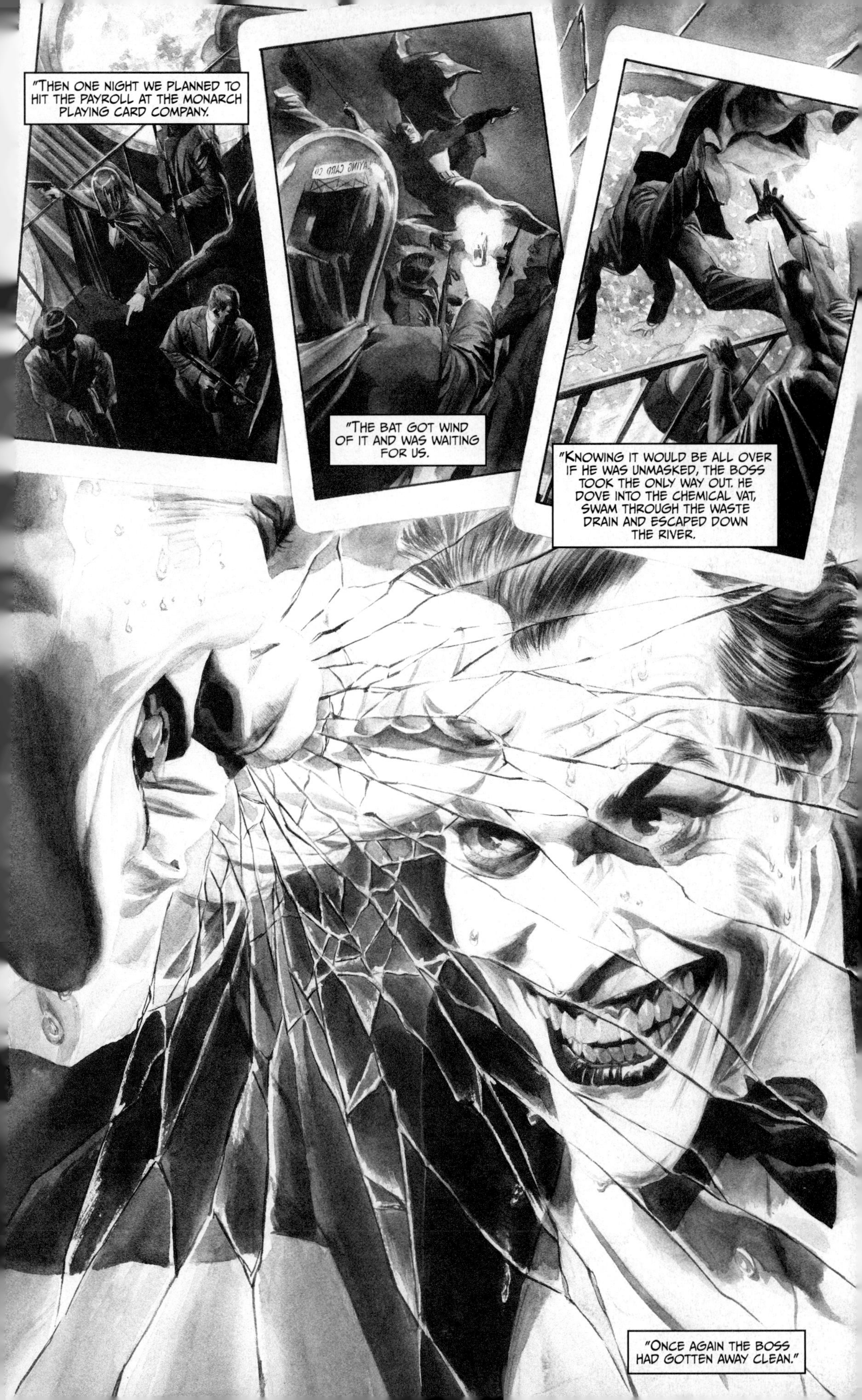
"THEN ONE NIGHT WE PLANNED TO HIT THE PAYROLL AT THE MONARCH PLAYING CARD COMPANY.
"THE BAT GOT WIND OF IT AND WAS WAITING FOR US.
"KNOWING IT WOULD BE ALL OVER IF HE WAS UNMASKED, THE BOSS TOOK THE ONLY WAY OUT. HE DOVE INTO THE CHEMICAL VAT, SWAM THROUGH THE WASTE DRAIN AND ESCAPED DOWN THE RIVER.
"ONCE AGAIN THE BOSS HAD GOTTEN AWAY CLEAN."

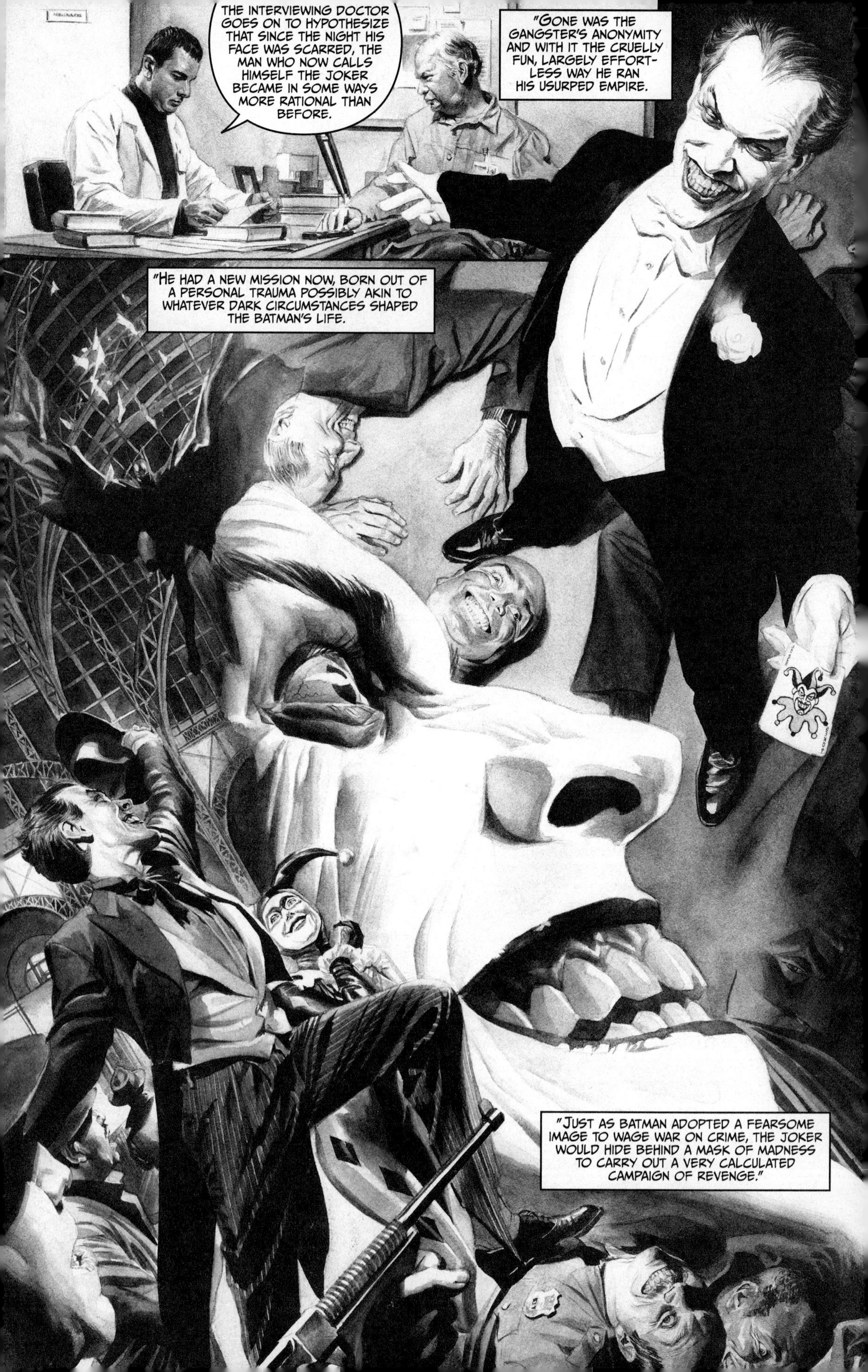
THE INTERVIEWING DOCTOR GOES ON TO HYPOTHESIZE THAT SINCE THE NIGHT HIS FACE WAS SCARRED, THE MAN WHO NOW CALLS HIMSELF THE JOKER BECAME IN SOME WAYS MORE RATIONAL THAN BEFORE.
"GONE WAS THE GANGSTER'S ANONYMITY AND WITH IT THE CRUELLY FUN, LARGELY EFFORTLESS WAY HE RAN HIS USURPED EMPIRE.
"HE HAD A NEW MISSION NOW, BORN OUT OF A PERSONAL TRAUMA POSSIBLY AKIN TO WHATEVER DARK CIRCUMSTANCES SHAPED THE BATMAN'S LIFE.
"JUST AS BATMAN ADOPTED A FEARSOME IMAGE TO WAGE WAR ON CRIME, THE JOKER WOULD HIDE BEHIND A MASK OF MADNESS TO CARRY OUT A VERY CALCULATED CAMPAIGN OF REVENGE."

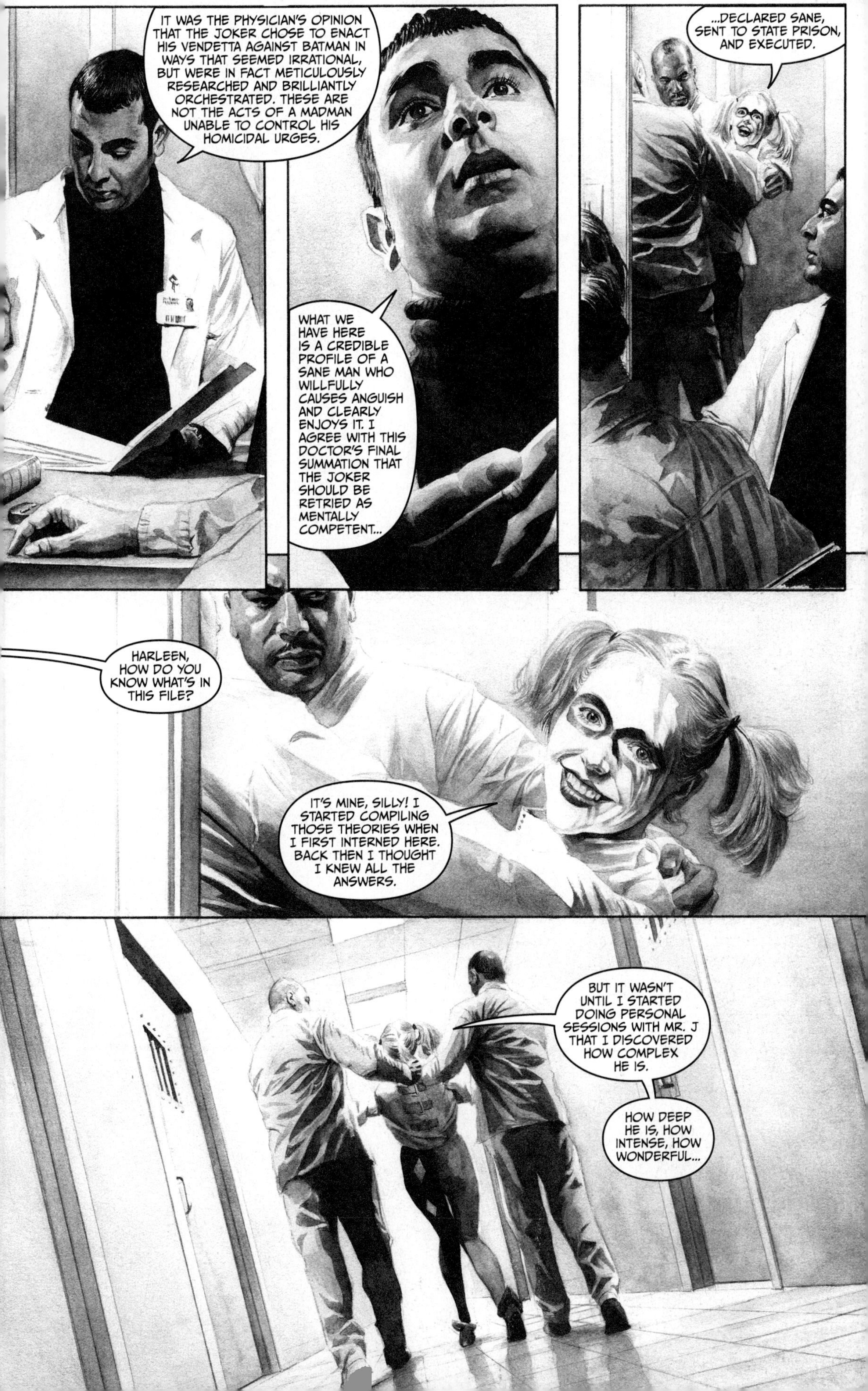
IT WAS THE PHYSICIAN'S OPINION THAT THE JOKER CHOSE TO ENACT HIS VENDETTA AGAINST BATMAN IN WAYS THAT SEEMED IRRATIONAL, BUT WERE IN FACT METICULOUSLY RESEARCHED AND BRILLIANTLY ORCHESTRATED. THESE ARE NOT THE ACTS OF A MADMAN UNABLE TO CONTROL HIS HOMICIDAL URGES.
WHAT WE HAVE HERE IS A CREDIBLE PROFILE OF A SANE MAN WHO WILLFULLY CAUSES ANGUISH AND CLEARLY ENJOYS IT. I AGREE WITH THIS DOCTOR'S FINAL SUMMATION THAT THE JOKER SHOULD BE RETRIED AS MENTALLY COMPETENT...
...DECLARED SANE, SENT TO STATE PRISON, AND EXECUTED.
HARLEEN, HOW DO YOU KNOW WHAT'S IN THIS FILE?
IT'S MINE, SILLY! I STARTED COMPILING THOSE THEORIES WHEN I FIRST INTERNED HERE. BACK THEN I THOUGHT I KNEW ALL THE ANSWERS.
BUT IT WASN'T UNTIL I STARTED DOING PERSONAL SESSIONS WITH MR. J THAT I DISCOVERED HOW COMPLEX HE IS.
HOW DEEP HE IS, HOW INTENSE, HOW WONDERFUL...

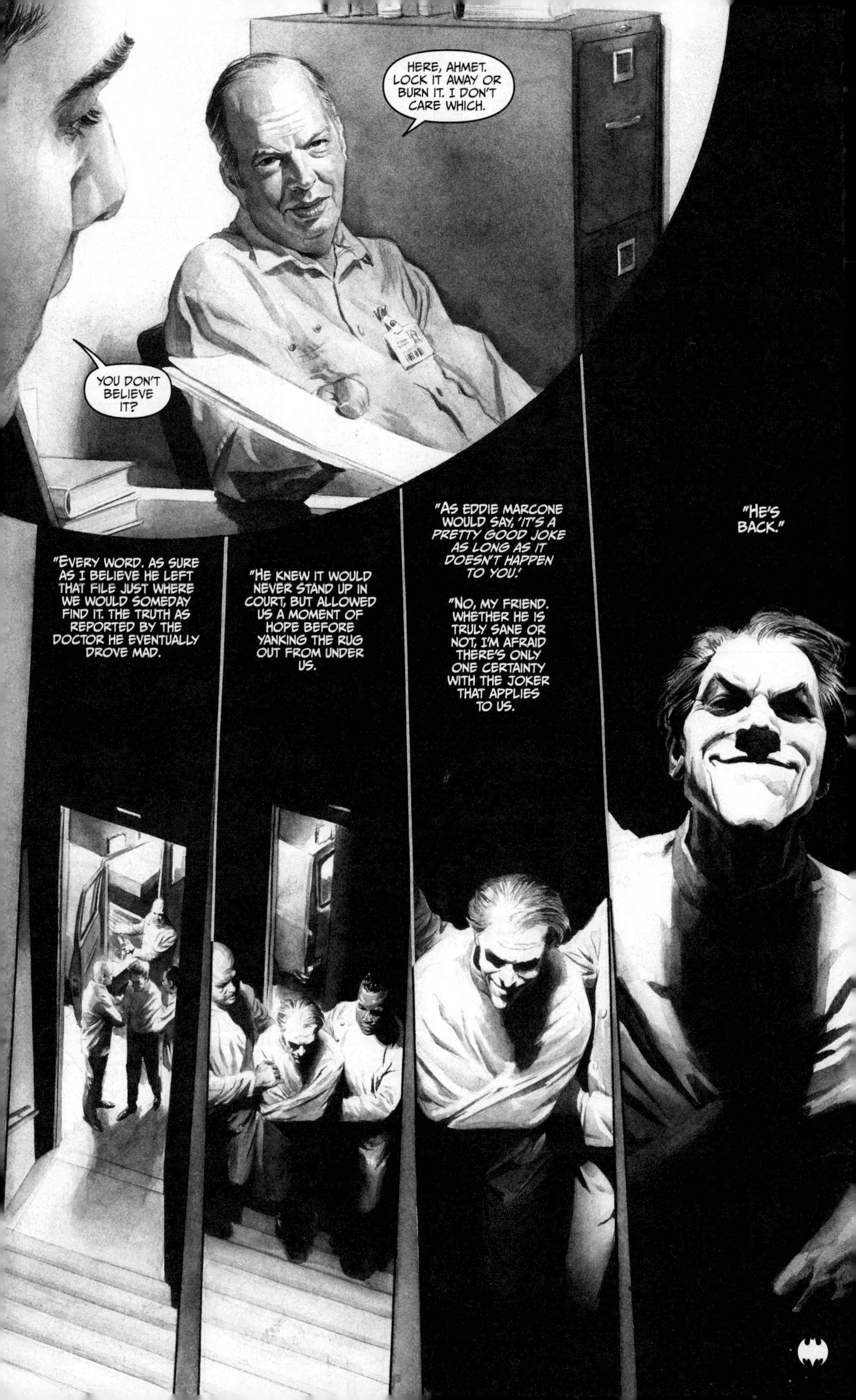
HERE, AHMET. LOCK IT AWAY OR BURN IT. I DON'T CARE WHICH.
YOU DON'T BELIEVE IT?
"EVERY WORD. AS SURE AS I BELIEVE HE LEFT THAT FILE JUST WHERE WE WOULD SOMEDAY FIND IT. THE TRUTH AS REPORTED BY THE DOCTOR HE EVENTUALLY DROVE MAD.
"HE KNEW IT WOULD NEVER STAND UP IN COURT, BUT ALLOWED US A MOMENT OF HOPE BEFORE YANKING THE RUG OUT FROM UNDER US.
"AS EDDIE MARCONE WOULD SAY, '*IT'S A PRETTY GOOD JOKE AS LONG AS IT DOESN'T HAPPEN TO YOU.*'
"NO, MY FRIEND. WHETHER HE IS TRULY SANE OR NOT, I'M AFRAID THERE'S ONLY ONE CERTAINTY WITH THE JOKER THAT APPLIES TO US.
"HE'S BACK."

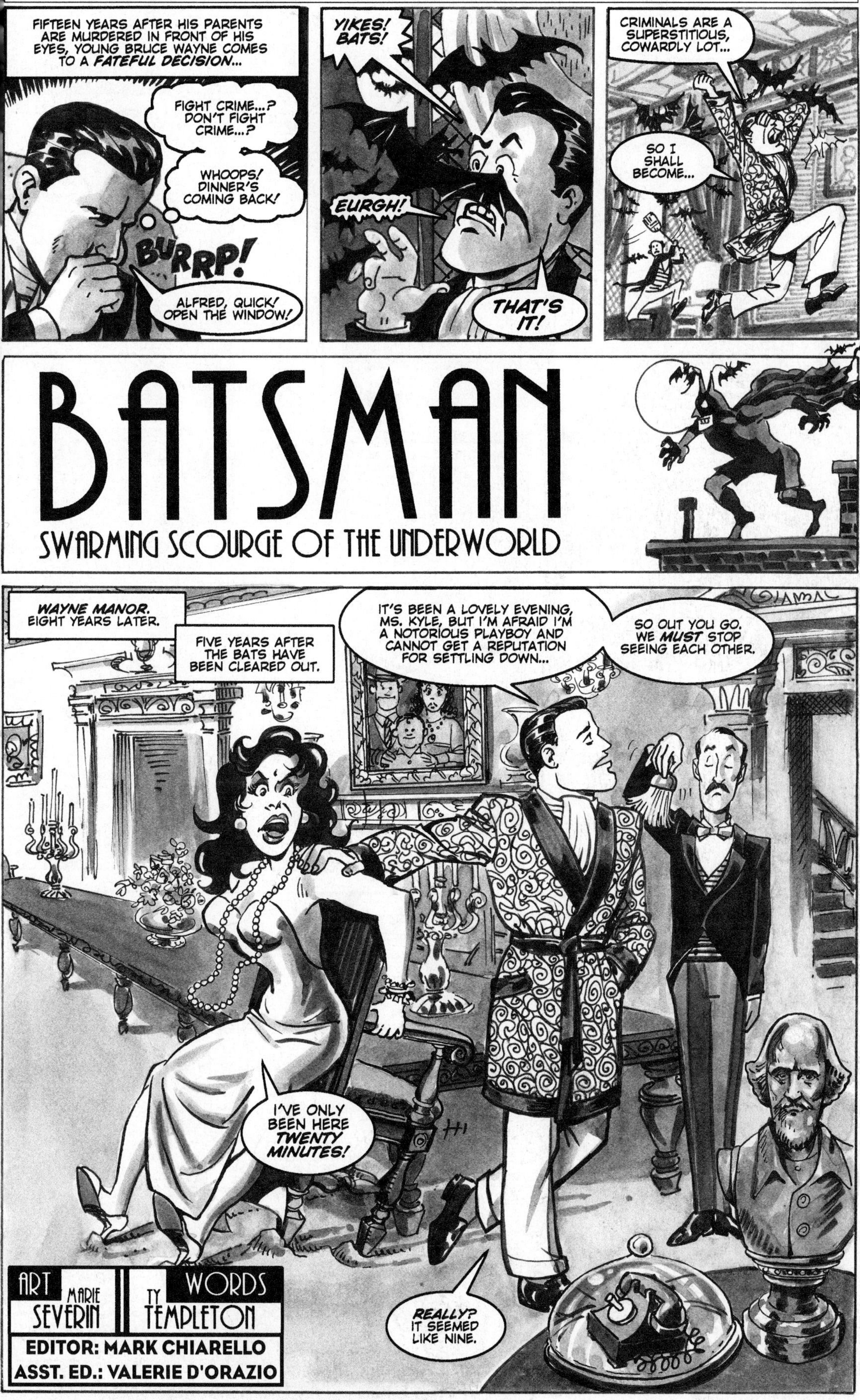
FIFTEEN YEARS AFTER HIS PARENTS ARE MURDERED IN FRONT OF HIS EYES, YOUNG BRUCE WAYNE COMES TO A FATEFUL DECISION...
FIGHT CRIME...? DON'T FIGHT CRIME...?
WHOOPS! DINNER'S COMING BACK!
BURRP!
ALFRED, QUICK! OPEN THE WINDOW!
YIKES! BATS!
EURGH!
THAT'S IT!
CRIMINALS ARE A SUPERSTITIOUS, COWARDLY LOT...
SO I SHALL BECOME...
BATSMAN
SWARMING SCOURGE OF THE UNDERWORLD
WAYNE MANOR. EIGHT YEARS LATER.
FIVE YEARS AFTER THE BATS HAVE BEEN CLEARED OUT.
IT'S BEEN A LOVELY EVENING, MS. KYLE, BUT I'M AFRAID I'M A NOTORIOUS PLAYBOY AND CANNOT GET A REPUTATION FOR SETTLING DOWN...
SO OUT YOU GO. WE MUST STOP SEEING EACH OTHER.
I'VE ONLY BEEN HERE TWENTY MINUTES!
REALLY? IT SEEMED LIKE NINE.
ART MARIE SEVERIN
WORDS TY TEMPLETON
EDITOR: MARK CHIARELLO
ASST. ED.: VALERIE D'ORAZIO

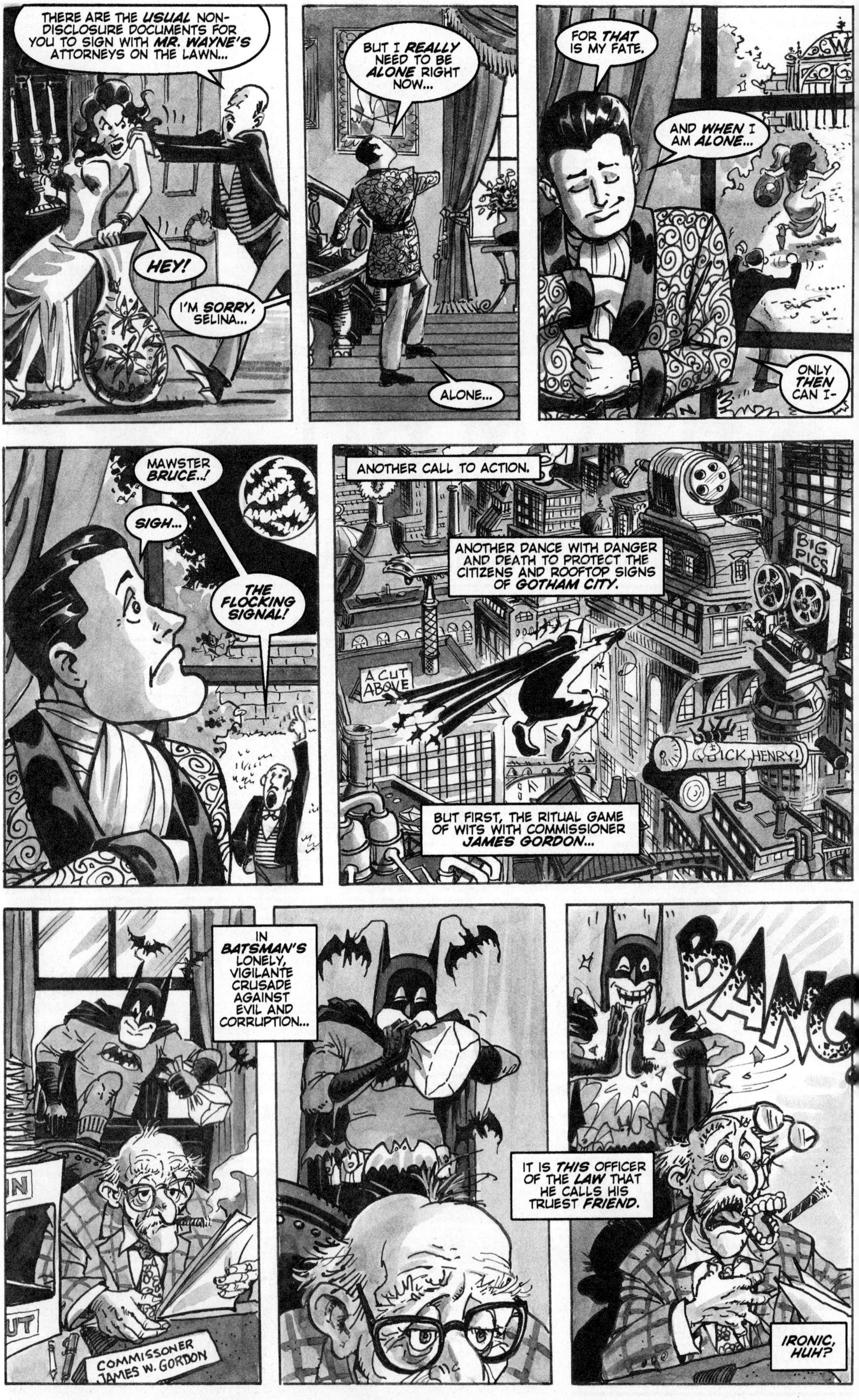

THERE ARE THE USUAL NON-DISCLOSURE DOCUMENTS FOR YOU TO SIGN WITH MR. WAYNE'S ATTORNEYS ON THE LAWN...
HEY!
I'M SORRY, SELINA...
BUT I REALLY NEED TO BE ALONE RIGHT NOW...
ALONE...
FOR THAT IS MY FATE.
AND WHEN I AM ALONE...
ONLY THEN CAN I-
MAWSTER BRUCE..!
SIGH...
THE FLOCKING SIGNAL!
ANOTHER CALL TO ACTION.
ANOTHER DANCE WITH DANGER AND DEATH TO PROTECT THE CITIZENS AND ROOFTOP SIGNS OF GOTHAM CITY.
BIG PICS
A CUT ABOVE
QUICK, HENRY!
BUT FIRST, THE RITUAL GAME OF WITS WITH COMMISSIONER JAMES GORDON...
IN
OUT
COMMISSONER JAMES W. GORDON
IN BATSMAN'S LONELY, VIGILANTE CRUSADE AGAINST EVIL AND CORRUPTION...
BANG
IT IS THIS OFFICER OF THE LAW THAT HE CALLS HIS TRUEST FRIEND.
IRONIC, HUH?

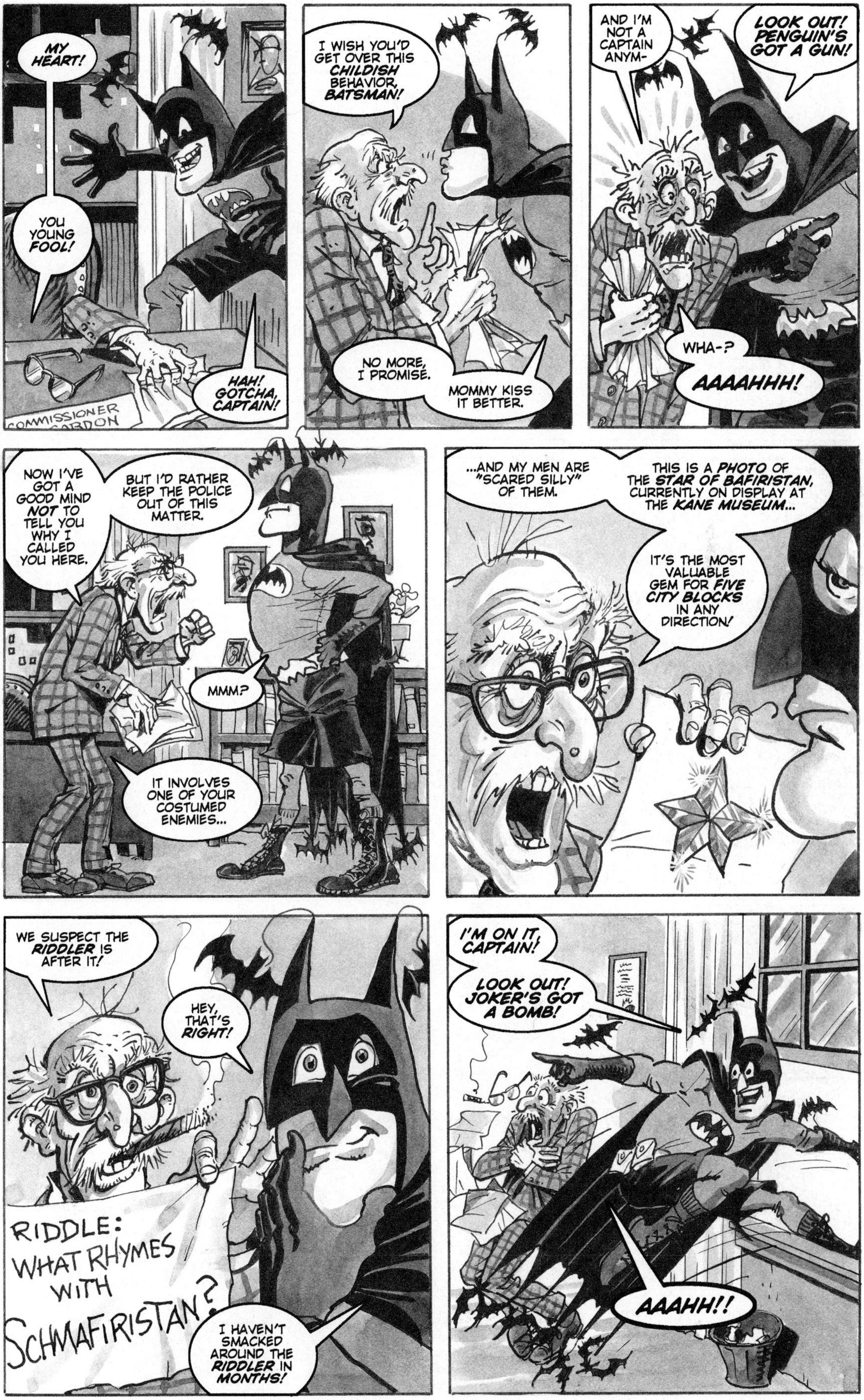
MY HEART!
YOU YOUNG FOOL!
COMMISSIONER GORDON
HAH! GOTCHA, CAPTAIN!
I WISH YOU'D GET OVER THIS CHILDISH BEHAVIOR, BATSMAN!
NO MORE, I PROMISE.
MOMMY KISS IT BETTER.
AND I'M NOT A CAPTAIN ANYM-
LOOK OUT! PENGUIN'S GOT A GUN!
WHA-?
AAAAHHH!
NOW I'VE GOT A GOOD MIND NOT TO TELL YOU WHY I CALLED YOU HERE.
BUT I'D RATHER KEEP THE POLICE OUT OF THIS MATTER.
MMM?
IT INVOLVES ONE OF YOUR COSTUMED ENEMIES...
...AND MY MEN ARE "SCARED SILLY" OF THEM.
THIS IS A PHOTO OF THE STAR OF BAFIRISTAN, CURRENTLY ON DISPLAY AT THE KANE MUSEUM...
IT'S THE MOST VALUABLE GEM FOR FIVE CITY BLOCKS IN ANY DIRECTION!
WE SUSPECT THE RIDDLER IS AFTER IT!
HEY, THAT'S RIGHT!
RIDDLE: WHAT RHYMES WITH SCHMAFIRISTAN?
I HAVEN'T SMACKED AROUND THE RIDDLER IN MONTHS!
I'M ON IT, CAPTAIN!
LOOK OUT! JOKER'S GOT A BOMB!
AAAHH!!

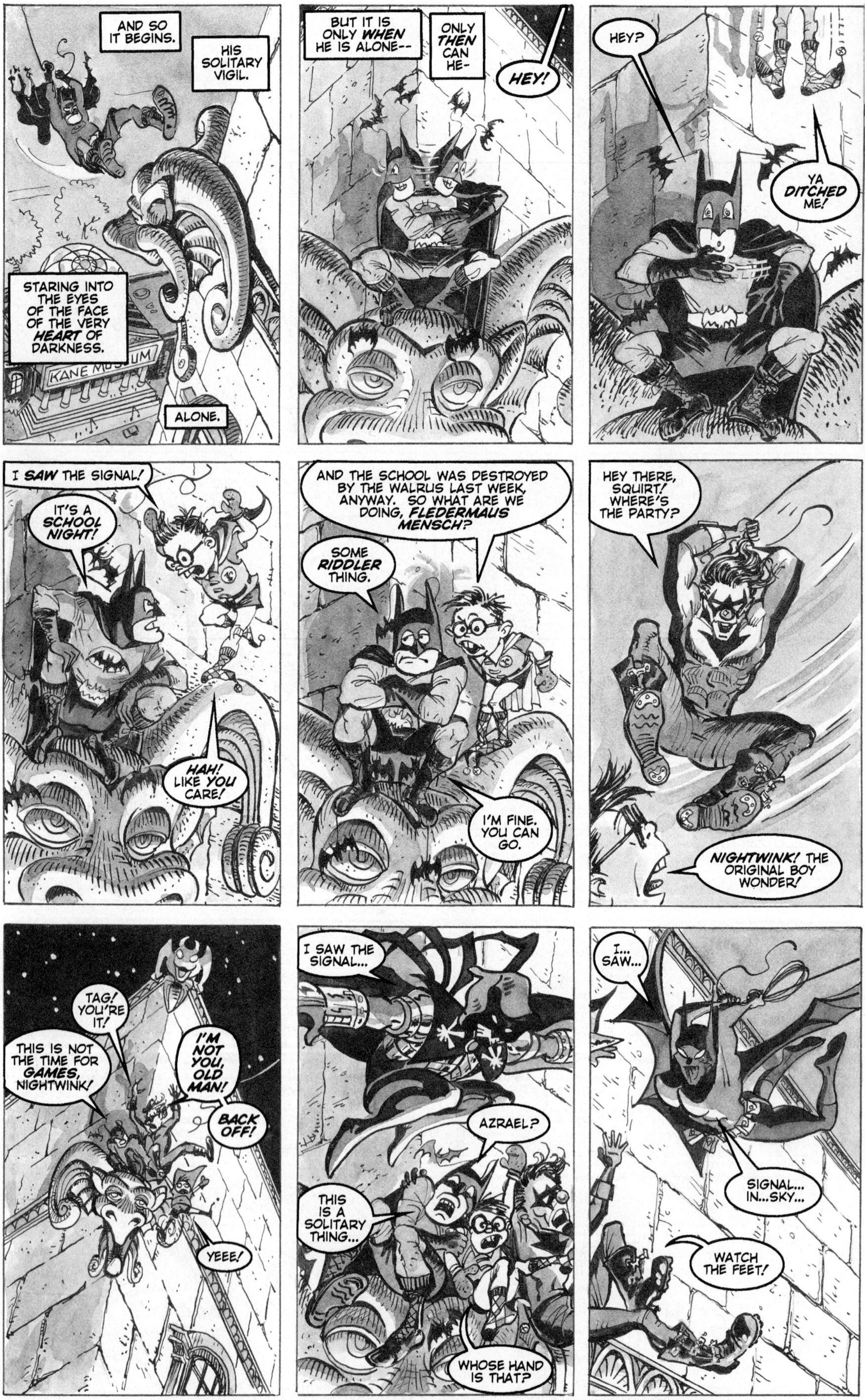
AND SO IT BEGINS.
HIS SOLITARY VIGIL.
STARING INTO THE EYES OF THE FACE OF THE VERY HEART OF DARKNESS.
KANE MUSEUM
ALONE.
BUT IT IS ONLY WHEN HE IS ALONE--
ONLY THEN CAN HE-
HEY!
HEY?
YA DITCHED ME!
I SAW THE SIGNAL!
IT'S A SCHOOL NIGHT!
HAH! LIKE YOU CARE!
AND THE SCHOOL WAS DESTROYED BY THE WALRUS LAST WEEK, ANYWAY. SO WHAT ARE WE DOING, FLEDERMAUS MENSCH?
SOME RIDDLER THING.
I'M FINE. YOU CAN GO.
HEY THERE, SQUIRT! WHERE'S THE PARTY?
NIGHTWINK! THE ORIGINAL BOY WONDER!
TAG! YOU'RE IT!
THIS IS NOT THE TIME FOR GAMES, NIGHTWINK!
I'M NOT YOU, OLD MAN!
BACK OFF!
YEEE!
I SAW THE SIGNAL...
AZRAEL?
THIS IS A SOLITARY THING...
WHOSE HAND IS THAT?
I... SAW...
SIGNAL... IN...SKY...
WATCH THE FEET!

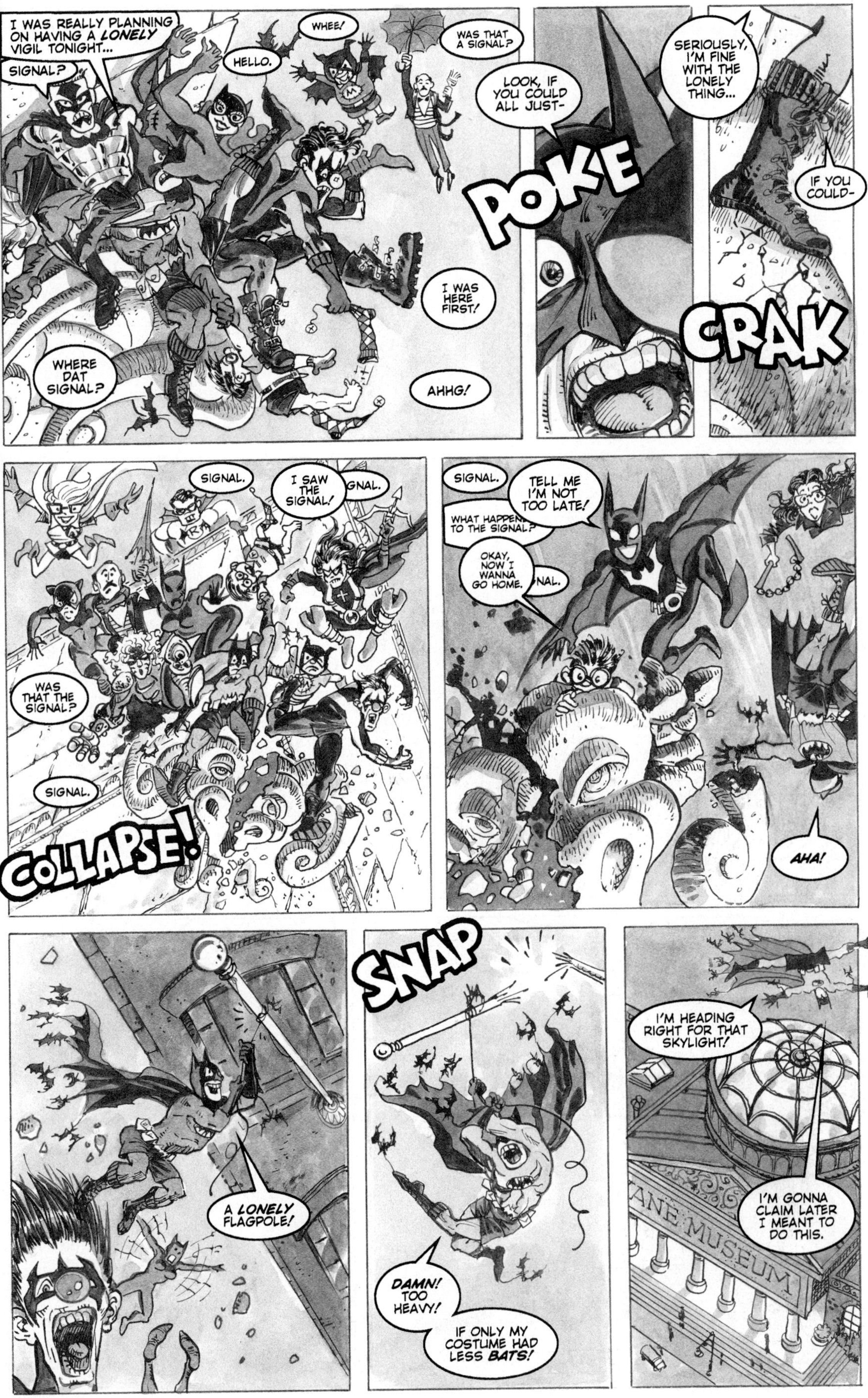
I WAS REALLY PLANNING ON HAVING A *LONELY* VIGIL TONIGHT...
SIGNAL?
HELLO.
WHEE!
WAS THAT A SIGNAL?
I WAS HERE FIRST!
WHERE DAT SIGNAL?
AHHG!
LOOK, IF YOU COULD ALL JUST-
POKE
SERIOUSLY, I'M FINE WITH THE LONELY THING...
IF YOU COULD-
CRAK
SIGNAL.
I SAW THE SIGNAL!
GNAL.
WAS THAT THE SIGNAL?
SIGNAL.
COLLAPSE!
SIGNAL.
TELL ME I'M NOT TOO LATE!
WHAT HAPPEN
TO THE SIGNAL?
OKAY, NOW I WANNA GO HOME.
NAL.
AHA!
A *LONELY* FLAGPOLE!
SNAP
DAMN! TOO HEAVY!
IF ONLY MY COSTUME HAD LESS *BATS!*
I'M HEADING RIGHT FOR THAT SKYLIGHT!
I'M GONNA CLAIM LATER I MEANT TO DO THIS.
ANE MUSEUM

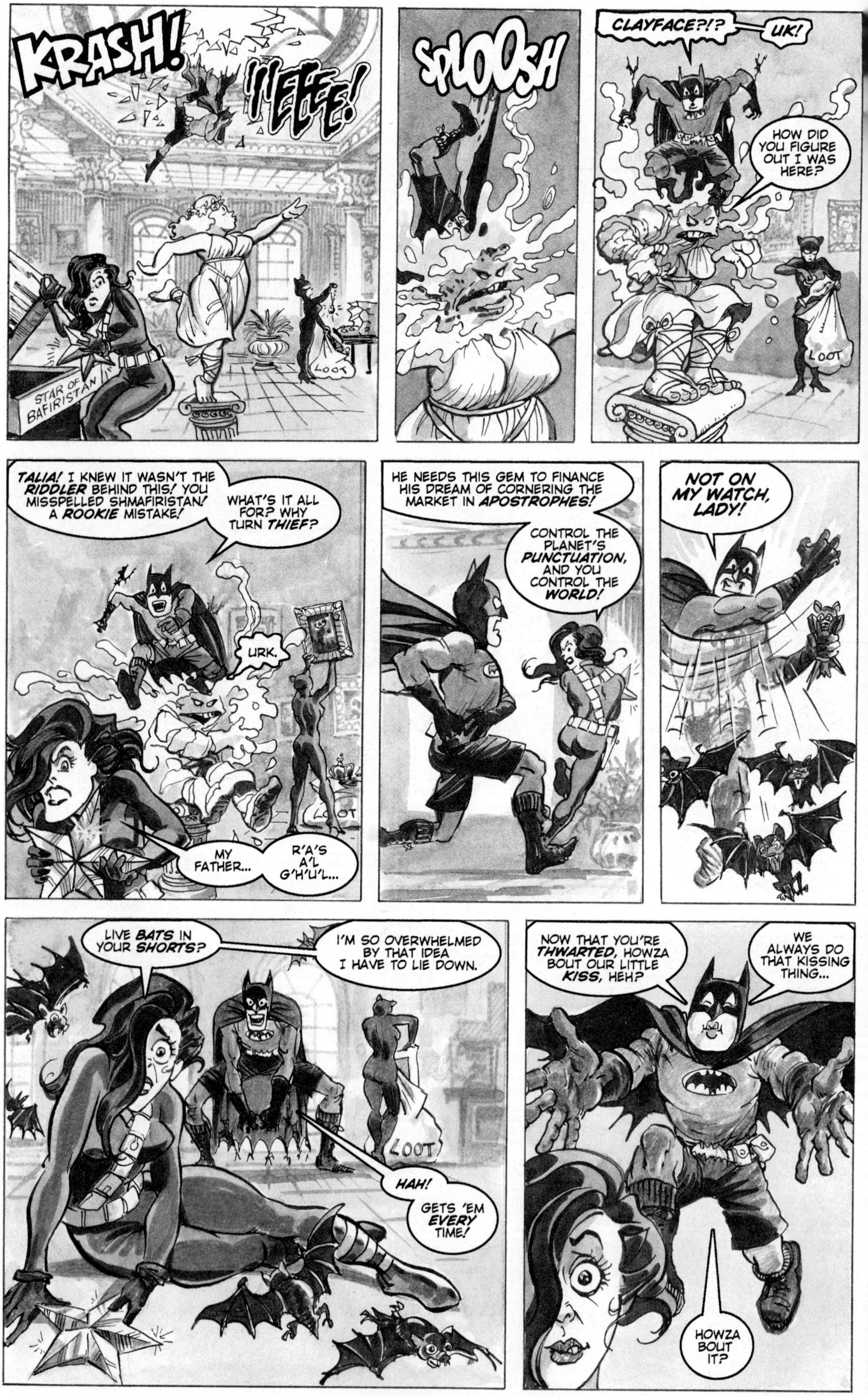

KRASH!
I'IEEEE!
STAR OF BAFIRISTAN
LOOT
SPLOOSH
CLAYFACE?!?
UK!
HOW DID YOU FIGURE OUT I WAS HERE?
LOOT
TALIA! I KNEW IT WASN'T THE RIDDLER BEHIND THIS! YOU MISSPELLED SHMAFIRISTAN! A ROOKIE MISTAKE!
WHAT'S IT ALL FOR? WHY TURN THIEF?
URK.
LOOT
MY FATHER...
R'A'S A'L G'H'U'L...
HE NEEDS THIS GEM TO FINANCE HIS DREAM OF CORNERING THE MARKET IN APOSTROPHES!
CONTROL THE PLANET'S PUNCTUATION, AND YOU CONTROL THE WORLD!
NOT ON MY WATCH, LADY!
LIVE BATS IN YOUR SHORTS?
I'M SO OVERWHELMED BY THAT IDEA I HAVE TO LIE DOWN.
LOOT
HAH!
GETS 'EM EVERY TIME!
NOW THAT YOU'RE THWARTED, HOWZA BOUT OUR LITTLE KISS, HEH?
WE ALWAYS DO THAT KISSING THING...
HOWZA BOUT IT?

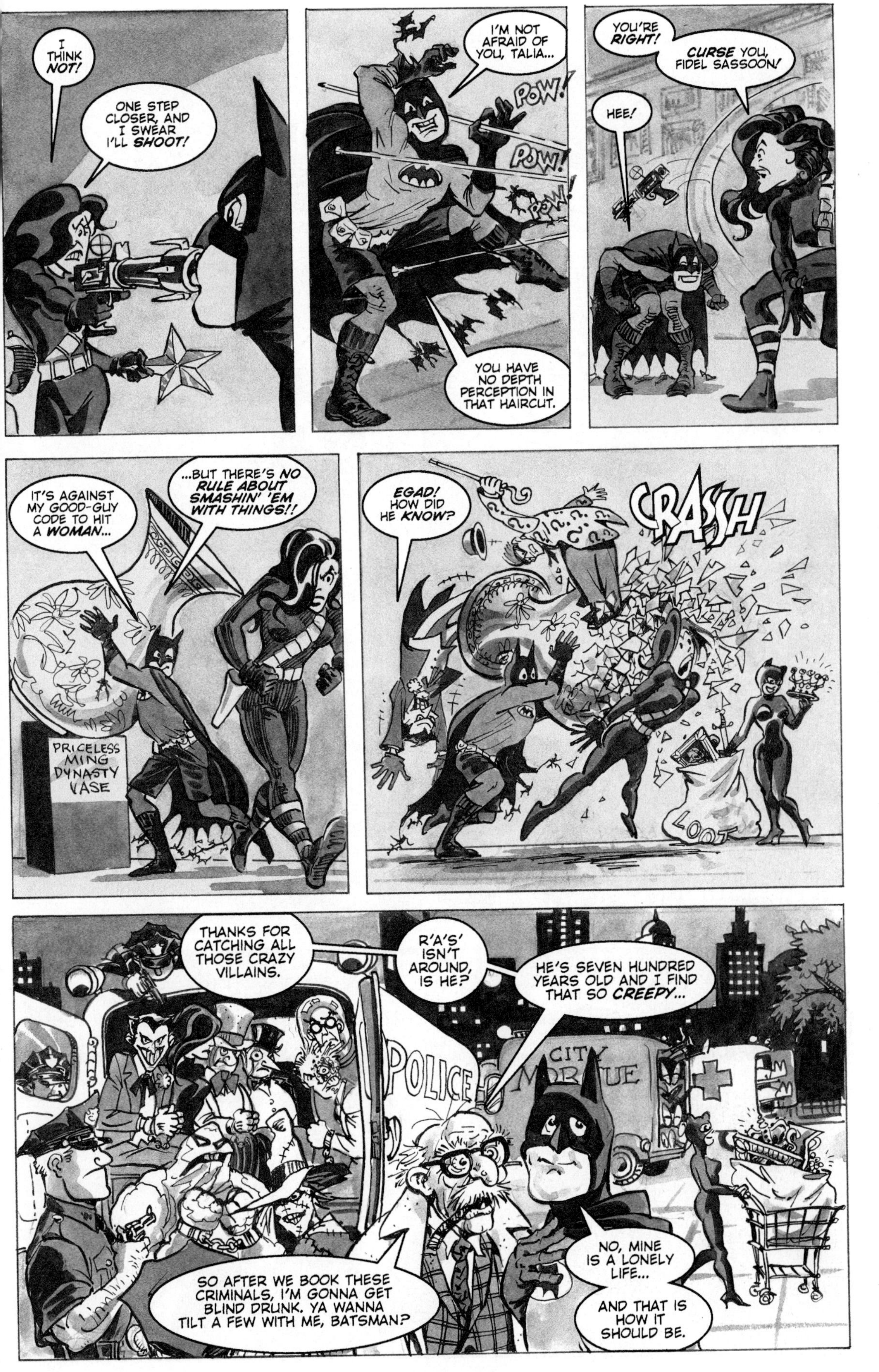

I THINK NOT!
ONE STEP CLOSER, AND I SWEAR I'LL SHOOT!
I'M NOT AFRAID OF YOU, TALIA...
POW!
POW!
POW!
YOU HAVE NO DEPTH PERCEPTION IN THAT HAIRCUT.
YOU'RE RIGHT!
CURSE YOU, FIDEL SASSOON!
HEE!
IT'S AGAINST MY GOOD-GUY CODE TO HIT A WOMAN...
...BUT THERE'S NO RULE ABOUT SMASHIN' 'EM WITH THINGS!!
PRICELESS MING DYNASTY VASE
EGAD! HOW DID HE KNOW?
CRASH
LOOT
THANKS FOR CATCHING ALL THOSE CRAZY VILLAINS.
R'A'S' ISN'T AROUND, IS HE?
HE'S SEVEN HUNDRED YEARS OLD AND I FIND THAT SO CREEPY...
POLICE
CITY MORGUE
SO AFTER WE BOOK THESE CRIMINALS, I'M GONNA GET BLIND DRUNK. YA WANNA TILT A FEW WITH ME, BATSMAN?
NO, MINE IS A LONELY LIFE...
AND THAT IS HOW IT SHOULD BE.

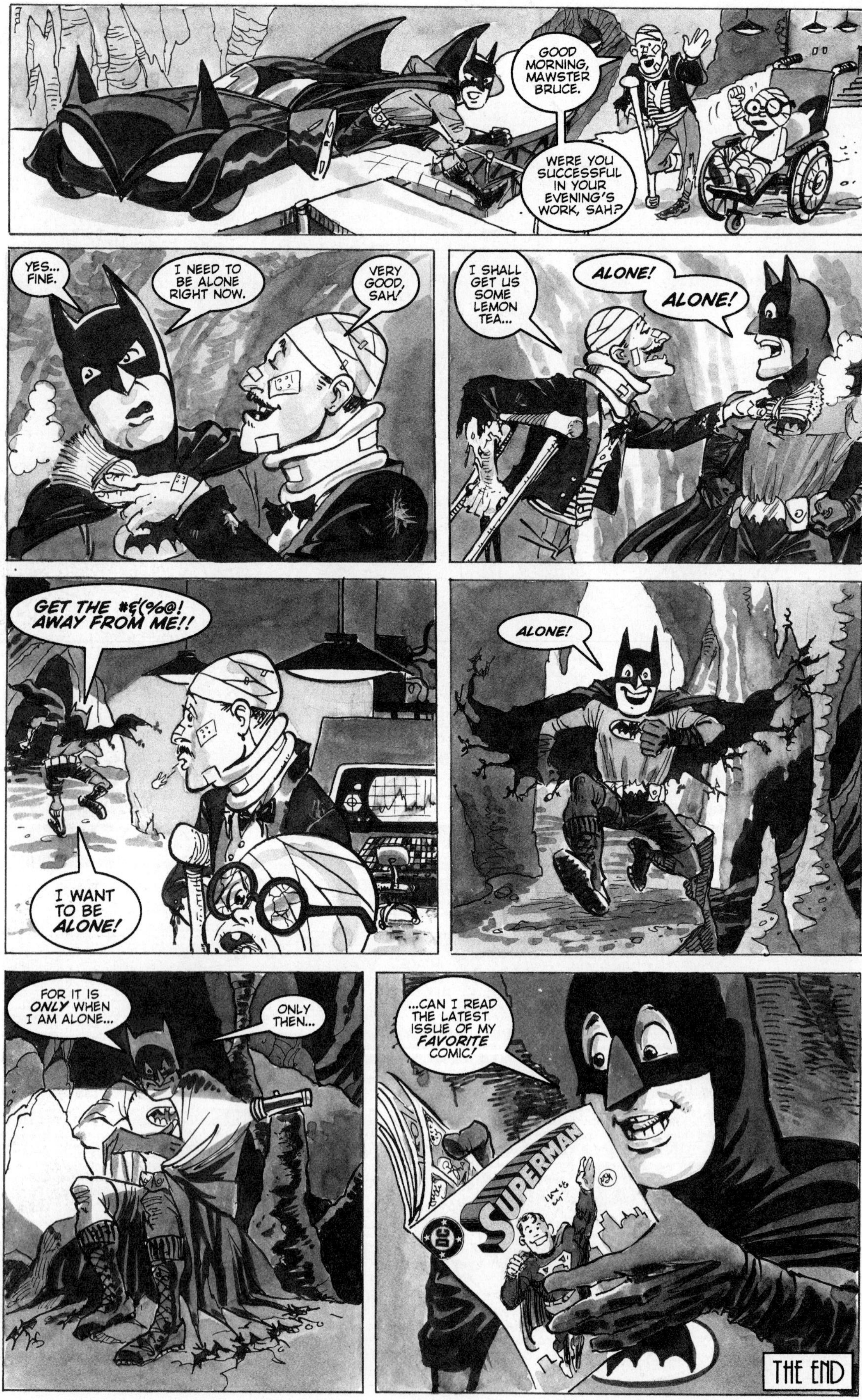
GOOD MORNING, MAWSTER BRUCE.
WERE YOU SUCCESSFUL IN YOUR EVENING'S WORK, SAH?
YES... FINE.
I NEED TO BE ALONE RIGHT NOW.
VERY GOOD, SAH.
I SHALL GET US SOME LEMON TEA...
ALONE!
ALONE!
GET THE #€(%@! AWAY FROM ME!!
I WANT TO BE ALONE!
ALONE!
FOR IT IS ONLY WHEN I AM ALONE...
ONLY THEN...
...CAN I READ THE LATEST ISSUE OF MY FAVORITE COMIC!
SUPERMAN
THE END

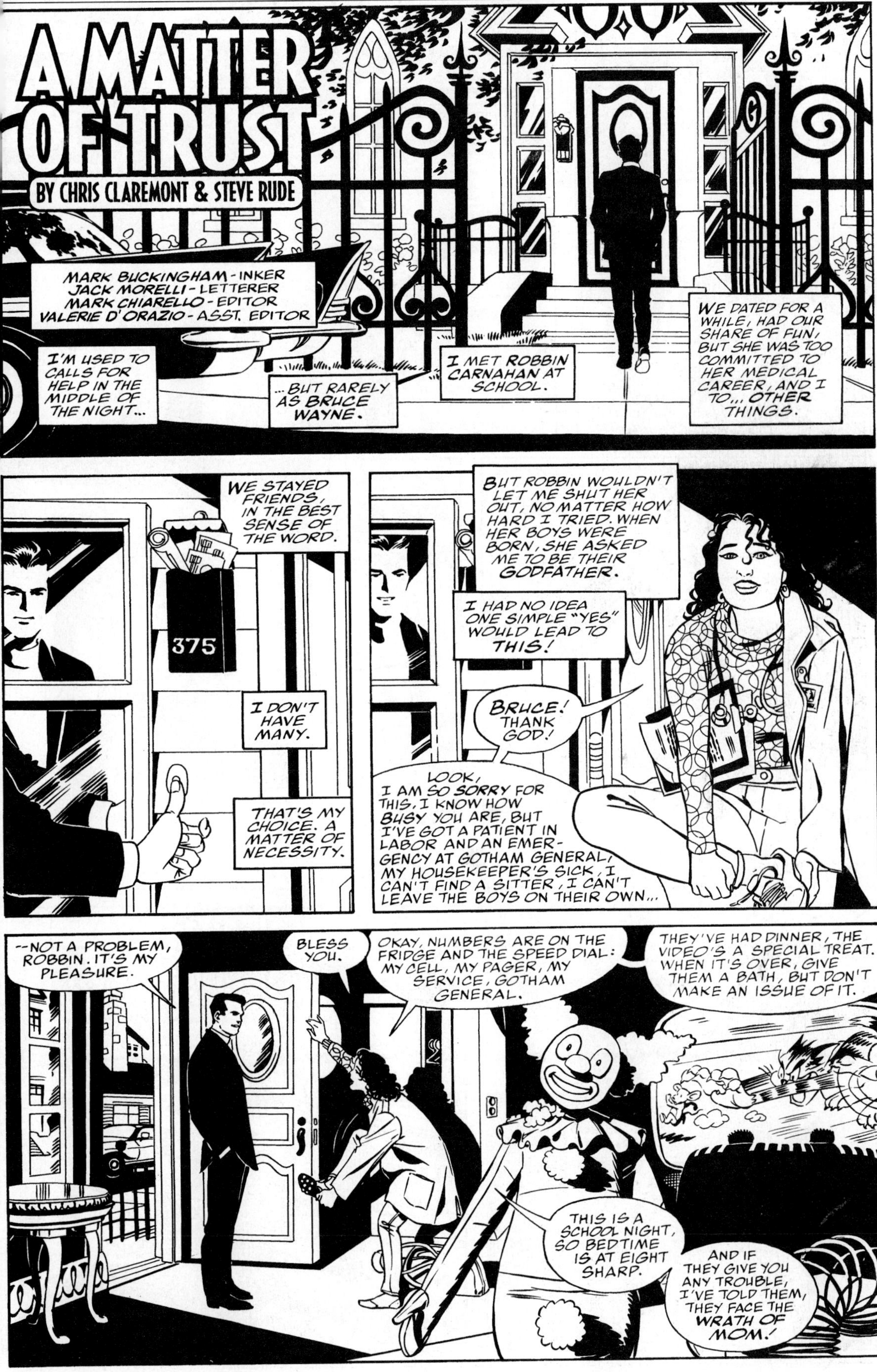
A MATTER OF TRUST
BY CHRIS CLAREMONT & STEVE RUDE
MARK BUCKINGHAM - INKER
JACK MORELLI - LETTERER
MARK CHIARELLO - EDITOR
VALERIE D'ORAZIO - ASST. EDITOR
I'M USED TO CALLS FOR HELP IN THE MIDDLE OF THE NIGHT...
...BUT RARELY AS BRUCE WAYNE.
I MET ROBBIN CARNAHAN AT SCHOOL.
WE DATED FOR A WHILE, HAD OUR SHARE OF FUN, BUT SHE WAS TOO COMMITTED TO HER MEDICAL CAREER, AND I TO... OTHER THINGS.
WE STAYED FRIENDS, IN THE BEST SENSE OF THE WORD.
375
I DON'T HAVE MANY.
THAT'S MY CHOICE. A MATTER OF NECESSITY.
BUT ROBBIN WOULDN'T LET ME SHUT HER OUT, NO MATTER HOW HARD I TRIED. WHEN HER BOYS WERE BORN, SHE ASKED ME TO BE THEIR GODFATHER.
I HAD NO IDEA ONE SIMPLE "YES" WOULD LEAD TO THIS!
BRUCE! THANK GOD!
LOOK, I AM SO SORRY FOR THIS. I KNOW HOW BUSY YOU ARE, BUT I'VE GOT A PATIENT IN LABOR AND AN EMERGENCY AT GOTHAM GENERAL, MY HOUSEKEEPER'S SICK, I CAN'T FIND A SITTER, I CAN'T LEAVE THE BOYS ON THEIR OWN...
--NOT A PROBLEM, ROBBIN. IT'S MY PLEASURE.
BLESS YOU.
OKAY, NUMBERS ARE ON THE FRIDGE AND THE SPEED DIAL: MY CELL, MY PAGER, MY SERVICE, GOTHAM GENERAL.
THEY'VE HAD DINNER, THE VIDEO'S A SPECIAL TREAT. WHEN IT'S OVER, GIVE THEM A BATH, BUT DON'T MAKE AN ISSUE OF IT.
THIS IS A SCHOOL NIGHT, SO BEDTIME IS AT EIGHT SHARP.
AND IF THEY GIVE YOU ANY TROUBLE, I'VE TOLD THEM, THEY FACE THE WRATH OF MOM!

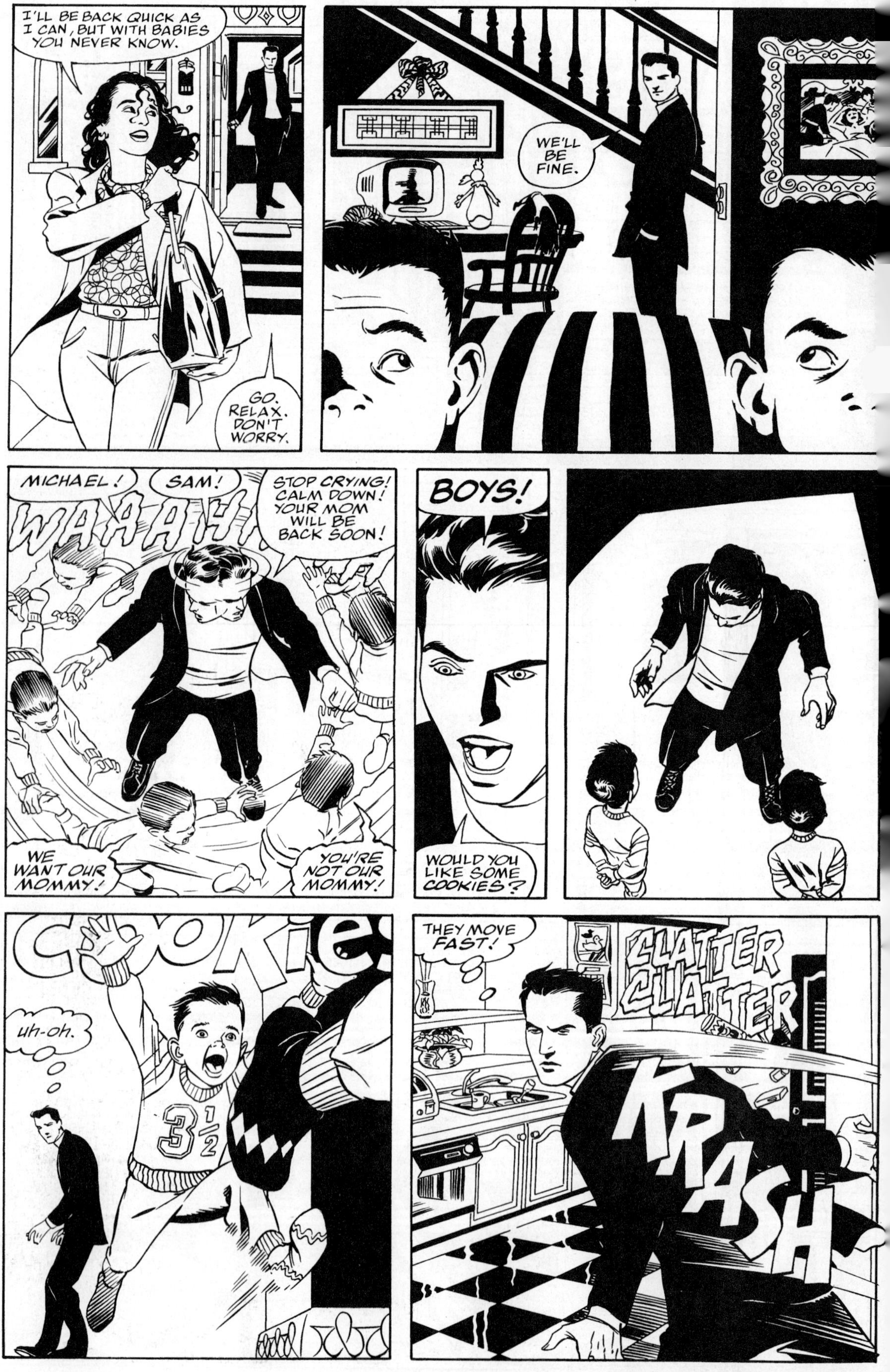

I'LL BE BACK QUICK AS I CAN, BUT WITH BABIES YOU NEVER KNOW.
GO. RELAX. DON'T WORRY.
WE'LL BE FINE.
MICHAEL!
SAM!
WAAAHH
STOP CRYING! CALM DOWN! YOUR MOM WILL BE BACK SOON!
WE WANT OUR MOMMY!
YOU'RE NOT OUR MOMMY!
BOYS!
WOULD YOU LIKE SOME COOKIES?
COOKIES
uh-oh.
THEY MOVE FAST!
CLATTER CLATTER
KRASH

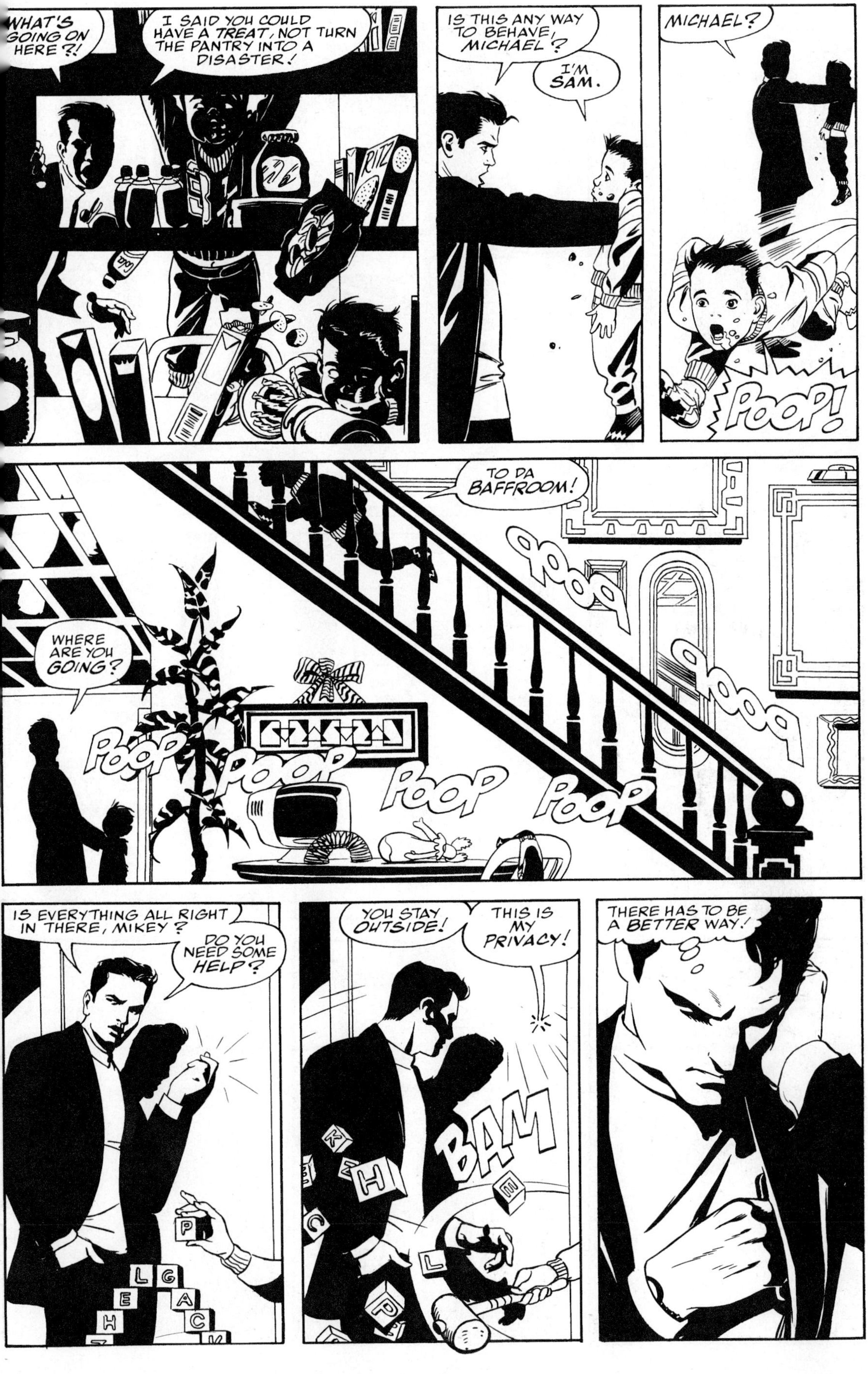
WHAT'S GOING ON HERE ?!
I SAID YOU COULD HAVE A TREAT, NOT TURN THE PANTRY INTO A DISASTER!
IS THIS ANY WAY TO BEHAVE, MICHAEL ?
I'M SAM.
MICHAEL?
POOP!
TO DA BAFFROOM!
WHERE ARE YOU GOING?
POOP POOP POOP POOP POOP POOP POOP
IS EVERYTHING ALL RIGHT IN THERE, MIKEY?
DO YOU NEED SOME HELP?
YOU STAY OUTSIDE!
THIS IS MY PRIVACY!
BAM
THERE HAS TO BE A BETTER WAY!

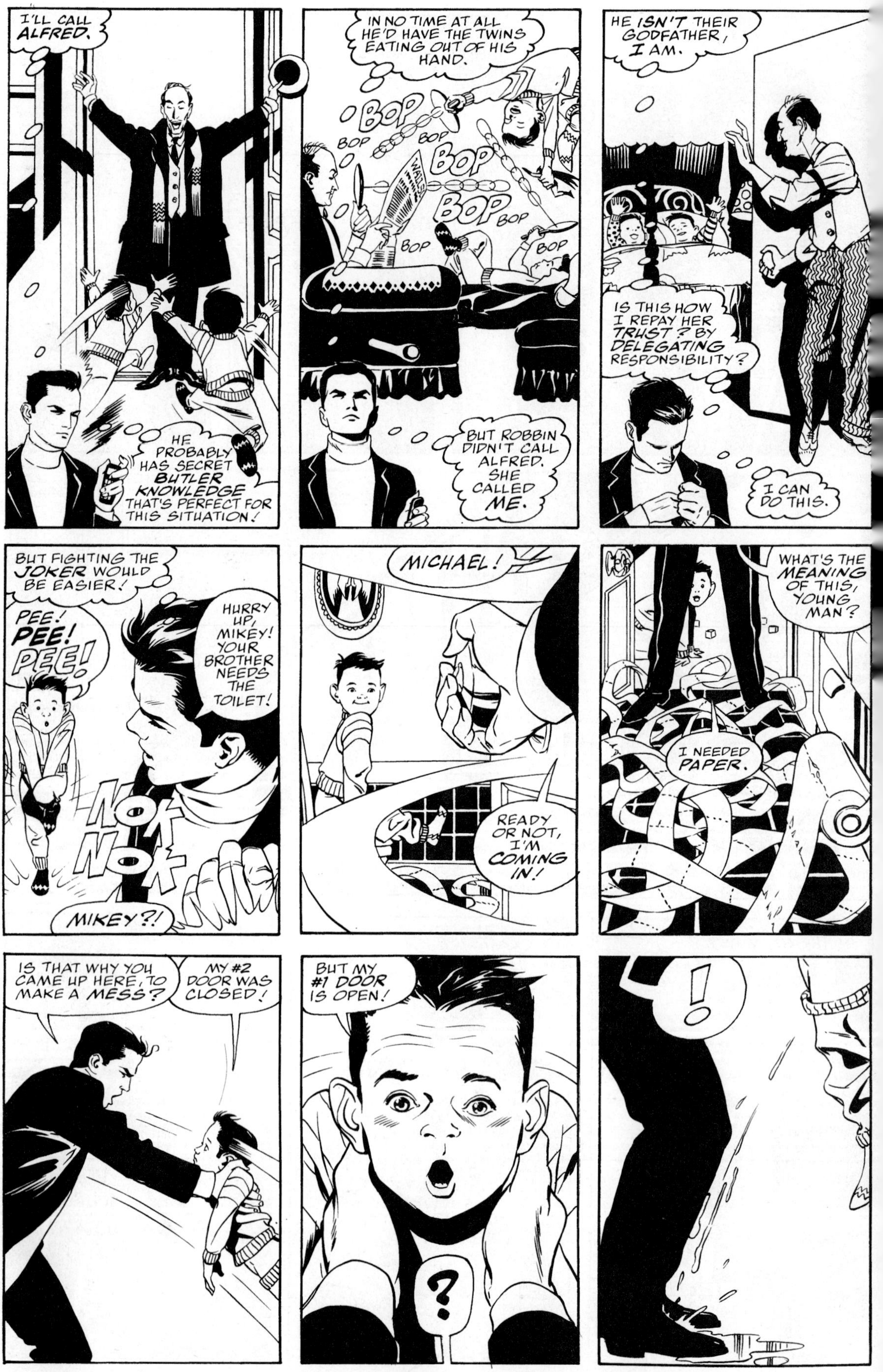
I'LL CALL ALFRED.
HE PROBABLY HAS SECRET BUTLER KNOWLEDGE THAT'S PERFECT FOR THIS SITUATION!
IN NO TIME AT ALL HE'D HAVE THE TWINS EATING OUT OF HIS HAND.
BOP BOP BOP BOP BOP BOP BOP BOP
BUT ROBBIN DIDN'T CALL ALFRED. SHE CALLED ME.
HE ISN'T THEIR GODFATHER, I AM.
IS THIS HOW I REPAY HER TRUST? BY DELEGATING RESPONSIBILITY?
I CAN DO THIS.
BUT FIGHTING THE JOKER WOULD BE EASIER!
PEE! PEE! PEE!
HURRY UP, MIKEY! YOUR BROTHER NEEDS THE TOILET!
NOK NOK
MIKEY?!
MICHAEL!
READY OR NOT, I'M COMING IN!
WHAT'S THE MEANING OF THIS, YOUNG MAN?
I NEEDED PAPER.
IS THAT WHY YOU CAME UP HERE, TO MAKE A MESS?
MY #2 DOOR WAS CLOSED!
BUT MY #1 DOOR IS OPEN!
?
!

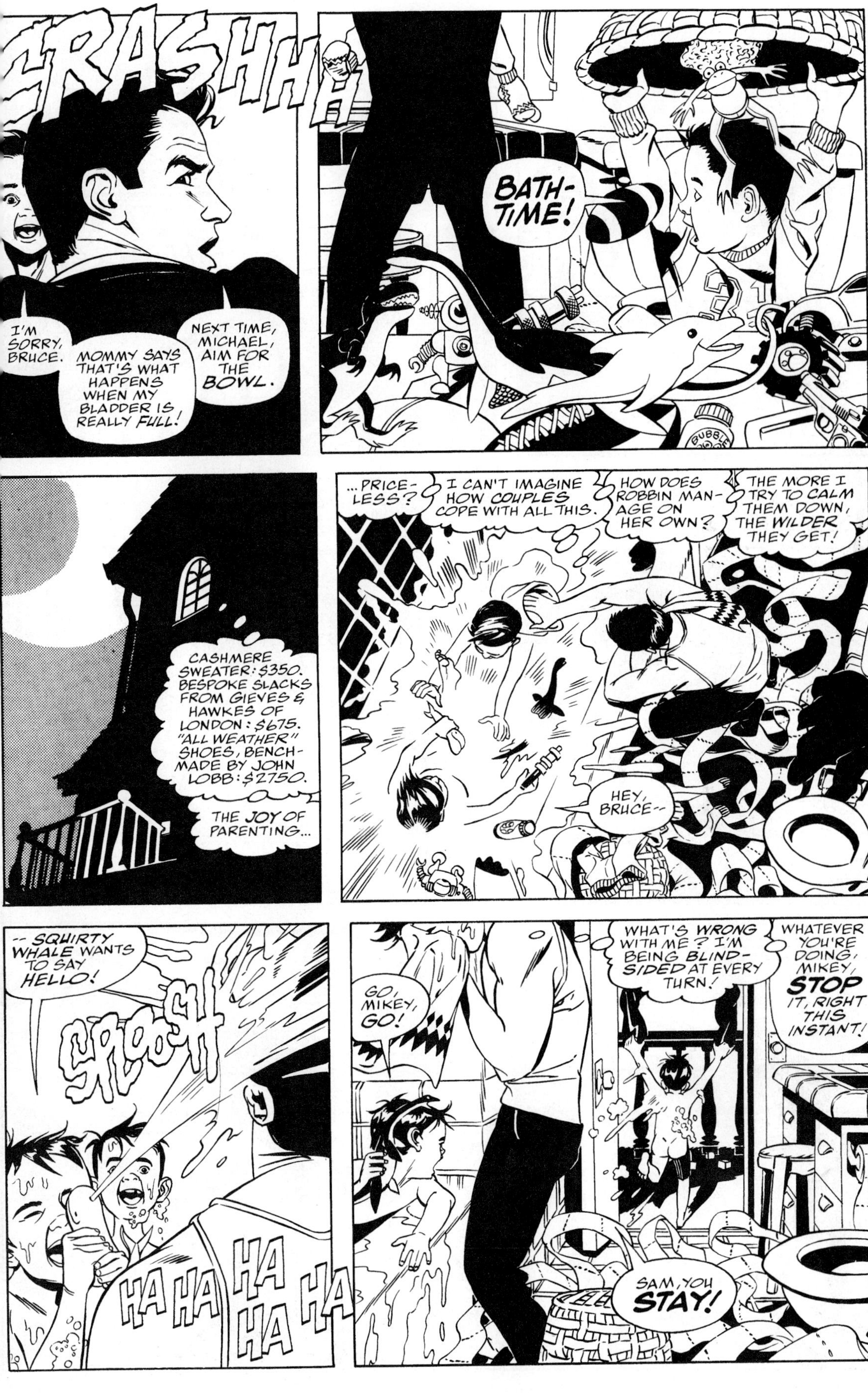
CRASHHH
I'M SORRY, BRUCE.
MOMMY SAYS THAT'S WHAT HAPPENS WHEN MY BLADDER IS REALLY FULL!
NEXT TIME, MICHAEL, AIM FOR THE BOWL.
BATH-TIME!
BUBBLE
CASHMERE SWEATER: $350. BESPOKE SLACKS FROM GIEVES & HAWKES OF LONDON: $675. "ALL WEATHER" SHOES, BENCH-MADE BY JOHN LOBB: $2750.
THE JOY OF PARENTING...
...PRICE-LESS?
I CAN'T IMAGINE HOW COUPLES COPE WITH ALL THIS.
HOW DOES ROBBIN MAN-AGE ON HER OWN?
THE MORE I TRY TO CALM THEM DOWN, THE WILDER THEY GET!
HEY, BRUCE--
--SQUIRTY WHALE WANTS TO SAY HELLO!
SPLOOSH
HA HA HA HA HA HA
GO, MIKEY, GO!
WHAT'S WRONG WITH ME? I'M BEING BLIND-SIDED AT EVERY TURN!
WHATEVER YOU'RE DOING, MIKEY, STOP IT, RIGHT THIS INSTANT!
SAM, YOU STAY!

WATER-SLIDE!

MIKEY--

--NO!

YA-HOOOO

I GUESS HE'S DONE THIS BEFORE, HE'S GOT A GOOD GRIP...HE'S OKAY.

LET MY GUARD DOWN FOR AN INSTANT, AND SEE WHAT HAPPENS? THIS COULD HAVE BEEN A DISASTER!

NO MORE FOOLING YOUNG MAN!

YOU'RE IN BIG TROUBLE!

NOW MARCH YOURSELF BACK UP-STAIRS--!

GUN! GUN! GUN!

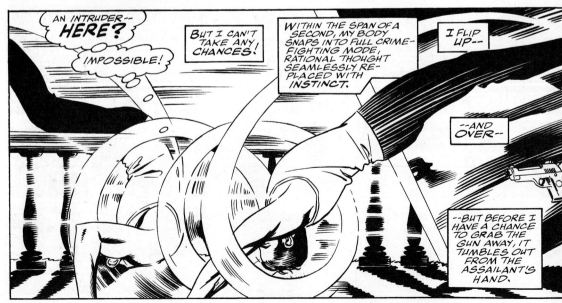

AN INTRUDER-- HERE?

IMPOSSIBLE!

BUT I CAN'T TAKE ANY CHANCES!

WITHIN THE SPAN OF A SECOND, MY BODY SNAPS INTO FULL CRIME-FIGHTING MODE, RATIONAL THOUGHT SEAMLESSLY RE-PLACED WITH INSTINCT.

I FLIP UP--

--AND OVER--

--BUT BEFORE I HAVE A CHANCE TO GRAB THE GUN AWAY, IT TUMBLES OUT FROM THE ASSAILANT'S HAND.

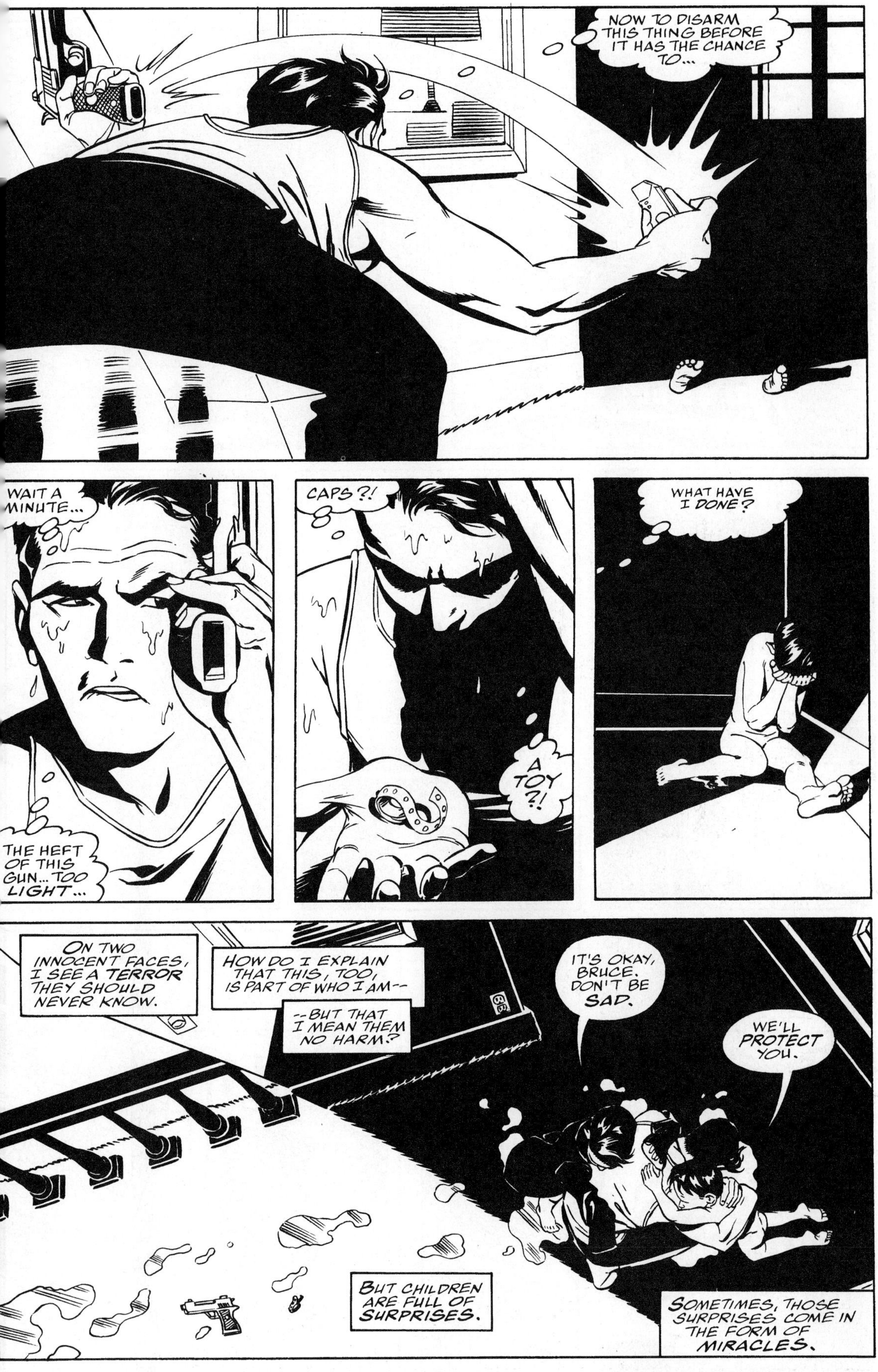
NOW TO DISARM THIS THING BEFORE IT HAS THE CHANCE TO...
WAIT A MINUTE...
THE HEFT OF THIS GUN... TOO LIGHT...
CAPS?!
A TOY?!
WHAT HAVE I DONE?
ON TWO INNOCENT FACES, I SEE A TERROR THEY SHOULD NEVER KNOW.
HOW DO I EXPLAIN THAT THIS, TOO, IS PART OF WHO I AM--
--BUT THAT I MEAN THEM NO HARM?
IT'S OKAY, BRUCE. DON'T BE SAD.
WE'LL PROTECT YOU.
BUT CHILDREN ARE FULL OF SURPRISES.
SOMETIMES, THOSE SURPRISES COME IN THE FORM OF MIRACLES.

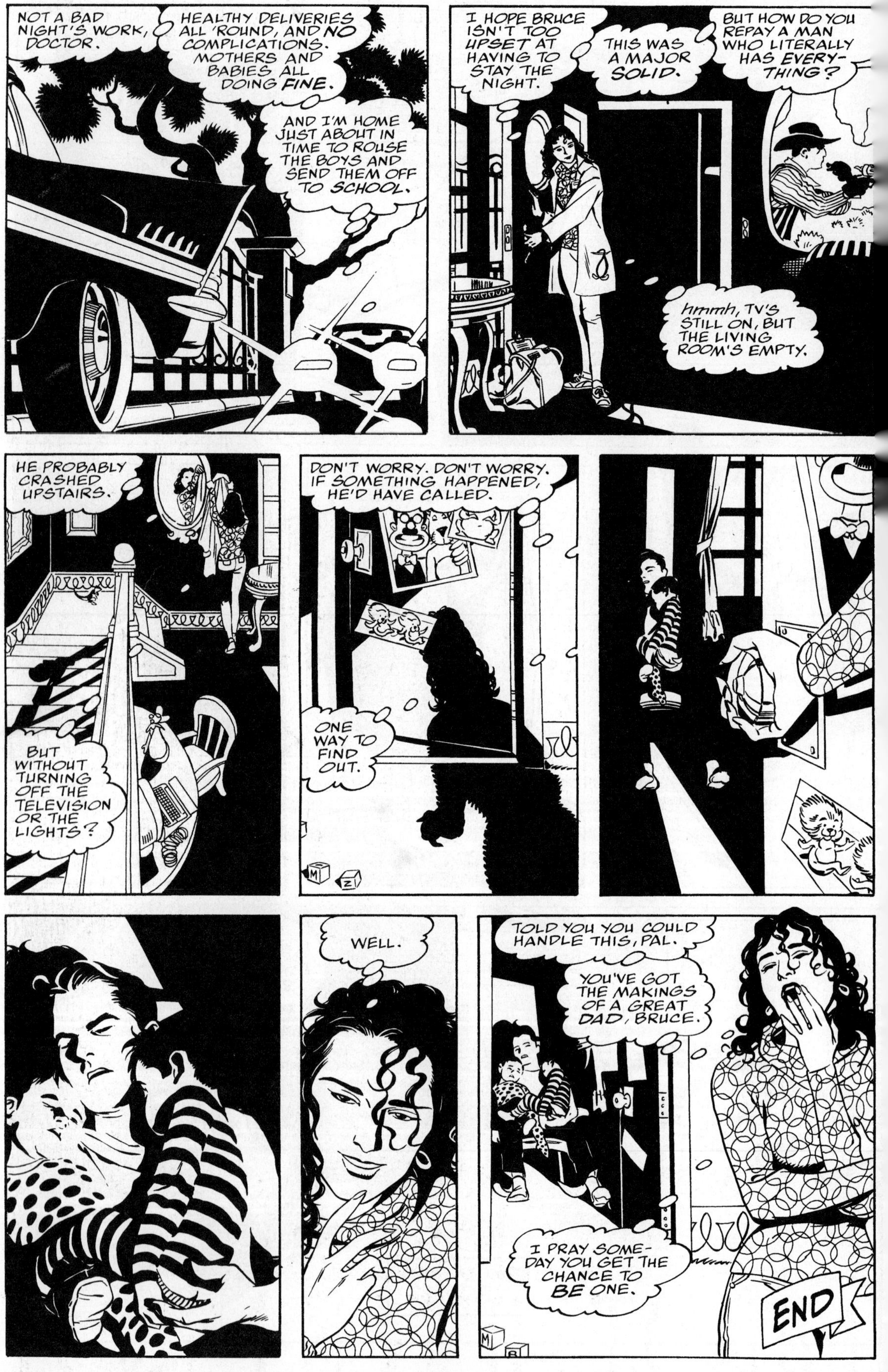
NOT A BAD NIGHT'S WORK, DOCTOR.
HEALTHY DELIVERIES ALL 'ROUND, AND NO COMPLICATIONS. MOTHERS AND BABIES ALL DOING FINE.
AND I'M HOME JUST ABOUT IN TIME TO ROUSE THE BOYS AND SEND THEM OFF TO SCHOOL.
I HOPE BRUCE ISN'T TOO UPSET AT HAVING TO STAY THE NIGHT.
THIS WAS A MAJOR SOLID.
BUT HOW DO YOU REPAY A MAN WHO LITERALLY HAS EVERYTHING?
hmmh, TV'S STILL ON, BUT THE LIVING ROOM'S EMPTY.
HE PROBABLY CRASHED UPSTAIRS.
BUT WITHOUT TURNING OFF THE TELEVISION OR THE LIGHTS?
DON'T WORRY. DON'T WORRY. IF SOMETHING HAPPENED, HE'D HAVE CALLED.
ONE WAY TO FIND OUT.
WELL.
TOLD YOU YOU COULD HANDLE THIS, PAL.
YOU'VE GOT THE MAKINGS OF A GREAT DAD, BRUCE.
I PRAY SOMEDAY YOU GET THE CHANCE TO BE ONE.
END

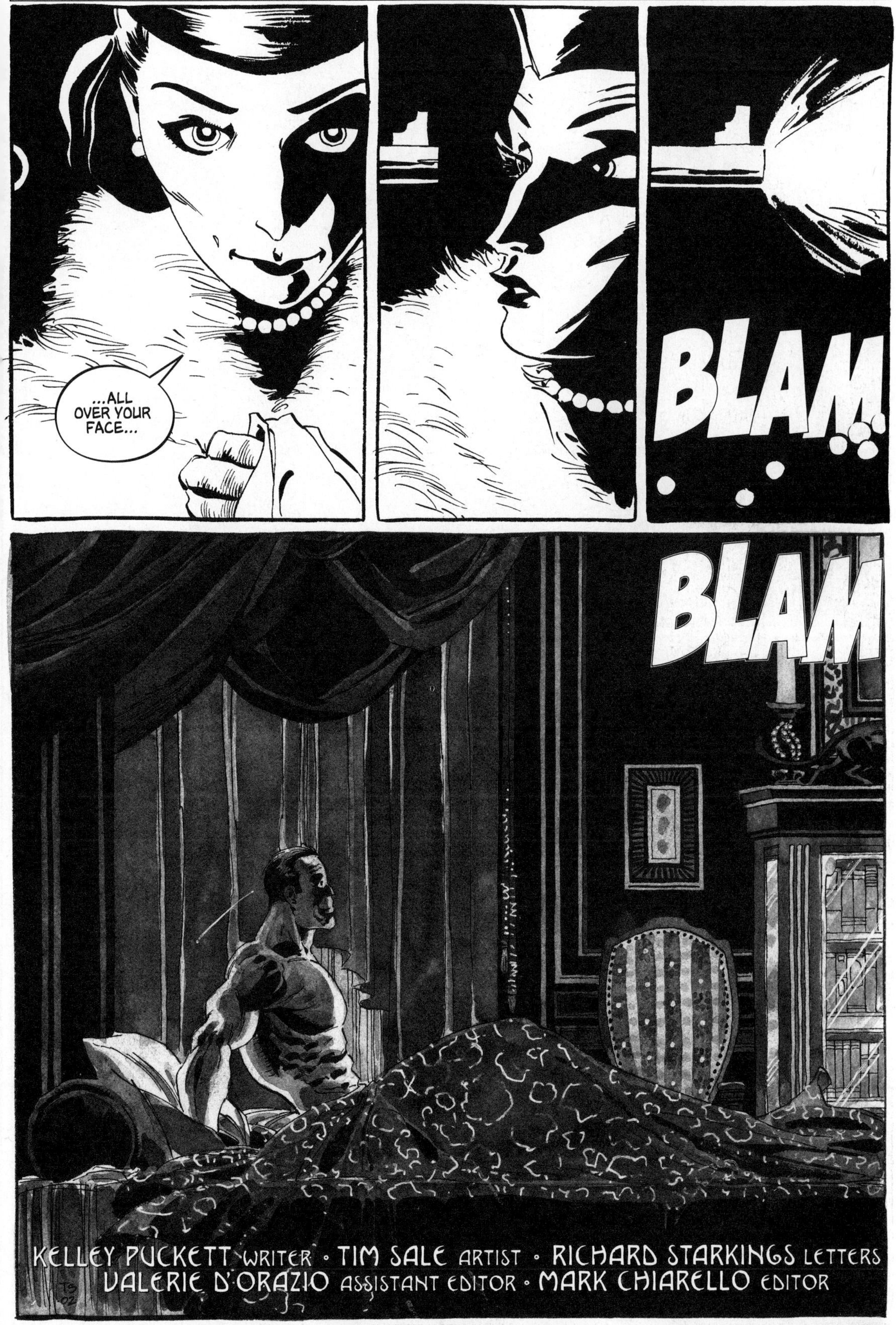
...ALL OVER YOUR FACE...
BLAM
BLAM
KELLEY PUCKETT WRITER • TIM SALE ARTIST • RICHARD STARKINGS LETTERS
VALERIE D'ORAZIO ASSISTANT EDITOR • MARK CHIARELLO EDITOR

NIGHT AFTER NIGHT

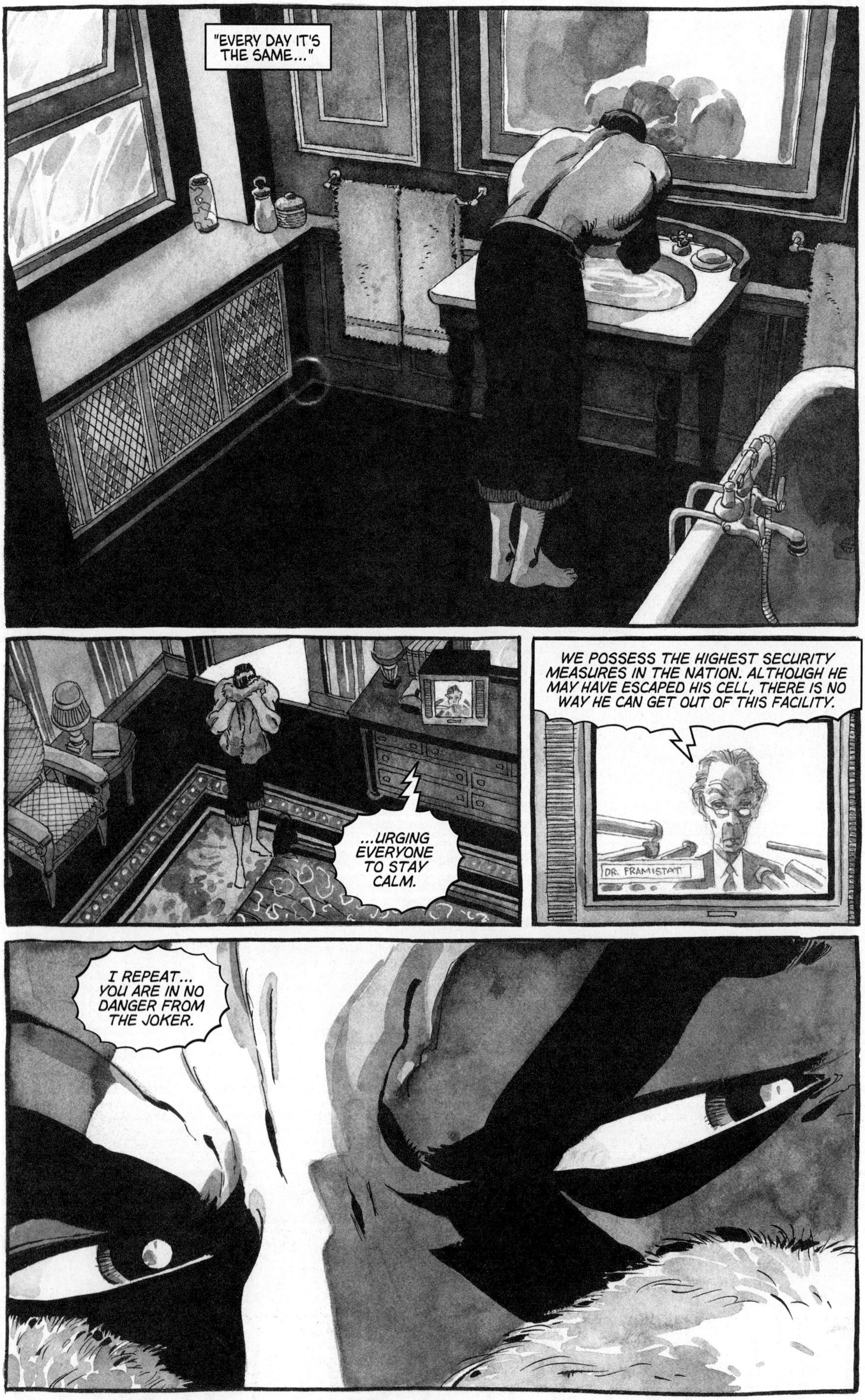
"EVERY DAY IT'S THE SAME..."
...URGING EVERYONE TO STAY CALM.
WE POSSESS THE HIGHEST SECURITY MEASURES IN THE NATION. ALTHOUGH HE MAY HAVE ESCAPED HIS CELL, THERE IS NO WAY HE CAN GET OUT OF THIS FACILITY.
DR. FRAMISTAT
I REPEAT... YOU ARE IN NO DANGER FROM THE JOKER.

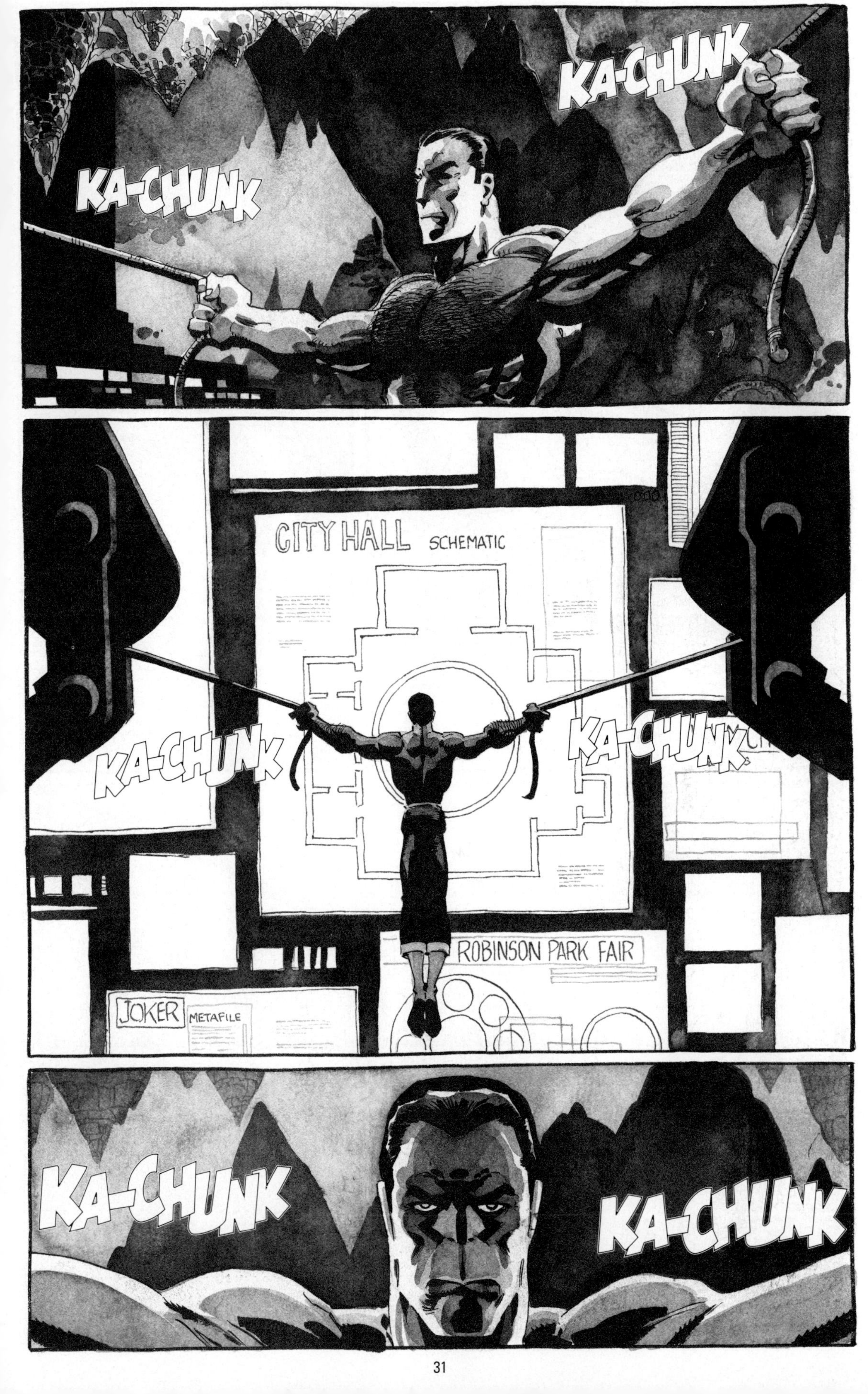
KA-CHUNK
KA-CHUNK
CITY HALL SCHEMATIC
KA-CHUNK
KA-CHUNK
ROBINSON PARK FAIR
JOKER METAFILE
KA-CHUNK
KA-CHUNK

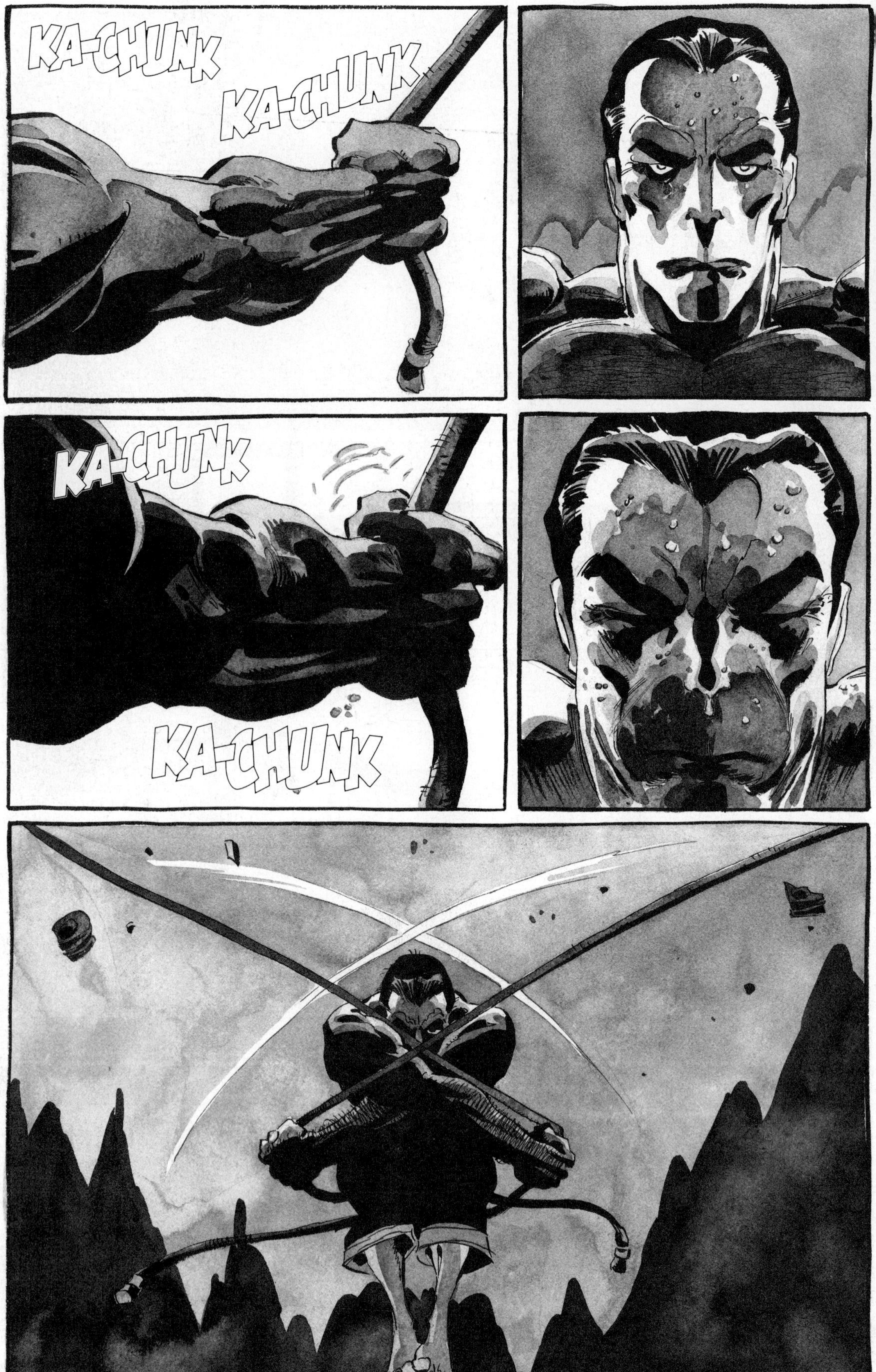
KA-CHUNK
KA-CHUNK
KA-CHUNK
KA-CHUNK

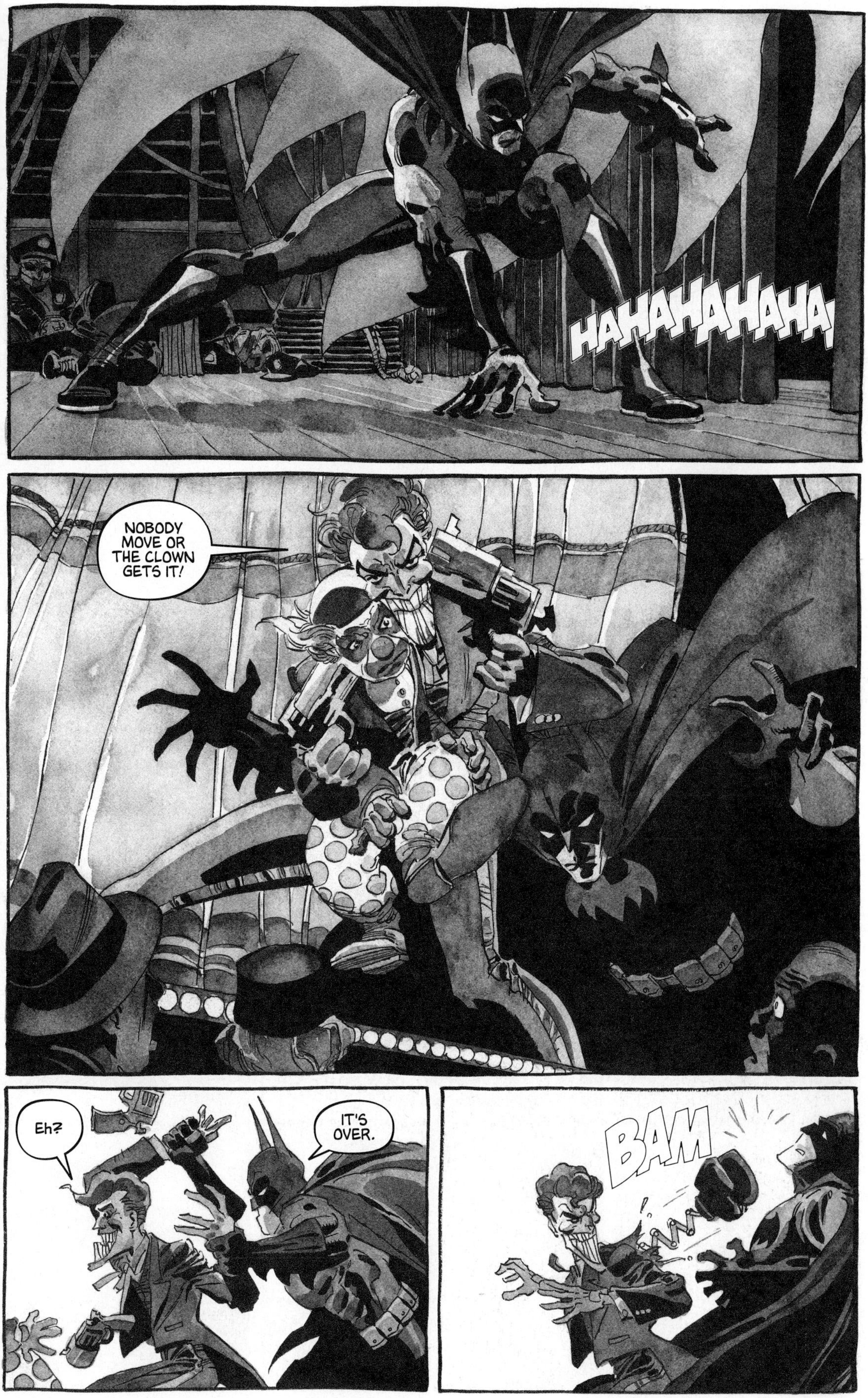
HAHAHAHAHA
NOBODY MOVE OR THE CLOWN GETS IT!
Eh?
IT'S OVER.
BAM

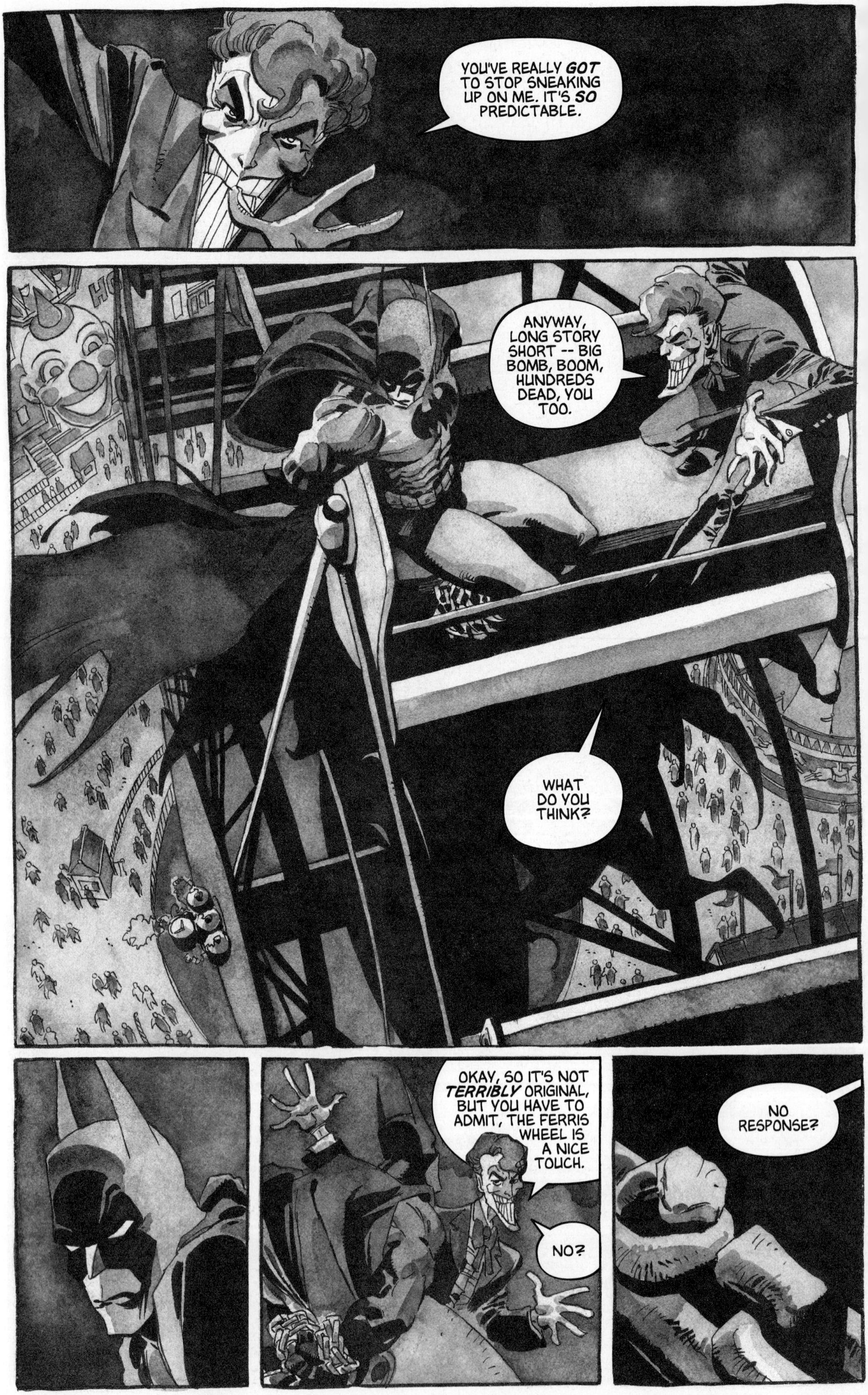
YOU'VE REALLY GOT TO STOP SNEAKING UP ON ME. IT'S SO PREDICTABLE.
ANYWAY, LONG STORY SHORT -- BIG BOMB, BOOM, HUNDREDS DEAD, YOU TOO.
WHAT DO YOU THINK?
OKAY, SO IT'S NOT TERRIBLY ORIGINAL, BUT YOU HAVE TO ADMIT, THE FERRIS WHEEL IS A NICE TOUCH.
NO?
NO RESPONSE?

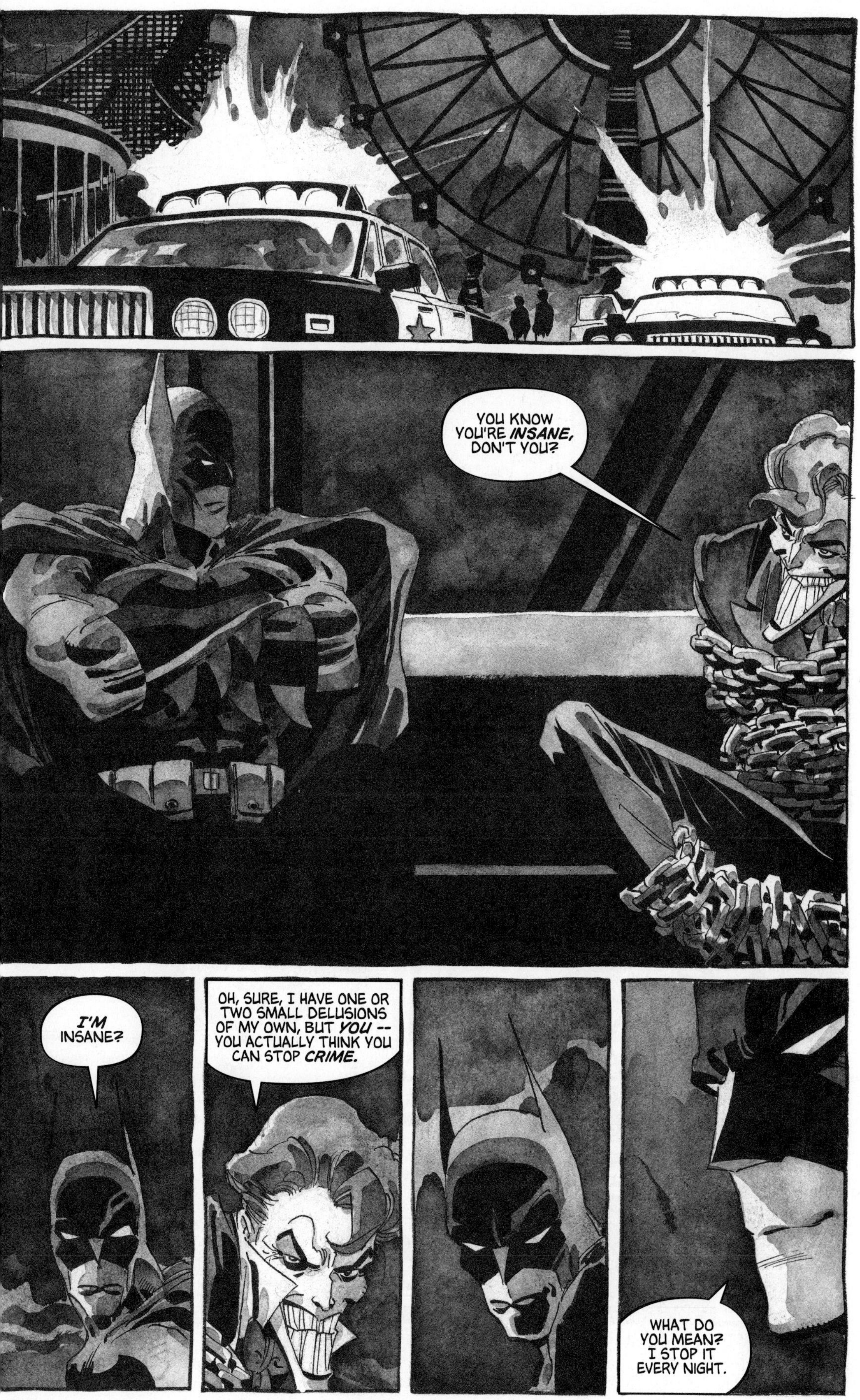

YOU KNOW YOU'RE *INSANE,* DON'T YOU?
I'M INSANE?
OH, SURE, I HAVE ONE OR TWO SMALL DELUSIONS OF MY OWN, BUT *YOU* -- YOU ACTUALLY THINK YOU CAN STOP *CRIME.*
WHAT DO YOU MEAN? I STOP IT EVERY NIGHT.

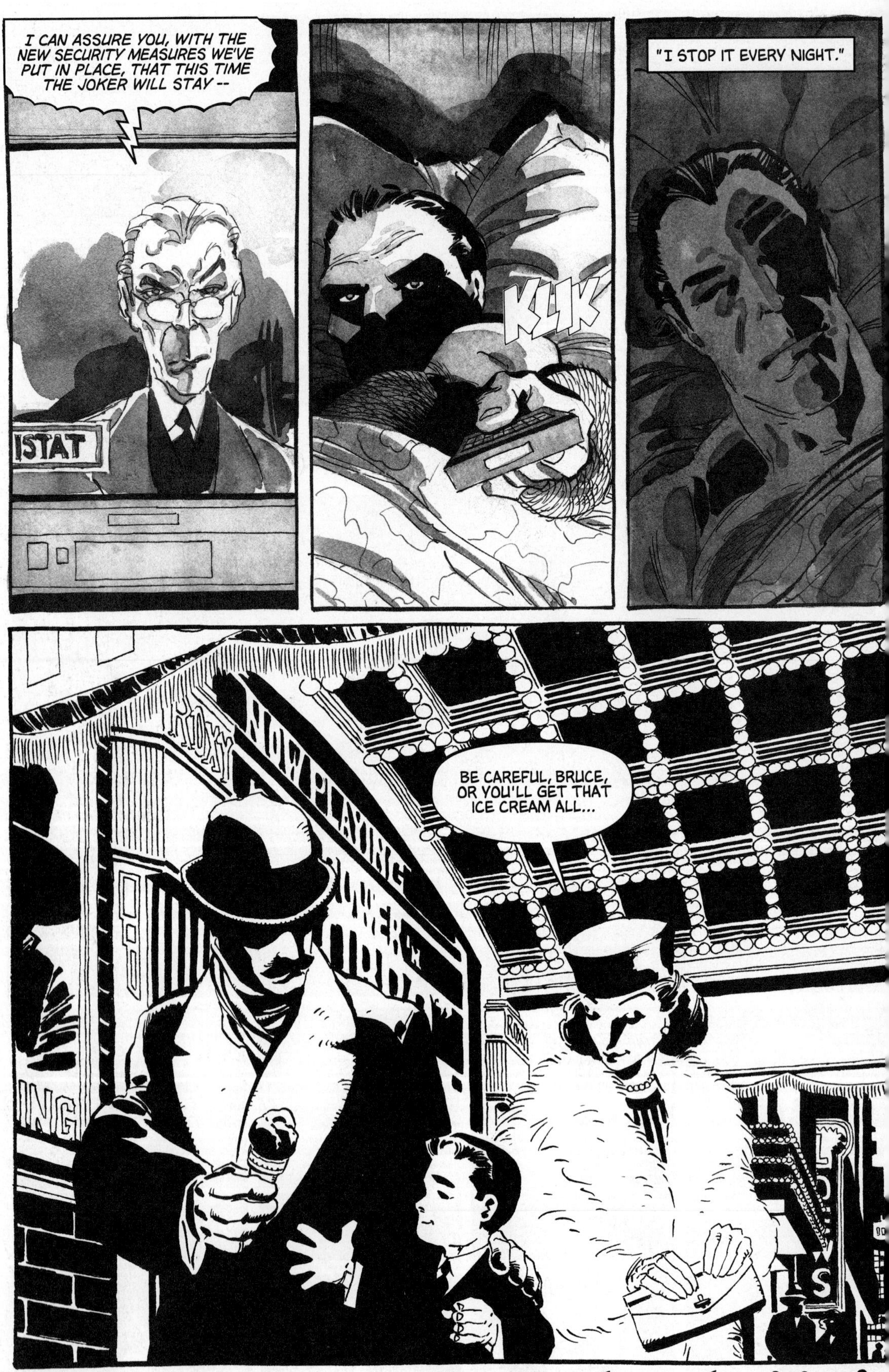
I CAN ASSURE YOU, WITH THE NEW SECURITY MEASURES WE'VE PUT IN PLACE, THAT THIS TIME THE JOKER WILL STAY --
ISTAT
KLIK
"I STOP IT EVERY NIGHT."
ROXY
NOW PLAYING
BE CAREFUL, BRUCE, OR YOU'LL GET THAT ICE CREAM ALL...
ING

KELLEY PUCKETT · TIM SALE · 2002

THE END

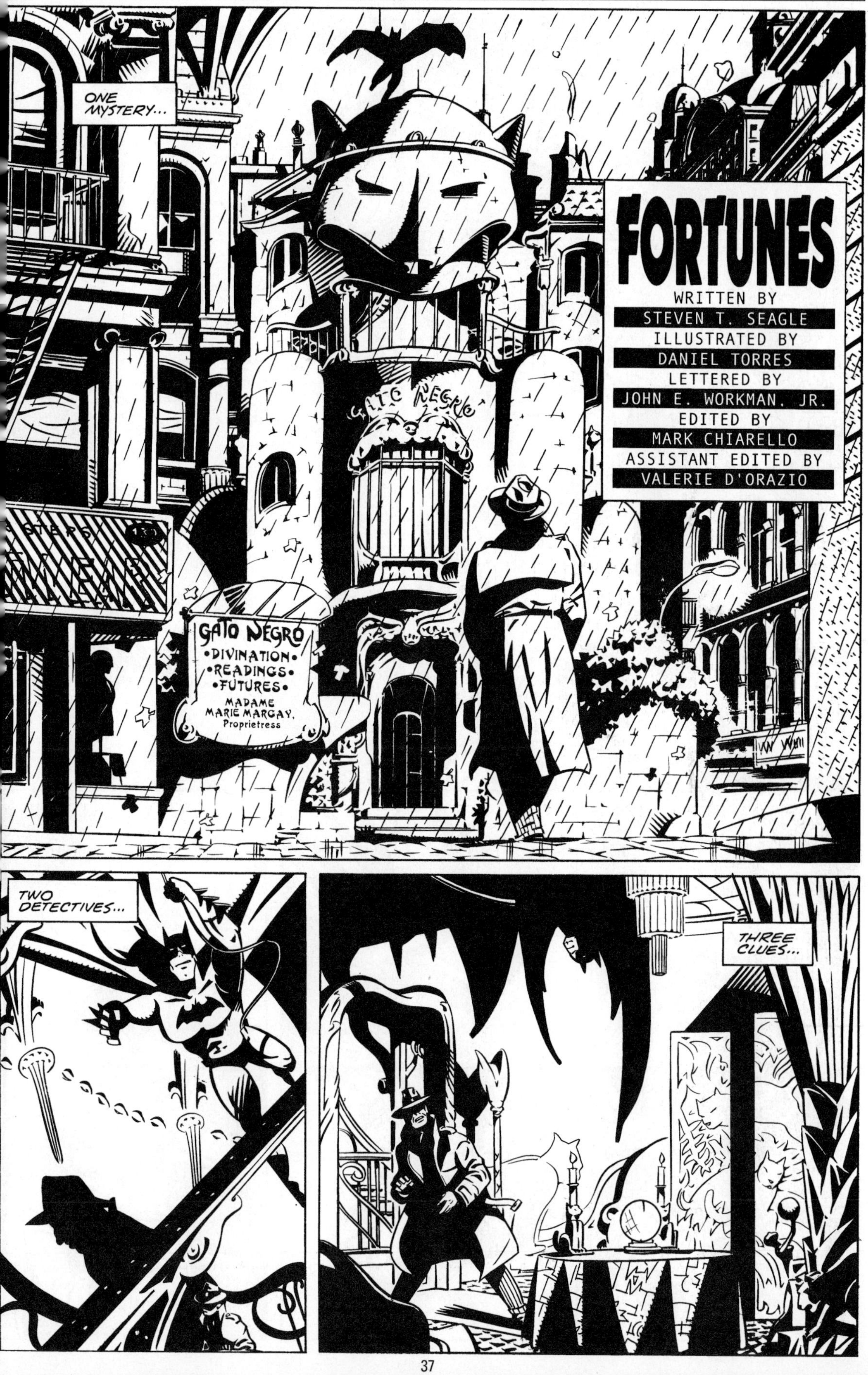
ONE MYSTERY...
FORTUNES
WRITTEN BY
STEVEN T. SEAGLE
ILLUSTRATED BY
DANIEL TORRES
LETTERED BY
JOHN E. WORKMAN, JR.
EDITED BY
MARK CHIARELLO
ASSISTANT EDITED BY
VALERIE D'ORAZIO
GATO NEGRO
GATO NEGRO
•DIVINATION•
•READINGS•
•FUTURES•
MADAME MARIE MARGAY, Proprietress
TWO DETECTIVES...
THREE CLUES...

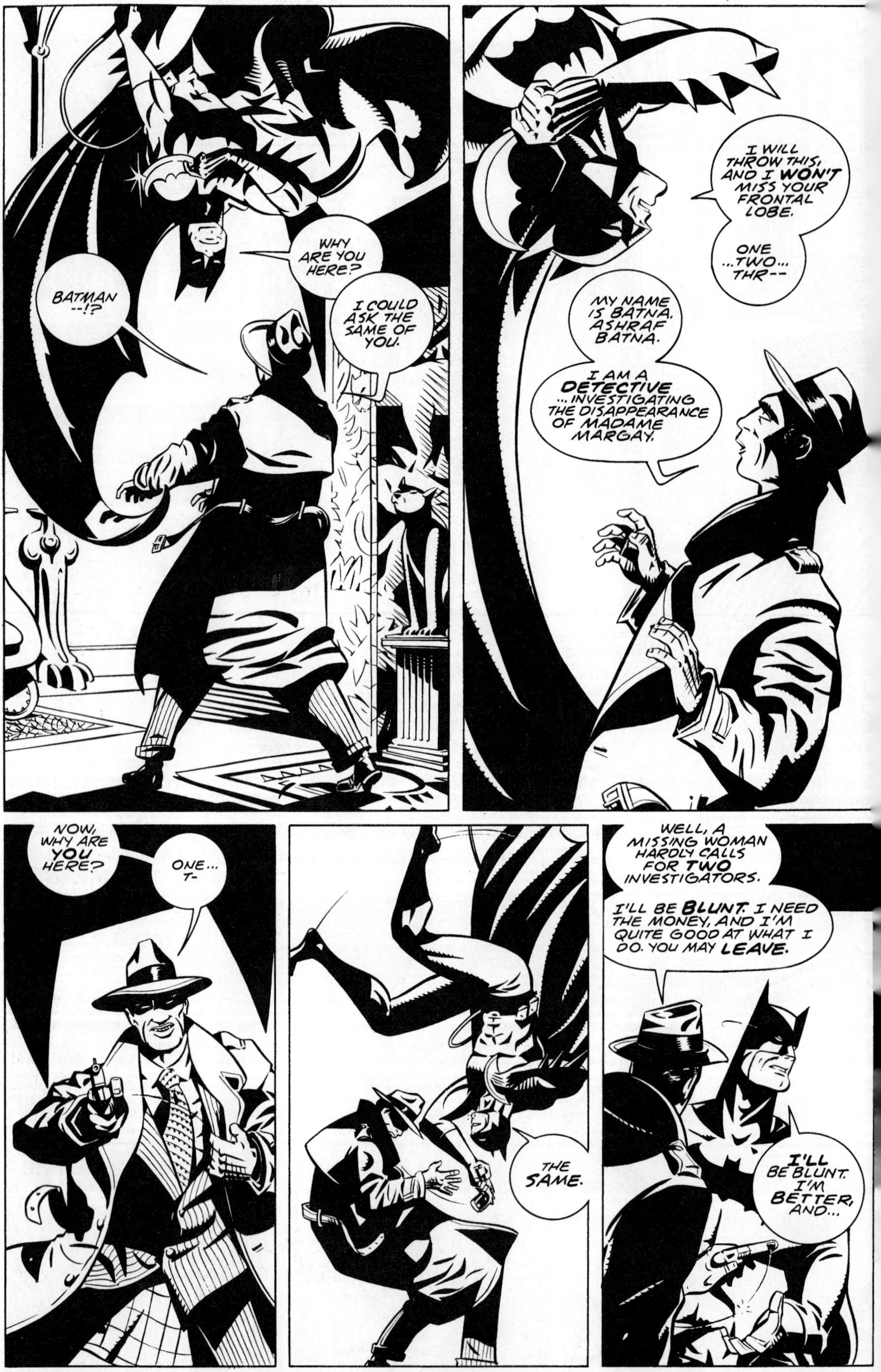
BATMAN --!?
WHY ARE YOU HERE?
I COULD ASK THE SAME OF YOU.
MY NAME IS BATNA. ASHRAF BATNA.
I AM A DETECTIVE ...INVESTIGATING THE DISAPPEARANCE OF MADAME MARGAY.
I WILL THROW THIS, AND I WON'T MISS YOUR FRONTAL LOBE.
ONE ...TWO... THR--
NOW, WHY ARE YOU HERE?
ONE... T-
THE SAME.
WELL, A MISSING WOMAN HARDLY CALLS FOR TWO INVESTIGATORS.
I'LL BE BLUNT. I NEED THE MONEY, AND I'M QUITE GOOD AT WHAT I DO. YOU MAY LEAVE.
I'LL BE BLUNT. I'M BETTER, AND...

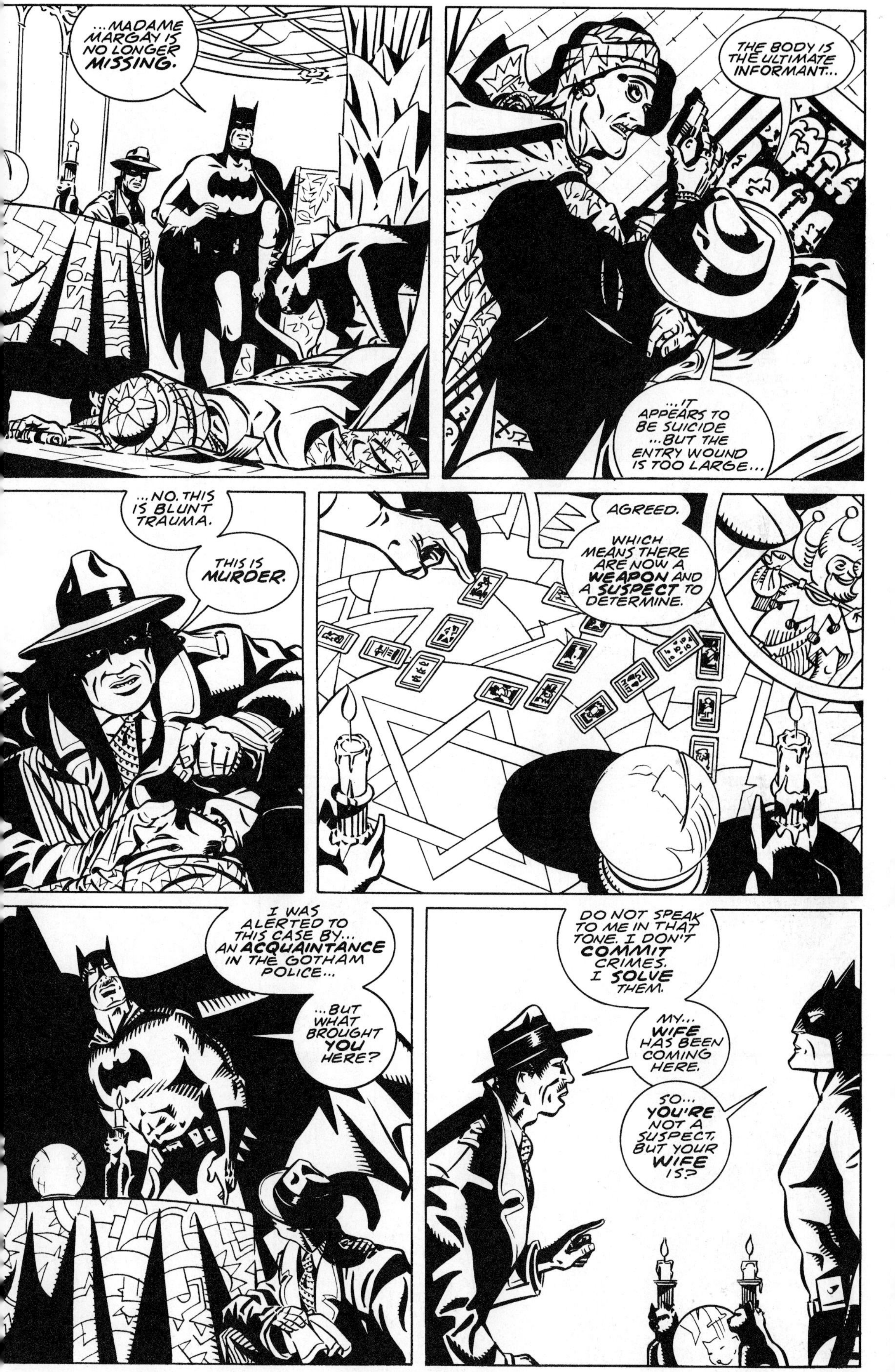
...MADAME MARGAY IS NO LONGER MISSING.
THE BODY IS THE ULTIMATE INFORMANT...
...IT APPEARS TO BE SUICIDE ...BUT THE ENTRY WOUND IS TOO LARGE...
...NO. THIS IS BLUNT TRAUMA.
THIS IS MURDER.
AGREED.
WHICH MEANS THERE ARE NOW A WEAPON AND A SUSPECT TO DETERMINE.
I WAS ALERTED TO THIS CASE BY... AN ACQUAINTANCE IN THE GOTHAM POLICE...
...BUT WHAT BROUGHT YOU HERE?
DO NOT SPEAK TO ME IN THAT TONE. I DON'T COMMIT CRIMES. I SOLVE THEM.
MY... WIFE HAS BEEN COMING HERE.
SO... YOU'RE NOT A SUSPECT, BUT YOUR WIFE IS?

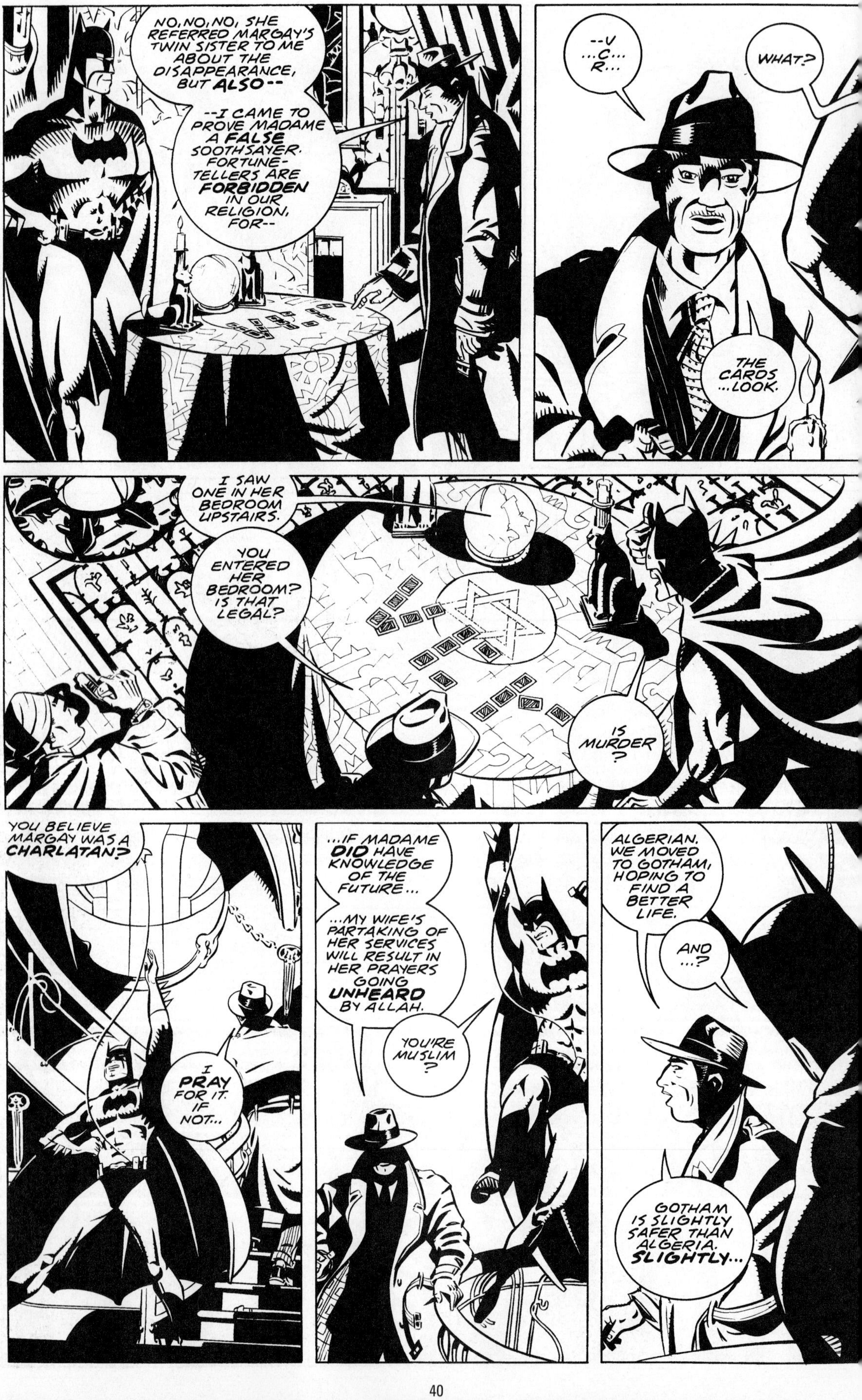
NO, NO, NO, SHE REFERRED MARGAY'S TWIN SISTER TO ME ABOUT THE DISAPPEARANCE, BUT ALSO--
--I CAME TO PROVE MADAME A FALSE SOOTHSAYER. FORTUNE-TELLERS ARE FORBIDDEN IN OUR RELIGION, FOR--
--V ...C... R...
WHAT?
THE CARDS ...LOOK.
I SAW ONE IN HER BEDROOM UPSTAIRS.
YOU ENTERED HER BEDROOM? IS THAT LEGAL?
IS MURDER?
YOU BELIEVE MARGAY WAS A CHARLATAN?
I PRAY FOR IT. IF NOT...
...IF MADAME DID HAVE KNOWLEDGE OF THE FUTURE...
...MY WIFE'S PARTAKING OF HER SERVICES WILL RESULT IN HER PRAYERS GOING UNHEARD BY ALLAH.
YOU'RE MUSLIM?
ALGERIAN. WE MOVED TO GOTHAM, HOPING TO FIND A BETTER LIFE.
AND ...?
GOTHAM IS SLIGHTLY SAFER THAN ALGERIA. SLIGHTLY...

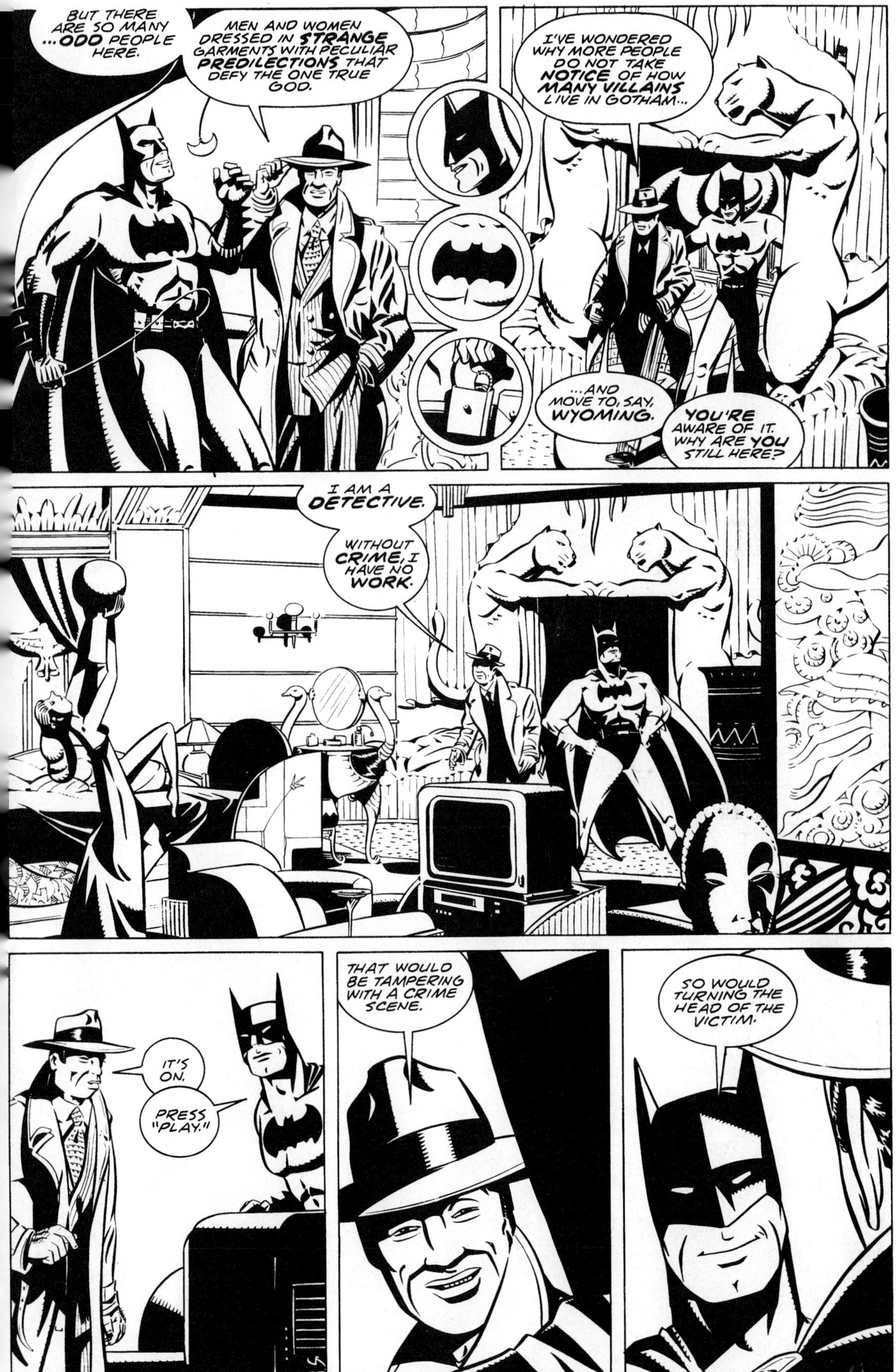
BUT THERE ARE SO MANY ...ODD PEOPLE HERE.
MEN AND WOMEN DRESSED IN STRANGE GARMENTS WITH PECULIAR PREDILECTIONS THAT DEFY THE ONE TRUE GOD.
I'VE WONDERED WHY MORE PEOPLE DO NOT TAKE NOTICE OF HOW MANY VILLAINS LIVE IN GOTHAM...
...AND MOVE TO, SAY, WYOMING.
YOU'RE AWARE OF IT. WHY ARE YOU STILL HERE?
I AM A DETECTIVE.
WITHOUT CRIME, I HAVE NO WORK.
IT'S ON.
PRESS "PLAY."
THAT WOULD BE TAMPERING WITH A CRIME SCENE.
SO WOULD TURNING THE HEAD OF THE VICTIM.

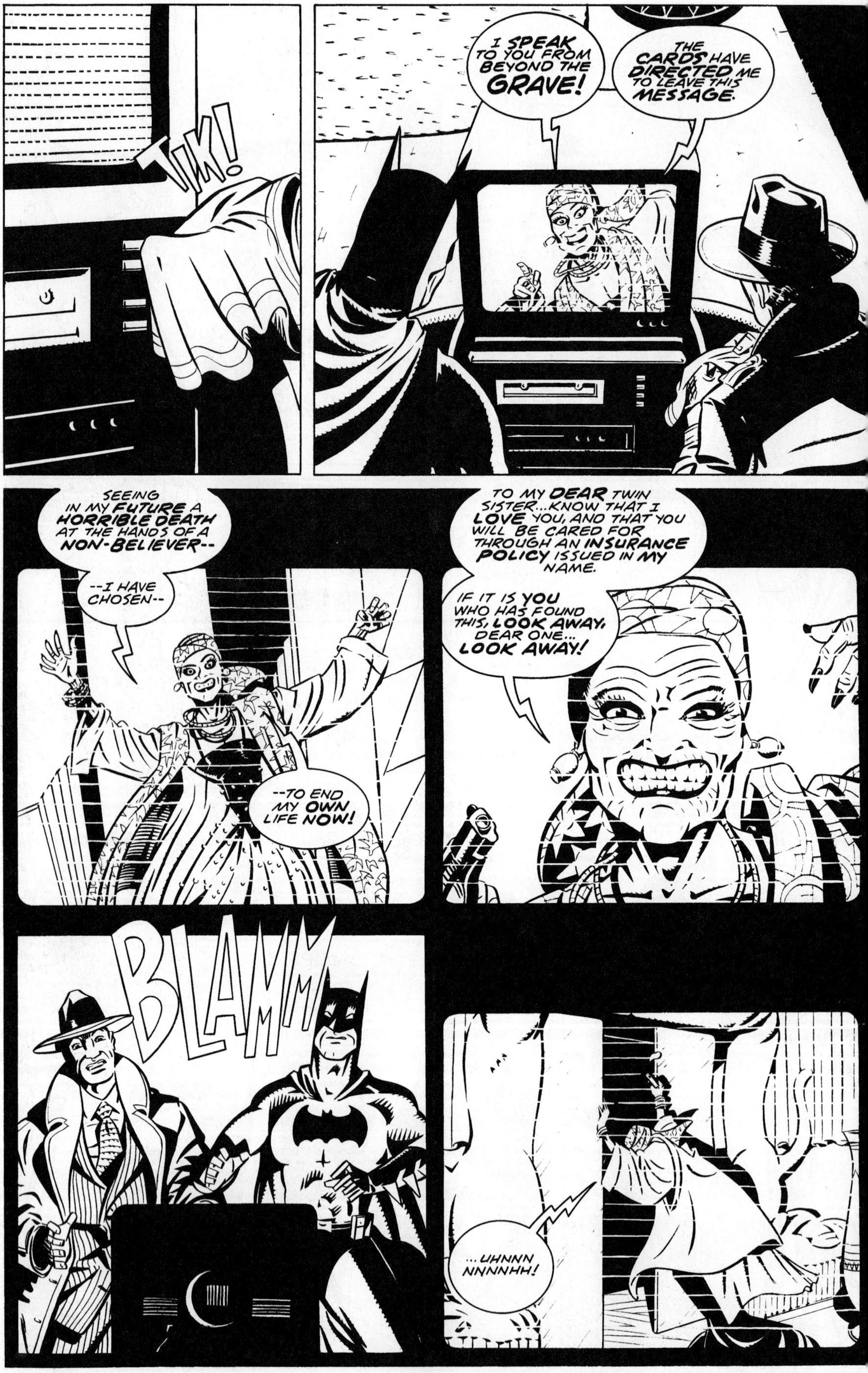
TIK!
I SPEAK TO YOU FROM BEYOND THE GRAVE!
THE CARDS HAVE DIRECTED ME TO LEAVE THIS MESSAGE.
SEEING IN MY FUTURE A HORRIBLE DEATH AT THE HANDS OF A NON-BELIEVER--
--I HAVE CHOSEN--
--TO END MY OWN LIFE NOW!
TO MY DEAR TWIN SISTER...KNOW THAT I LOVE YOU, AND THAT YOU WILL BE CARED FOR THROUGH AN INSURANCE POLICY ISSUED IN MY NAME.
IF IT IS YOU WHO HAS FOUND THIS, LOOK AWAY, DEAR ONE... LOOK AWAY!
BLAMM
...UHNNN NNNNHH!

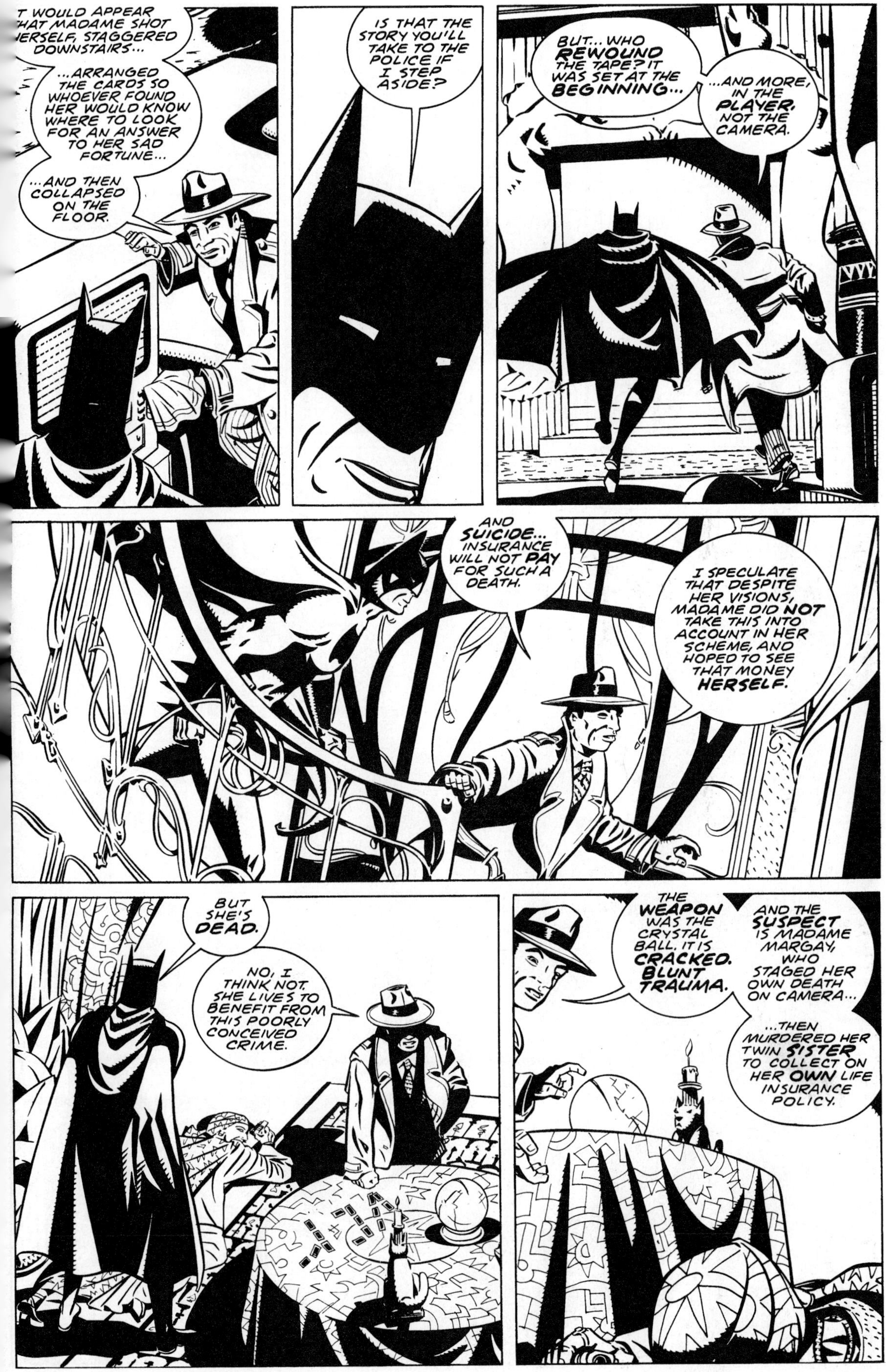
T WOULD APPEAR HAT MADAME SHOT IERSELF, STAGGERED DOWNSTAIRS...
...ARRANGED THE CARDS SO WHOEVER FOUND HER WOULD KNOW WHERE TO LOOK FOR AN ANSWER TO HER SAD FORTUNE...
...AND THEN COLLAPSED ON THE FLOOR.
IS THAT THE STORY YOU'LL TAKE TO THE POLICE IF I STEP ASIDE?
BUT... WHO REWOUND THE TAPE? IT WAS SET AT THE BEGINNING...
...AND MORE, IN THE PLAYER, NOT THE CAMERA.
AND SUICIDE... INSURANCE WILL NOT PAY FOR SUCH A DEATH.
I SPECULATE THAT DESPITE HER VISIONS, MADAME DID NOT TAKE THIS INTO ACCOUNT IN HER SCHEME, AND HOPED TO SEE THAT MONEY HERSELF.
BUT SHE'S DEAD.
NO, I THINK NOT. SHE LIVES TO BENEFIT FROM THIS POORLY CONCEIVED CRIME.
THE WEAPON WAS THE CRYSTAL BALL. IT IS CRACKED. BLUNT TRAUMA.
AND THE SUSPECT IS MADAME MARGAY, WHO STAGED HER OWN DEATH ON CAMERA...
...THEN MURDERED HER TWIN SISTER TO COLLECT ON HER OWN LIFE INSURANCE POLICY.

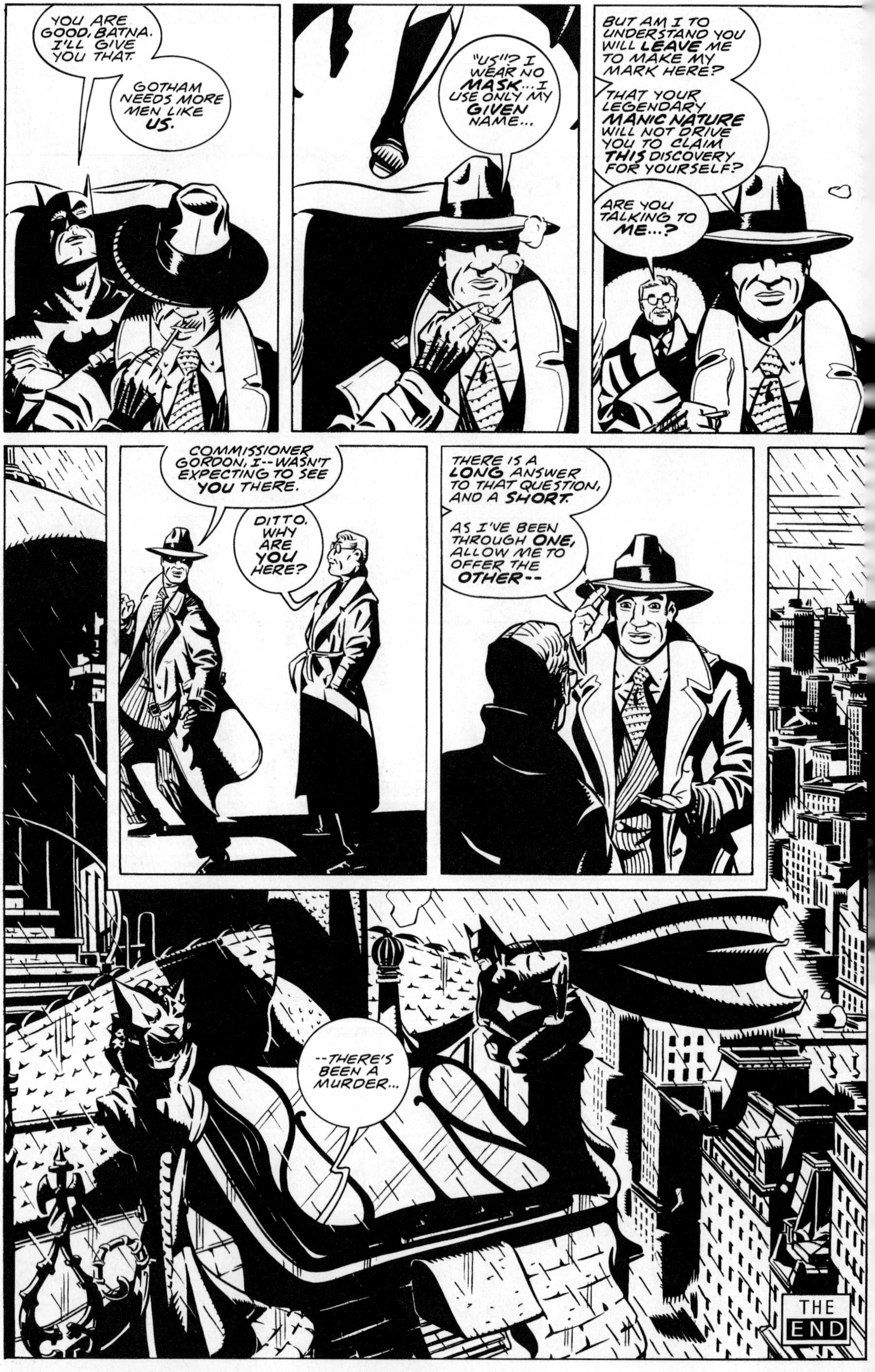

YOU ARE GOOD, BATNA. I'LL GIVE YOU THAT.
GOTHAM NEEDS MORE MEN LIKE US.
"US"? I WEAR NO MASK... I USE ONLY MY GIVEN NAME...
BUT AM I TO UNDERSTAND YOU WILL LEAVE ME TO MAKE MY MARK HERE?
THAT YOUR LEGENDARY MANIC NATURE WILL NOT DRIVE YOU TO CLAIM THIS DISCOVERY FOR YOURSELF?
ARE YOU TALKING TO ME...?
COMMISSIONER GORDON, I--WASN'T EXPECTING TO SEE YOU THERE.
DITTO. WHY ARE YOU HERE?
THERE IS A LONG ANSWER TO THAT QUESTION, AND A SHORT.
AS I'VE BEEN THROUGH ONE, ALLOW ME TO OFFER THE OTHER--
--THERE'S BEEN A MURDER...
THE END

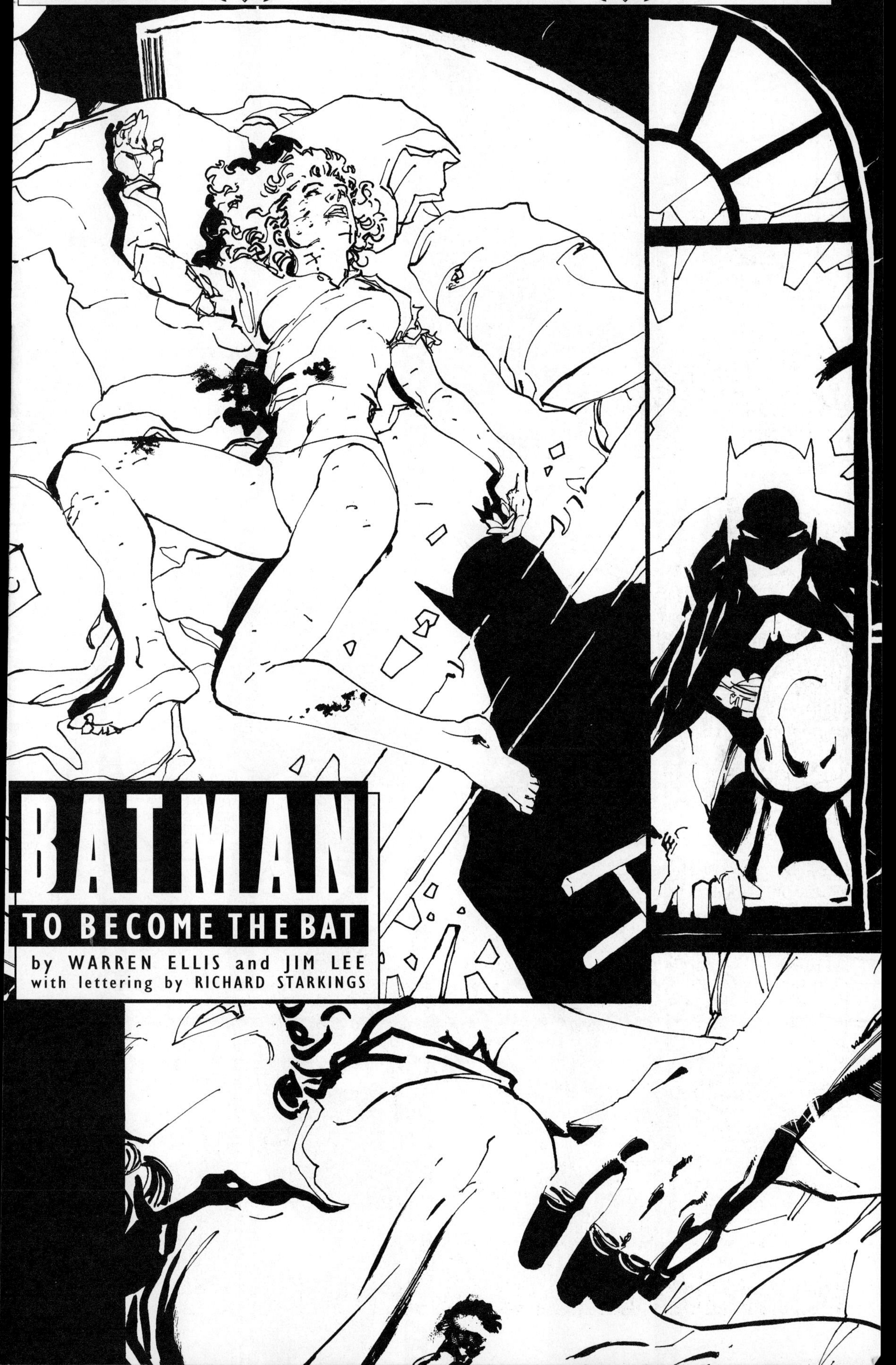
BATMAN
TO BECOME THE BAT
by WARREN ELLIS and JIM LEE
with lettering by RICHARD STARKINGS

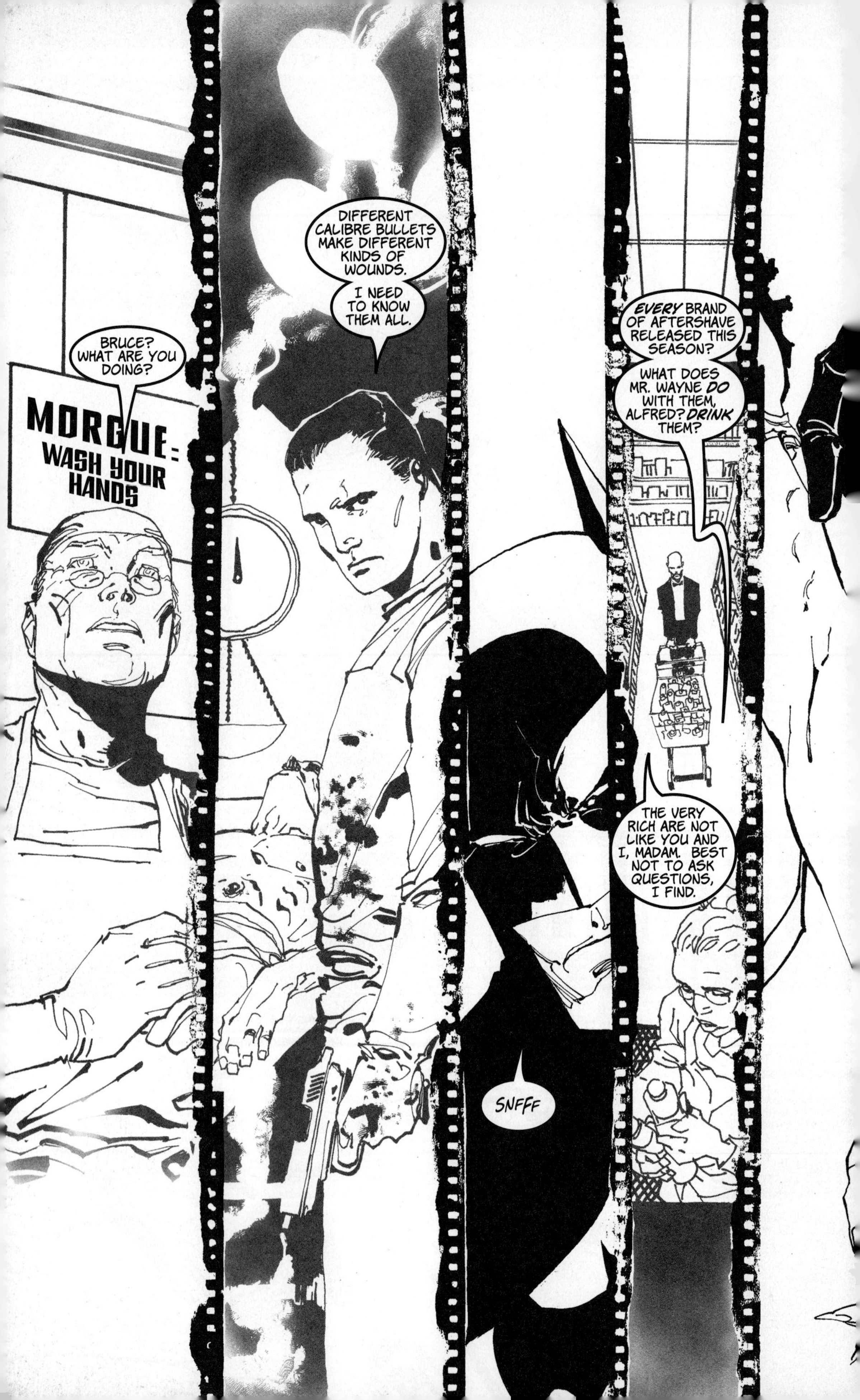

BRUCE? WHAT ARE YOU DOING?
MORGUE: WASH YOUR HANDS
DIFFERENT CALIBRE BULLETS MAKE DIFFERENT KINDS OF WOUNDS.
I NEED TO KNOW THEM ALL.
SNFFF
EVERY BRAND OF AFTERSHAVE RELEASED THIS SEASON?
WHAT DOES MR. WAYNE DO WITH THEM, ALFRED? DRINK THEM?
THE VERY RICH ARE NOT LIKE YOU AND I, MADAM. BEST NOT TO ASK QUESTIONS, I FIND.

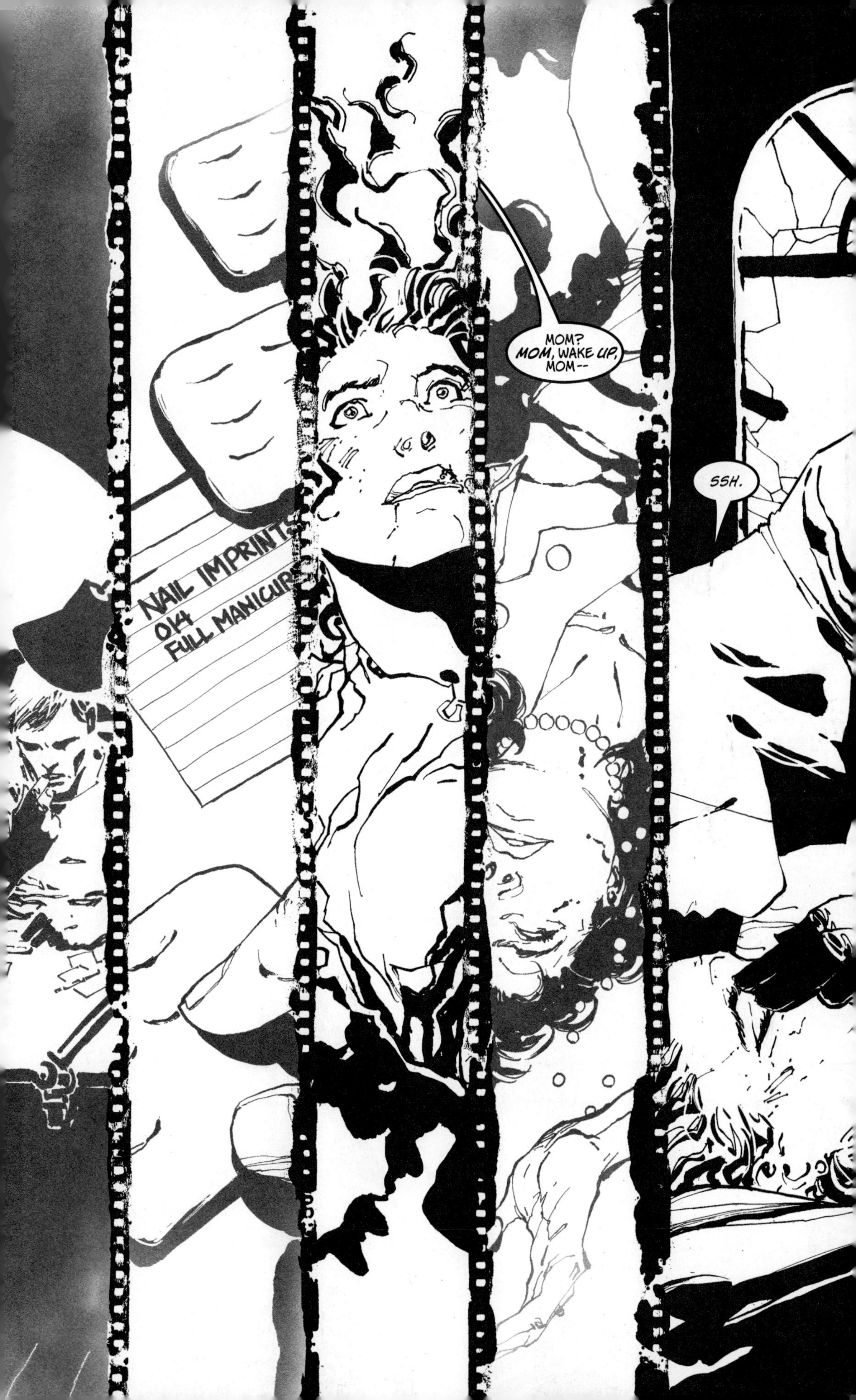
NAIL IMPRINTS
014
FULL MANICURE
MOM? MOM, WAKE UP, MOM--
SSH.

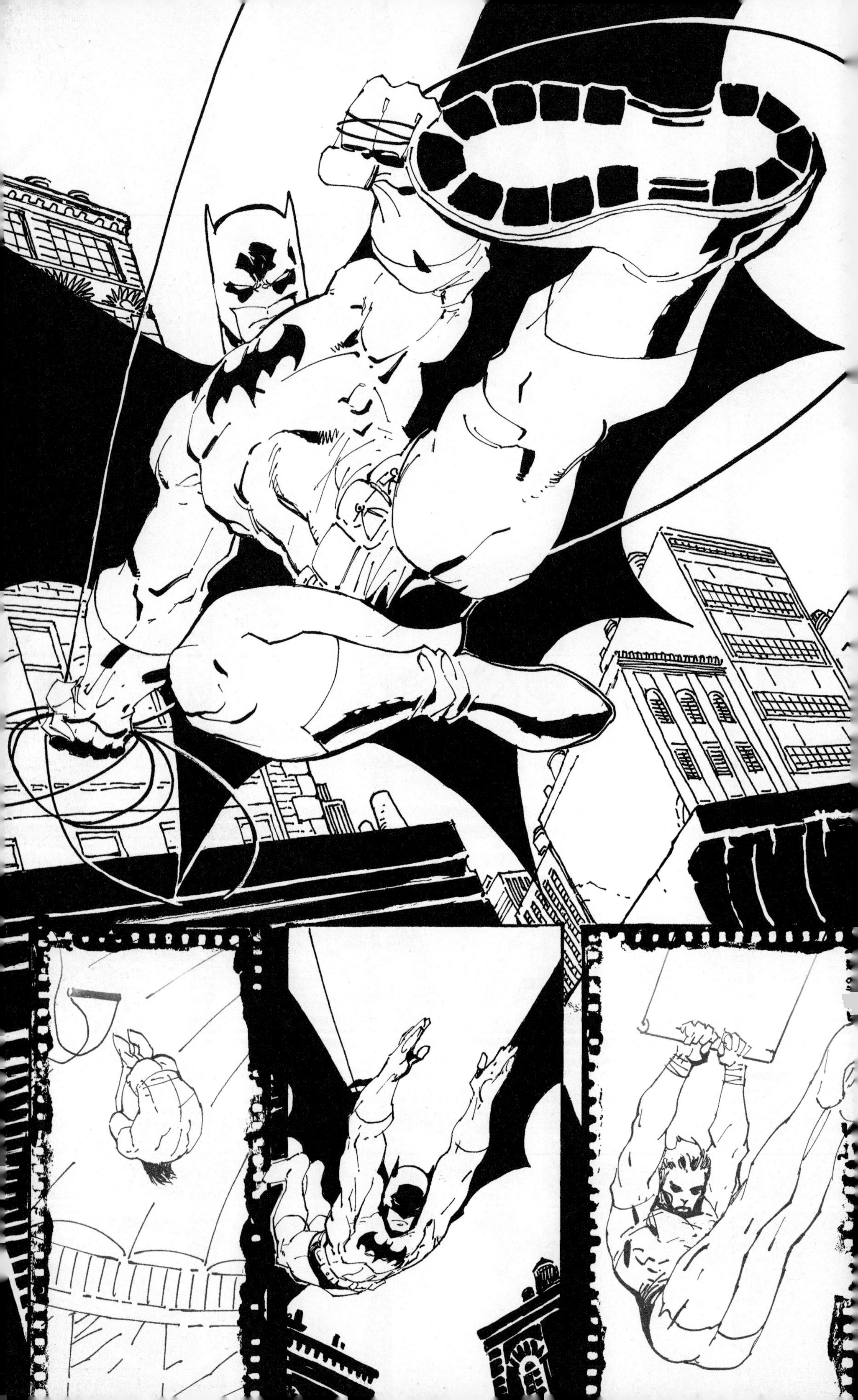

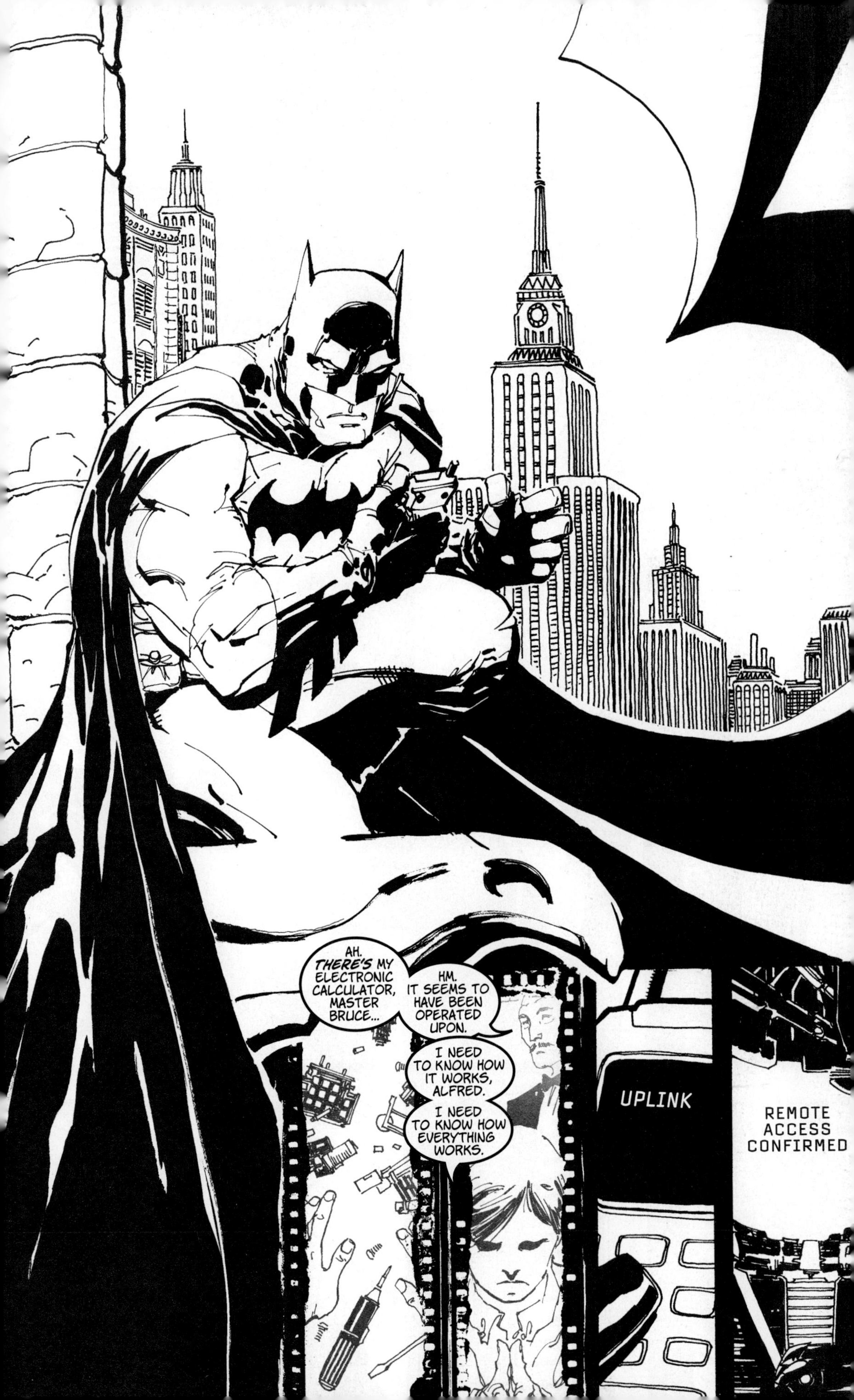
AH. THERE'S MY ELECTRONIC CALCULATOR, MASTER BRUCE...
HM. IT SEEMS TO HAVE BEEN OPERATED UPON.
I NEED TO KNOW HOW IT WORKS, ALFRED.
I NEED TO KNOW HOW EVERYTHING WORKS.
UPLINK
REMOTE ACCESS CONFIRMED

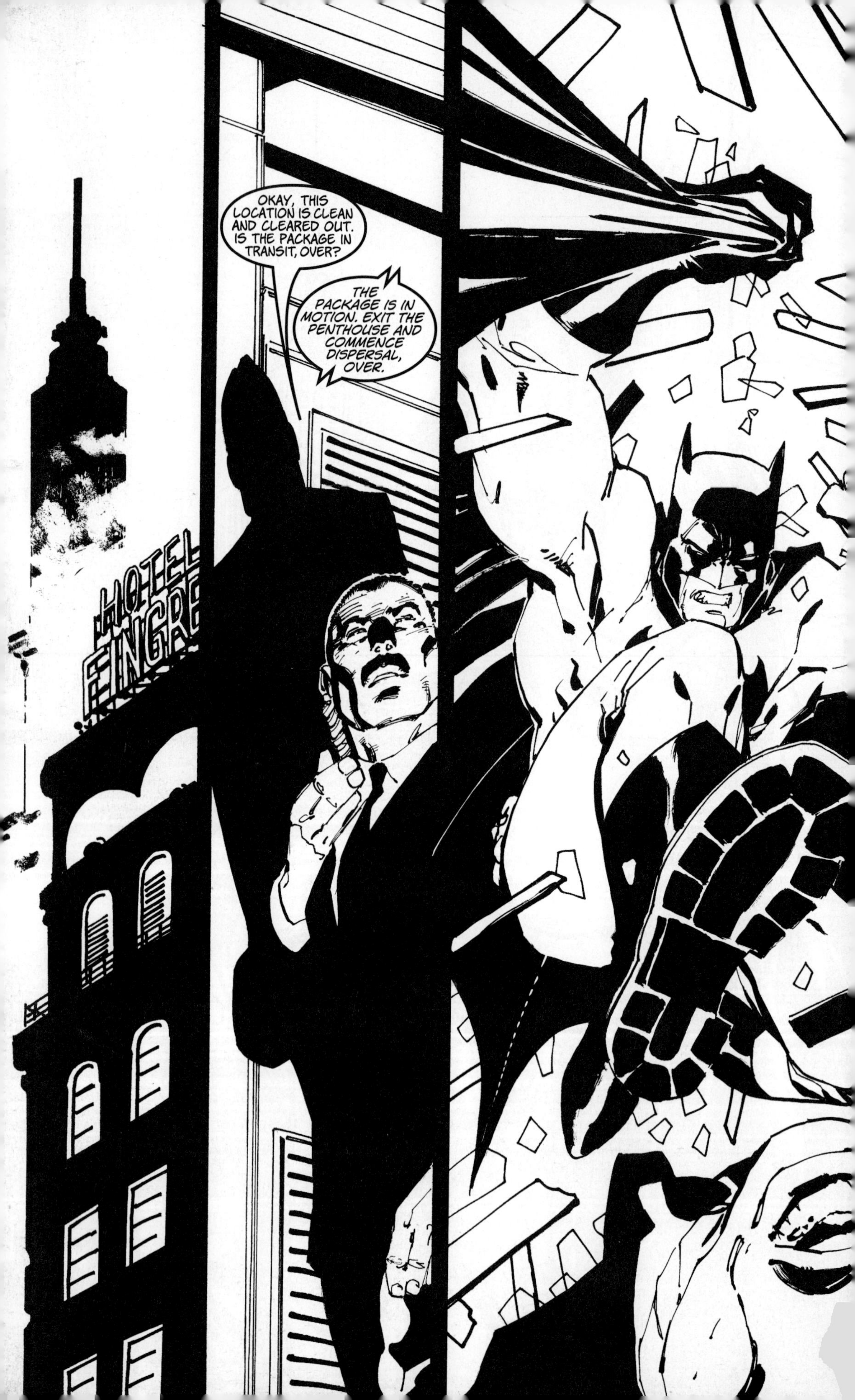
OKAY, THIS LOCATION IS CLEAN AND CLEARED OUT. IS THE PACKAGE IN TRANSIT, OVER?
THE PACKAGE IS IN MOTION. EXIT THE PENTHOUSE AND COMMENCE DISPERSAL, OVER.
HOTEL FINGR

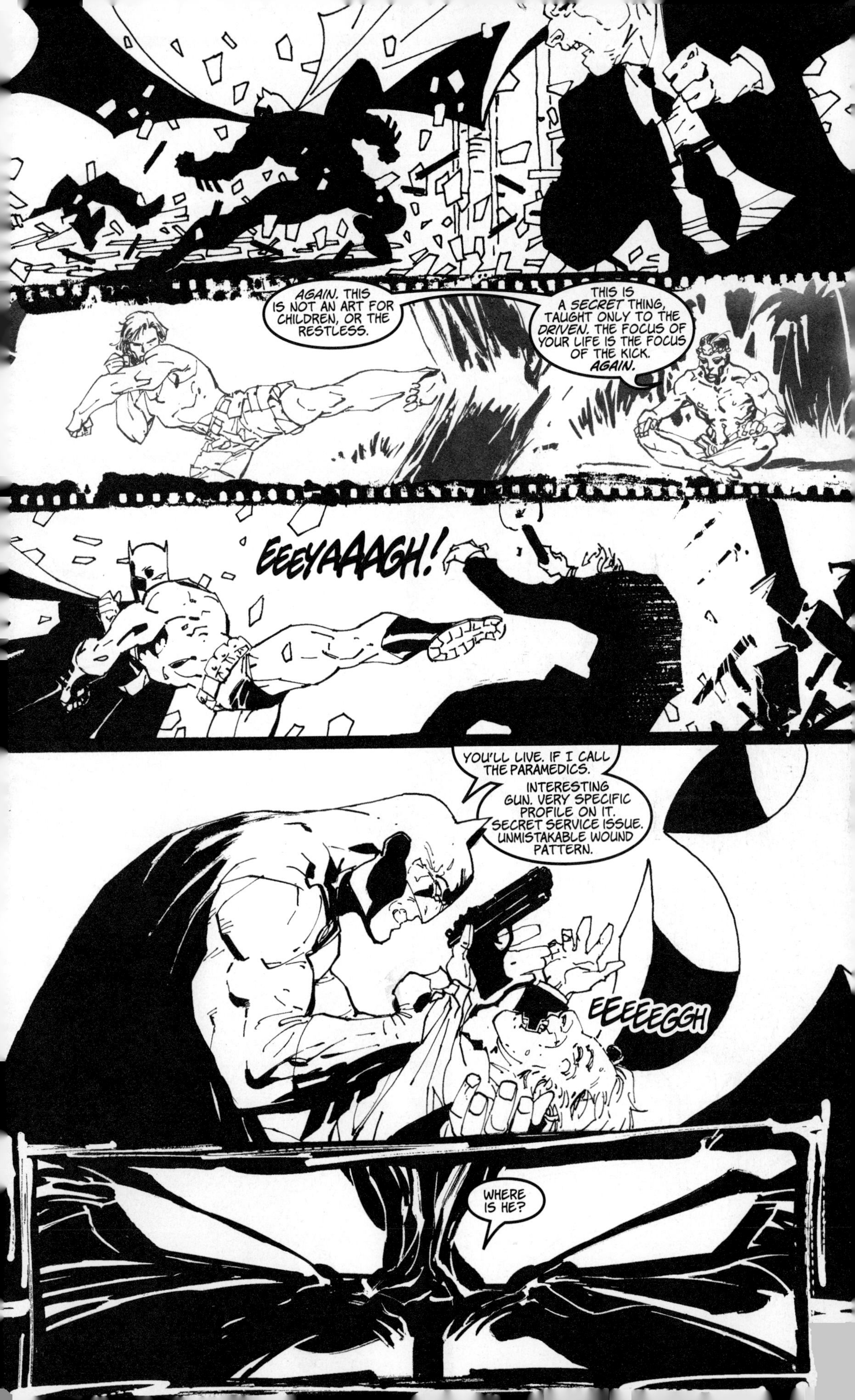
AGAIN. THIS IS NOT AN ART FOR CHILDREN, OR THE RESTLESS.
THIS IS A SECRET THING, TAUGHT ONLY TO THE DRIVEN. THE FOCUS OF YOUR LIFE IS THE FOCUS OF THE KICK. AGAIN.
EEEYAAAAGH!
YOU'LL LIVE. IF I CALL THE PARAMEDICS.
INTERESTING GUN. VERY SPECIFIC PROFILE ON IT. SECRET SERVICE ISSUE. UNMISTAKABLE WOUND PATTERN.
EEEEEEGGH
WHERE IS HE?

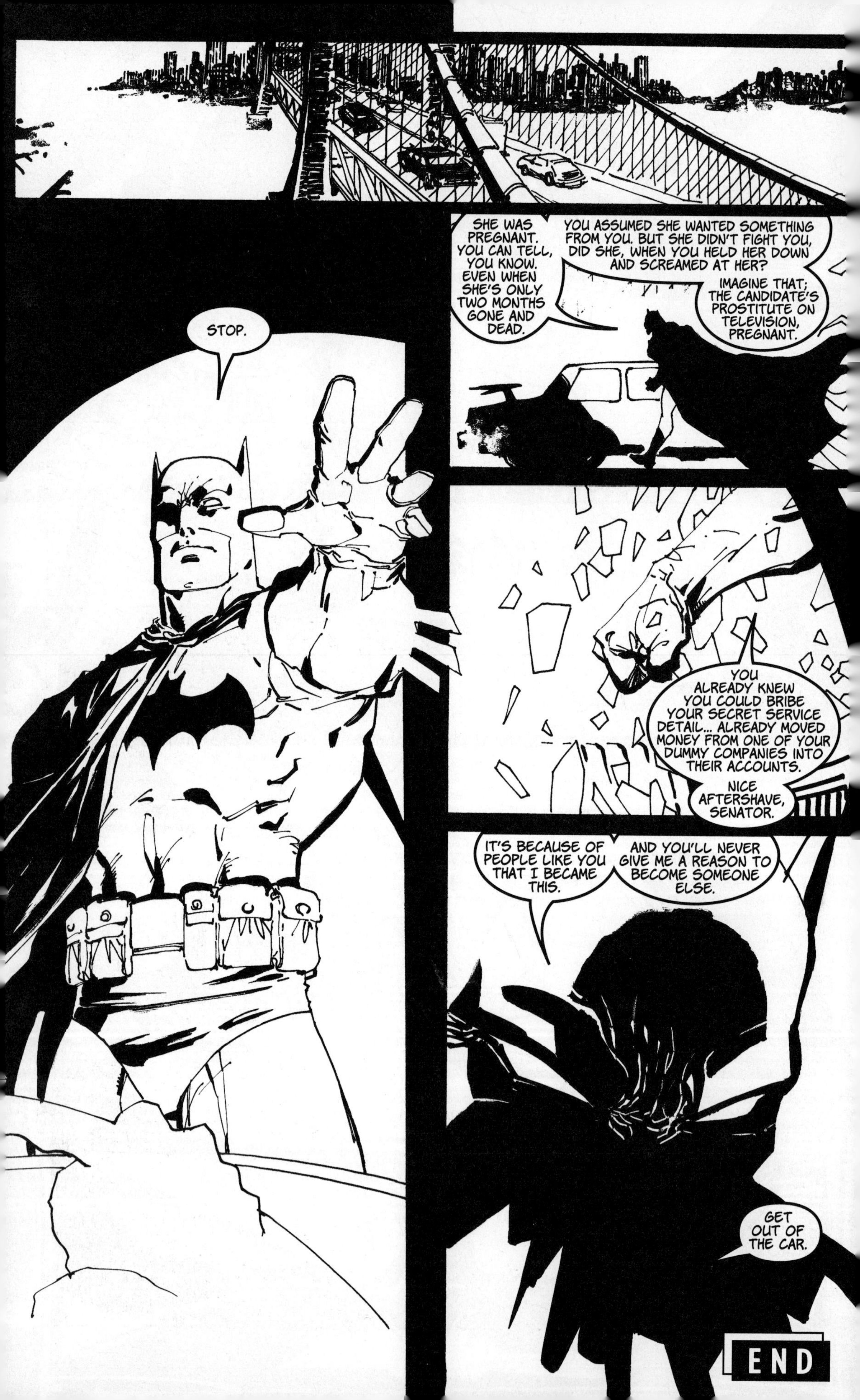
STOP.
SHE WAS PREGNANT. YOU CAN TELL, YOU KNOW. EVEN WHEN SHE'S ONLY TWO MONTHS GONE AND DEAD.
YOU ASSUMED SHE WANTED SOMETHING FROM YOU. BUT SHE DIDN'T FIGHT YOU, DID SHE, WHEN YOU HELD HER DOWN AND SCREAMED AT HER?
IMAGINE THAT; THE CANDIDATE'S PROSTITUTE ON TELEVISION, PREGNANT.
YOU ALREADY KNEW YOU COULD BRIBE YOUR SECRET SERVICE DETAIL... ALREADY MOVED MONEY FROM ONE OF YOUR DUMMY COMPANIES INTO THEIR ACCOUNTS.
NICE AFTERSHAVE, SENATOR.
IT'S BECAUSE OF PEOPLE LIKE YOU THAT I BECAME THIS.
AND YOU'LL NEVER GIVE ME A REASON TO BECOME SOMEONE ELSE.
GET OUT OF THE CAR.
END

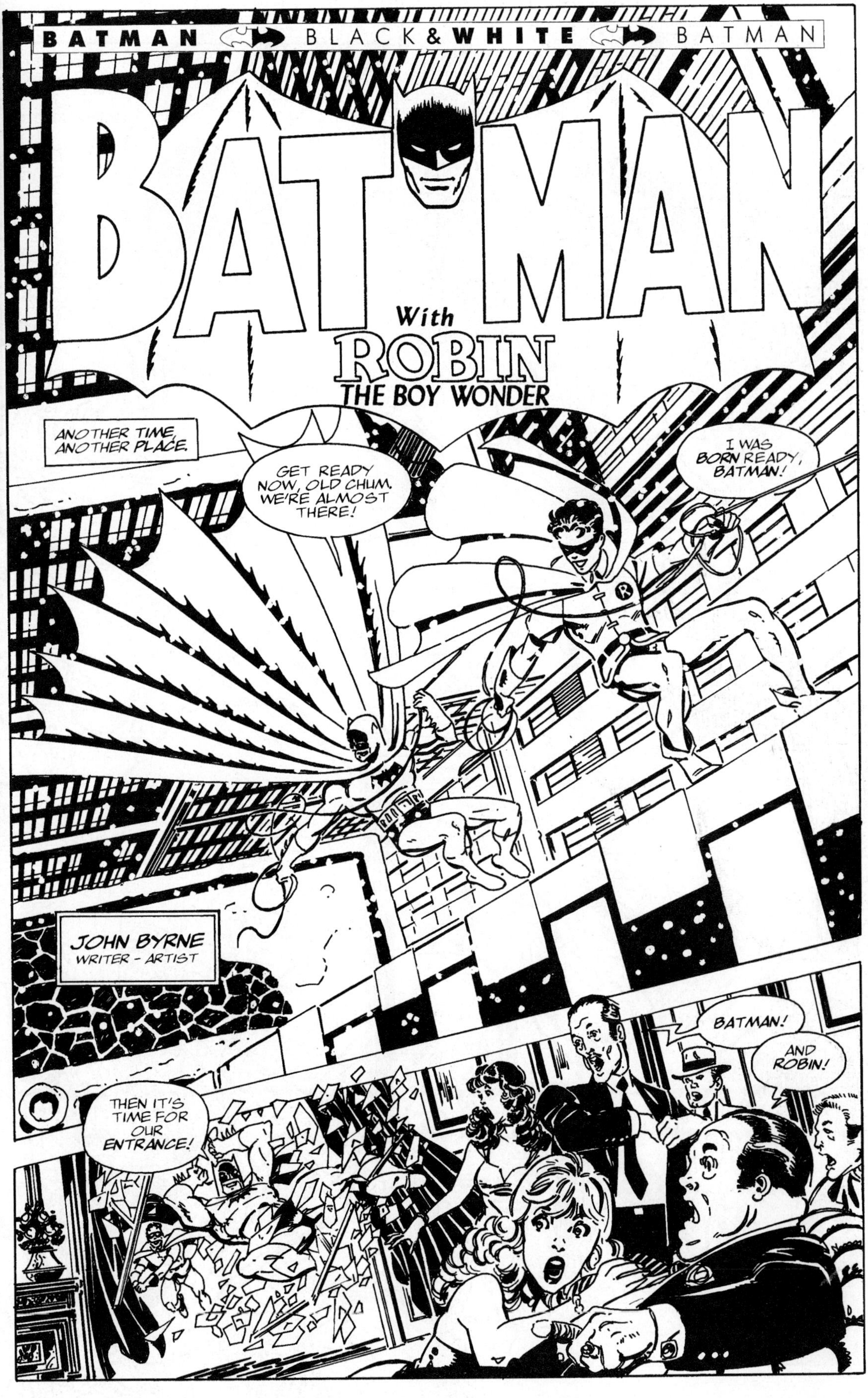

BATMAN BLACK & WHITE BATMAN
BATMAN
With ROBIN THE BOY WONDER
ANOTHER TIME, ANOTHER PLACE.
GET READY NOW, OLD CHUM. WE'RE ALMOST THERE!
I WAS BORN READY, BATMAN!
JOHN BYRNE WRITER - ARTIST
THEN IT'S TIME FOR OUR ENTRANCE!
BATMAN!
AND ROBIN!

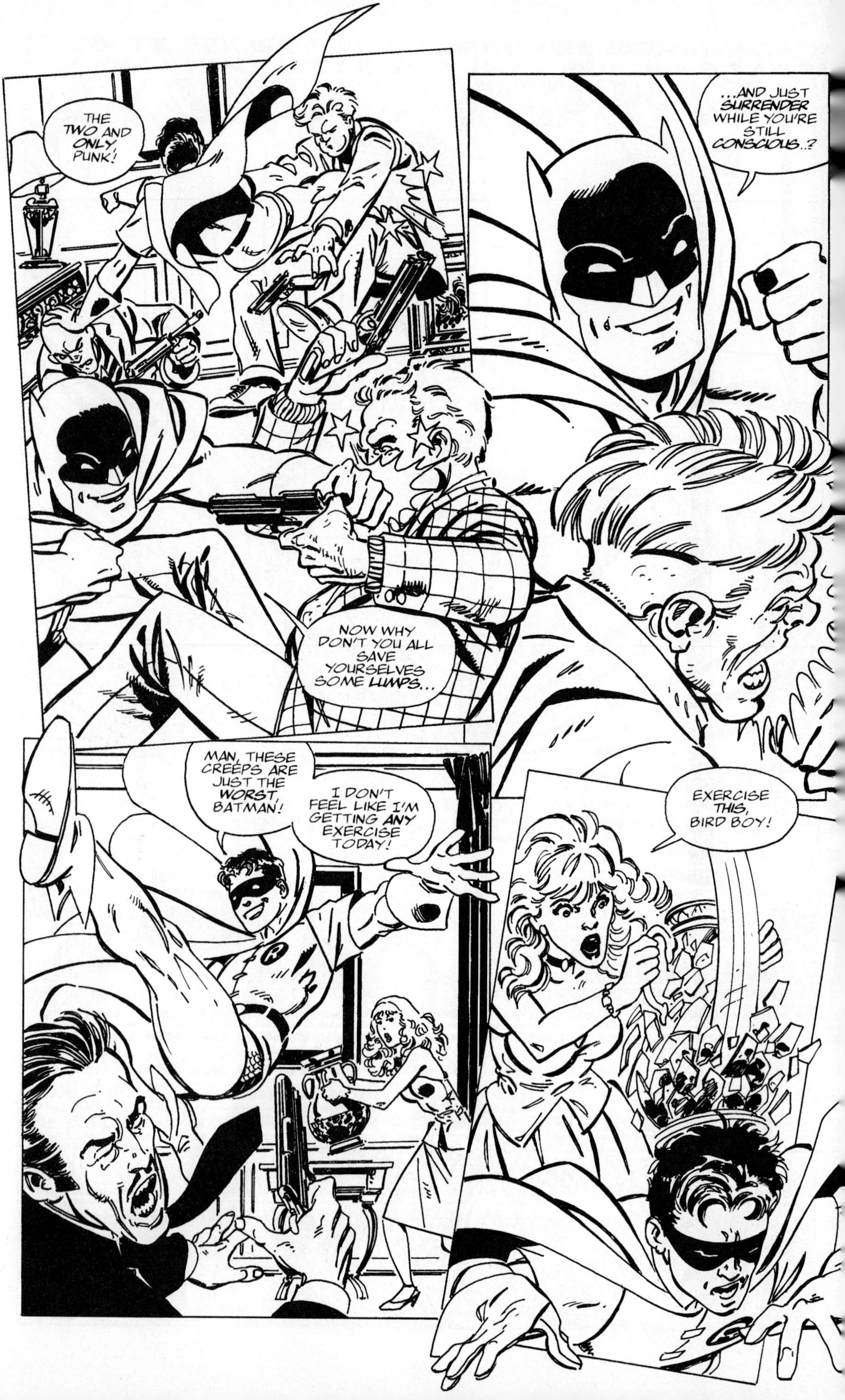
THE TWO AND ONLY PUNK!
...AND JUST SURRENDER WHILE YOU'RE STILL CONSCIOUS..?
NOW WHY DON'T YOU ALL SAVE YOURSELVES SOME LUMPS...
MAN, THESE CREEPS ARE JUST THE WORST, BATMAN!
I DON'T FEEL LIKE I'M GETTING ANY EXERCISE TODAY!
EXERCISE THIS, BIRD BOY!

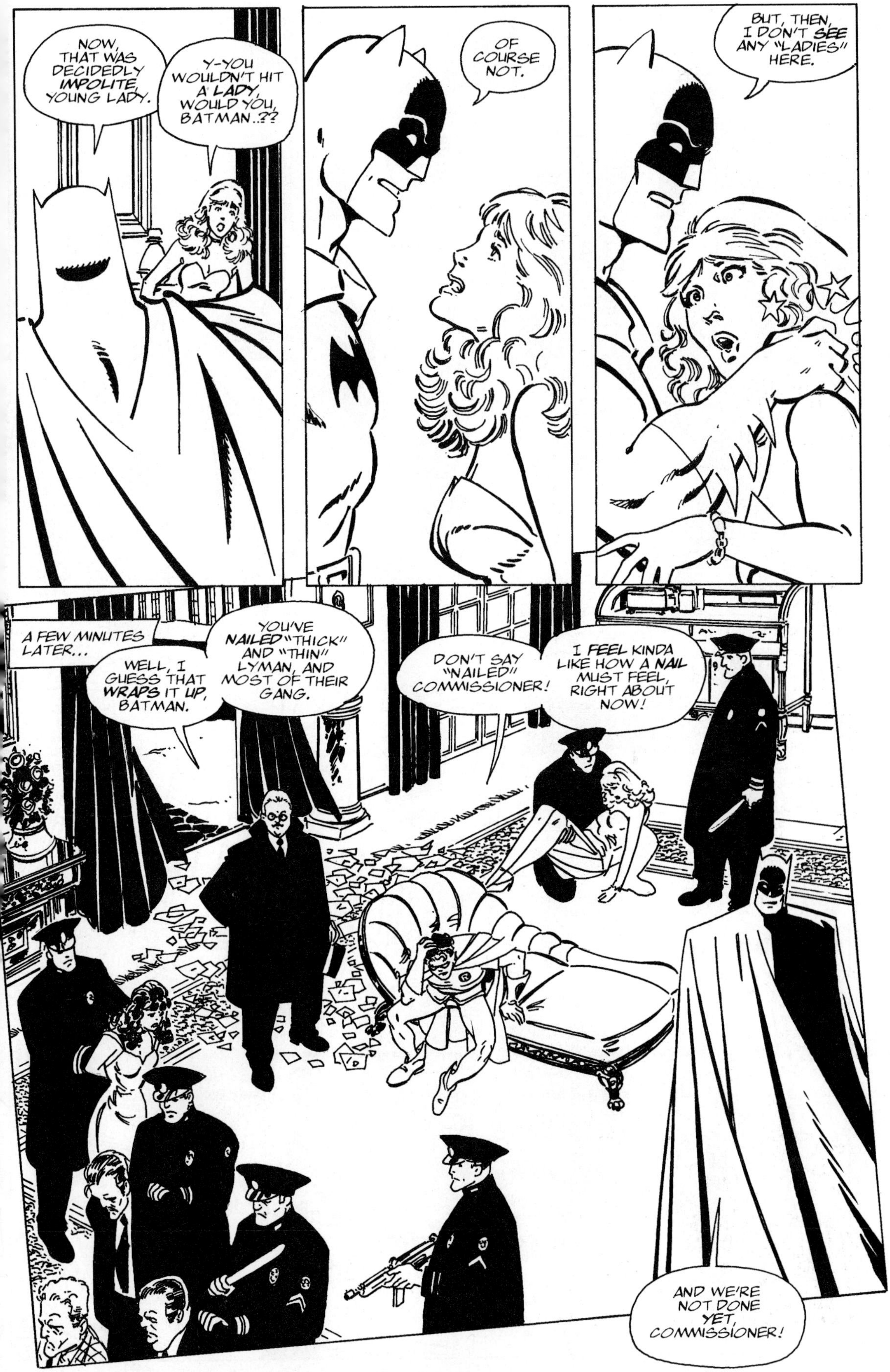
NOW, THAT WAS DECIDEDLY IMPOLITE, YOUNG LADY.
Y-YOU WOULDN'T HIT A LADY, WOULD YOU, BATMAN..??
OF COURSE NOT.
BUT, THEN, I DON'T SEE ANY "LADIES" HERE.
A FEW MINUTES LATER...
WELL, I GUESS THAT WRAPS IT UP, BATMAN.
YOU'VE NAILED "THICK" AND "THIN" LYMAN, AND MOST OF THEIR GANG.
DON'T SAY "NAILED" COMMISSIONER!
I FEEL KINDA LIKE HOW A NAIL MUST FEEL, RIGHT ABOUT NOW!
AND WE'RE NOT DONE YET, COMMISSIONER!

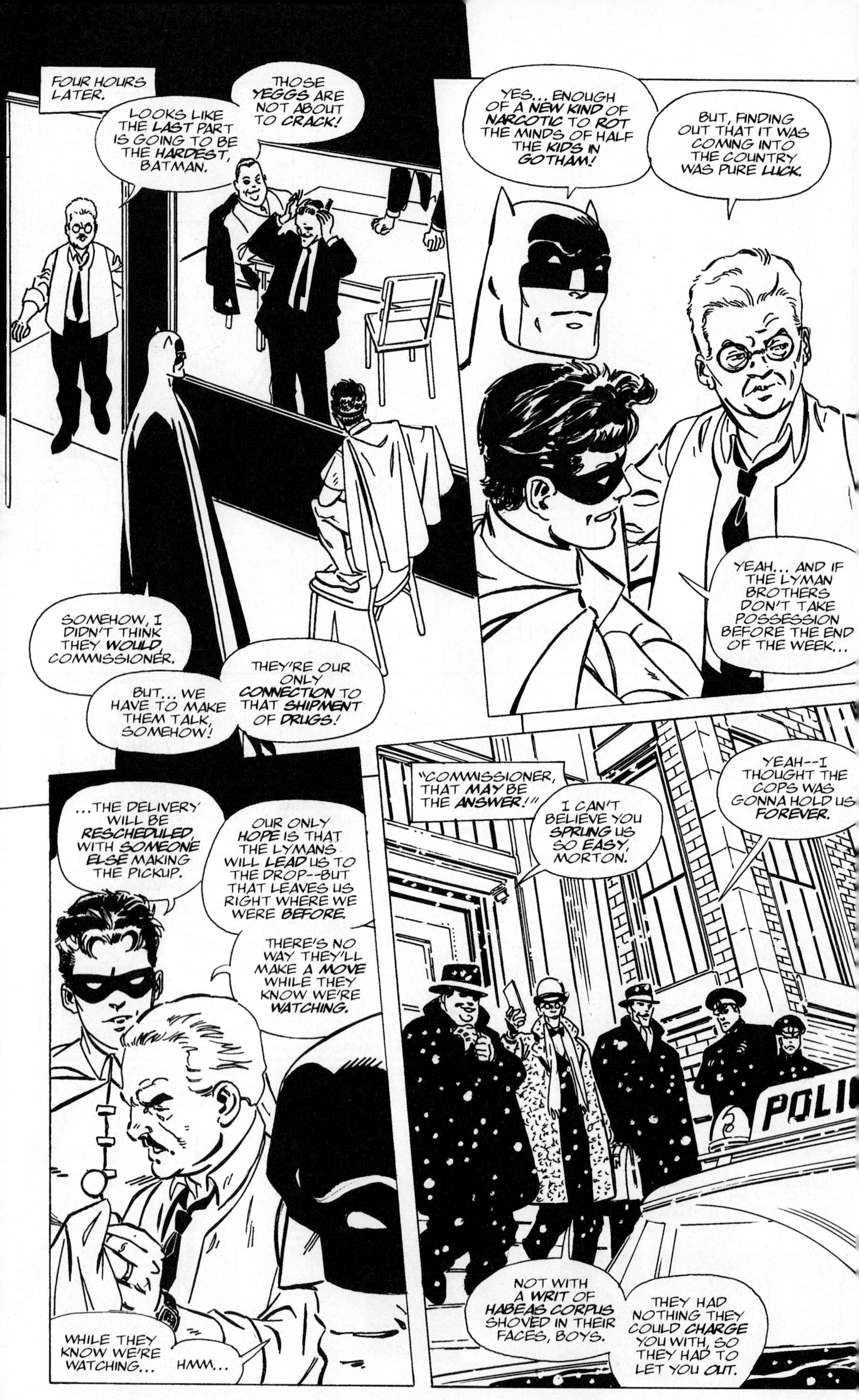

FOUR HOURS LATER.
LOOKS LIKE THE LAST PART IS GOING TO BE THE HARDEST, BATMAN.
THOSE YEGGS ARE NOT ABOUT TO CRACK!
SOMEHOW, I DIDN'T THINK THEY WOULD, COMMISSIONER.
BUT... WE HAVE TO MAKE THEM TALK, SOMEHOW!
THEY'RE OUR ONLY CONNECTION TO THAT SHIPMENT OF DRUGS!
YES... ENOUGH OF A NEW KIND OF NARCOTIC TO ROT THE MINDS OF HALF THE KIDS IN GOTHAM!
BUT, FINDING OUT THAT IT WAS COMING INTO THE COUNTRY WAS PURE LUCK.
YEAH... AND IF THE LYMAN BROTHERS DON'T TAKE POSSESSION BEFORE THE END OF THE WEEK...
...THE DELIVERY WILL BE RESCHEDULED, WITH SOMEONE ELSE MAKING THE PICKUP.
OUR ONLY HOPE IS THAT THE LYMANS WILL LEAD US TO THE DROP--BUT THAT LEAVES US RIGHT WHERE WE WERE BEFORE.
THERE'S NO WAY THEY'LL MAKE A MOVE WHILE THEY KNOW WE'RE WATCHING.
WHILE THEY KNOW WE'RE WATCHING... HMM...
"COMMISSIONER, THAT MAY BE THE ANSWER!"
I CAN'T BELIEVE YOU SPRUNG US SO EASY, MORTON.
YEAH--I THOUGHT THE COPS WAS GONNA HOLD US FOREVER.
NOT WITH A WRIT OF HABEAS CORPUS SHOVED IN THEIR FACES, BOYS.
THEY HAD NOTHING THEY COULD CHARGE YOU WITH, SO THEY HAD TO LET YOU OUT.
POLI

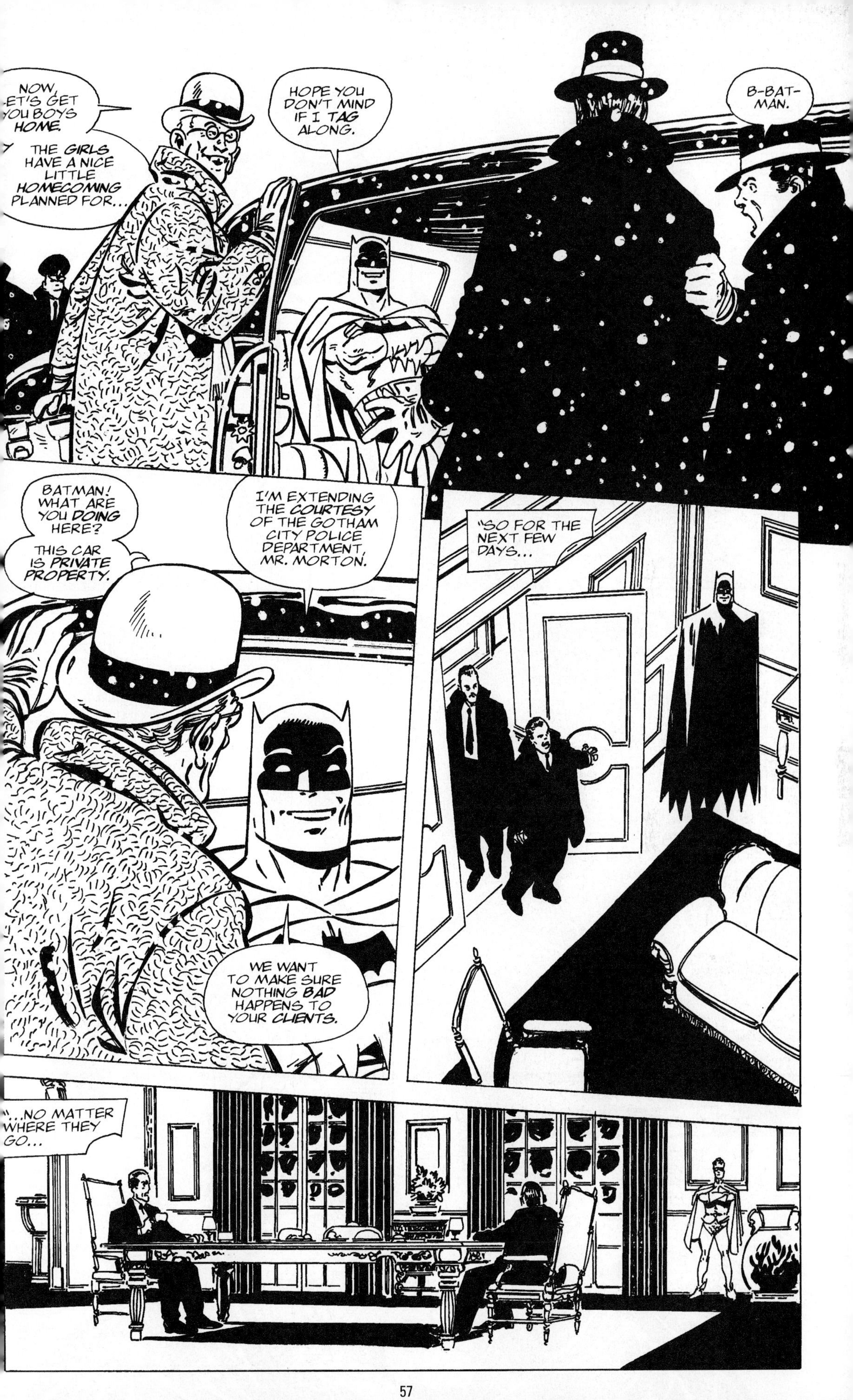
NOW, LET'S GET YOU BOYS HOME.
THE GIRLS HAVE A NICE LITTLE HOMECOMING PLANNED FOR...
HOPE YOU DON'T MIND IF I TAG ALONG.
B-BAT-MAN.
BATMAN! WHAT ARE YOU DOING HERE?
THIS CAR IS PRIVATE PROPERTY.
I'M EXTENDING THE COURTESY OF THE GOTHAM CITY POLICE DEPARTMENT, MR. MORTON.
WE WANT TO MAKE SURE NOTHING BAD HAPPENS TO YOUR CLIENTS.
"SO FOR THE NEXT FEW DAYS...
"...NO MATTER WHERE THEY GO...

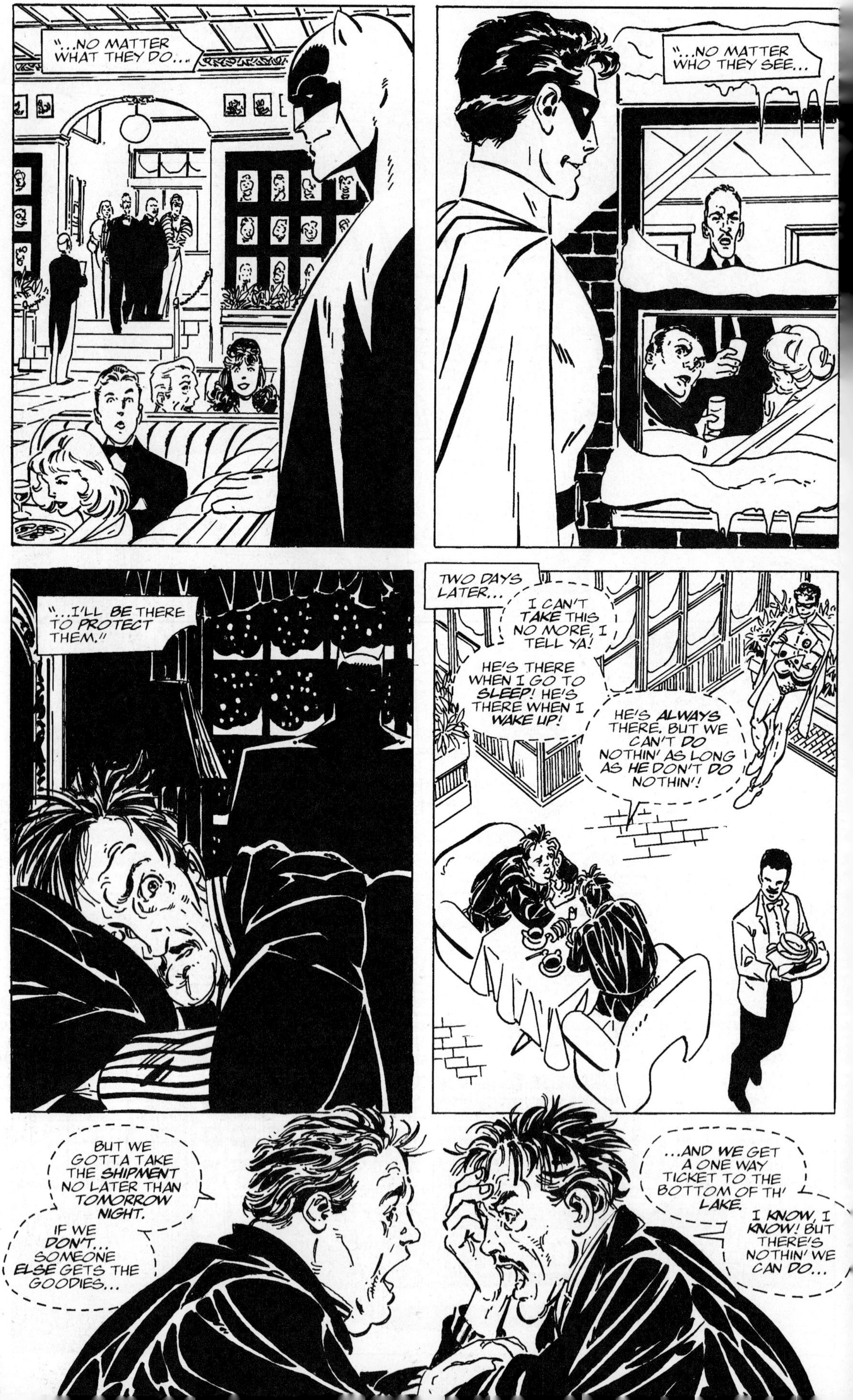
"...NO MATTER WHAT THEY DO..."
"...NO MATTER WHO THEY SEE..."
"...I'LL BE THERE TO PROTECT THEM."
TWO DAYS LATER...
I CAN'T TAKE THIS NO MORE, I TELL YA!
HE'S THERE WHEN I GO TO SLEEP! HE'S THERE WHEN I WAKE UP!
HE'S ALWAYS THERE. BUT WE CAN'T DO NOTHIN' AS LONG AS HE DON'T DO NOTHIN'!
BUT WE GOTTA TAKE THE SHIPMENT NO LATER THAN TOMORROW NIGHT.
IF WE DON'T... SOMEONE ELSE GETS THE GOODIES...
...AND WE GET A ONE WAY TICKET TO THE BOTTOM OF TH' LAKE.
I KNOW, I KNOW! BUT THERE'S NOTHIN' WE CAN DO...

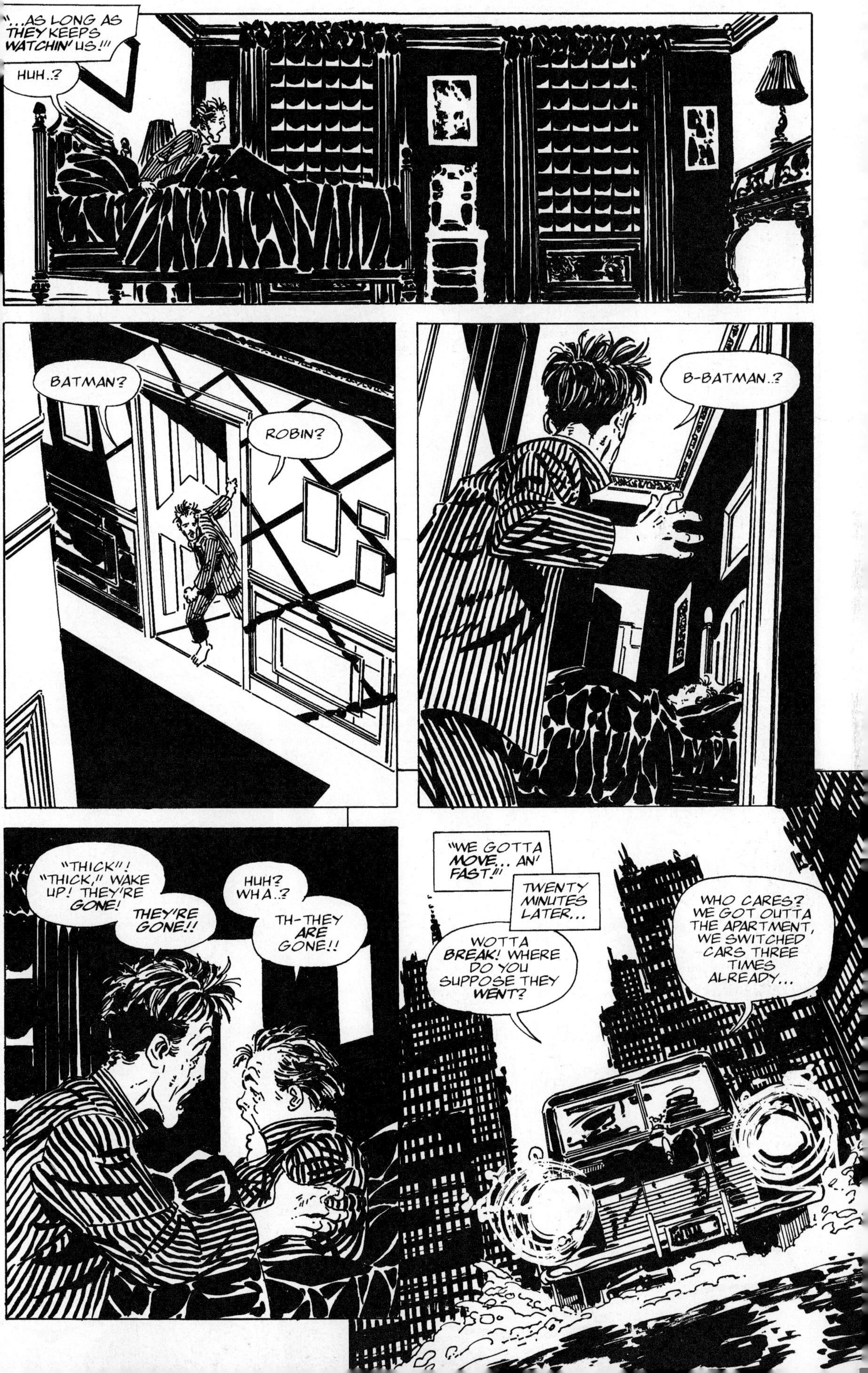
"...AS LONG AS THEY KEEPS WATCHIN' US!!"
HUH..?
BATMAN?
ROBIN?
B-BATMAN..?
"THICK"! "THICK," WAKE UP! THEY'RE GONE!
THEY'RE GONE!!
HUH? WHA..?
TH-THEY ARE GONE!!
"WE GOTTA MOVE... AN' FAST!!"
TWENTY MINUTES LATER...
WOTTA BREAK! WHERE DO YOU SUPPOSE THEY WENT?
WHO CARES? WE GOT OUTTA THE APARTMENT, WE SWITCHED CARS THREE TIMES ALREADY...

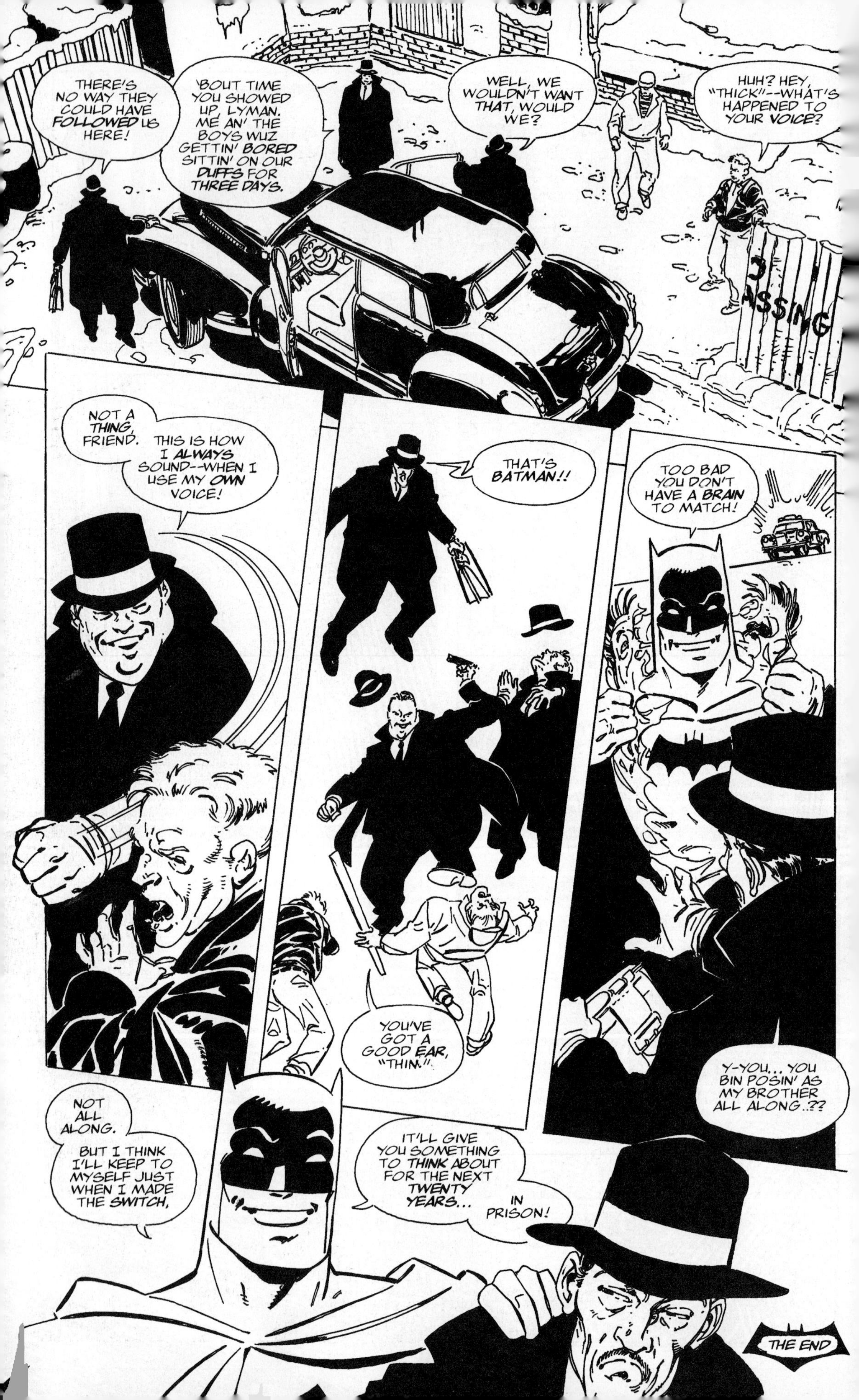
THERE'S NO WAY THEY COULD HAVE FOLLOWED US HERE!
'BOUT TIME YOU SHOWED UP, LYMAN. ME AN' THE BOYS WUZ GETTIN' BORED SITTIN' ON OUR DUFFS FOR THREE DAYS.
WELL, WE WOULDN'T WANT THAT, WOULD WE?
HUH? HEY, "THICK"--WHAT'S HAPPENED TO YOUR VOICE?
NOT A THING, FRIEND.
THIS IS HOW I ALWAYS SOUND--WHEN I USE MY OWN VOICE!
THAT'S BATMAN!!
YOU'VE GOT A GOOD EAR, "THIN".
TOO BAD YOU DON'T HAVE A BRAIN TO MATCH!
Y-YOU... YOU BIN POSIN' AS MY BROTHER ALL ALONG..??
NOT ALL ALONG.
BUT I THINK I'LL KEEP TO MYSELF JUST WHEN I MADE THE SWITCH,
IT'LL GIVE YOU SOMETHING TO THINK ABOUT FOR THE NEXT TWENTY YEARS...
IN PRISON!
THE END

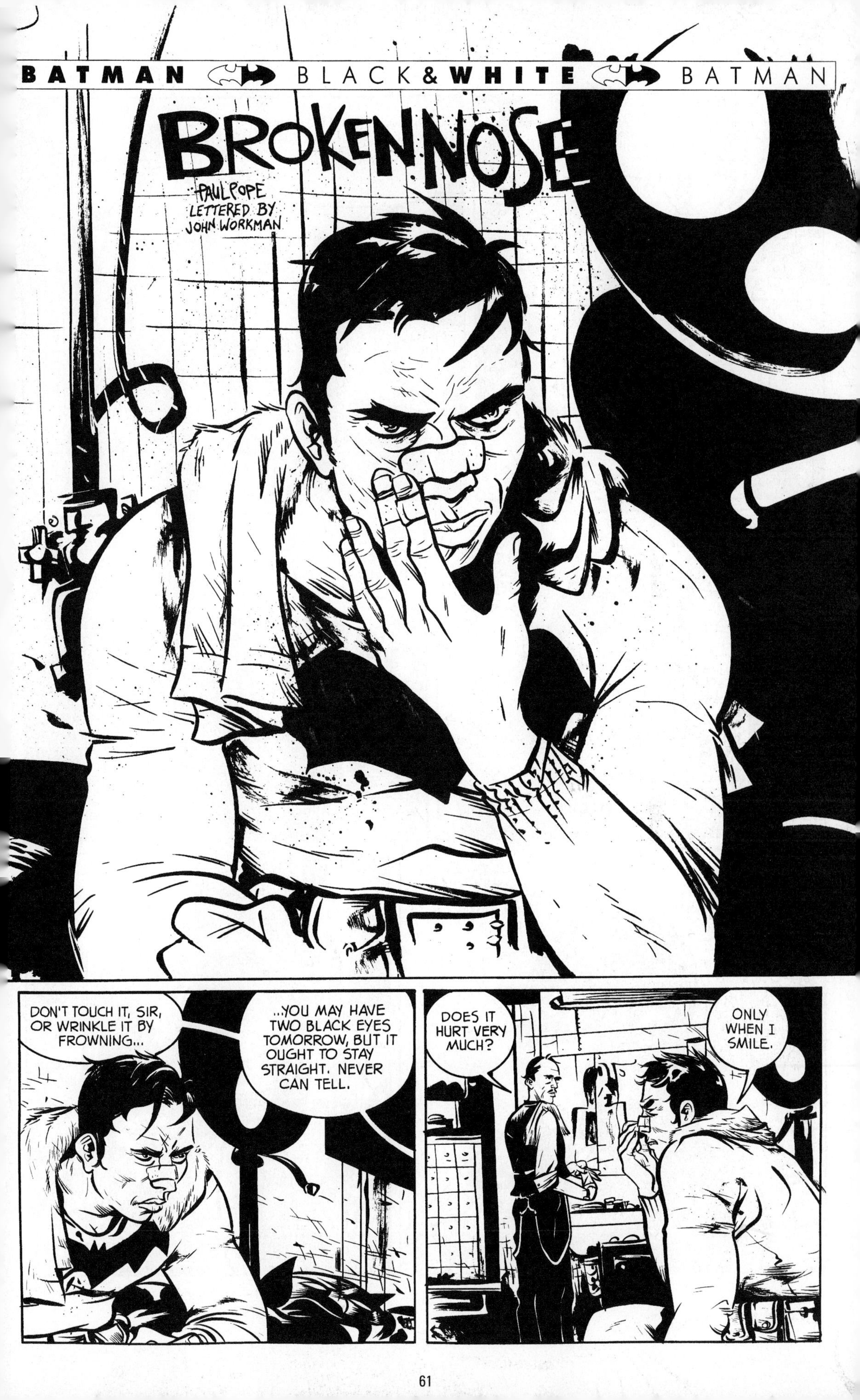
BROKENNOSE
PAUL POPE
LETTERED BY JOHN WORKMAN
DON'T TOUCH IT, SIR, OR WRINKLE IT BY FROWNING...
...YOU MAY HAVE TWO BLACK EYES TOMORROW, BUT IT OUGHT TO STAY STRAIGHT. NEVER CAN TELL.
DOES IT HURT VERY MUCH?
ONLY WHEN I SMILE.

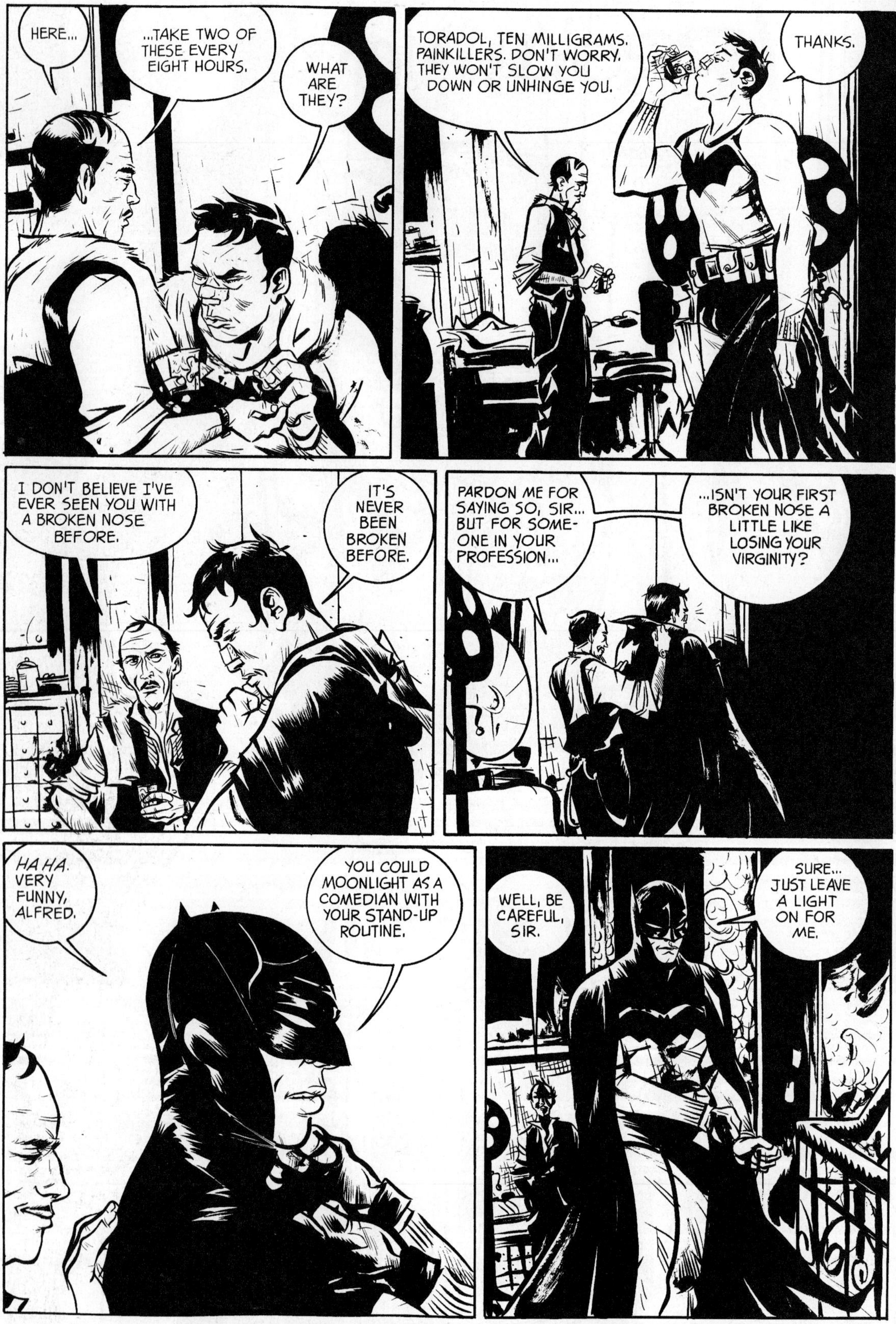
HERE...
...TAKE TWO OF THESE EVERY EIGHT HOURS.
WHAT ARE THEY?
TORADOL, TEN MILLIGRAMS. PAINKILLERS. DON'T WORRY. THEY WON'T SLOW YOU DOWN OR UNHINGE YOU.
THANKS.
I DON'T BELIEVE I'VE EVER SEEN YOU WITH A BROKEN NOSE BEFORE.
IT'S NEVER BEEN BROKEN BEFORE.
PARDON ME FOR SAYING SO, SIR... BUT FOR SOME-ONE IN YOUR PROFESSION...
...ISN'T YOUR FIRST BROKEN NOSE A LITTLE LIKE LOSING YOUR VIRGINITY?
HA HA. VERY FUNNY, ALFRED.
YOU COULD MOONLIGHT AS A COMEDIAN WITH YOUR STAND-UP ROUTINE.
WELL, BE CAREFUL, SIR.
SURE... JUST LEAVE A LIGHT ON FOR ME.

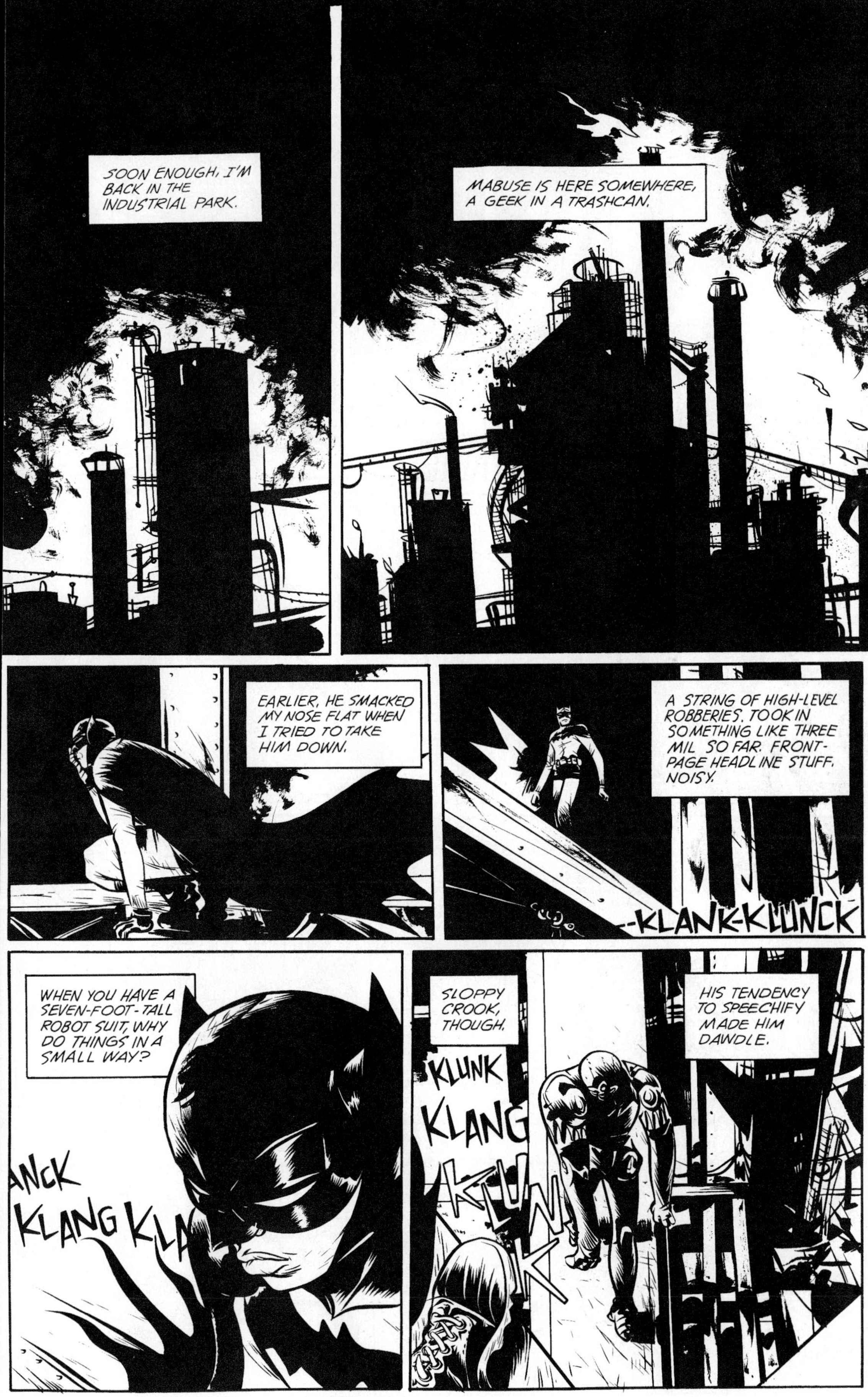
SOON ENOUGH, I'M BACK IN THE INDUSTRIAL PARK.
MABUSE IS HERE SOMEWHERE, A GEEK IN A TRASHCAN.
EARLIER, HE SMACKED MY NOSE FLAT WHEN I TRIED TO TAKE HIM DOWN.
A STRING OF HIGH-LEVEL ROBBERIES. TOOK IN SOMETHING LIKE THREE MIL SO FAR. FRONT-PAGE HEADLINE STUFF. NOISY.
-KLANK-KLUNCK
WHEN YOU HAVE A SEVEN-FOOT-TALL ROBOT SUIT, WHY DO THINGS IN A SMALL WAY?
ANCK
KLANG KLA
SLOPPY CROOK, THOUGH.
HIS TENDENCY TO SPEECHIFY MADE HIM DAWDLE.
KLUNK
KLANG
KLUN
K

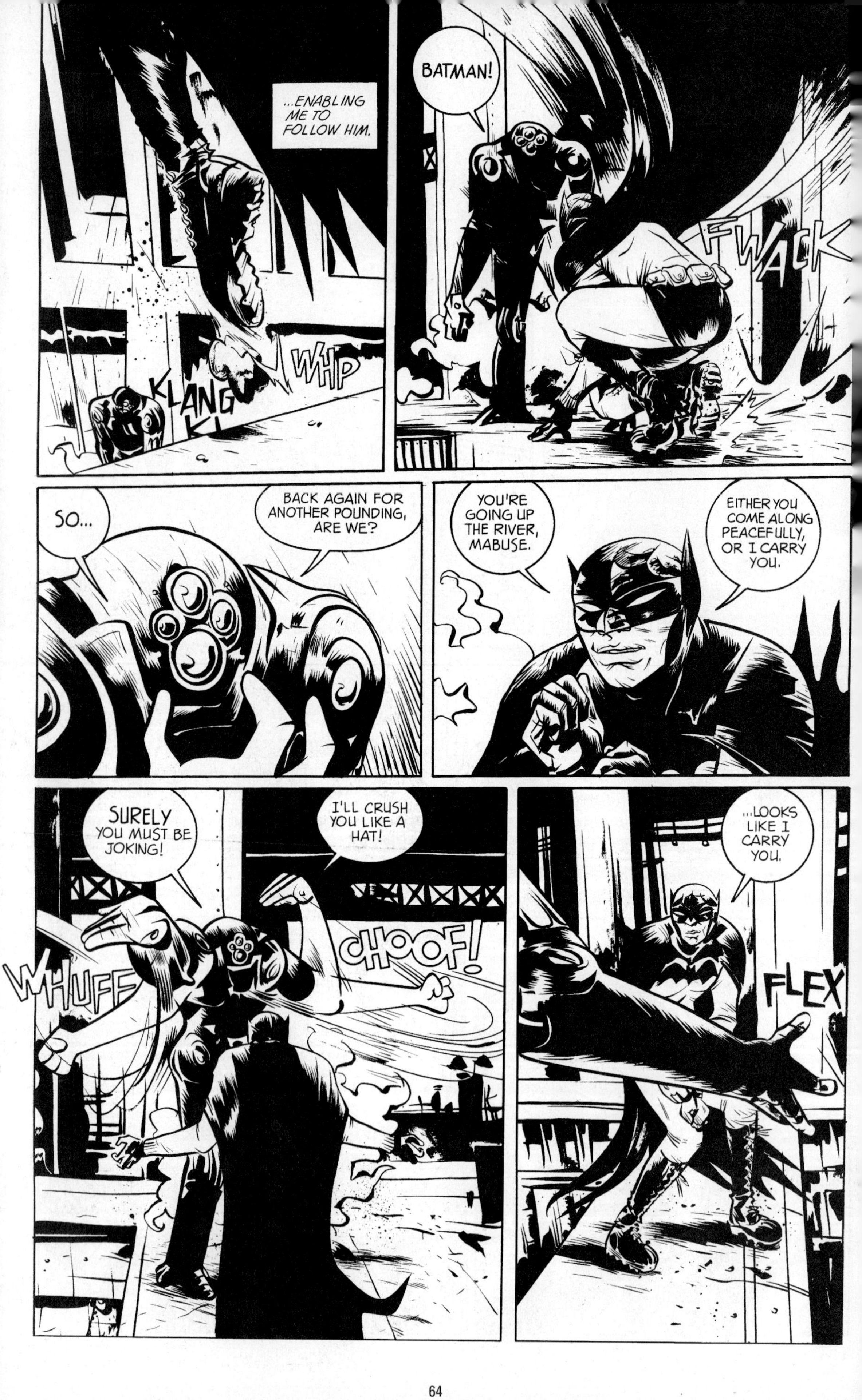
...ENABLING ME TO FOLLOW HIM.
KLANG
KL
WHIP
BATMAN!
FWACK
SO...
BACK AGAIN FOR ANOTHER POUNDING, ARE WE?
YOU'RE GOING UP THE RIVER, MABUSE.
EITHER YOU COME ALONG PEACEFULLY, OR I CARRY YOU.
SURELY YOU MUST BE JOKING!
I'LL CRUSH YOU LIKE A HAT!
CHOOF!
WHUFF
...LOOKS LIKE I CARRY YOU.
FLEX

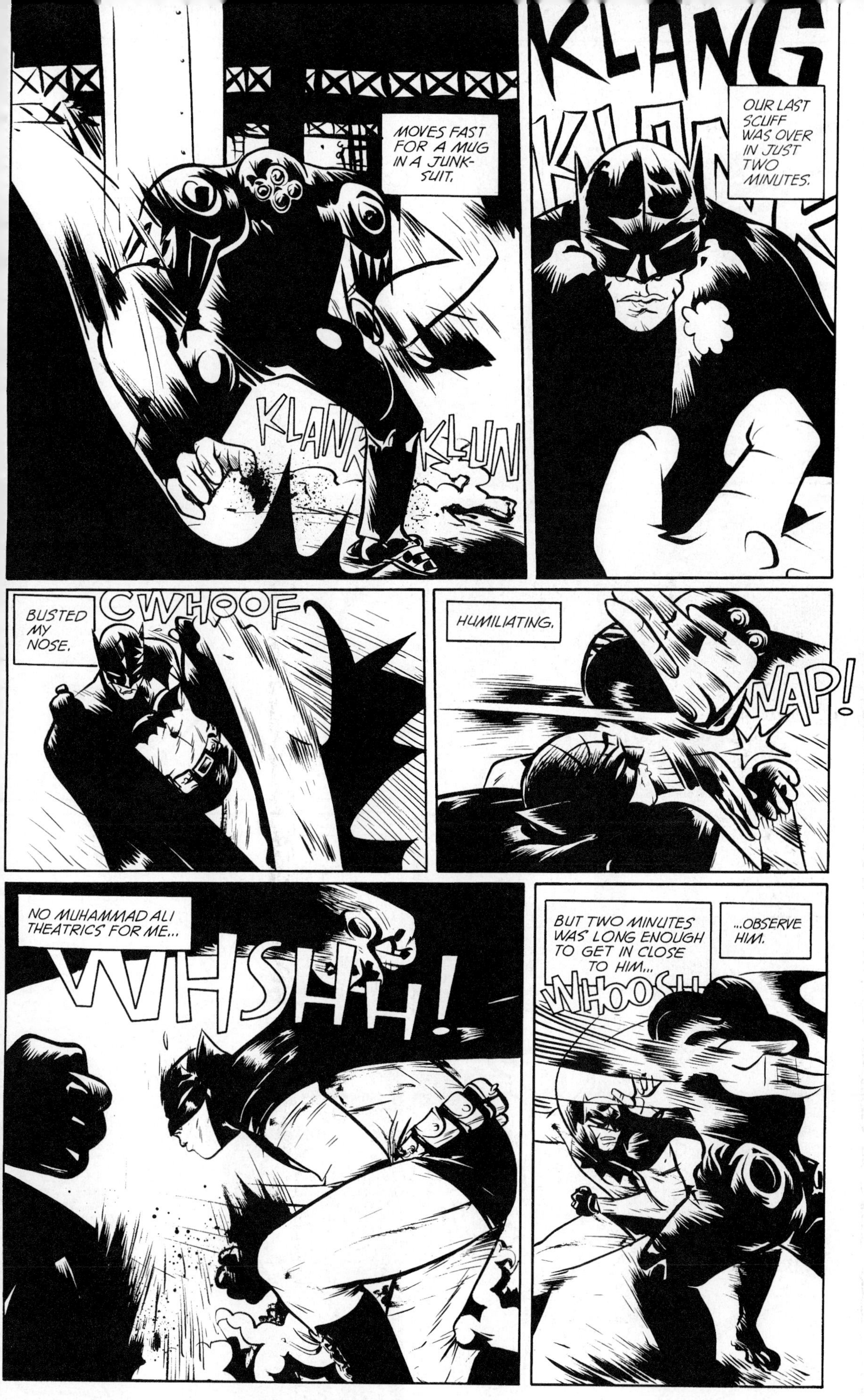
MOVES FAST FOR A MUG IN A JUNK-SUIT.
KLANK
KLUN
KLANG
OUR LAST SCUFF WAS OVER IN JUST TWO MINUTES.
BUSTED MY NOSE.
CWHOOF
HUMILIATING.
WAP!
NO MUHAMMAD ALI THEATRICS FOR ME...
WHSHH!
BUT TWO MINUTES WAS LONG ENOUGH TO GET IN CLOSE TO HIM...
...OBSERVE HIM.

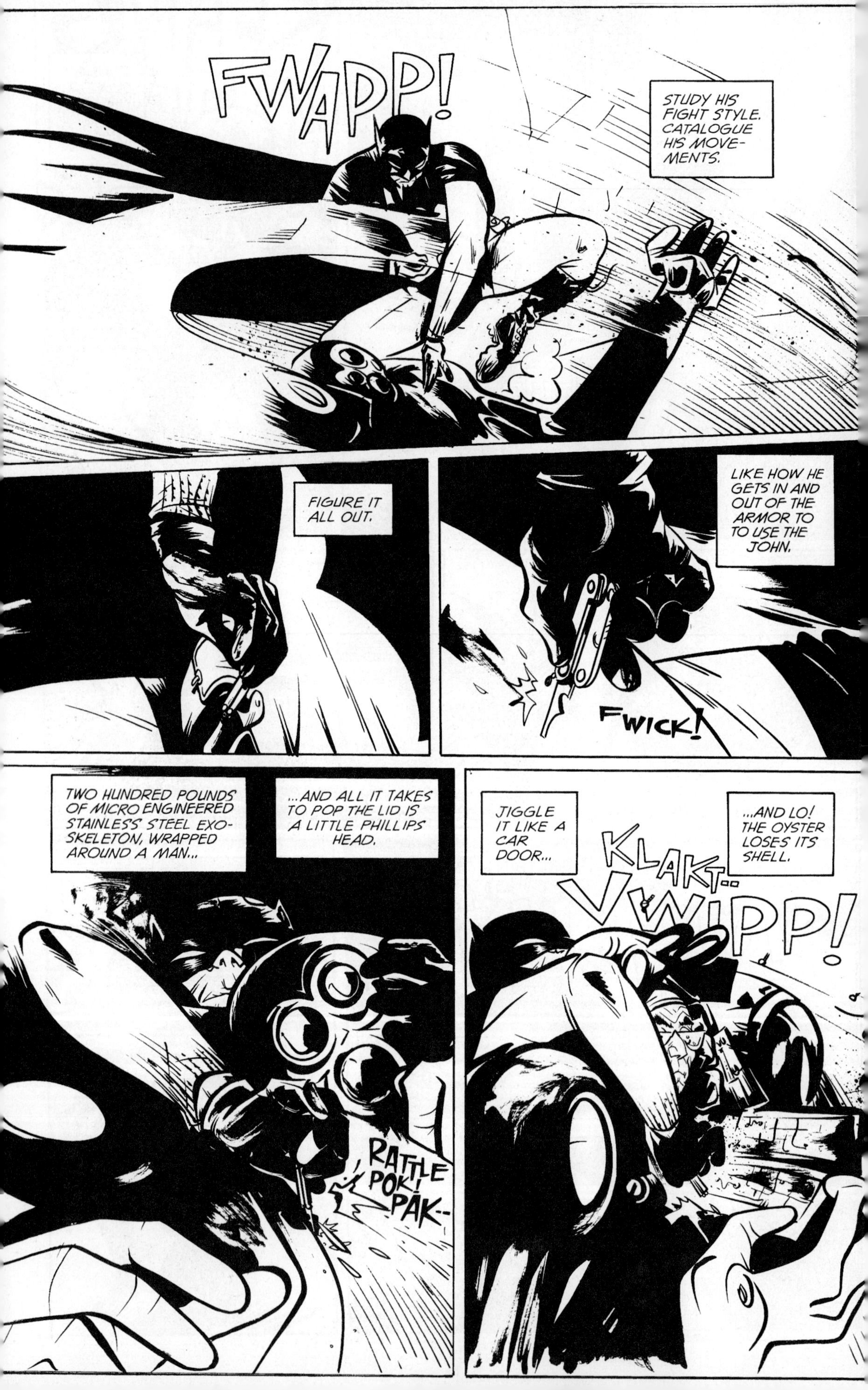
FWAPP!
STUDY HIS FIGHT STYLE. CATALOGUE HIS MOVEMENTS.
FIGURE IT ALL OUT.
LIKE HOW HE GETS IN AND OUT OF THE ARMOR TO TO USE THE JOHN.
FWICK!
TWO HUNDRED POUNDS OF MICRO ENGINEERED STAINLESS STEEL EXO-SKELETON, WRAPPED AROUND A MAN...
...AND ALL IT TAKES TO POP THE LID IS A LITTLE PHILLIPS HEAD.
RATTLE
POK!
PAK--
JIGGLE IT LIKE A CAR DOOR...
...AND LO! THE OYSTER LOSES ITS SHELL.
KLAKT--
VWIPP!

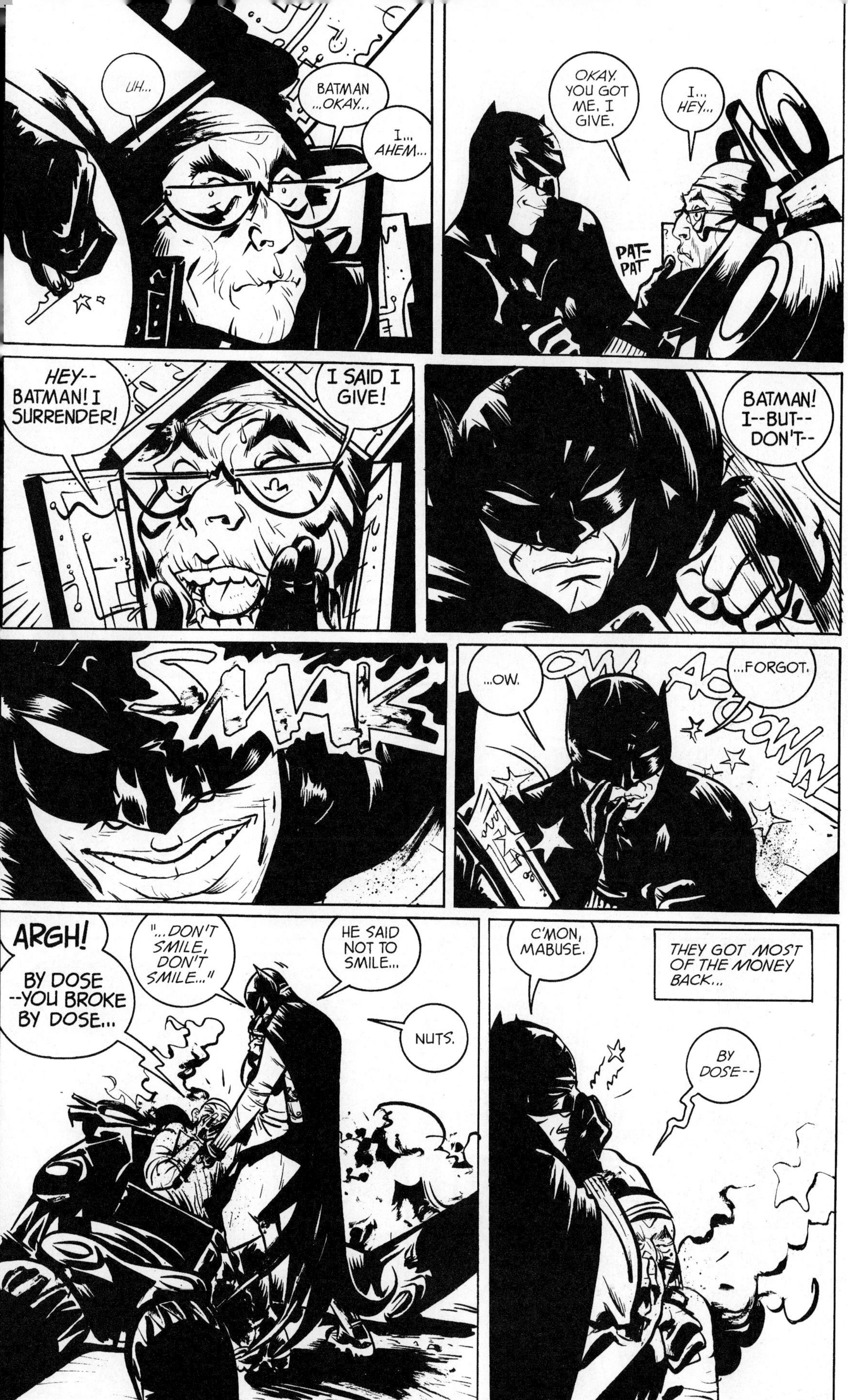

UH...
BATMAN ...OKAY...
I... AHEM...
OKAY. YOU GOT ME. I GIVE.
I... HEY...
PAT-PAT
HEY-- BATMAN! I SURRENDER!
I SAID I GIVE!
BATMAN! I--BUT-- DON'T--
SMAK
...OW.
OW! AOOOWWW
...FORGOT.
ARGH!
BY DOSE --YOU BROKE BY DOSE...
"...DON'T SMILE, DON'T SMILE..."
HE SAID NOT TO SMILE...
NUTS.
C'MON, MABUSE.
THEY GOT MOST OF THE MONEY BACK...
BY DOSE--

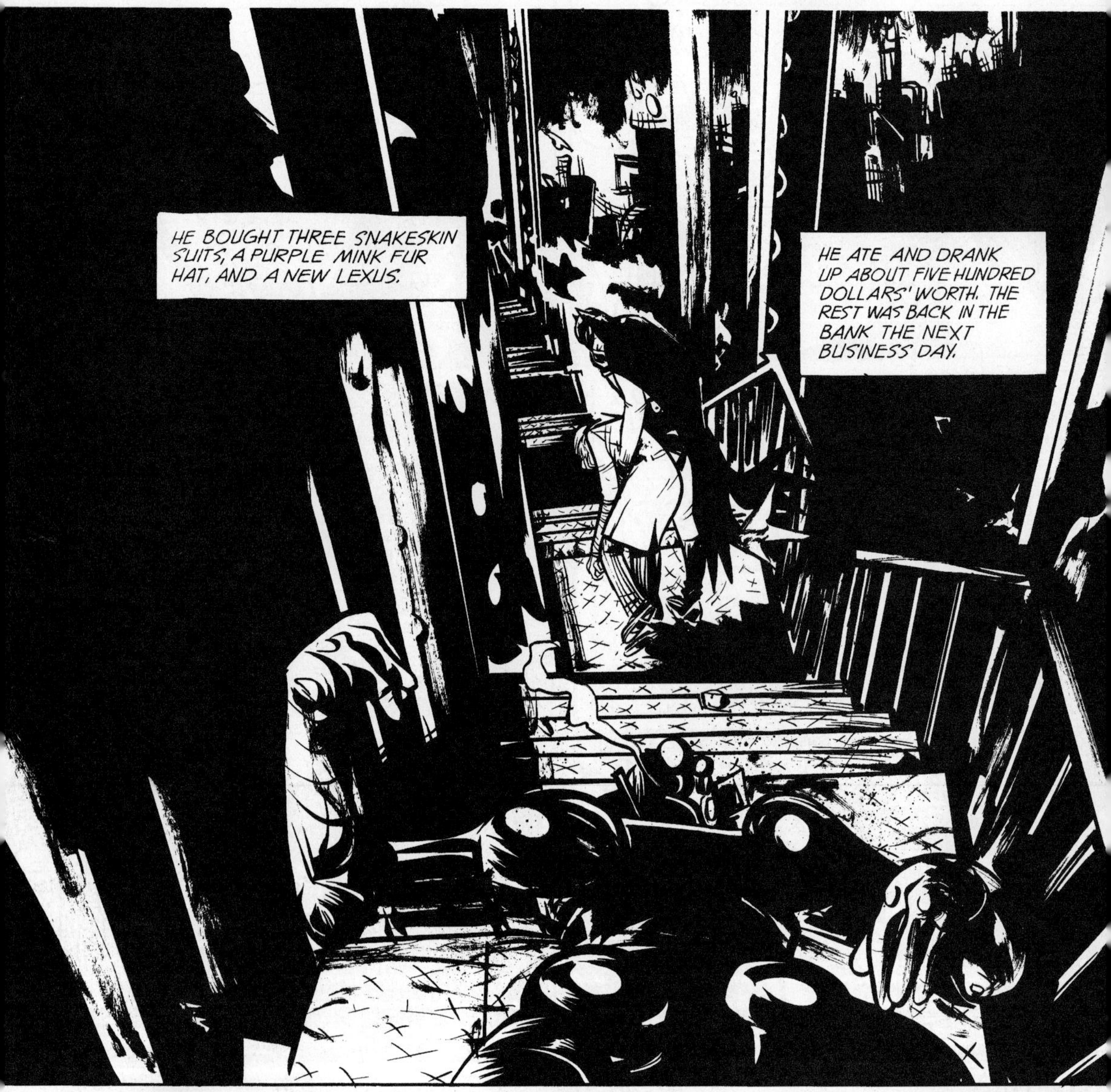
HE BOUGHT THREE SNAKESKIN SUITS, A PURPLE MINK FUR HAT, AND A NEW LEXUS.
HE ATE AND DRANK UP ABOUT FIVE HUNDRED DOLLARS' WORTH. THE REST WAS BACK IN THE BANK THE NEXT BUSINESS DAY.

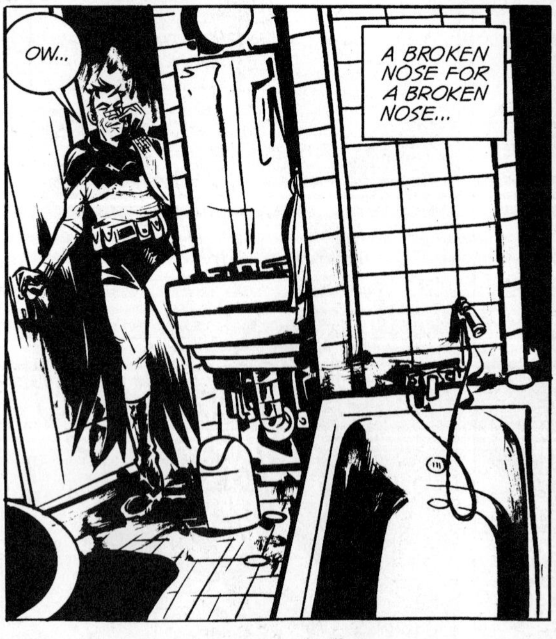
OW...
A BROKEN NOSE FOR A BROKEN NOSE...

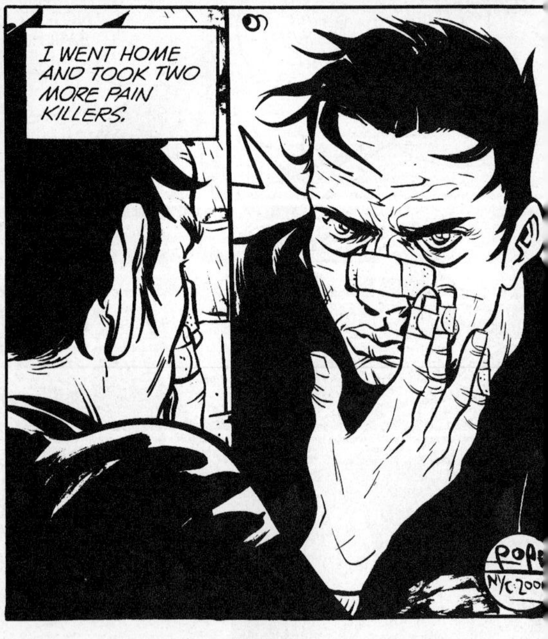
I WENT HOME AND TOOK TWO MORE PAIN KILLERS.
POPE
NYC 2000

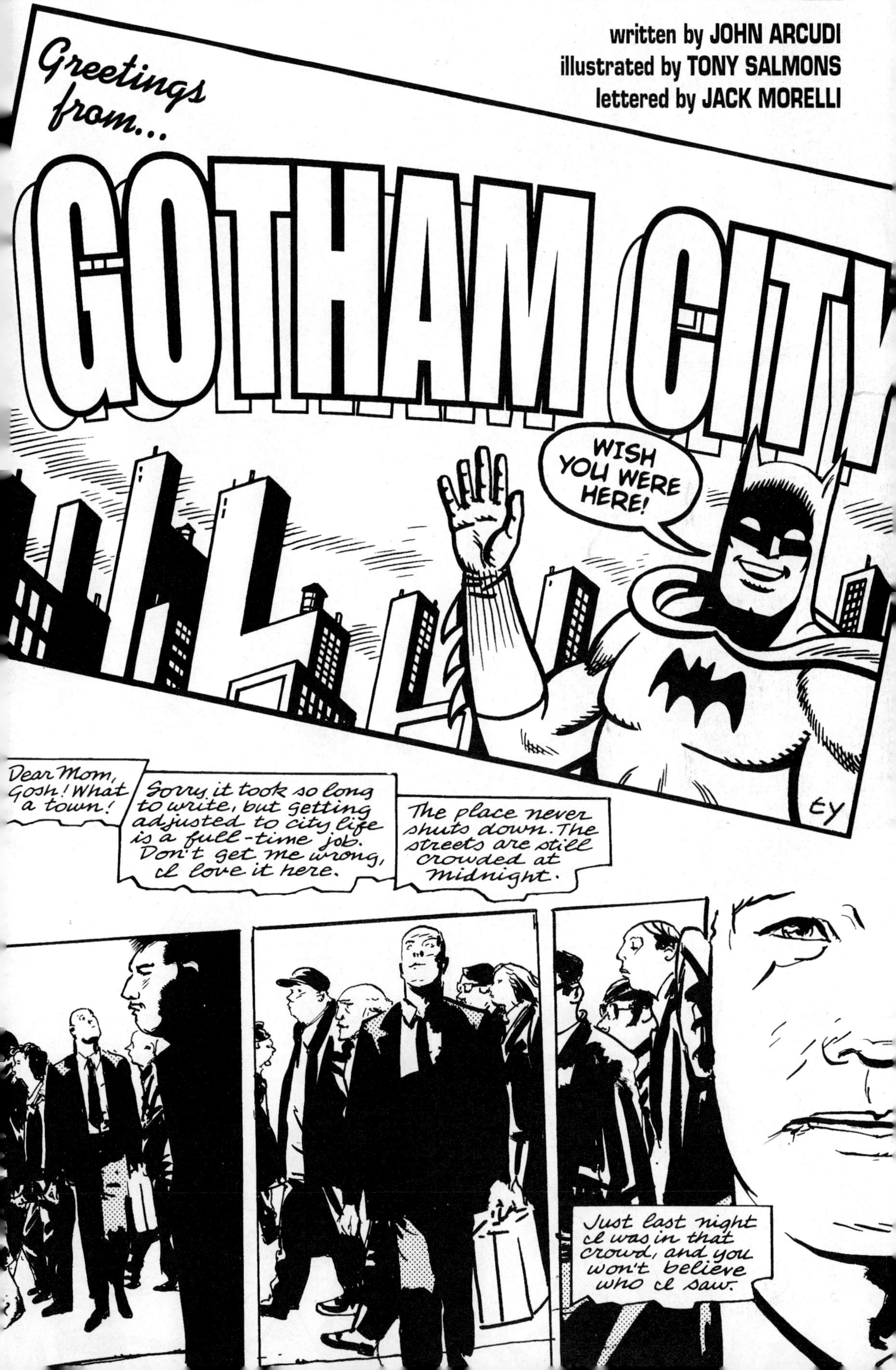
Greetings from...
GOTHAM CITY
written by JOHN ARCUDI
illustrated by TONY SALMONS
lettered by JACK MORELLI
WISH YOU WERE HERE!
Dear Mom, Gosh! What a town!
Sorry it took so long to write, but getting adjusted to city life is a full-time job. Don't get me wrong, I love it here.
The place never shuts down. The streets are still crowded at midnight.
Just last night I was in that crowd, and you won't believe who I saw.

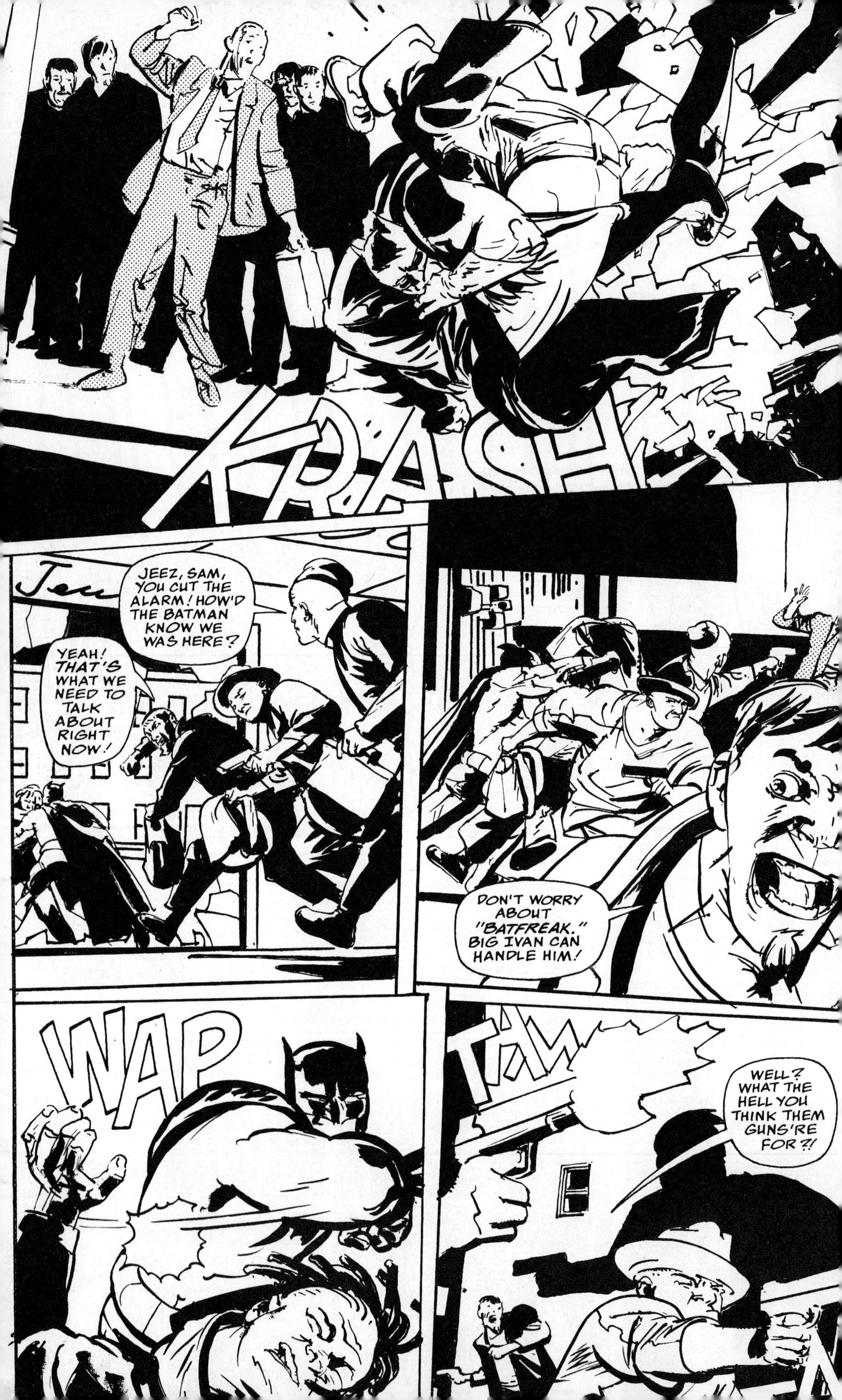
KRASH
JEEZ, SAM, YOU CUT THE ALARM! HOW'D THE BATMAN KNOW WE WAS HERE?
YEAH! THAT'S WHAT WE NEED TO TALK ABOUT RIGHT NOW!
DON'T WORRY ABOUT "BATFREAK." BIG IVAN CAN HANDLE HIM!
WAP
TAW
WELL? WHAT THE HELL YOU THINK THEM GUNS'RE FOR?!

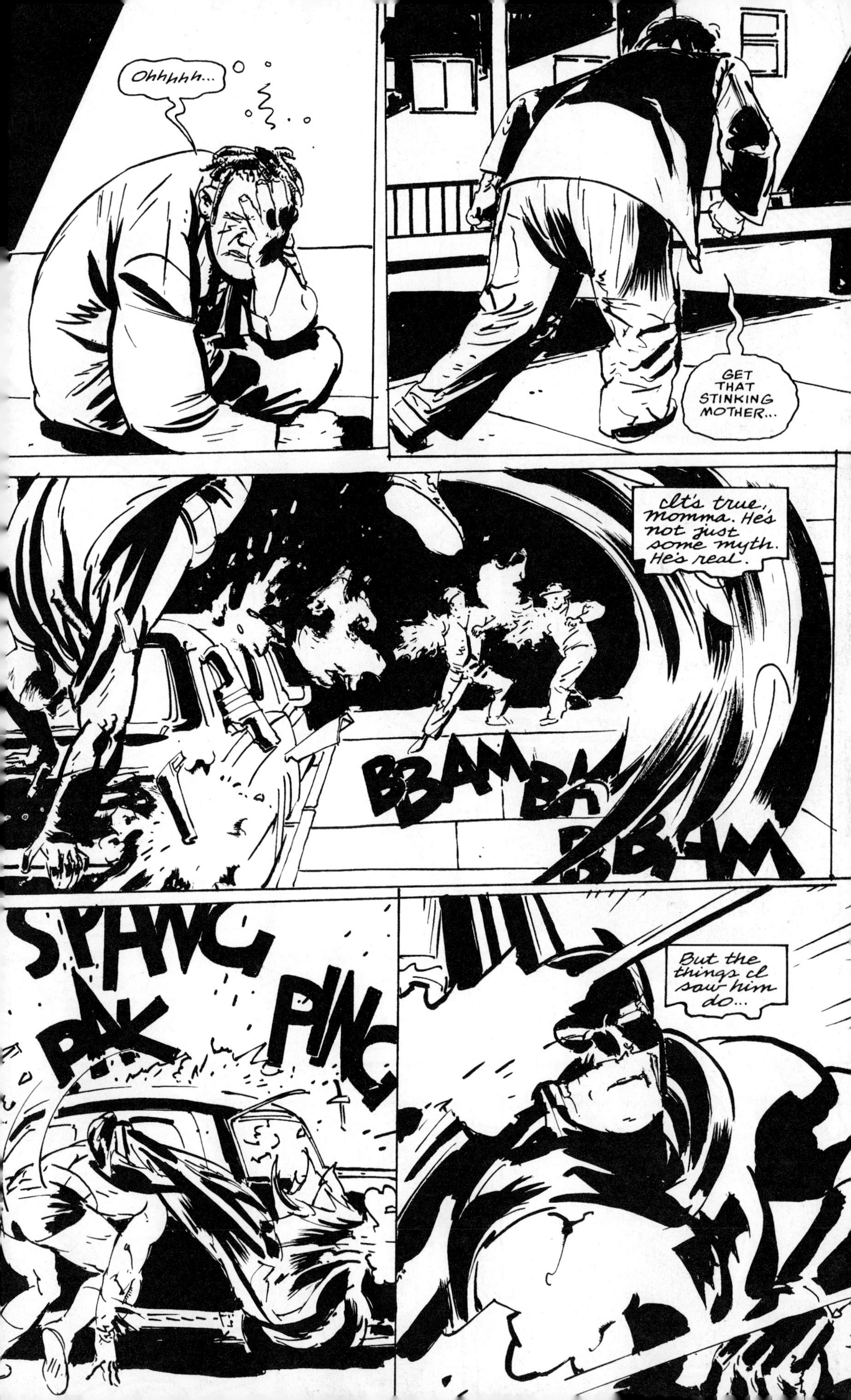
Ohhhhh...
GET THAT STINKING MOTHER...
I't's true, momma. He's not just some myth. He's real.
BBAM BAM
BBAM
SPANG
PAK
PING
But the things I saw him do...

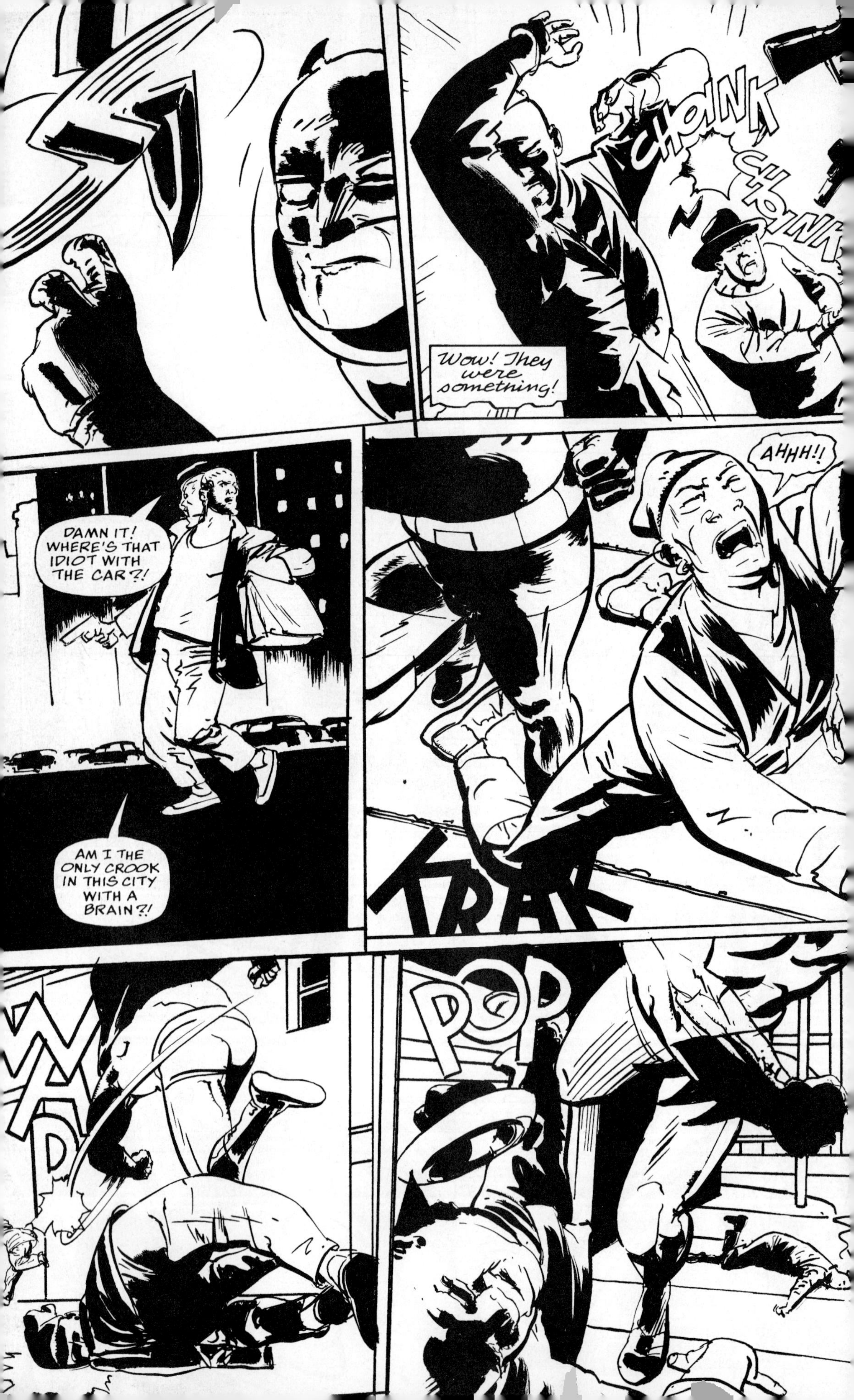

CHOINK
CHOINK
Wow! They were something!
DAMN IT! WHERE'S THAT IDIOT WITH THE CAR?!
AM I THE ONLY CROOK IN THIS CITY WITH A BRAIN?!
AHHH!!
TRAK
WAP
POP

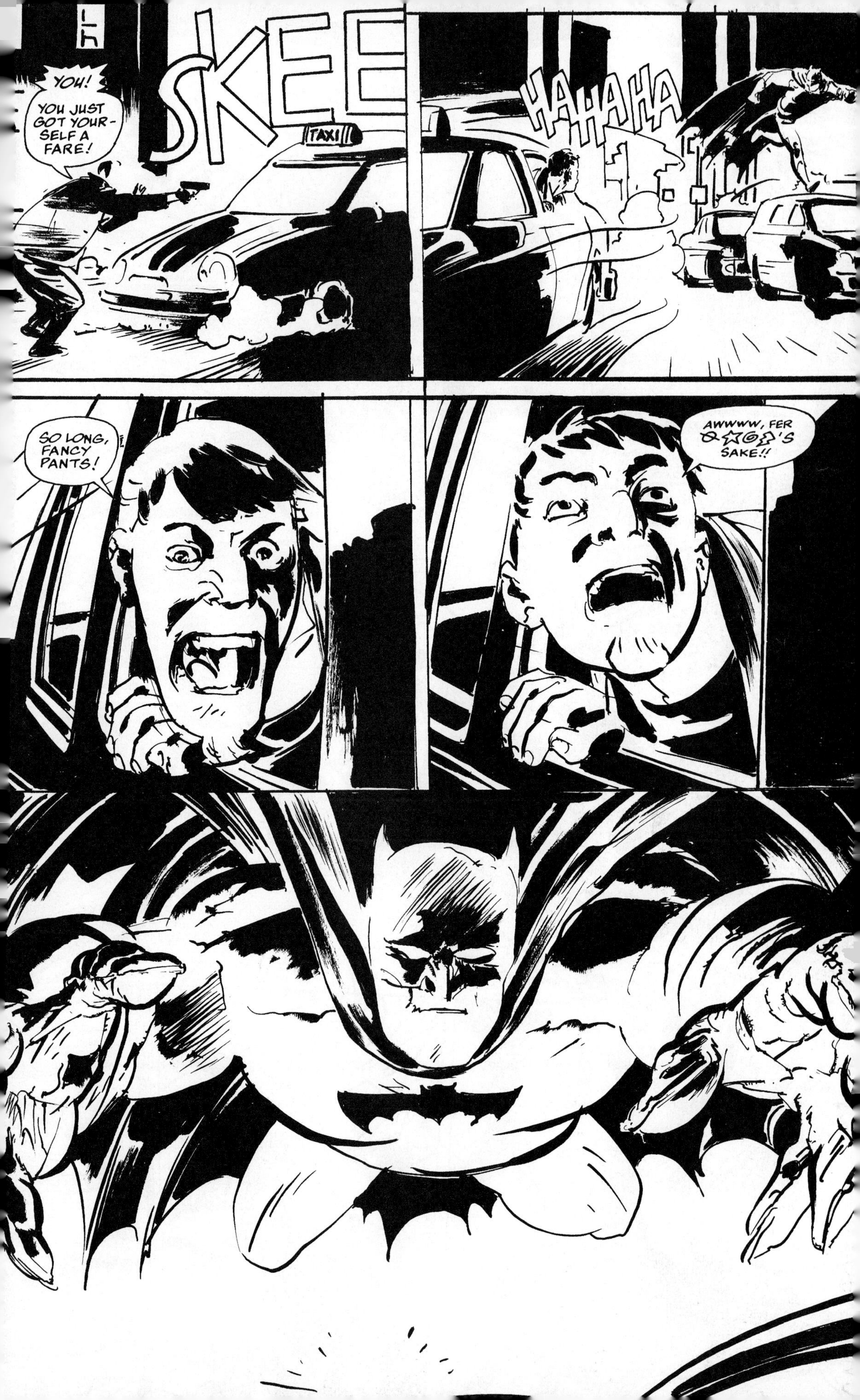

YOU!
YOU JUST GOT YOURSELF A FARE!
SKEE
TAXI
HAHAHA
SO LONG, FANCY PANTS!
AWWWW, FER 'S SAKE!!

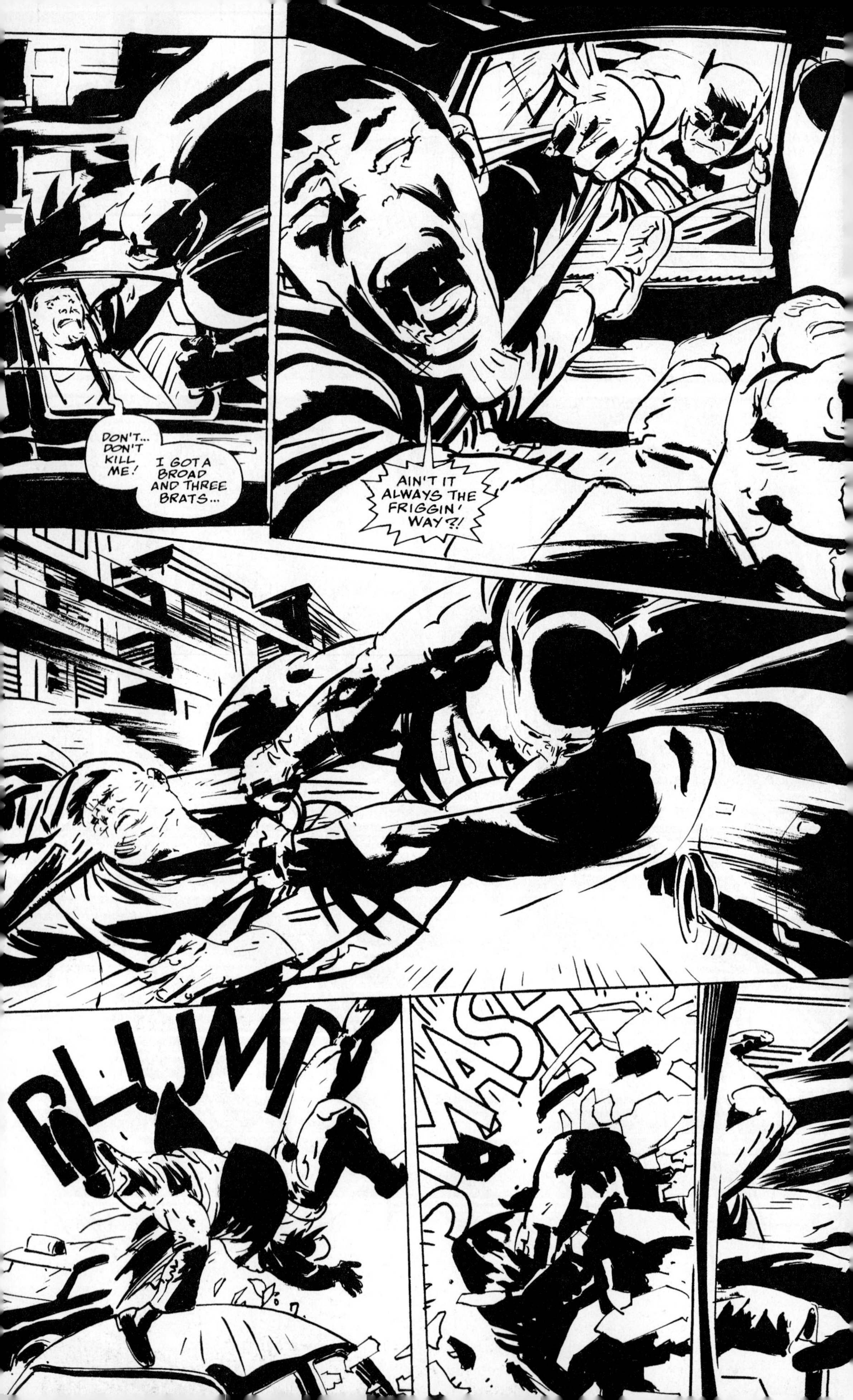
DON'T... DON'T KILL ME!
I GOT A BROAD AND THREE BRATS...
AIN'T IT ALWAYS THE FRIGGIN' WAY?!
PLUMP

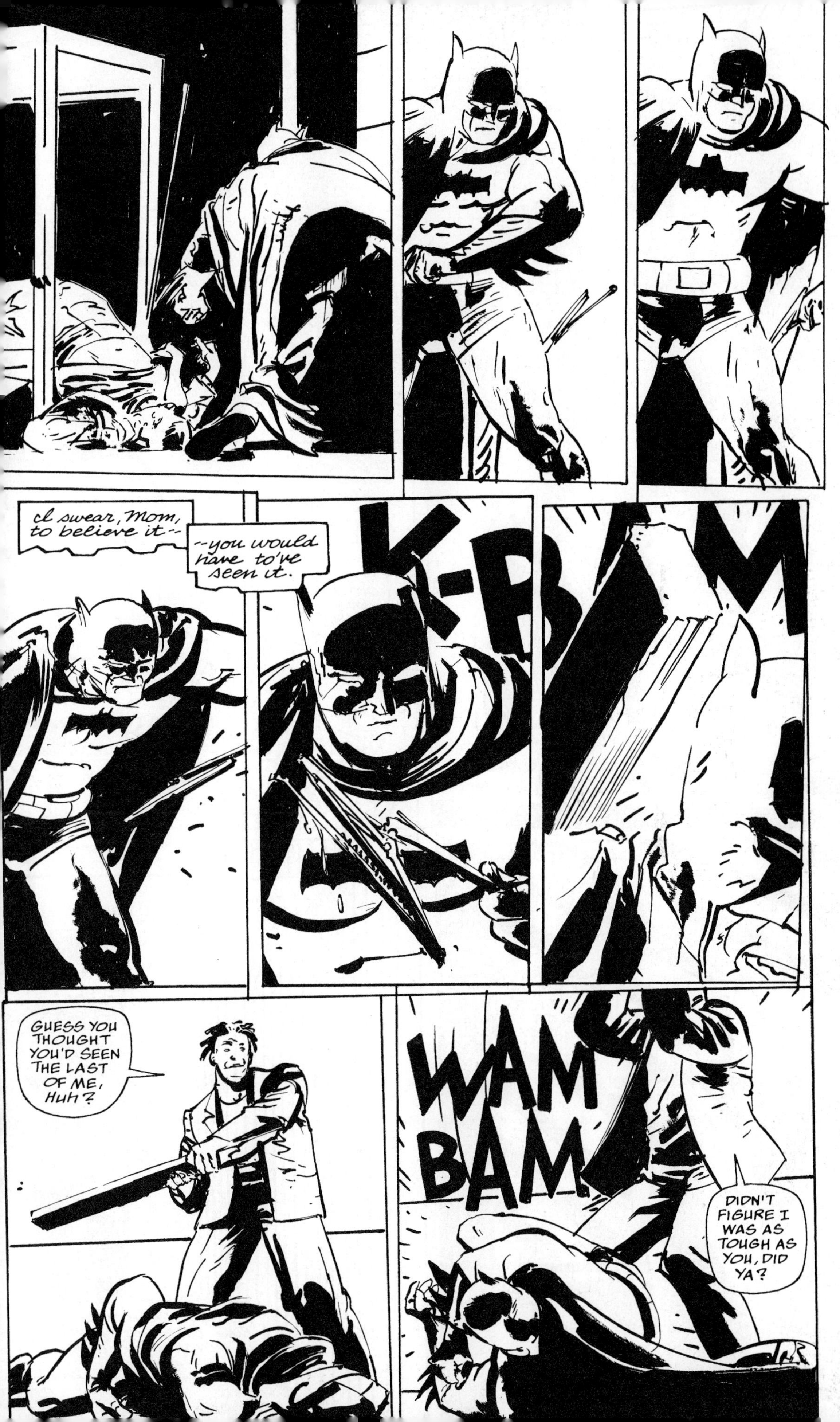
I swear, Mom, to believe it--
--you would have to've seen it.
K-BAM
GUESS YOU THOUGHT YOU'D SEEN THE LAST OF ME, HUH?
WAM BAM
DIDN'T FIGURE I WAS AS TOUGH AS YOU, DID YA?

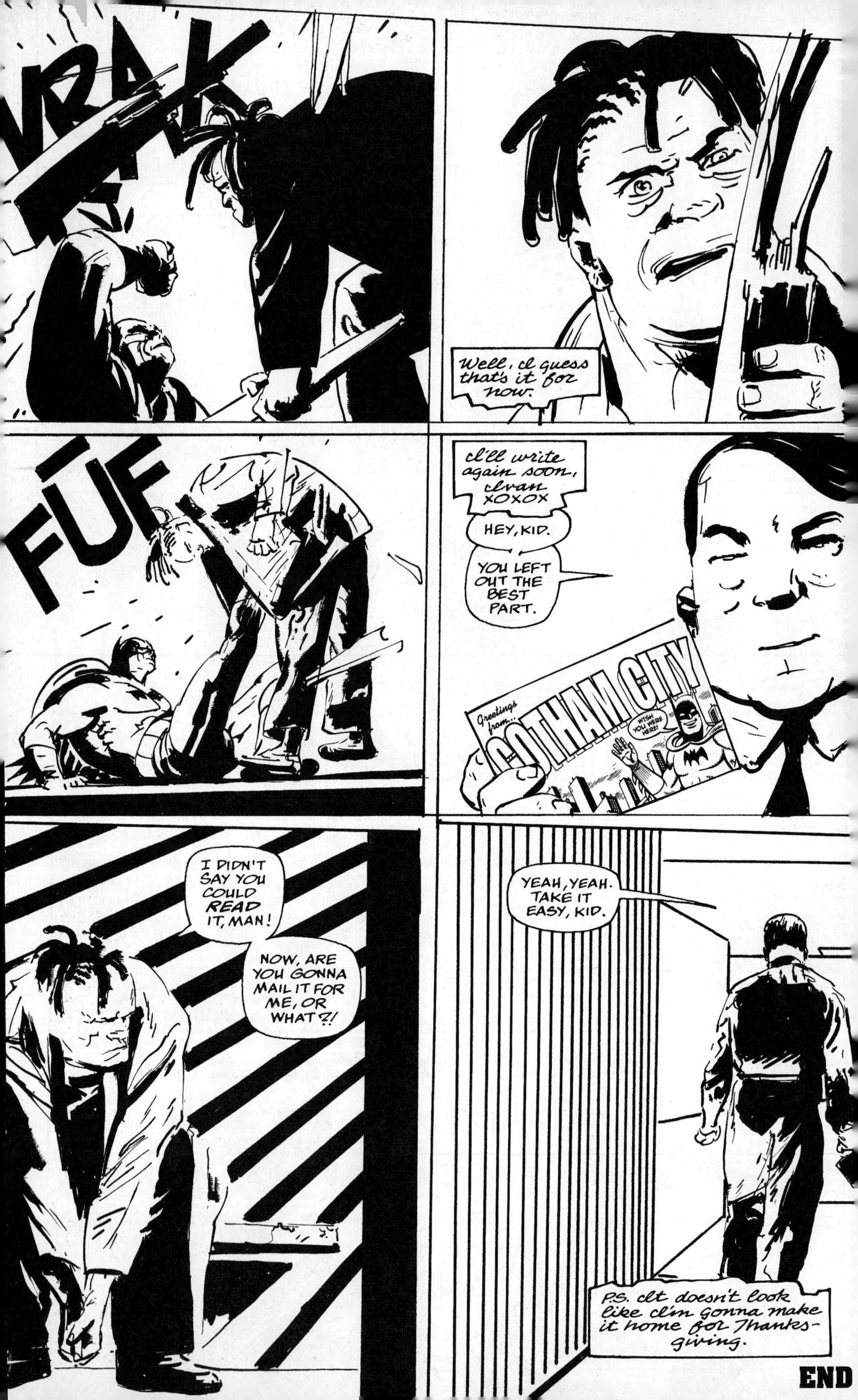
VRAK
Well, I guess that's it for now.
FUF
I'll write again soon, Ivan XOXOX
HEY, KID.
YOU LEFT OUT THE BEST PART.
Greetings from... GOTHAM CITY
WISH YOU WERE HERE!
I DIDN'T SAY YOU COULD READ IT, MAN!
NOW, ARE YOU GONNA MAIL IT FOR ME, OR WHAT?!
YEAH, YEAH. TAKE IT EASY, KID.
P.S. It doesn't look like I'm gonna make it home for Thanksgiving.
END

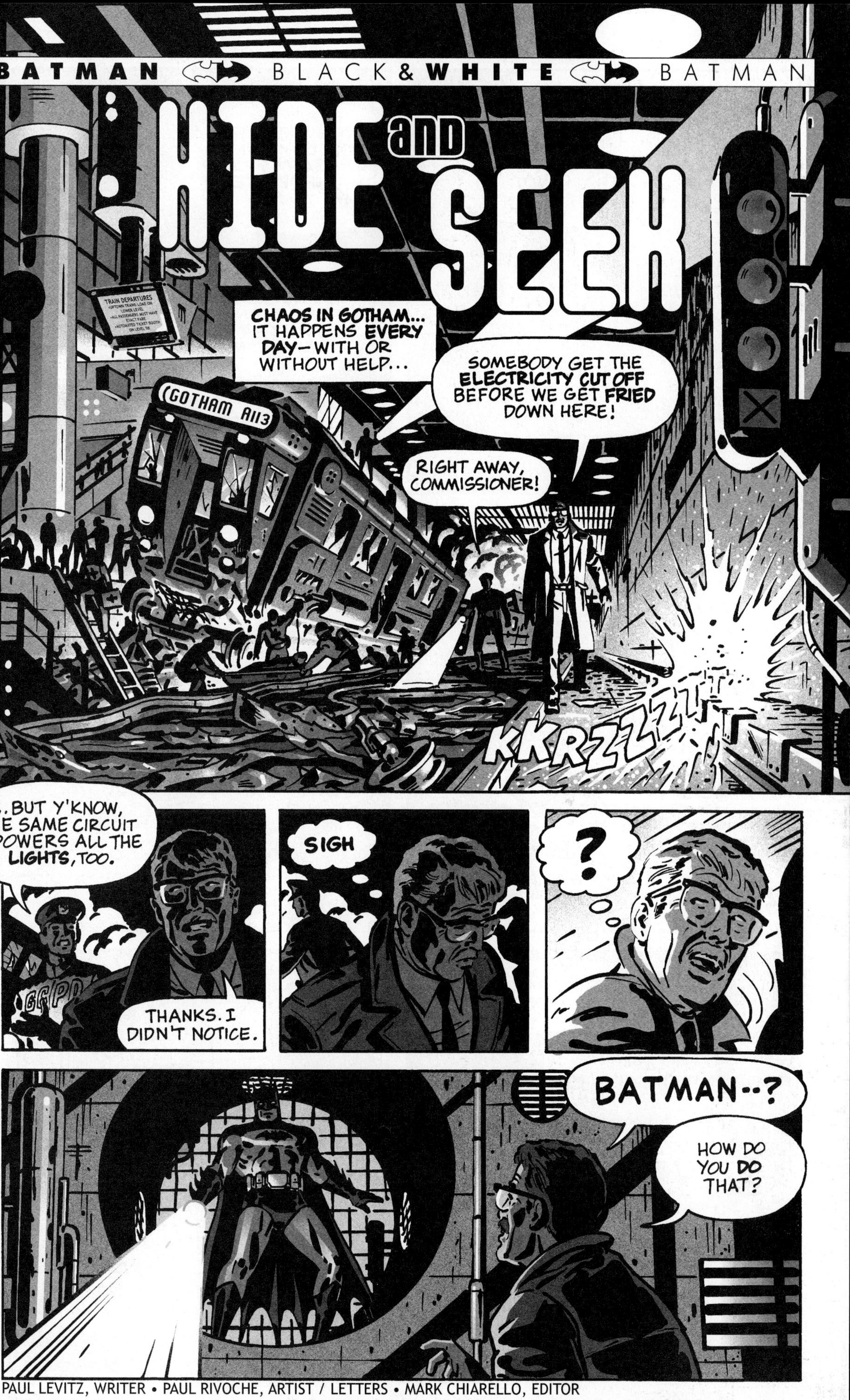

BATMAN BLACK & WHITE BATMAN
HIDE and SEEK
TRAIN DEPARTURES
CHAOS IN GOTHAM... IT HAPPENS EVERY DAY– WITH OR WITHOUT HELP...
GOTHAM A113
SOMEBODY GET THE ELECTRICITY CUT OFF BEFORE WE GET FRIED DOWN HERE!
RIGHT AWAY, COMMISSIONER!
KKRZZ
..BUT Y'KNOW, E SAME CIRCUIT OWERS ALL THE LIGHTS, TOO.
THANKS. I DIDN'T NOTICE.
SIGH
?
BATMAN--?
HOW DO YOU DO THAT?

PAUL LEVITZ, WRITER • PAUL RIVOCHE, ARTIST / LETTERS • MARK CHIARELLO, EDITOR

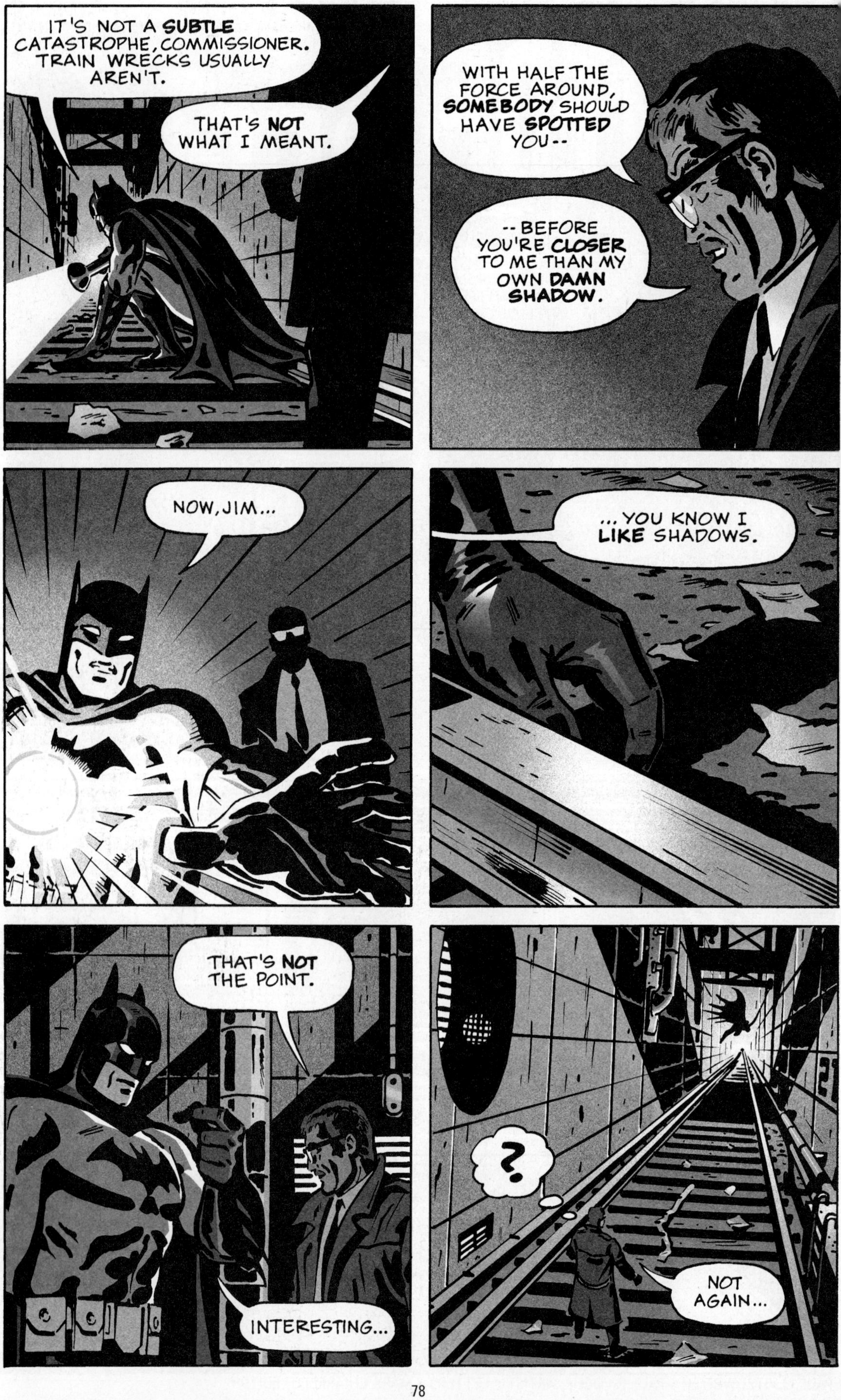
IT'S NOT A SUBTLE CATASTROPHE, COMMISSIONER. TRAIN WRECKS USUALLY AREN'T.
THAT'S NOT WHAT I MEANT.
WITH HALF THE FORCE AROUND, SOMEBODY SHOULD HAVE SPOTTED YOU--
--BEFORE YOU'RE CLOSER TO ME THAN MY OWN DAMN SHADOW.
NOW, JIM...
...YOU KNOW I LIKE SHADOWS.
THAT'S NOT THE POINT.
INTERESTING...
?
NOT AGAIN...

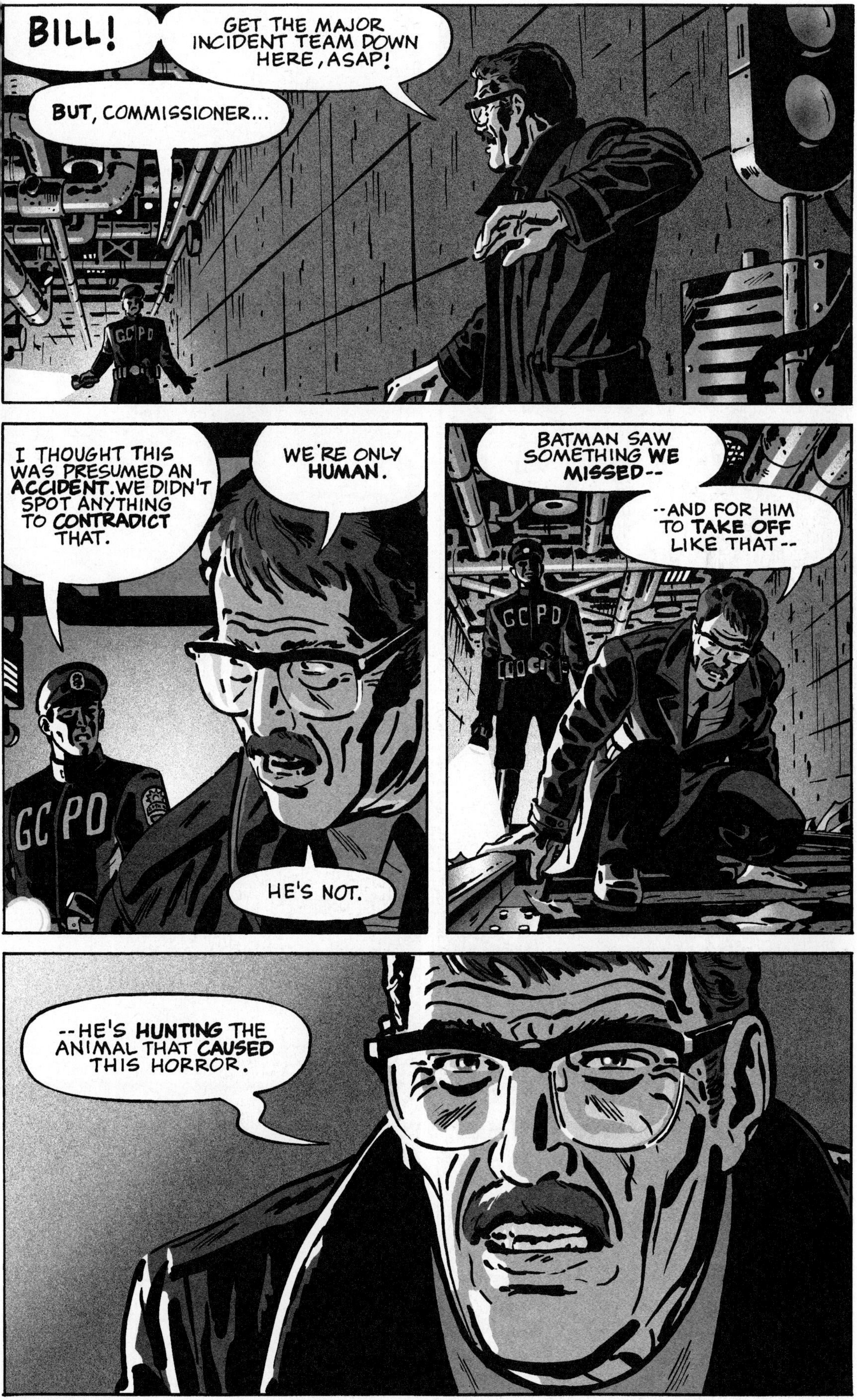
BILL!
GET THE MAJOR INCIDENT TEAM DOWN HERE, ASAP!
BUT, COMMISSIONER...
I THOUGHT THIS WAS PRESUMED AN ACCIDENT. WE DIDN'T SPOT ANYTHING TO CONTRADICT THAT.
WE'RE ONLY HUMAN.
HE'S NOT.
BATMAN SAW SOMETHING WE MISSED--
--AND FOR HIM TO TAKE OFF LIKE THAT--
--HE'S HUNTING THE ANIMAL THAT CAUSED THIS HORROR.
GCPD
GCPD
GCPD

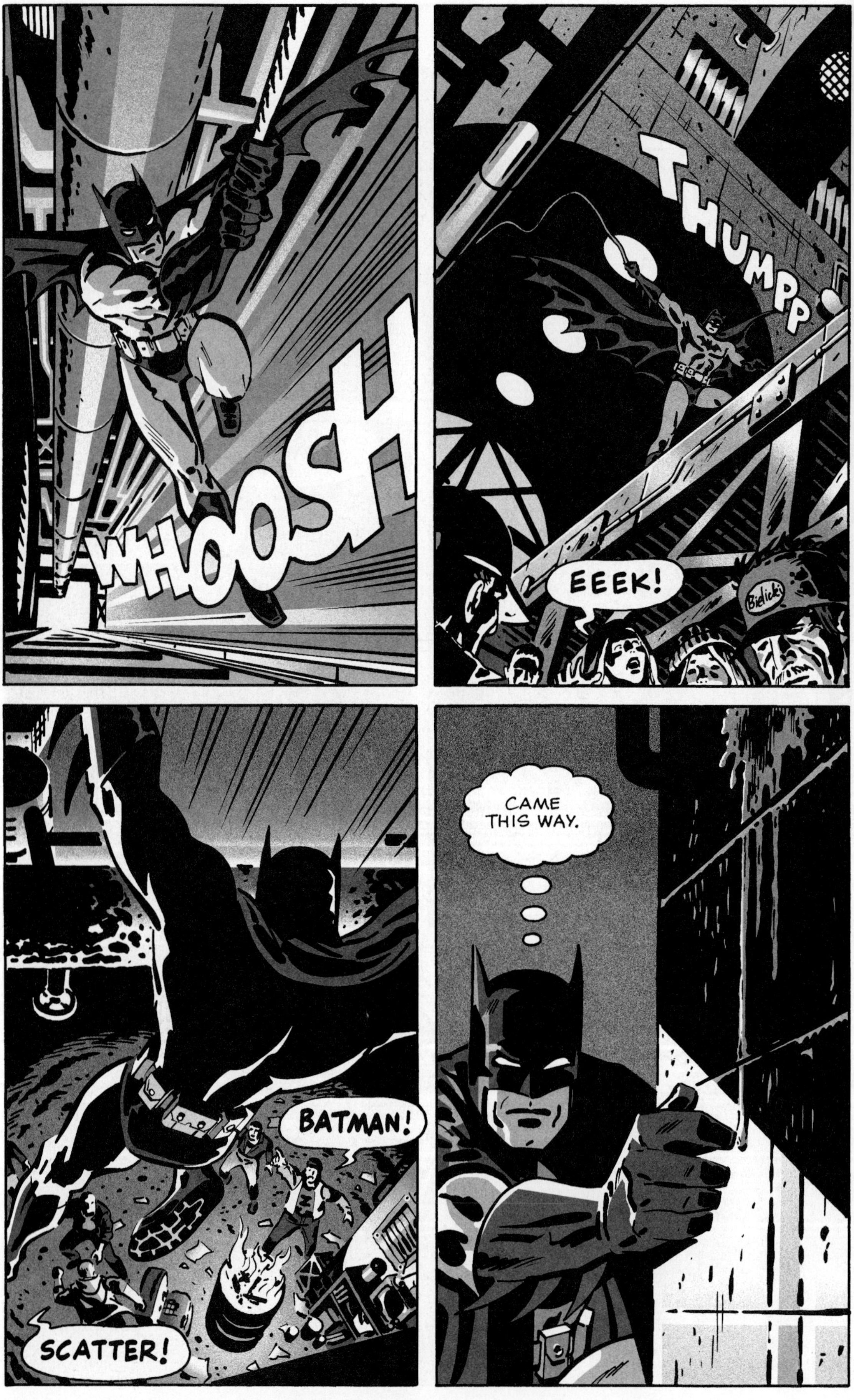

WHOOSH
THUMPP
EEEK!
Bielicki
BATMAN!
SCATTER!
CAME THIS WAY.

BLOOD'S **FRESH**, TOO.

JUMPED FROM THE UPPER TRACK-- OR **FELL**?

EASY TO **MISCALCULATE** THE DISTANCE--

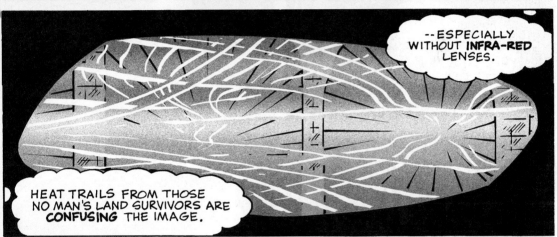

--ESPECIALLY WITHOUT **INFRA-RED** LENSES.

HEAT TRAILS FROM THOSE NO MAN'S LAND SURVIVORS ARE **CONFUSING** THE IMAGE.

NOTE: GET LESLIE THOMPKINS ON A PROJECT TO **MAINSTREAM** THEM-- SOMEHOW.

SHE'S **BETTER** AT THAT.

WE **EACH** HAVE OUR **CALLING**.

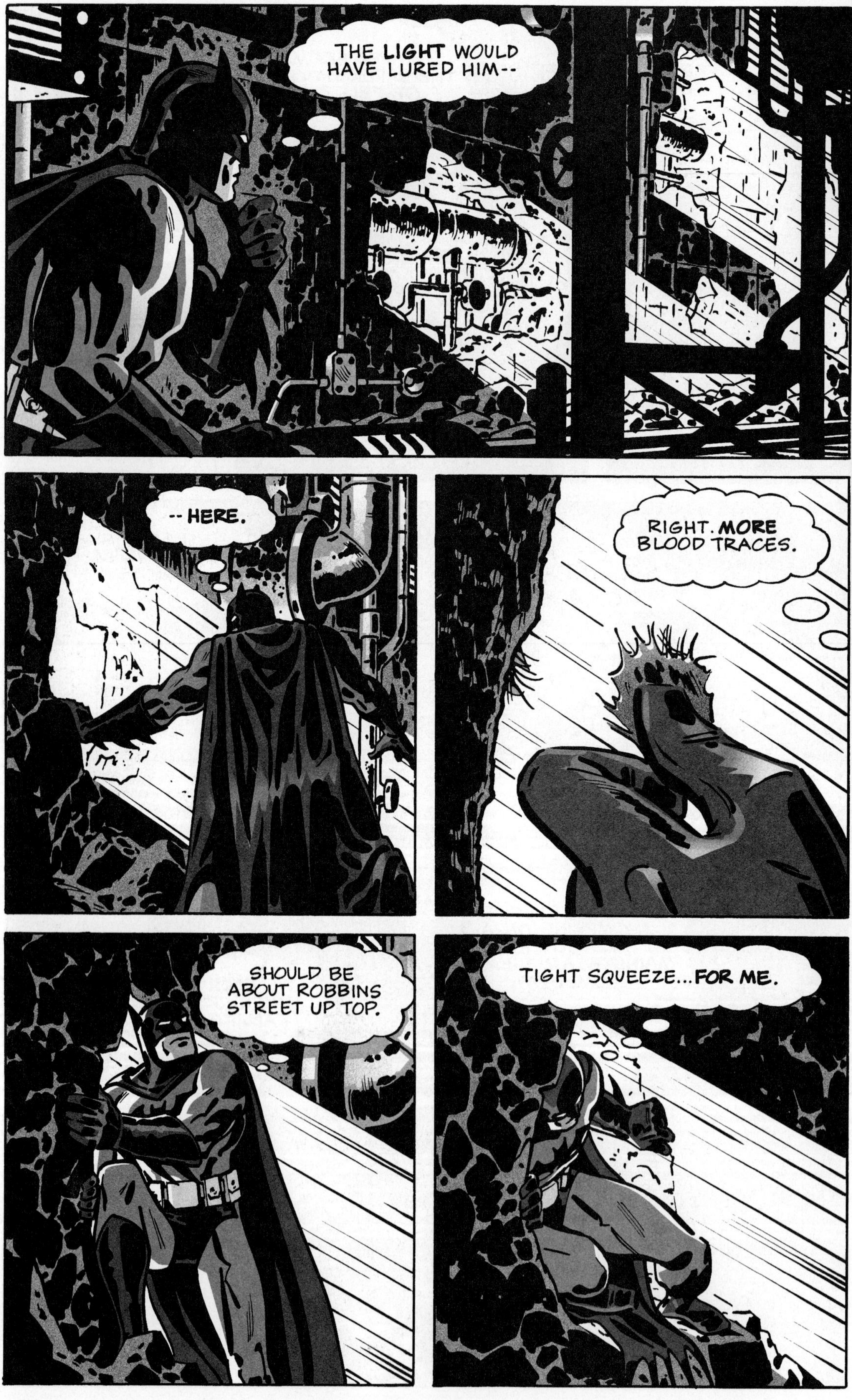
THE LIGHT WOULD HAVE LURED HIM--
--HERE.
RIGHT. MORE BLOOD TRACES.
SHOULD BE ABOUT ROBBINS STREET UP TOP.
TIGHT SQUEEZE...FOR ME.

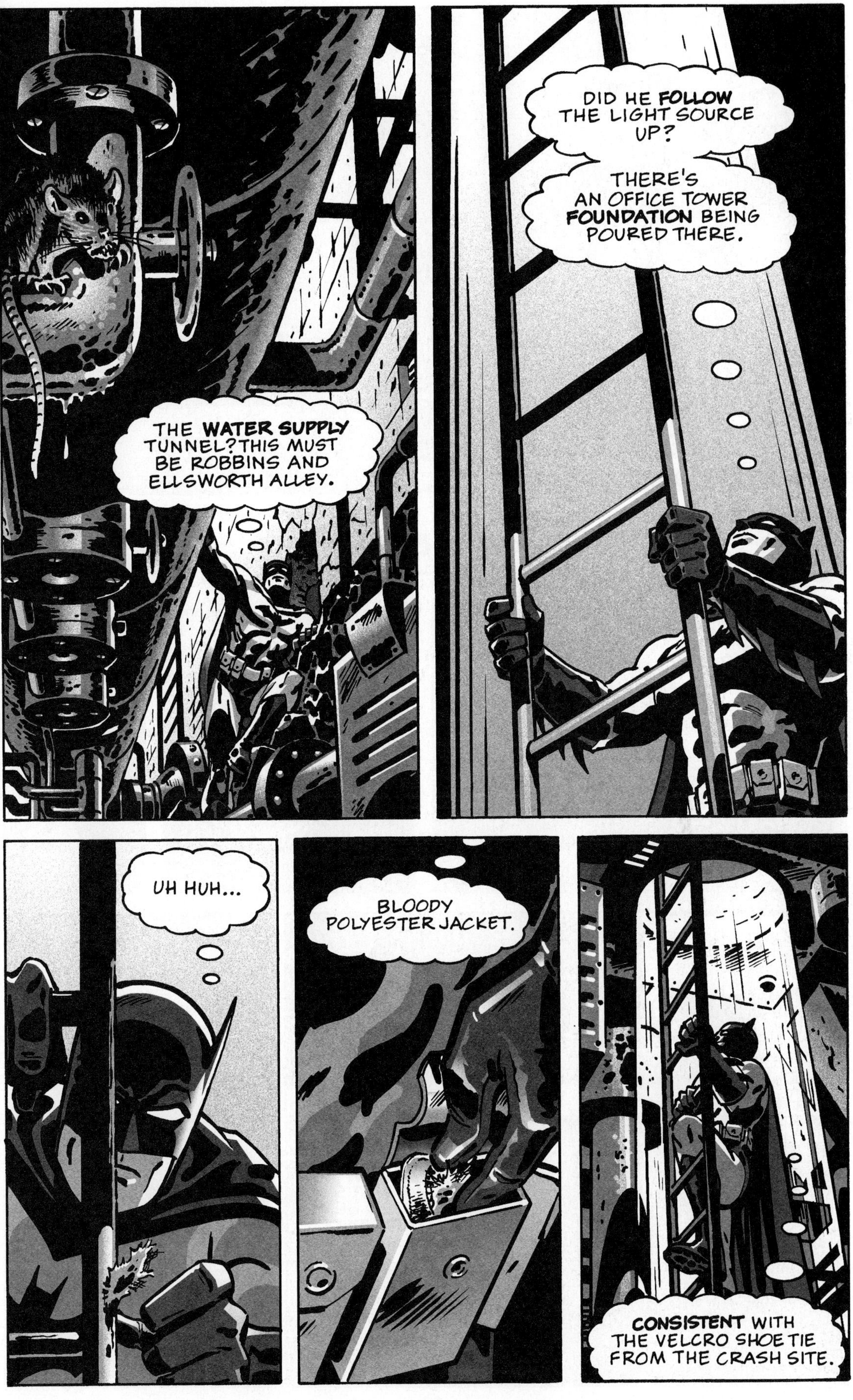
THE WATER SUPPLY TUNNEL? THIS MUST BE ROBBINS AND ELLSWORTH ALLEY.
DID HE FOLLOW THE LIGHT SOURCE UP?
THERE'S AN OFFICE TOWER FOUNDATION BEING POURED THERE.
UH HUH...
BLOODY POLYESTER JACKET.
CONSISTENT WITH THE VELCRO SHOE TIE FROM THE CRASH SITE.

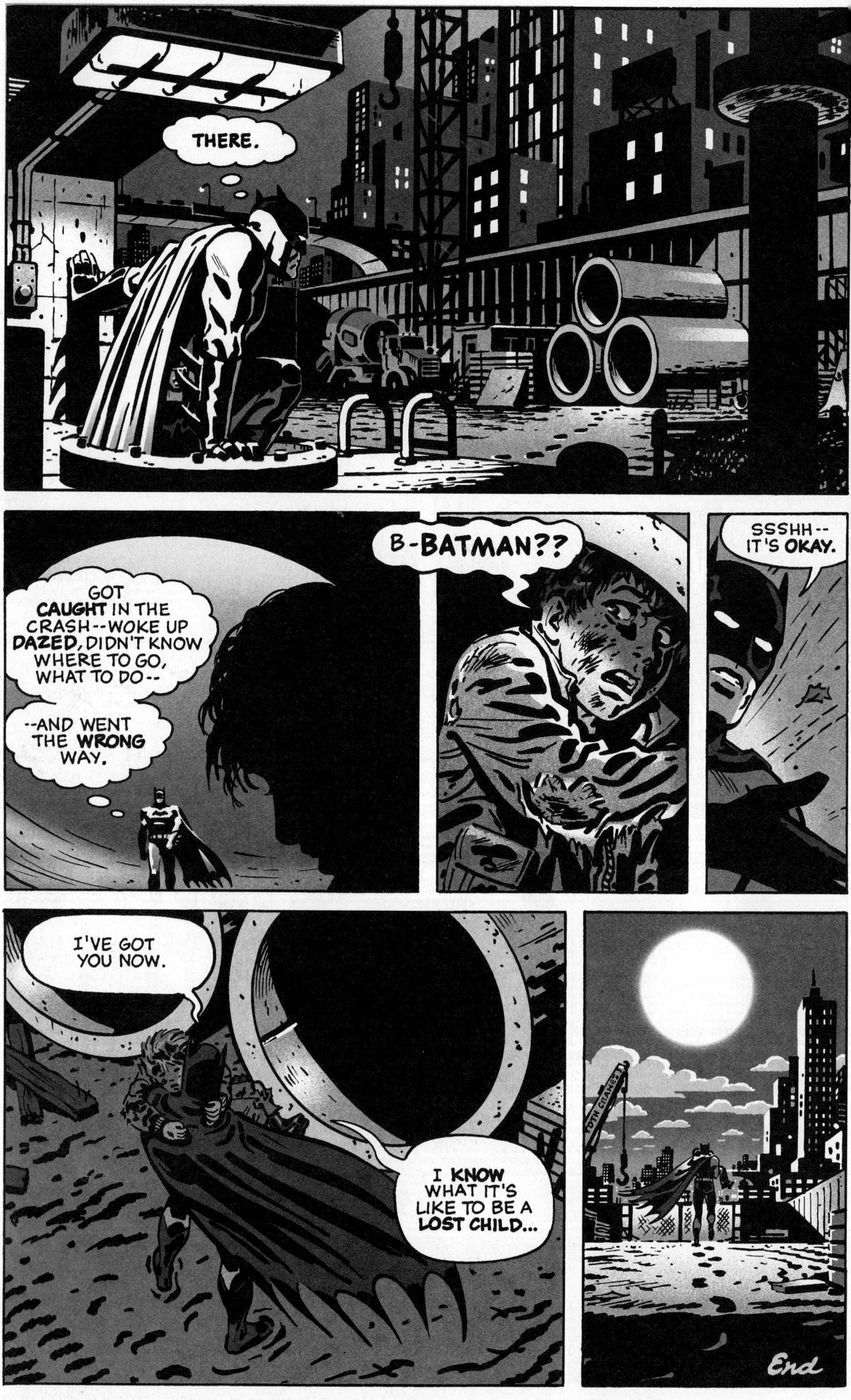
THERE.
GOT CAUGHT IN THE CRASH--WOKE UP DAZED, DIDN'T KNOW WHERE TO GO, WHAT TO DO--
--AND WENT THE WRONG WAY.
B-BATMAN??
SSSHH-- IT'S OKAY.
I'VE GOT YOU NOW.
I KNOW WHAT IT'S LIKE TO BE A LOST CHILD...
End

"THE HATTER OPENED HIS EYES VERY WIDE ON HEARING THIS; BUT ALL HE SAID WAS, 'WHY IS A RAVEN LIKE A WRITING DESK?'"

--ALICE'S ADVENTURES IN WONDERLAND

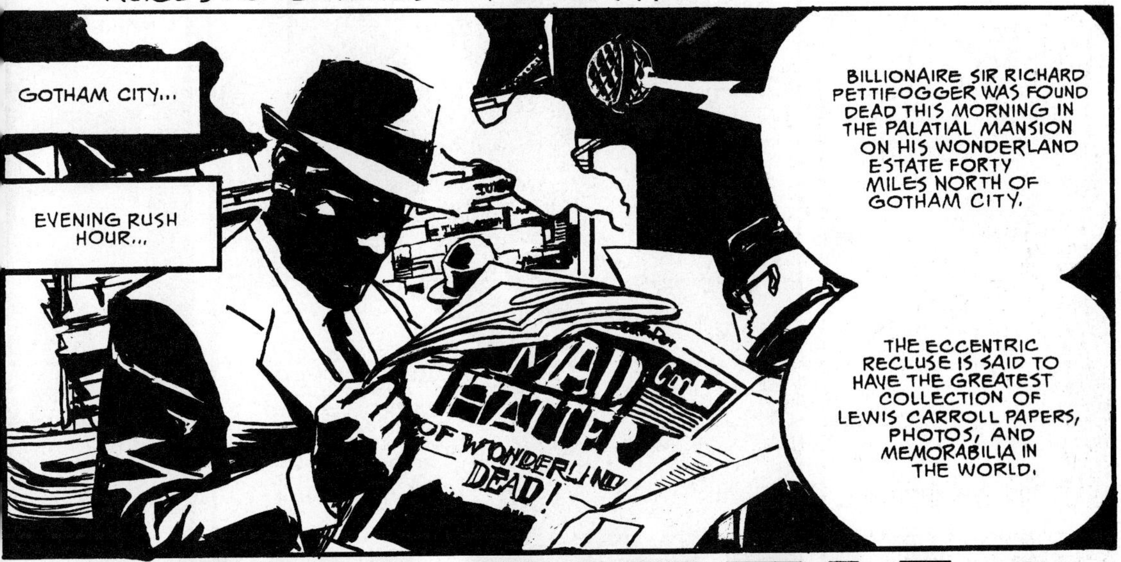
GOTHAM CITY...
EVENING RUSH HOUR...
BILLIONAIRE SIR RICHARD PETTIFOGGER WAS FOUND DEAD THIS MORNING IN THE PALATIAL MANSION ON HIS WONDERLAND ESTATE FORTY MILES NORTH OF GOTHAM CITY.
THE ECCENTRIC RECLUSE IS SAID TO HAVE THE GREATEST COLLECTION OF LEWIS CARROLL PAPERS, PHOTOS, AND MEMORABILIA IN THE WORLD.
MAD HATTER OF WONDERLAND DEAD!

THE RIDDLE

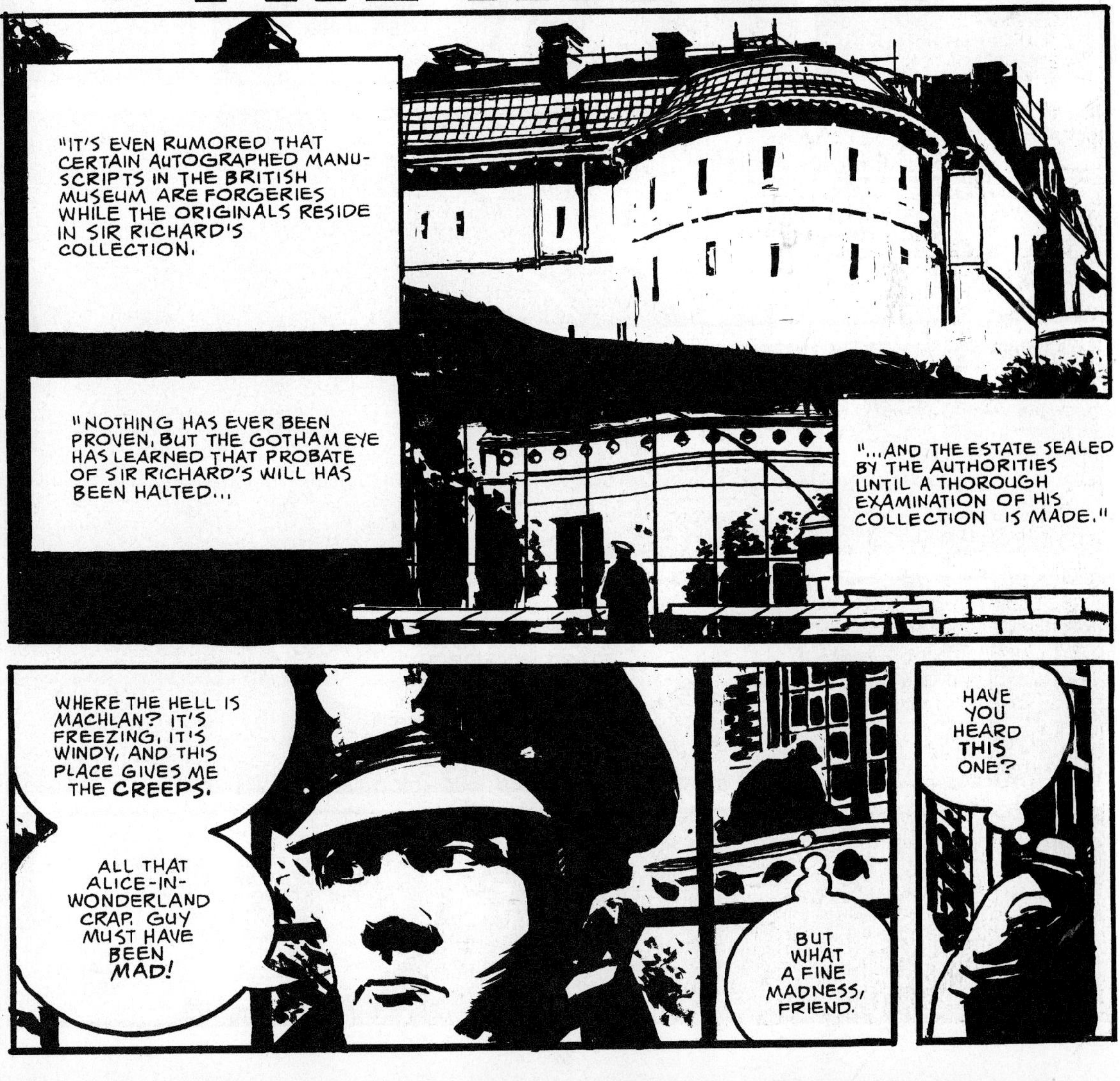
"IT'S EVEN RUMORED THAT CERTAIN AUTOGRAPHED MANUSCRIPTS IN THE BRITISH MUSEUM ARE FORGERIES WHILE THE ORIGINALS RESIDE IN SIR RICHARD'S COLLECTION.
"NOTHING HAS EVER BEEN PROVEN, BUT THE GOTHAM EYE HAS LEARNED THAT PROBATE OF SIR RICHARD'S WILL HAS BEEN HALTED...
"...AND THE ESTATE SEALED BY THE AUTHORITIES UNTIL A THOROUGH EXAMINATION OF HIS COLLECTION IS MADE."
WHERE THE HELL IS MACHLAN? IT'S FREEZING, IT'S WINDY, AND THIS PLACE GIVES ME THE CREEPS.
ALL THAT ALICE-IN-WONDERLAND CRAP. GUY MUST HAVE BEEN MAD!
BUT WHAT A FINE MADNESS, FRIEND.
HAVE YOU HEARD THIS ONE?

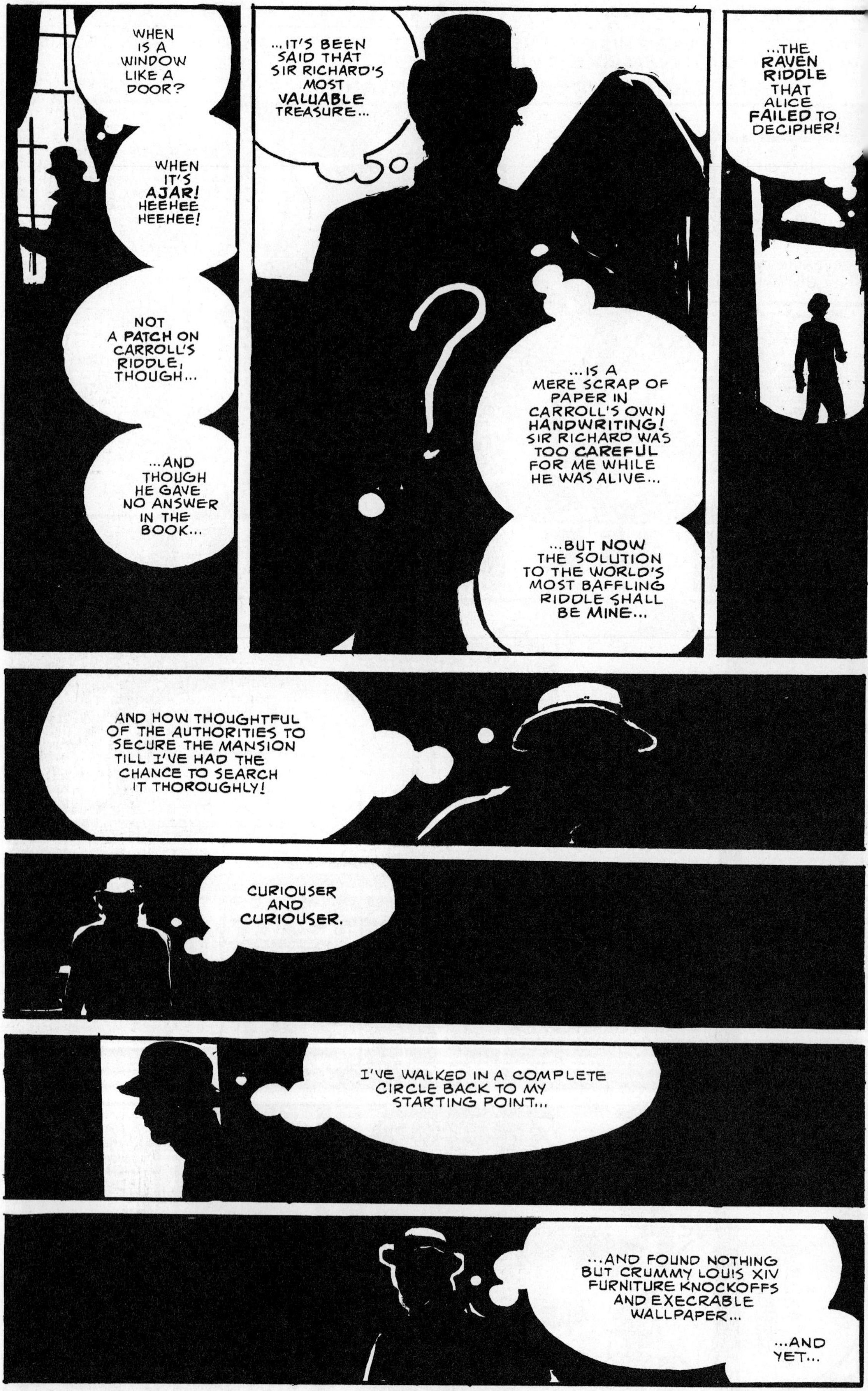
WHEN IS A WINDOW LIKE A DOOR?
WHEN IT'S AJAR! HEEHEE HEEHEE!
NOT A PATCH ON CARROLL'S RIDDLE, THOUGH...
...AND THOUGH HE GAVE NO ANSWER IN THE BOOK...
...IT'S BEEN SAID THAT SIR RICHARD'S MOST VALUABLE TREASURE...
...IS A MERE SCRAP OF PAPER IN CARROLL'S OWN HANDWRITING! SIR RICHARD WAS TOO CAREFUL FOR ME WHILE HE WAS ALIVE...
...BUT NOW THE SOLUTION TO THE WORLD'S MOST BAFFLING RIDDLE SHALL BE MINE...
...THE RAVEN RIDDLE THAT ALICE FAILED TO DECIPHER!
AND HOW THOUGHTFUL OF THE AUTHORITIES TO SECURE THE MANSION TILL I'VE HAD THE CHANCE TO SEARCH IT THOROUGHLY!
CURIOUSER AND CURIOUSER.
I'VE WALKED IN A COMPLETE CIRCLE BACK TO MY STARTING POINT...
...AND FOUND NOTHING BUT CRUMMY LOUIS XIV FURNITURE KNOCKOFFS AND EXECRABLE WALLPAPER...
...AND YET...

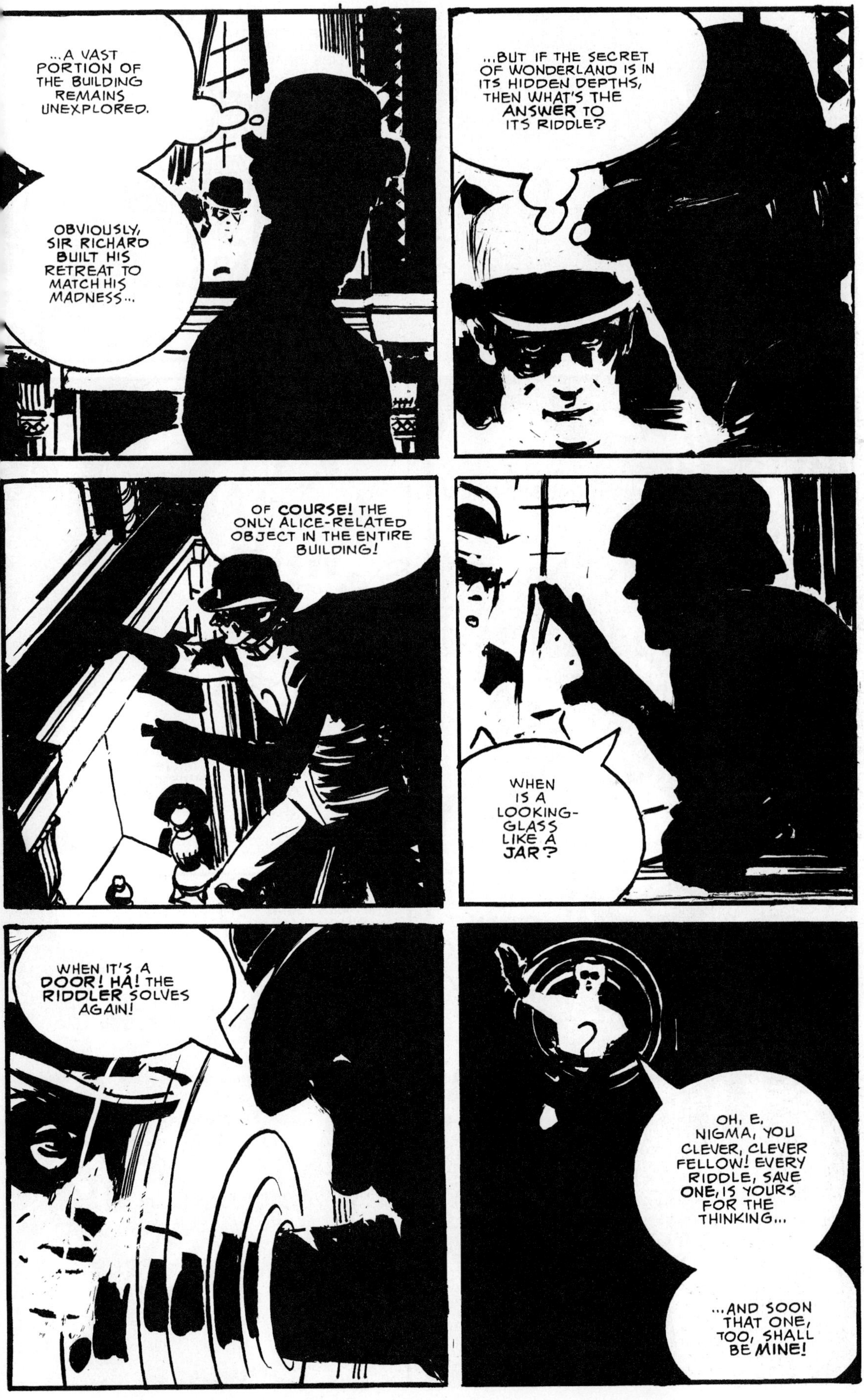
...A VAST PORTION OF THE BUILDING REMAINS UNEXPLORED.
OBVIOUSLY, SIR RICHARD BUILT HIS RETREAT TO MATCH HIS MADNESS...
...BUT IF THE SECRET OF WONDERLAND IS IN ITS HIDDEN DEPTHS, THEN WHAT'S THE ANSWER TO ITS RIDDLE?
OF COURSE! THE ONLY ALICE-RELATED OBJECT IN THE ENTIRE BUILDING!
WHEN IS A LOOKING-GLASS LIKE A JAR?
WHEN IT'S A DOOR! HA! THE RIDDLER SOLVES AGAIN!
OH, E. NIGMA, YOU CLEVER, CLEVER FELLOW! EVERY RIDDLE, SAVE ONE, IS YOURS FOR THE THINKING...
...AND SOON THAT ONE, TOO, SHALL BE MINE!

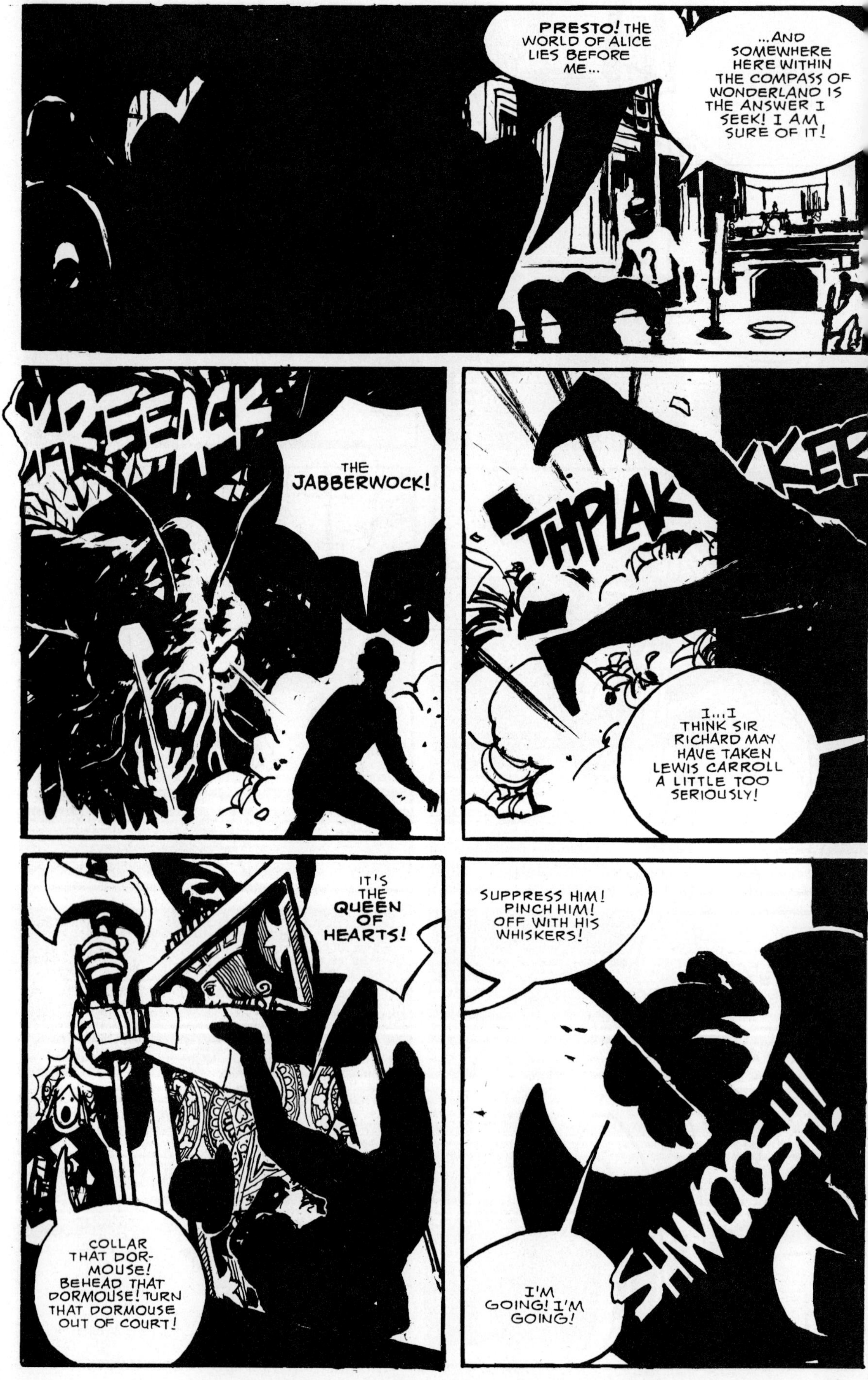
PRESTO! THE WORLD OF ALICE LIES BEFORE ME...
...AND SOMEWHERE HERE WITHIN THE COMPASS OF WONDERLAND IS THE ANSWER I SEEK! I AM SURE OF IT!
KREEACK
THE JABBERWOCK!
THPLAK
KER
I...I THINK SIR RICHARD MAY HAVE TAKEN LEWIS CARROLL A LITTLE TOO SERIOUSLY!
IT'S THE QUEEN OF HEARTS!
COLLAR THAT DOR-MOUSE! BEHEAD THAT DORMOUSE! TURN THAT DORMOUSE OUT OF COURT!
SUPPRESS HIM! PINCH HIM! OFF WITH HIS WHISKERS!
SHWOOSH!
I'M GOING! I'M GOING!

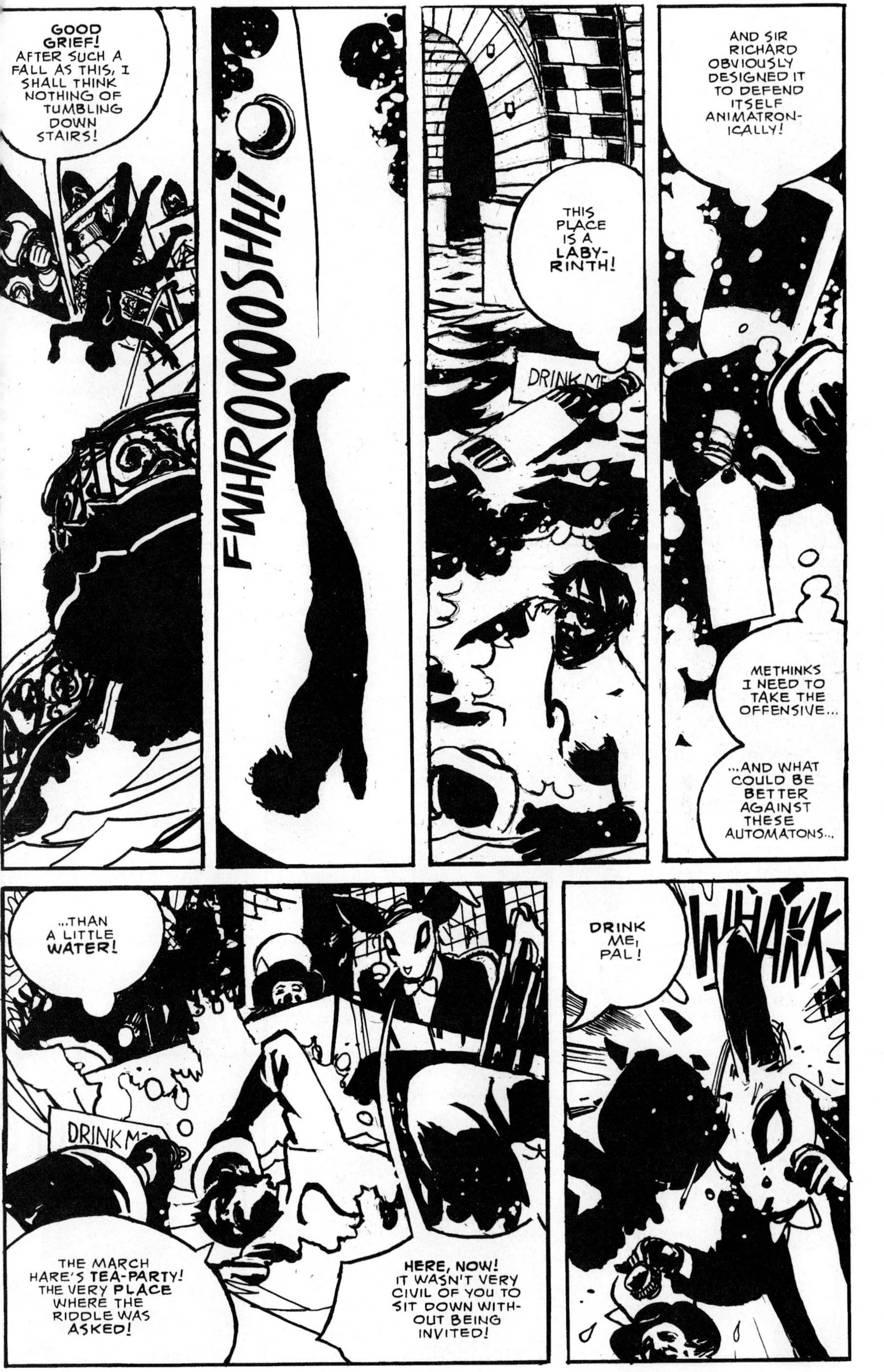
GOOD GRIEF! AFTER SUCH A FALL AS THIS, I SHALL THINK NOTHING OF TUMBLING DOWN STAIRS!
FWHROOOOOSHH!
THIS PLACE IS A LABYRINTH!
DRINK ME
AND SIR RICHARD OBVIOUSLY DESIGNED IT TO DEFEND ITSELF ANIMATRONICALLY!
METHINKS I NEED TO TAKE THE OFFENSIVE...
...AND WHAT COULD BE BETTER AGAINST THESE AUTOMATONS...
...THAN A LITTLE WATER!
DRINK ME
THE MARCH HARE'S TEA-PARTY! THE VERY PLACE WHERE THE RIDDLE WAS ASKED!
HERE, NOW! IT WASN'T VERY CIVIL OF YOU TO SIT DOWN WITHOUT BEING INVITED!
DRINK ME, PAL!
WHAKK

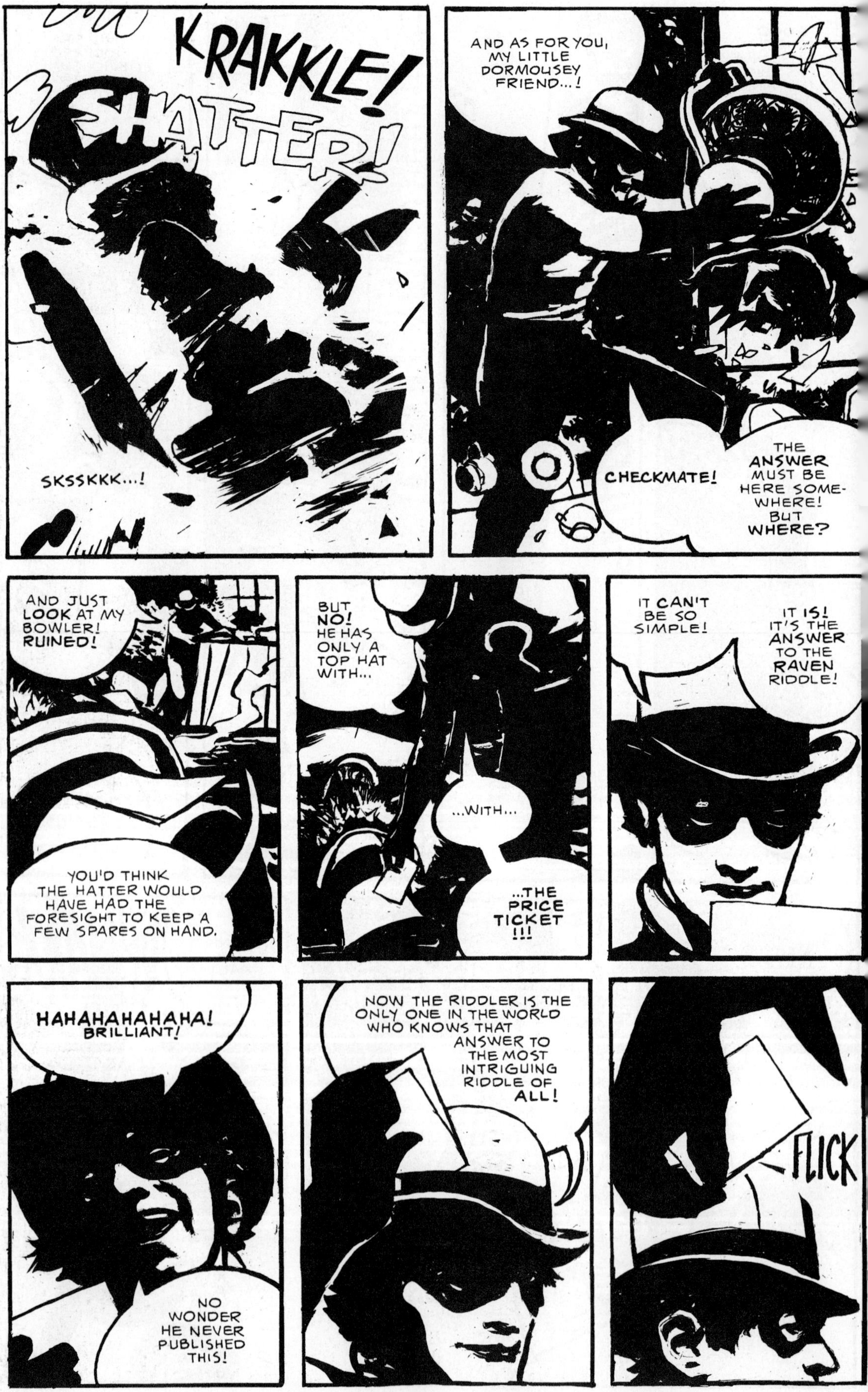
KRAKKLE!
SHATTER!
SKSSKKK...!
AND AS FOR YOU, MY LITTLE DORMOUSEY FRIEND...!
CHECKMATE!
THE ANSWER MUST BE HERE SOMEWHERE! BUT WHERE?
AND JUST LOOK AT MY BOWLER! RUINED!
YOU'D THINK THE HATTER WOULD HAVE HAD THE FORESIGHT TO KEEP A FEW SPARES ON HAND.
BUT NO! HE HAS ONLY A TOP HAT WITH...
...WITH...
...THE PRICE TICKET!!!
IT CAN'T BE SO SIMPLE!
IT IS! IT'S THE ANSWER TO THE RAVEN RIDDLE!
HAHAHAHAHAHA! BRILLIANT!
NO WONDER HE NEVER PUBLISHED THIS!
NOW THE RIDDLER IS THE ONLY ONE IN THE WORLD WHO KNOWS THAT ANSWER TO THE MOST INTRIGUING RIDDLE OF ALL!
FLICK

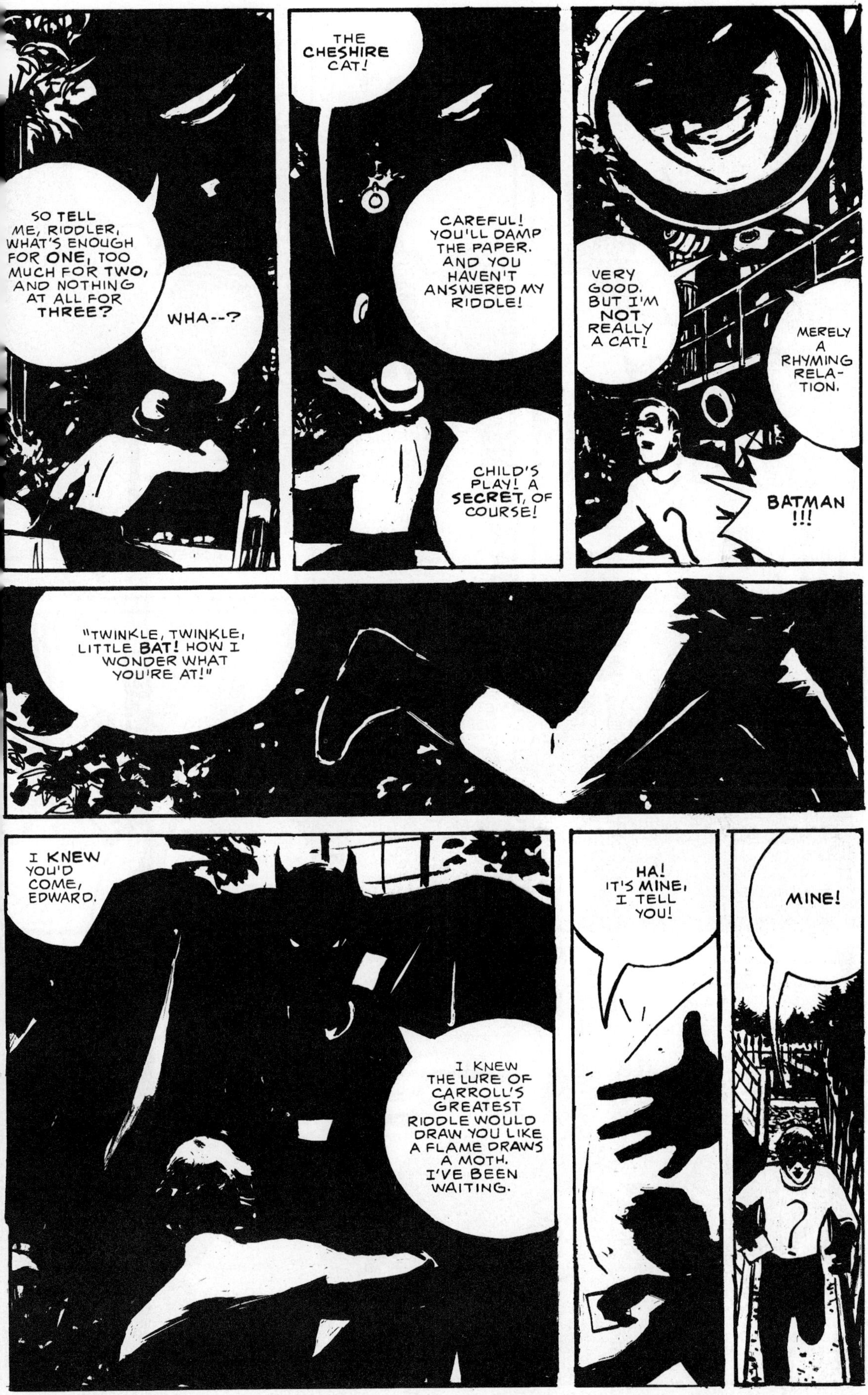
SO TELL ME, RIDDLER, WHAT'S ENOUGH FOR ONE, TOO MUCH FOR TWO, AND NOTHING AT ALL FOR THREE?
WHA--?
THE CHESHIRE CAT!
CAREFUL! YOU'LL DAMP THE PAPER. AND YOU HAVEN'T ANSWERED MY RIDDLE!
CHILD'S PLAY! A SECRET, OF COURSE!
VERY GOOD. BUT I'M NOT REALLY A CAT!
MERELY A RHYMING RELA-TION.
BATMAN!!!
"TWINKLE, TWINKLE, LITTLE BAT! HOW I WONDER WHAT YOU'RE AT!"
I KNEW YOU'D COME, EDWARD.
I KNEW THE LURE OF CARROLL'S GREATEST RIDDLE WOULD DRAW YOU LIKE A FLAME DRAWS A MOTH. I'VE BEEN WAITING.
HA! IT'S MINE, I TELL YOU!
MINE!

I THOUGHT I HEARD SOME COMMOTION COMING FROM THE HOUSE!

GRAB HIM, MACHLAN!

NOOOO!

IT'S GONE, EDWARD. CARRIED BY THE WIND AND TAKEN BY THE NIGHT.

BUT NEVER MIND. IT WASN'T THE REAL ANSWER, ANYWAY.

WHAT?

I SAID I KNEW YOU'D COME. I ARRIVED AN HOUR EARLIER, SOLVED THE LABYRINTH, JUST AS YOU DID...

...AND FOUND THE HIDDEN RIDDLE.

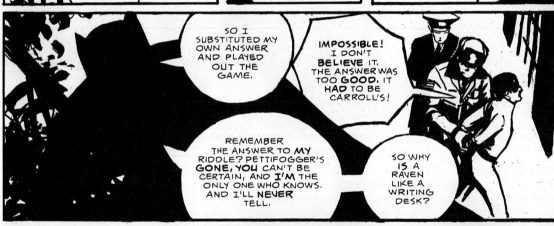

SO I SUBSTITUTED MY OWN ANSWER AND PLAYED OUT THE GAME.

REMEMBER THE ANSWER TO MY RIDDLE? PETTIFOGGER'S GONE, YOU CAN'T BE CERTAIN, AND I'M THE ONLY ONE WHO KNOWS. AND I'LL NEVER TELL.

IMPOSSIBLE! I DON'T BELIEVE IT. THE ANSWER WAS TOO GOOD. IT HAD TO BE CARROLL'S!

SO WHY IS A RAVEN LIKE A WRITING DESK?

COME BACK. COME BACK HERE! YOU CAN'T LEAVE ME LIKE THIS, YOU COSTUMED FREAK! COME BACK HERE!

'S ALL RIGHT, PAL. YOU'LL BE HAPPY ENOUGH ONCE YER BACK IN ARKHAM ASYLUM.

JUST THINK OF IT AS ONE MORE RIDDLE, EDWARD, AND REMEMBER THE WORDS OF THE CHESHIRE BAT...

"...WE'RE ALL MAD HERE."

END

WALTER SIMONSON writer ■ JOHN PAUL LEON artist ■ JOHN WORKMAN letterer ■ MARK CHIARELLO editor

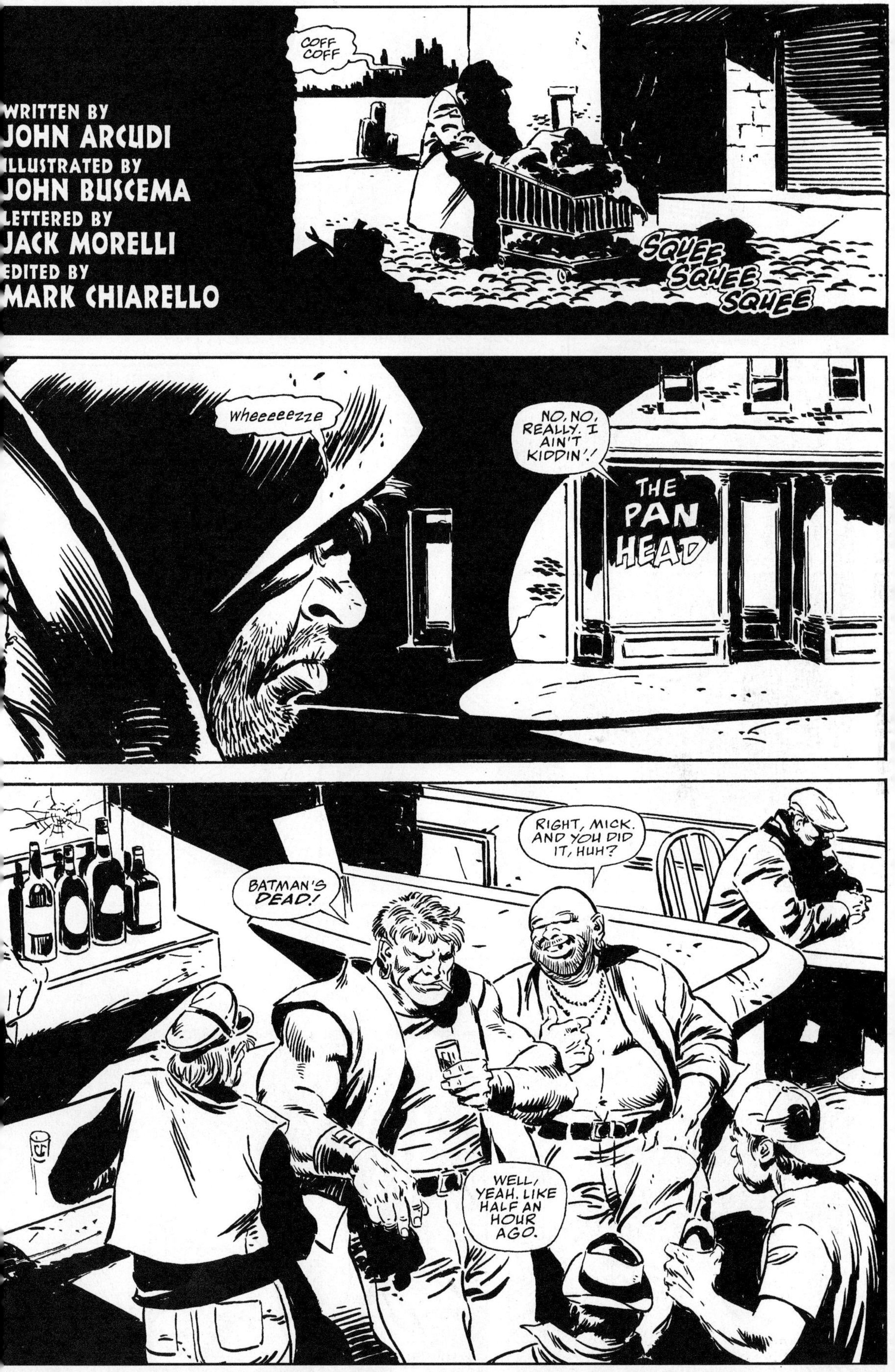
WRITTEN BY
JOHN ARCUDI
ILLUSTRATED BY
JOHN BUSCEMA
LETTERED BY
JACK MORELLI
EDITED BY
MARK CHIARELLO
COFF COFF
SQUEE SQUEE SQUEE
wheeeeezze
NO, NO, REALLY. I AIN'T KIDDIN'!
THE PAN HEAD
BATMAN'S DEAD!
RIGHT, MICK. AND YOU DID IT, HUH?
WELL, YEAH. LIKE HALF AN HOUR AGO.

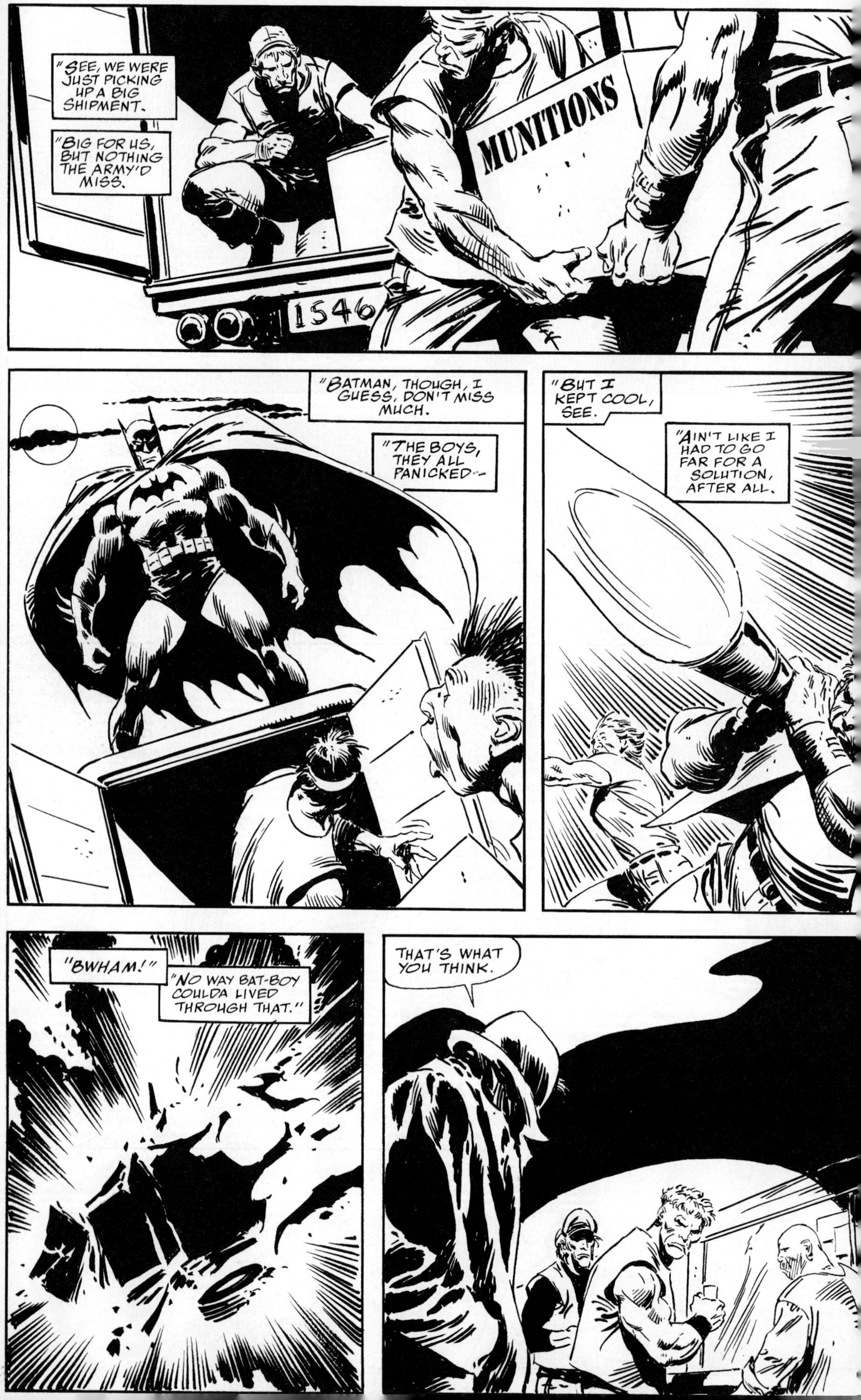
"SEE, WE WERE JUST PICKING UP A BIG SHIPMENT.
"BIG FOR US, BUT NOTHING THE ARMY'D MISS.
MUNITIONS
1546
"BATMAN, THOUGH, I GUESS, DON'T MISS MUCH.
"THE BOYS, THEY ALL PANICKED--
"BUT I KEPT COOL, SEE.
"AIN'T LIKE I HAD TO GO FAR FOR A SOLUTION, AFTER ALL.
"BWHAM!"
"NO WAY BAT-BOY COULDA LIVED THROUGH THAT."
THAT'S WHAT YOU THINK.

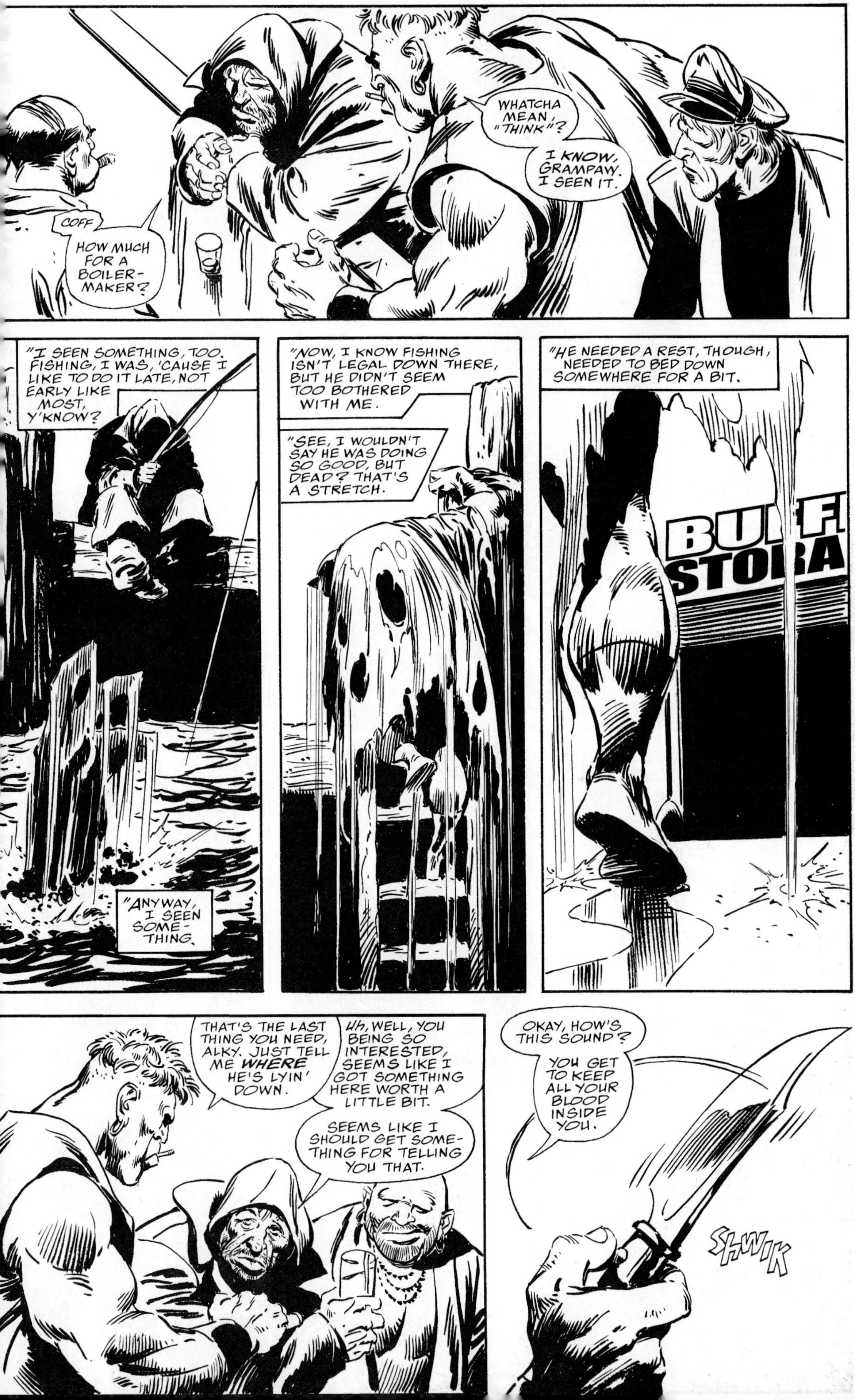
WHATCHA MEAN, "THINK"?
I KNOW, GRAMPAW. I SEEN IT.
COFF
HOW MUCH FOR A BOILER-MAKER?
"I SEEN SOMETHING, TOO. FISHING, I WAS, 'CAUSE I LIKE TO DO IT LATE, NOT EARLY LIKE MOST, Y'KNOW?
"ANYWAY, I SEEN SOME-THING.
"NOW, I KNOW FISHING ISN'T LEGAL DOWN THERE, BUT HE DIDN'T SEEM TOO BOTHERED WITH ME.
"SEE, I WOULDN'T SAY HE WAS DOING SO GOOD, BUT DEAD? THAT'S A STRETCH.
"HE NEEDED A REST, THOUGH, NEEDED TO BED DOWN SOMEWHERE FOR A BIT.
BUFF
STORA
THAT'S THE LAST THING YOU NEED, ALKY. JUST TELL ME WHERE HE'S LYIN' DOWN.
UH, WELL, YOU BEING SO INTERESTED, SEEMS LIKE I GOT SOMETHING HERE WORTH A LITTLE BIT.
SEEMS LIKE I SHOULD GET SOME-THING FOR TELLING YOU THAT.
OKAY, HOW'S THIS SOUND?
YOU GET TO KEEP ALL YOUR BLOOD INSIDE YOU.
SHWIK

BUFFEL STORAGE

MICK, IF HE CAN LIVE THROUGH THAT EXPLOSION, SHOULD WE REALLY BE DOWN HERE?

YOU HEARD THE BOOZE-HOUND. HE'S HURT, MAN, ALL MESSED UP. WHAT CAN HE DO TO US?

WOUNDED BEAR KILT MY UNCLE LOUIE.

SHUT UP, CLAUDE.

NOW I'LL TAKE POINT, CLAUDE AND RAFE ONNA LEFT, NED AND BRUNO--

--BRUNO?

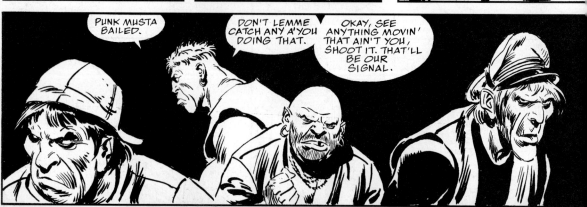

PUNK MUSTA BAILED.

DON'T LEMME CATCH ANY A'YOU DOING THAT.

OKAY, SEE ANYTHING MOVIN' THAT AIN'T YOU, SHOOT IT. THAT'LL BE OUR SIGNAL.

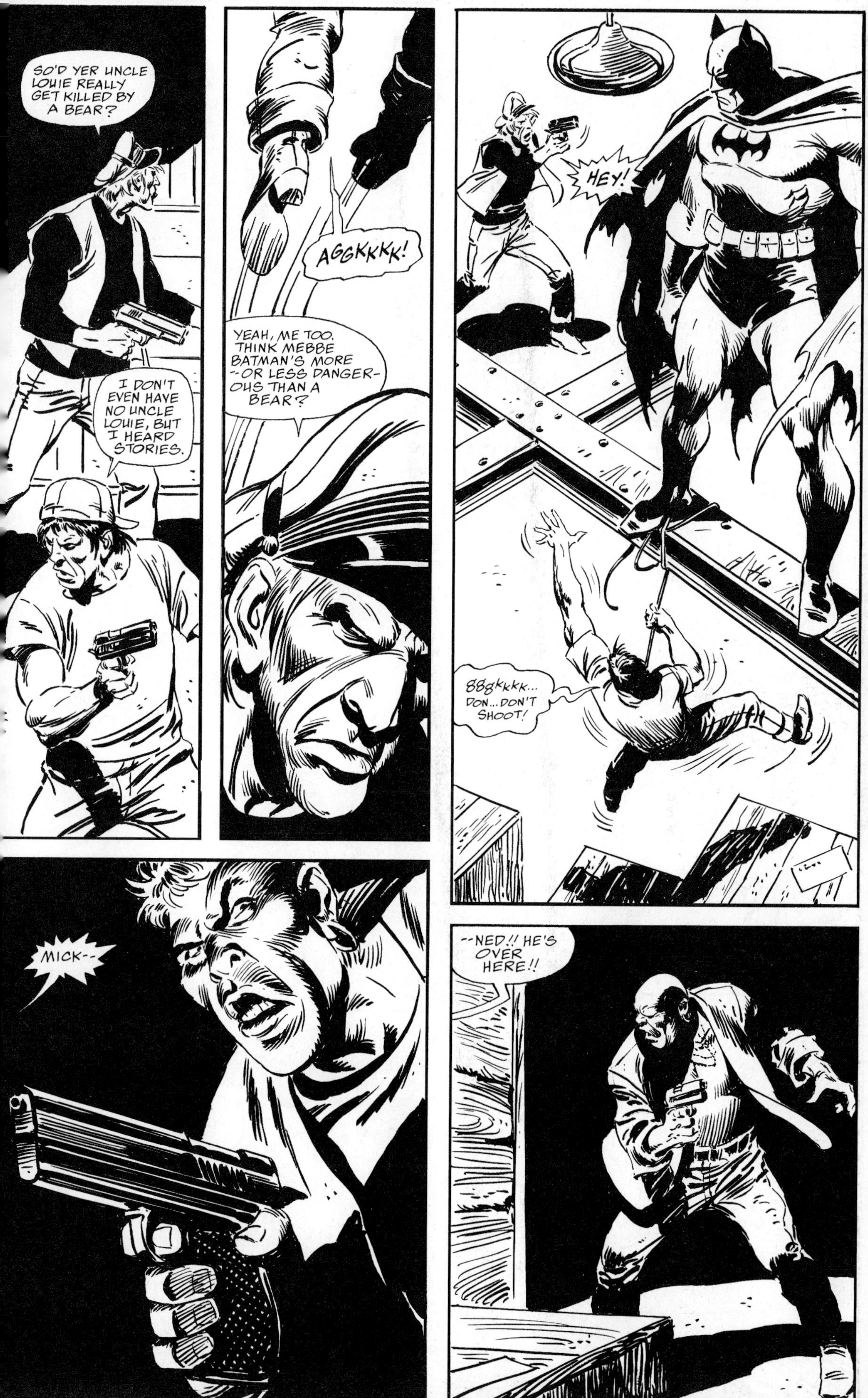

SO'D YER UNCLE LOUIE REALLY GET KILLED BY A BEAR?
I DON'T EVEN HAVE NO UNCLE LOUIE, BUT I HEARD STORIES.
YEAH, ME TOO. THINK MEBBE BATMAN'S MORE --OR LESS DANGER-OUS THAN A BEAR?
AGGKKKK!
HEY!
88gkkkk... DON... DON'T SHOOT!
MICK--
--NED!! HE'S OVER HERE!!

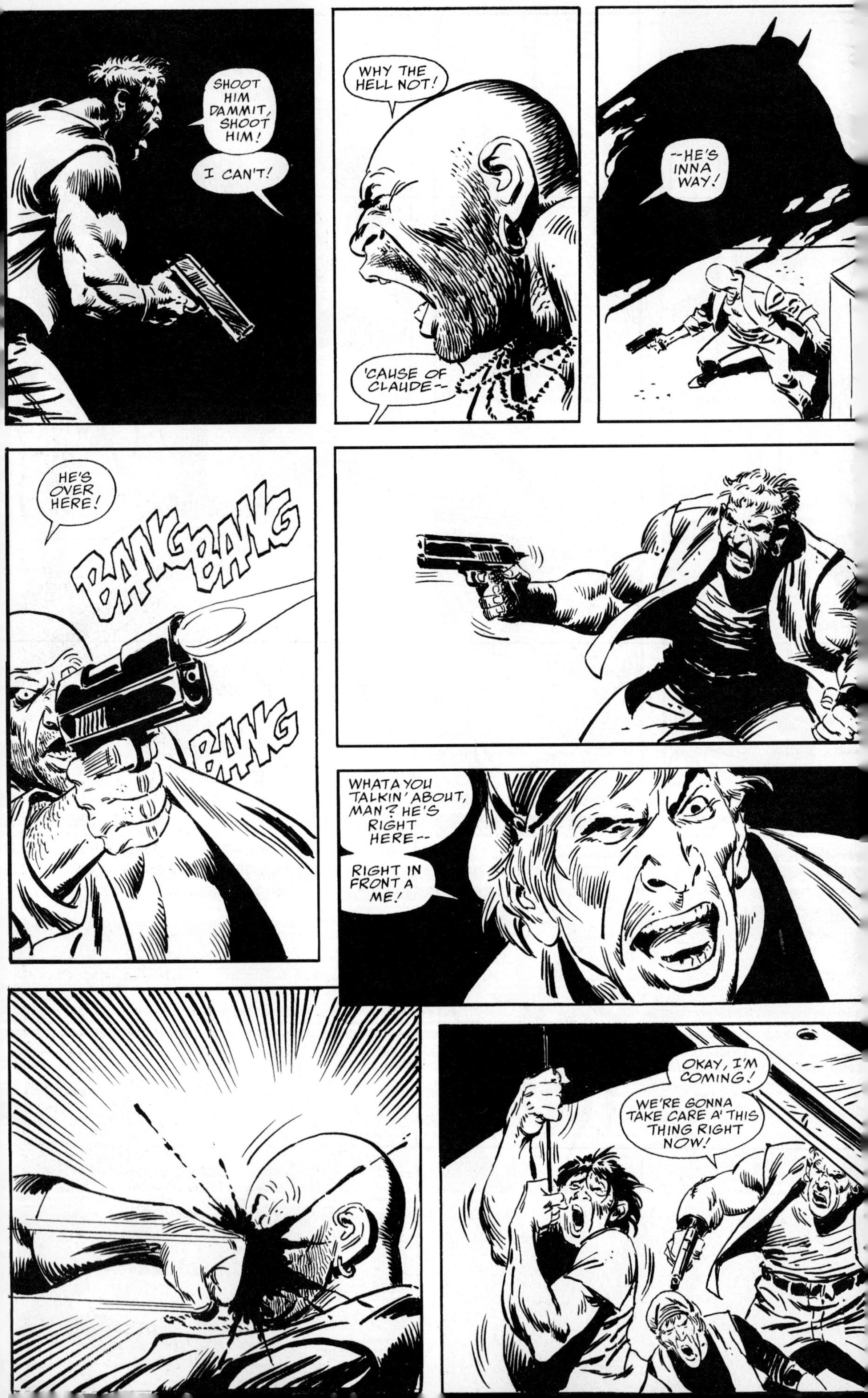
SHOOT HIM DAMMIT, SHOOT HIM!
I CAN'T!
WHY THE HELL NOT!
'CAUSE OF CLAUDE--
--HE'S INNA WAY!
HE'S OVER HERE!
BANG BANG
BANG
WHATA YOU TALKIN' ABOUT, MAN? HE'S RIGHT HERE--
RIGHT IN FRONT A ME!
OKAY, I'M COMING!
WE'RE GONNA TAKE CARE A' THIS THING RIGHT NOW!

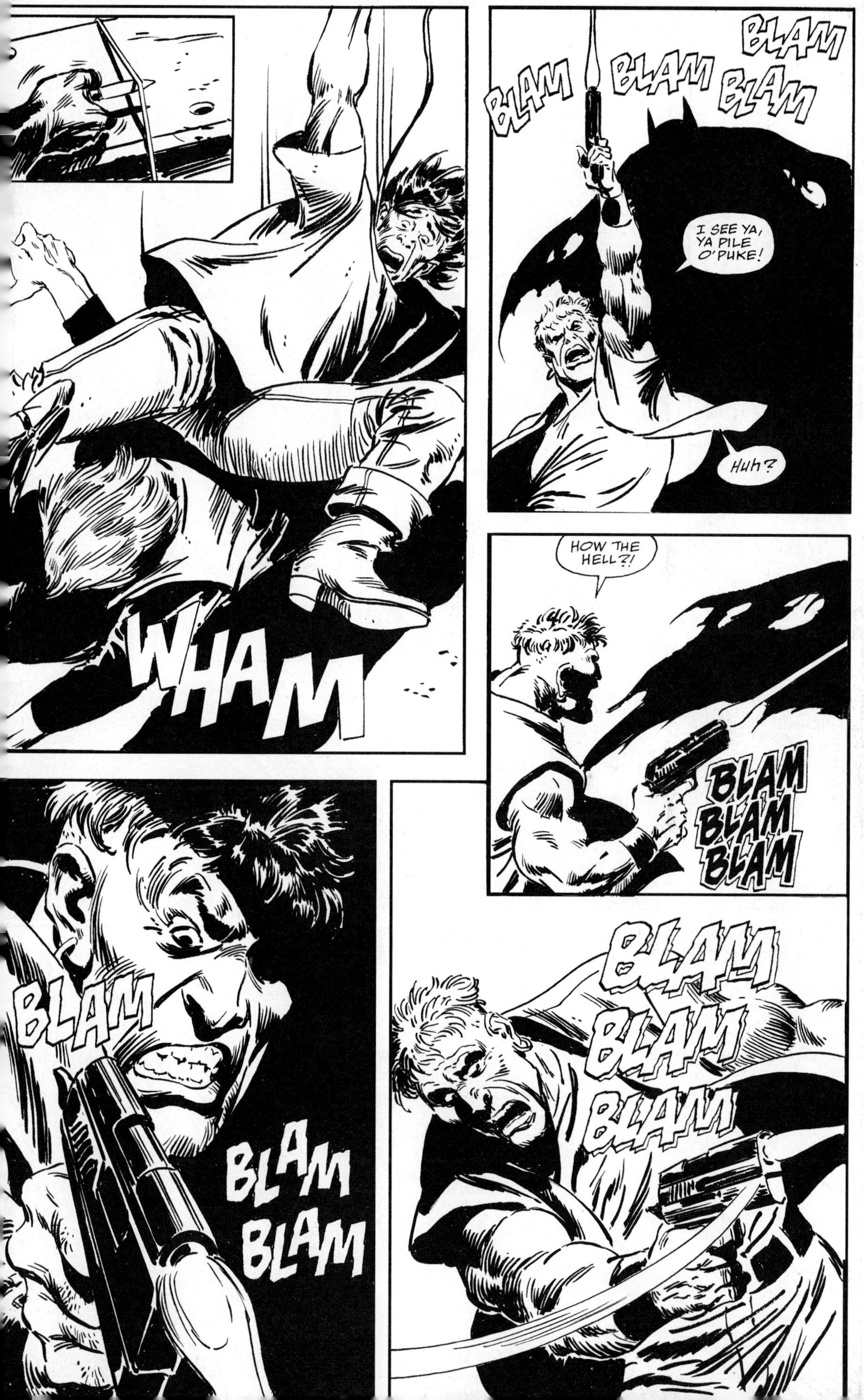
WHAM
BLAM
BLAM
BLAM
BLAM
I SEE YA, YA PILE O' PUKE!
Huh?
HOW THE HELL?!
BLAM
BLAM
BLAM
BLAM
BLAM
BLAM
BLAM
BLAM
BLAM

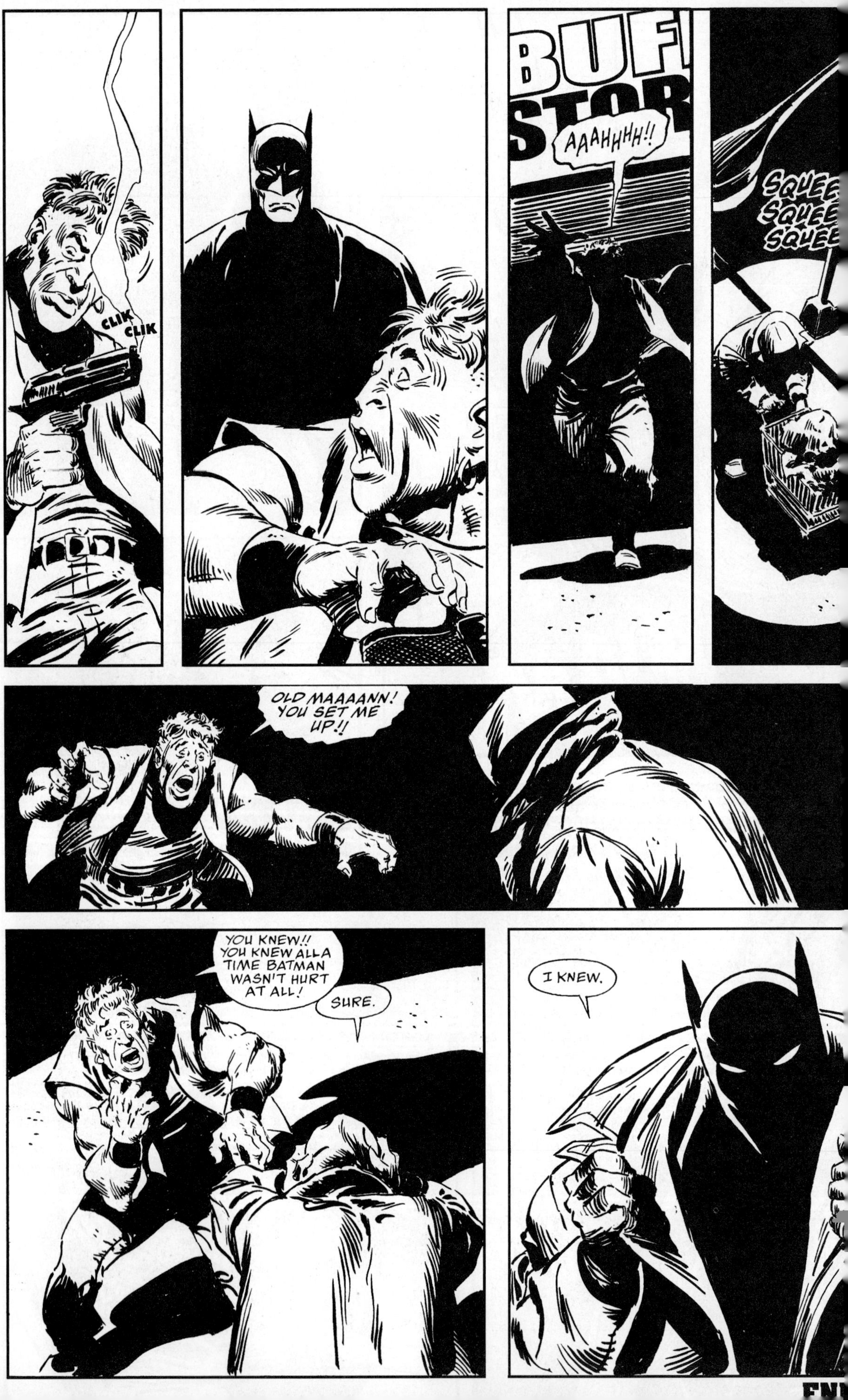
CLIK
CLIK
BUF
STOR
AAAHHHH!!
SQUEE
SQUEE
SQUEE
OLD MAAAANN! YOU SET ME UP!!
YOU KNEW!! YOU KNEW ALLA TIME BATMAN WASN'T HURT AT ALL!
SURE.
I KNEW.

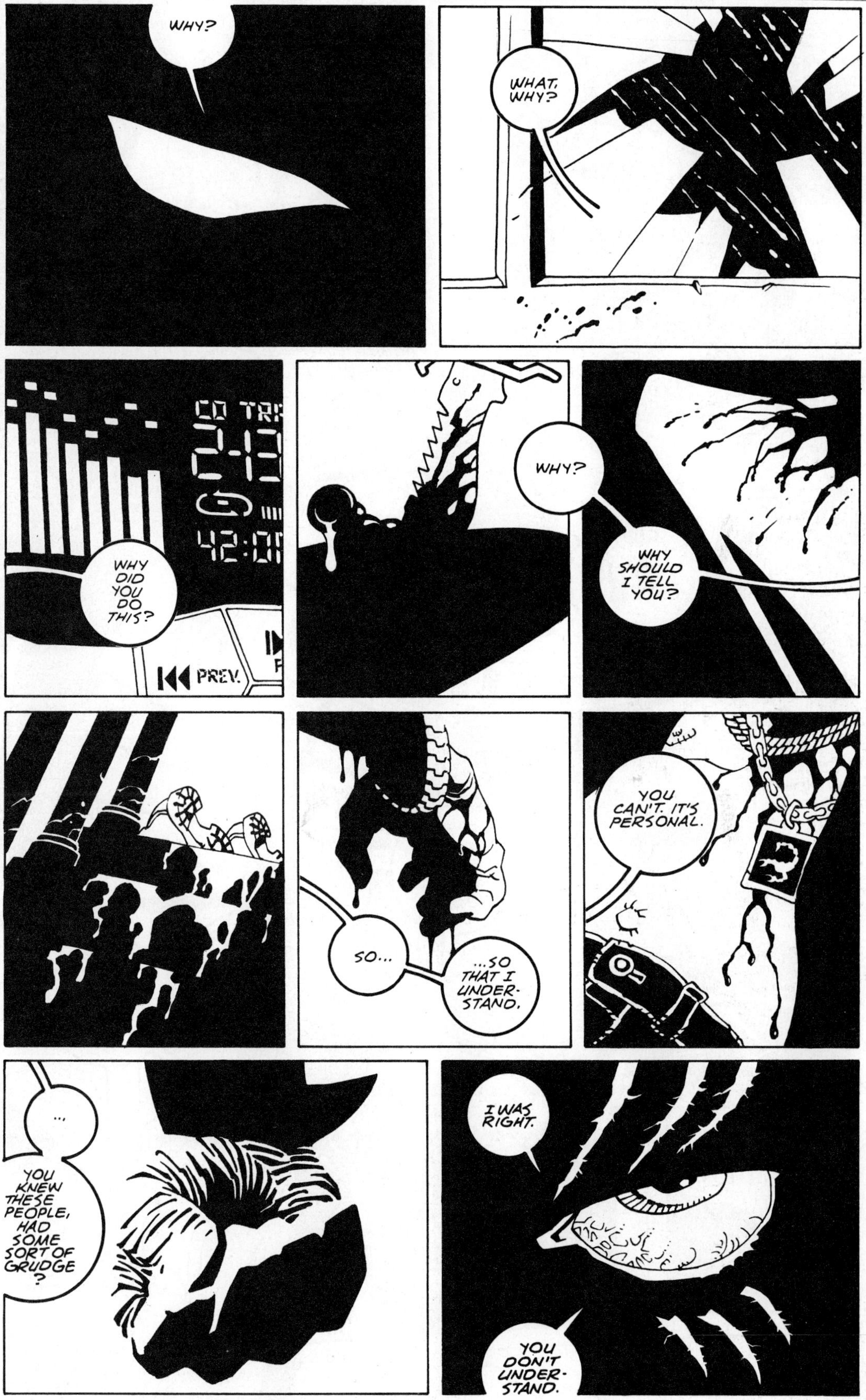
WHY?
WHAT, WHY?
CD TR
2-13
42:0
PREV.
WHY DID YOU DO THIS?
WHY?
WHY SHOULD I TELL YOU?
SO...
...SO THAT I UNDER-STAND.
YOU CAN'T. IT'S PERSONAL.
...
YOU KNEW THESE PEOPLE, HAD SOME SORT OF GRUDGE?
I WAS RIGHT.
YOU DON'T UNDER-STAND.

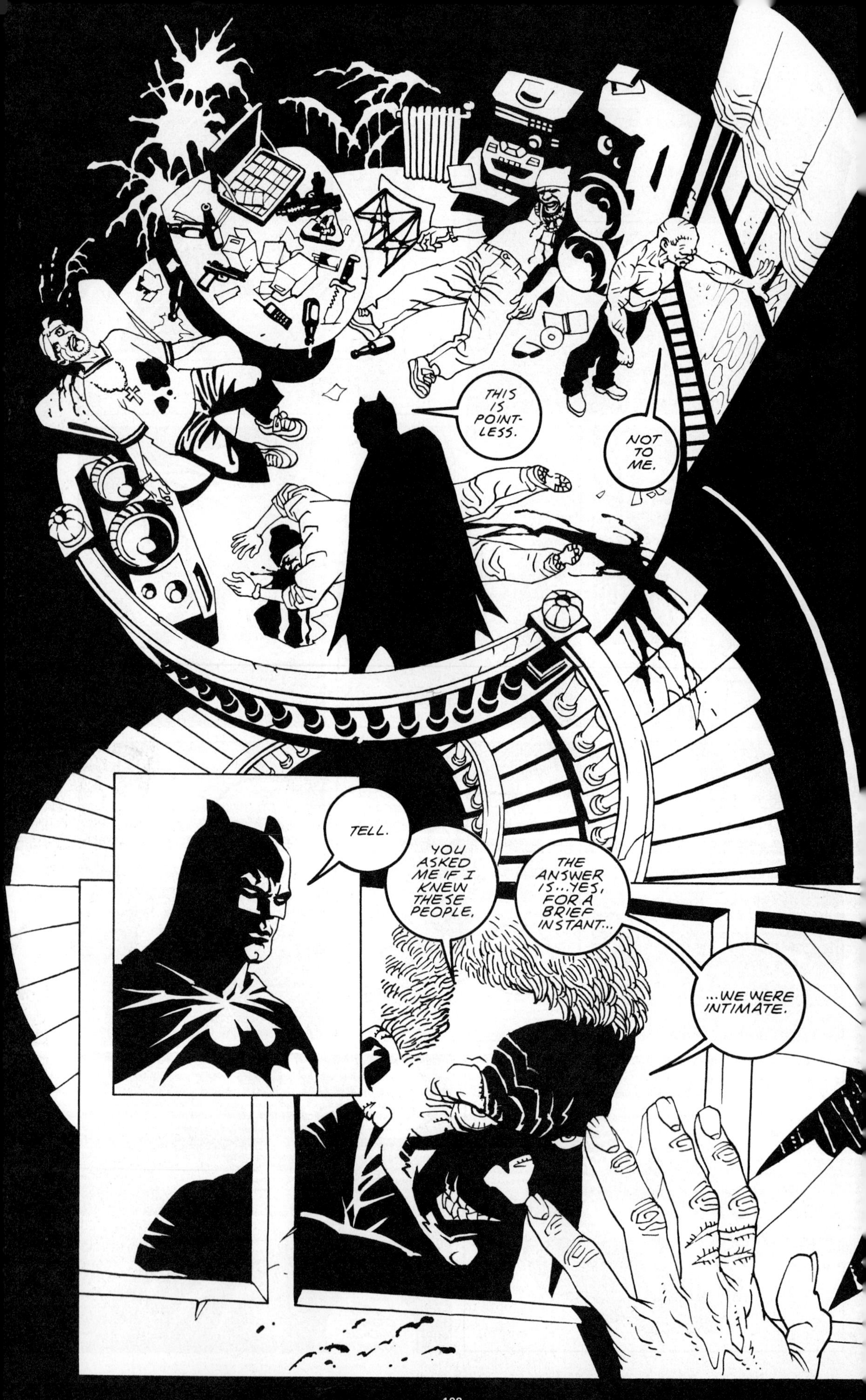

THIS IS POINTLESS.
NOT TO ME.
TELL.
YOU ASKED ME IF I KNEW THESE PEOPLE.
THE ANSWER IS...YES, FOR A BRIEF INSTANT...
...WE WERE INTIMATE.

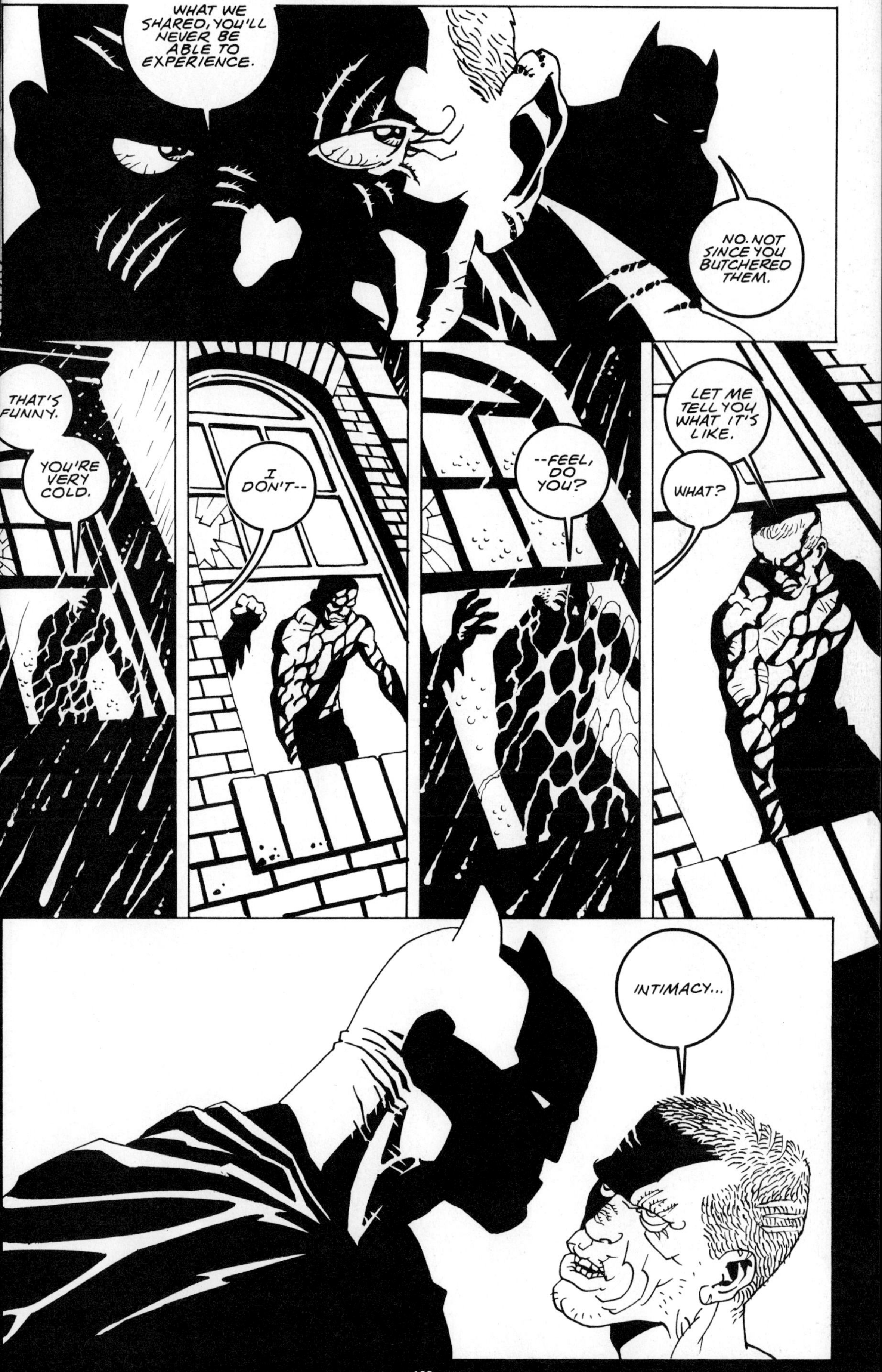
WHAT WE SHARED, YOU'LL NEVER BE ABLE TO EXPERIENCE.
NO. NOT SINCE YOU BUTCHERED THEM.
THAT'S FUNNY.
YOU'RE VERY COLD.
I DON'T--
--FEEL, DO YOU?
LET ME TELL YOU WHAT IT'S LIKE.
WHAT?
INTIMACY...

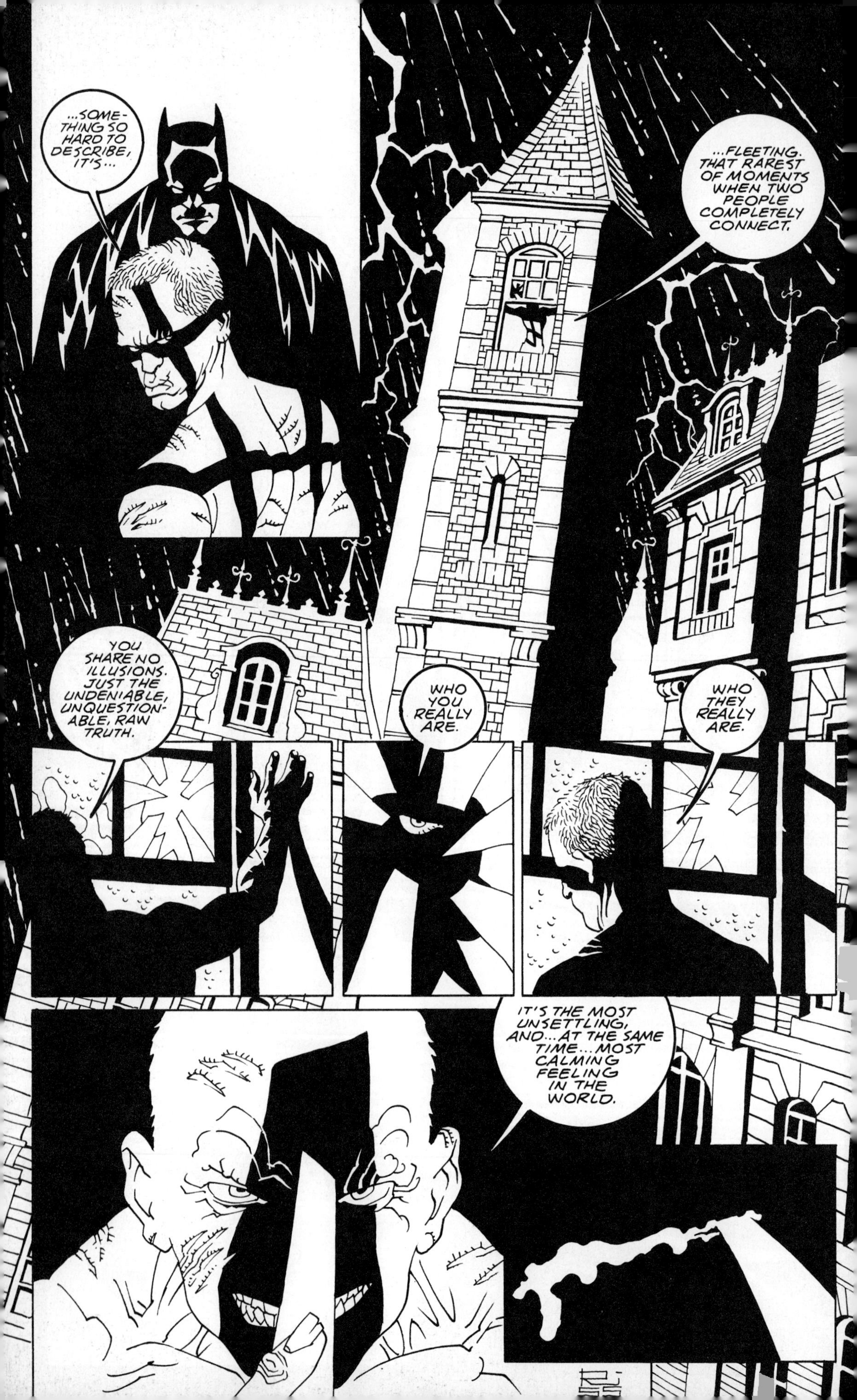

...SOME-THING SO HARD TO DESCRIBE, IT'S...
...FLEETING. THAT RAREST OF MOMENTS WHEN TWO PEOPLE COMPLETELY CONNECT.
YOU SHARE NO ILLUSIONS. JUST THE UNDENIABLE, UNQUESTION-ABLE, RAW TRUTH.
WHO YOU REALLY ARE.
WHO THEY REALLY ARE.
IT'S THE MOST UNSETTLING, AND...AT THE SAME TIME...MOST CALMING FEELING IN THE WORLD.

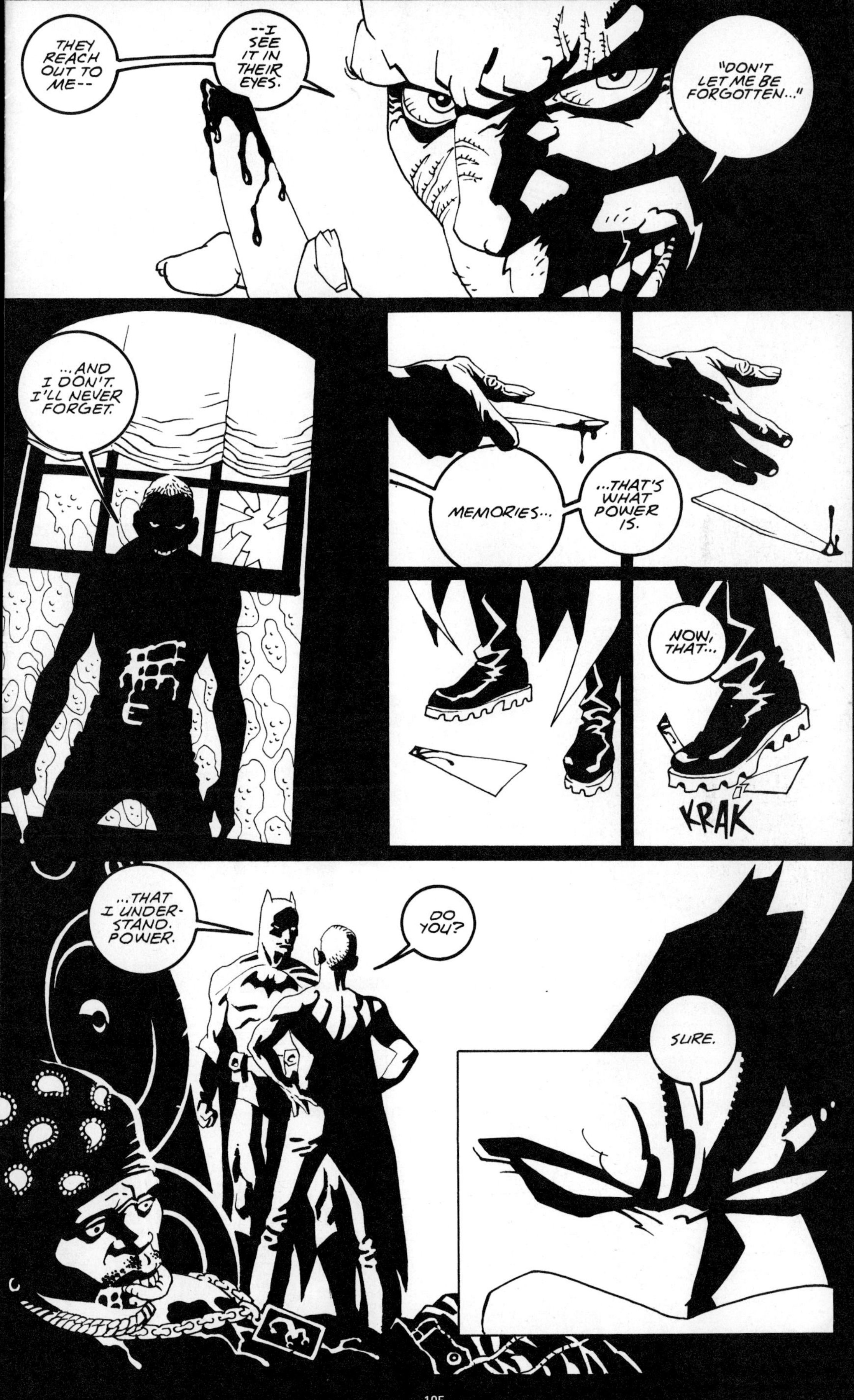
THEY REACH OUT TO ME--
--I SEE IT IN THEIR EYES.
"DON'T LET ME BE FORGOTTEN..."
...AND I DON'T. I'LL NEVER FORGET.
MEMORIES...
...THAT'S WHAT POWER IS.
NOW, THAT...
KRAK
...THAT I UNDER-STAND. POWER.
DO YOU?
SURE.

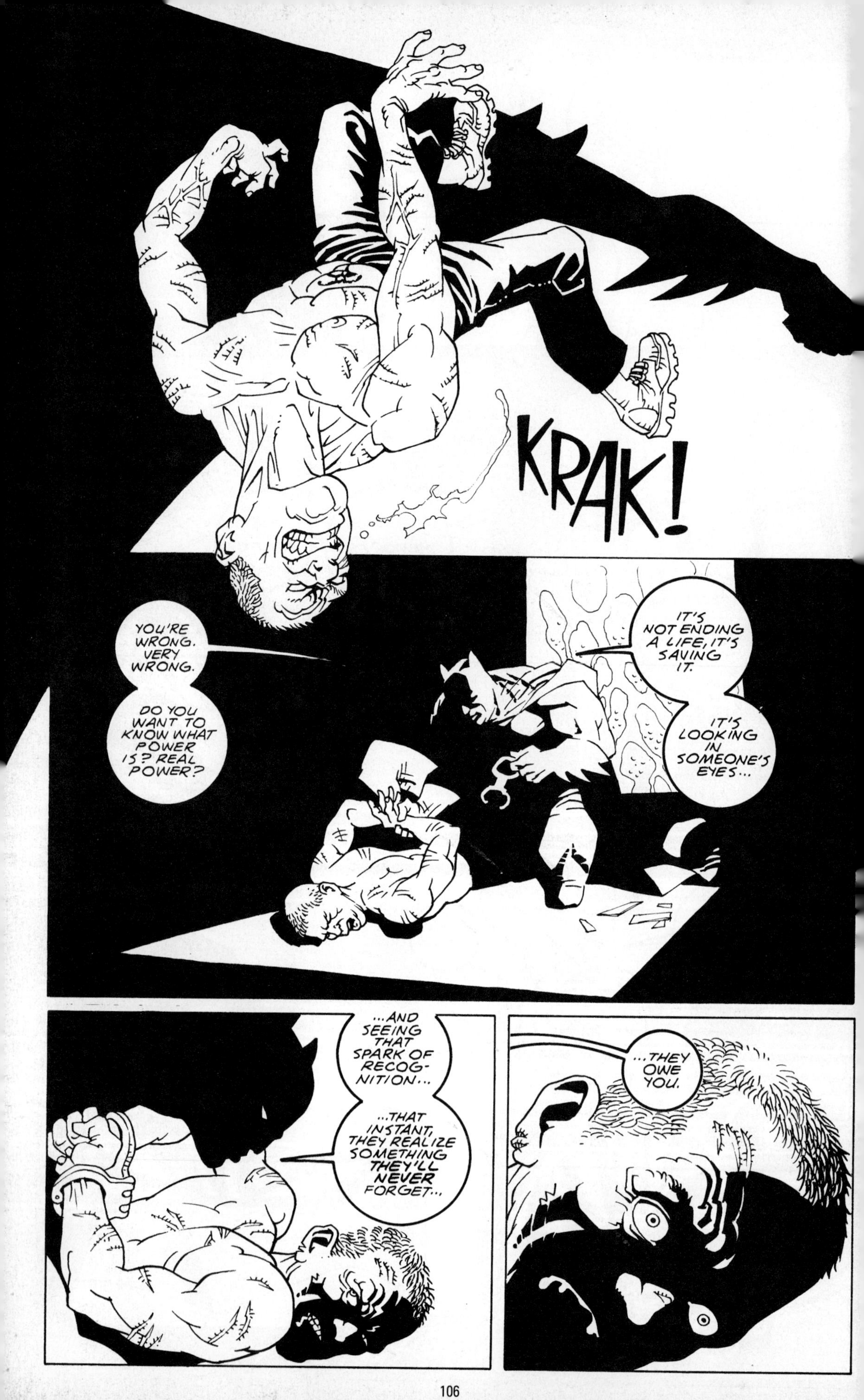
KRAK!
YOU'RE WRONG. VERY WRONG.
DO YOU WANT TO KNOW WHAT POWER IS? REAL POWER?
IT'S NOT ENDING A LIFE, IT'S SAVING IT.
IT'S LOOKING IN SOMEONE'S EYES...
...AND SEEING THAT SPARK OF RECOG-NITION...
...THAT INSTANT, THEY REALIZE SOMETHING THEY'LL NEVER FORGET...
...THEY OWE YOU.

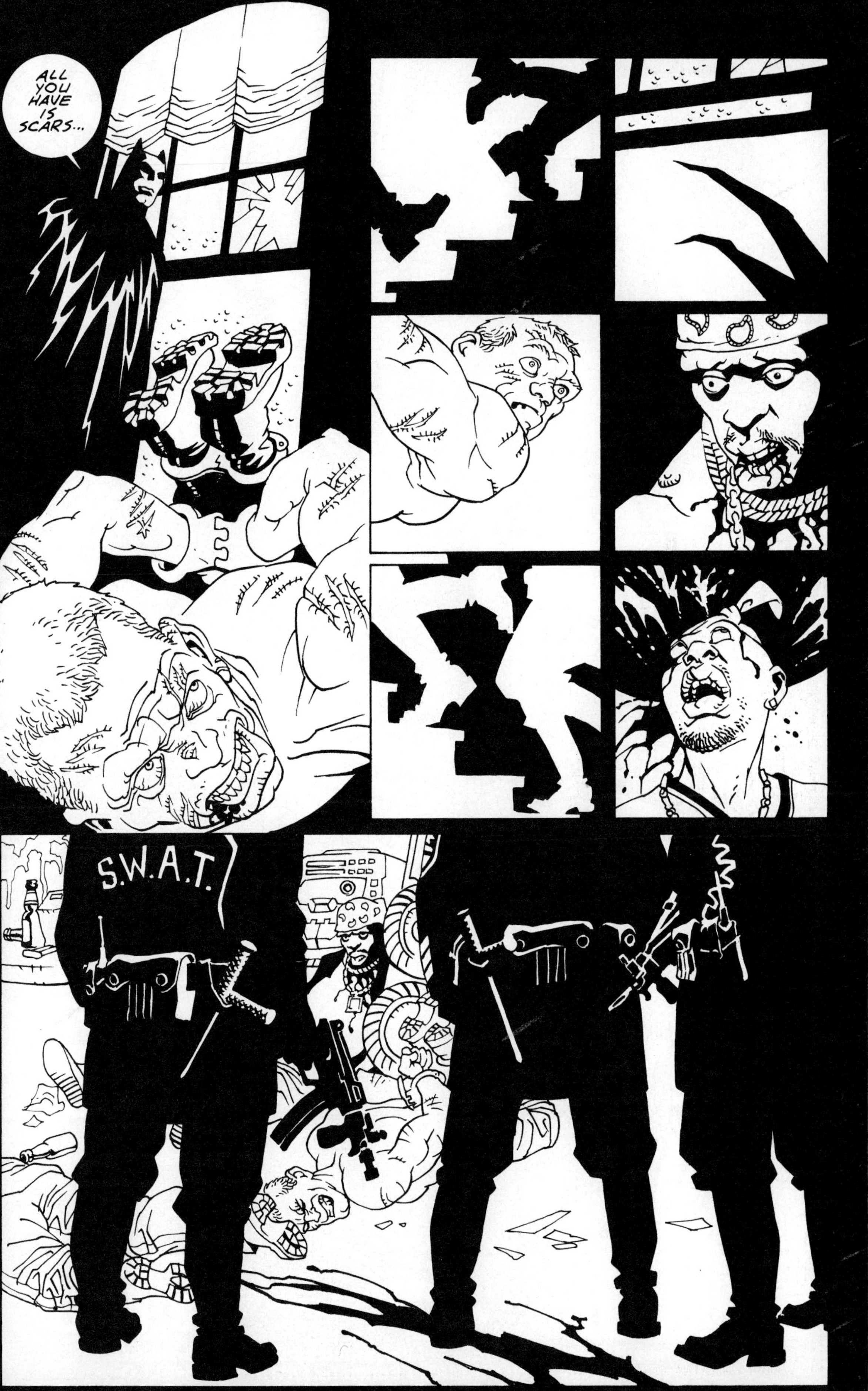
ALL YOU HAVE IS SCARS...
S.W.A.T.

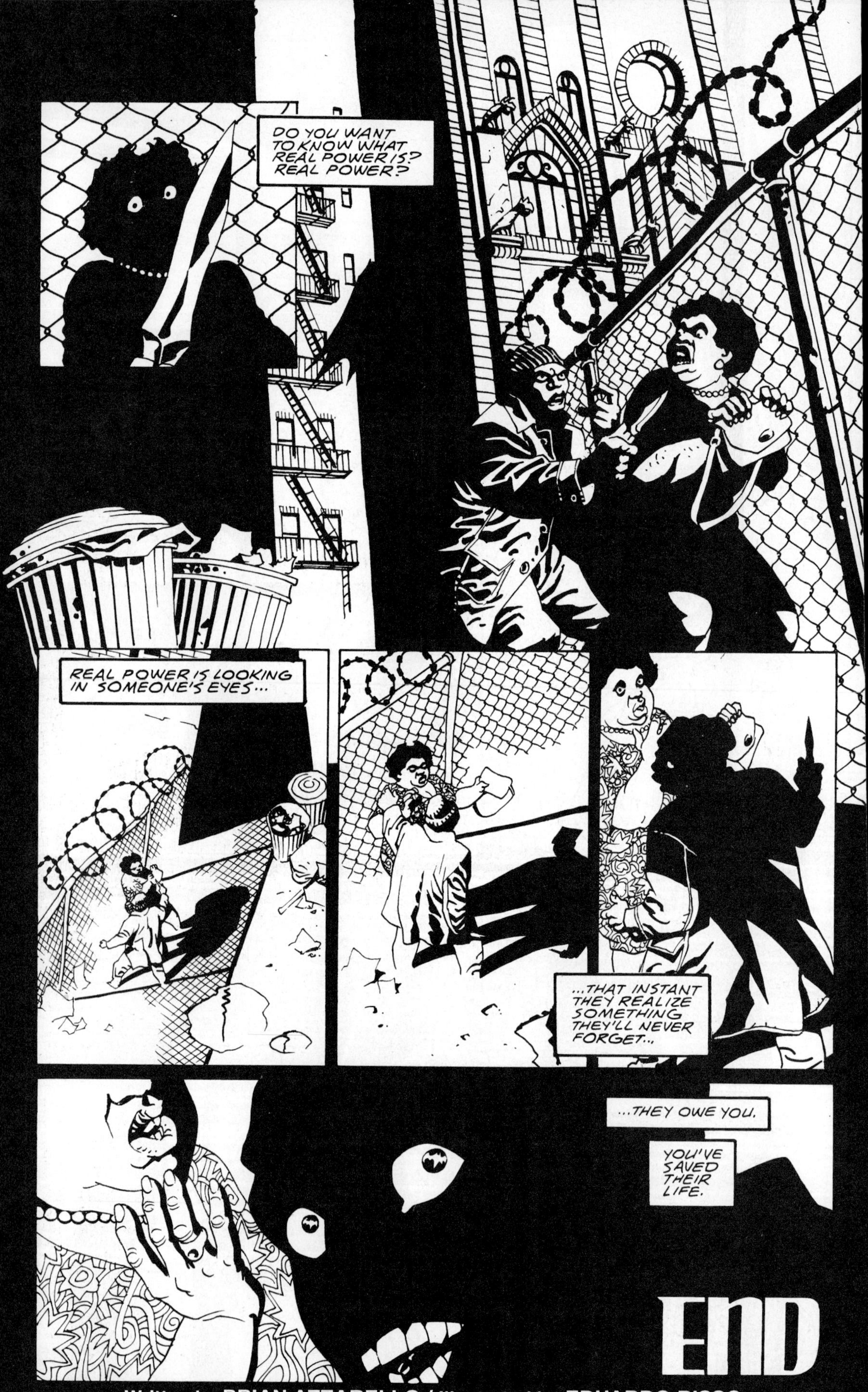
DO YOU WANT TO KNOW WHAT REAL POWER IS? REAL POWER?
REAL POWER IS LOOKING IN SOMEONE'S EYES...
...THAT INSTANT THEY REALIZE SOMETHING THEY'LL NEVER FORGET...
...THEY OWE YOU.
YOU'VE SAVED THEIR LIFE.
END

Written by BRIAN AZZARELLO / Illustrated by EDUARDO RISSO
Lettered by JOHN E. WORKMAN / Edited by MARK CHIARELLO

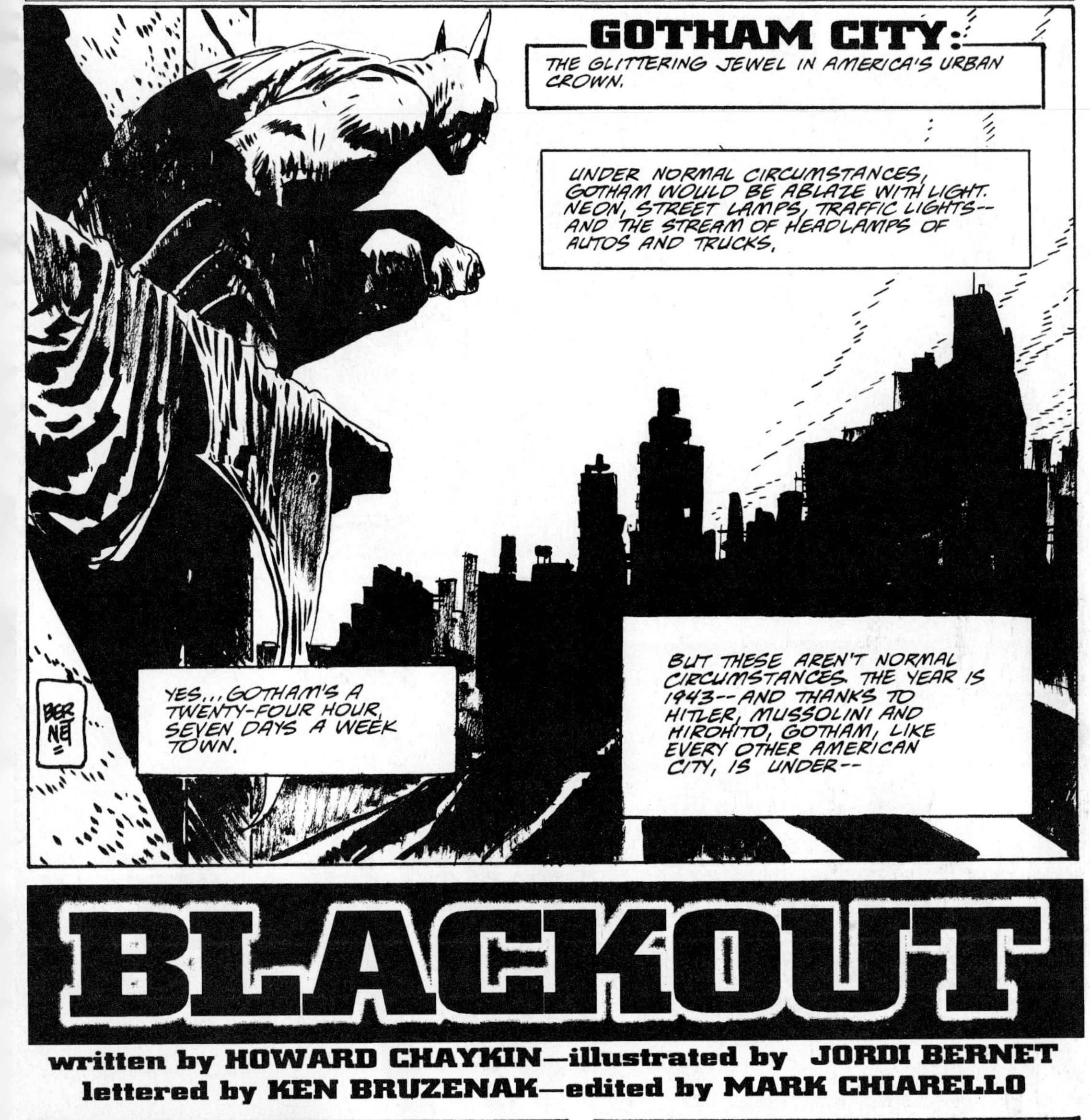
GOTHAM CITY:
THE GLITTERING JEWEL IN AMERICA'S URBAN CROWN.
UNDER NORMAL CIRCUMSTANCES, GOTHAM WOULD BE ABLAZE WITH LIGHT. NEON, STREET LAMPS, TRAFFIC LIGHTS-- AND THE STREAM OF HEADLAMPS OF AUTOS AND TRUCKS.
YES...GOTHAM'S A TWENTY-FOUR HOUR, SEVEN DAYS A WEEK TOWN.
BUT THESE AREN'T NORMAL CIRCUMSTANCES. THE YEAR IS 1943--AND THANKS TO HITLER, MUSSOLINI AND HIROHITO, GOTHAM, LIKE EVERY OTHER AMERICAN CITY, IS UNDER--
BERNET

BLACKOUT

written by HOWARD CHAYKIN—illustrated by JORDI BERNET
lettered by KEN BRUZENAK—edited by MARK CHIARELLO

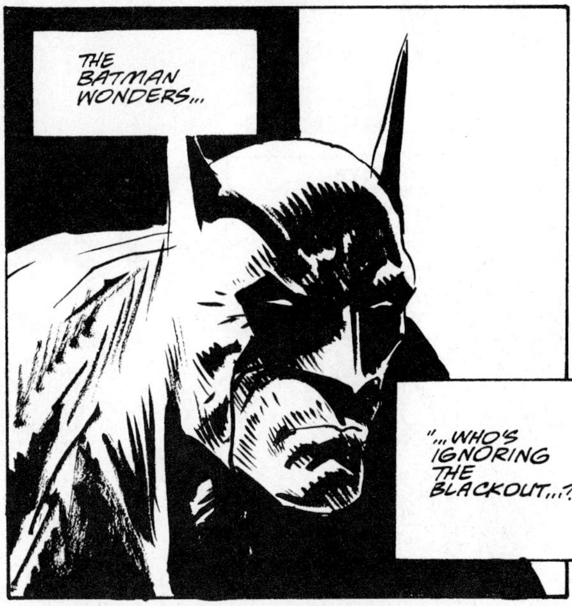
THE BATMAN WONDERS...
"...WHO'S IGNORING THE BLACKOUT...?"

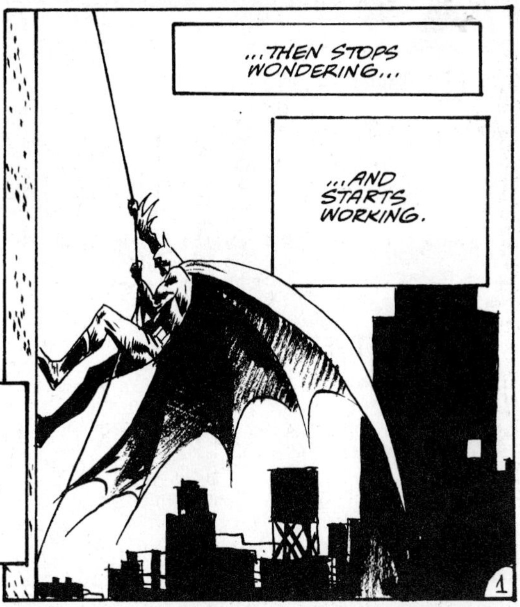
...THEN STOPS WONDERING...
...AND STARTS WORKING.
1

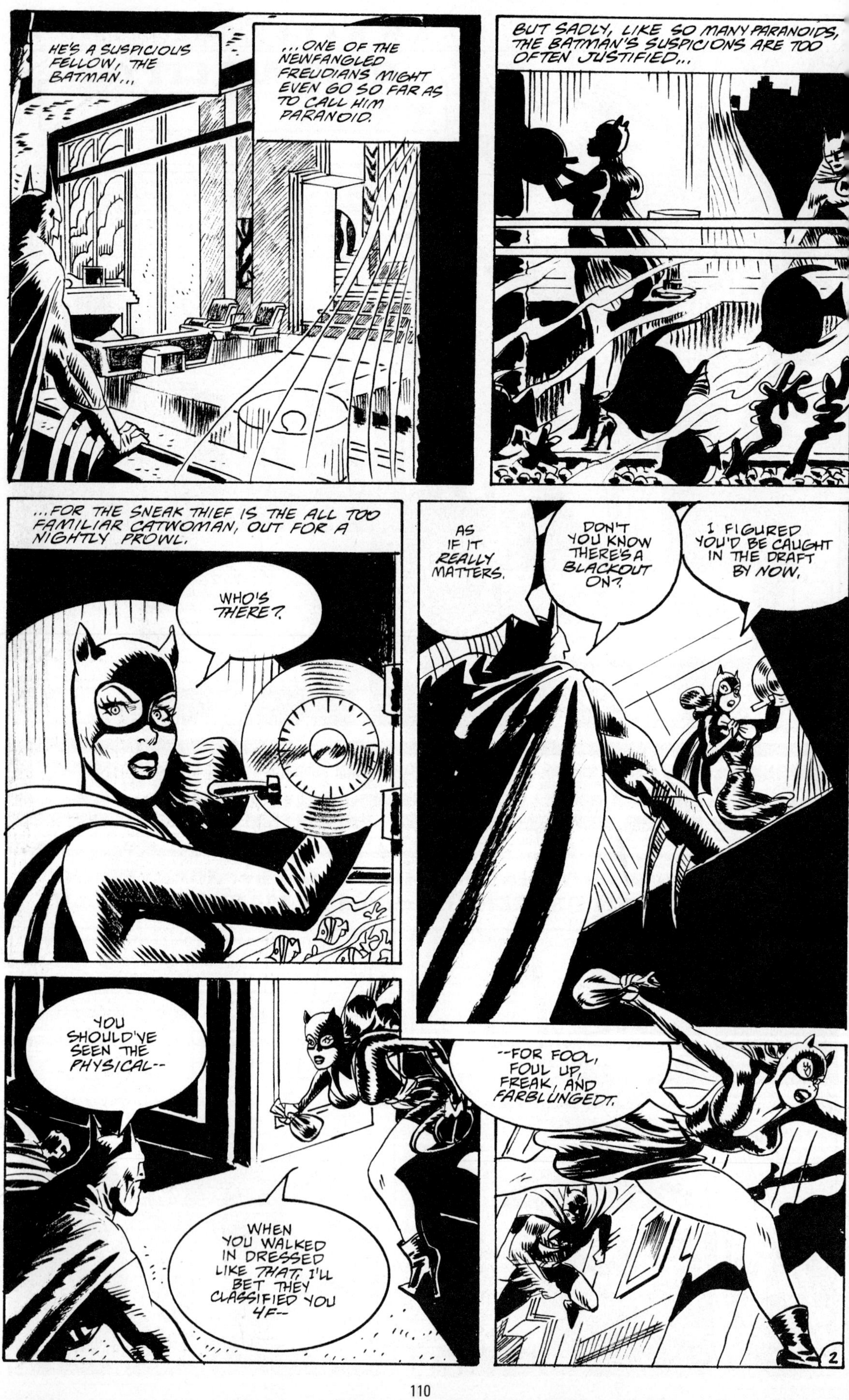

HE'S A SUSPICIOUS FELLOW, THE BATMAN...
...ONE OF THE NEWFANGLED FREUDIANS MIGHT EVEN GO SO FAR AS TO CALL HIM PARANOID.
BUT SADLY, LIKE SO MANY PARANOIDS, THE BATMAN'S SUSPICIONS ARE TOO OFTEN JUSTIFIED...
...FOR THE SNEAK THIEF IS THE ALL TOO FAMILIAR CATWOMAN, OUT FOR A NIGHTLY PROWL.
WHO'S THERE?
AS IF IT REALLY MATTERS.
DON'T YOU KNOW THERE'S A BLACKOUT ON?
I FIGURED YOU'D BE CAUGHT IN THE DRAFT BY NOW.
YOU SHOULD'VE SEEN THE PHYSICAL--
WHEN YOU WALKED IN DRESSED LIKE THAT, I'LL BET THEY CLASSIFIED YOU 4F--
--FOR FOOL, FOUL UP, FREAK, AND FARBLUNGEDT.
2

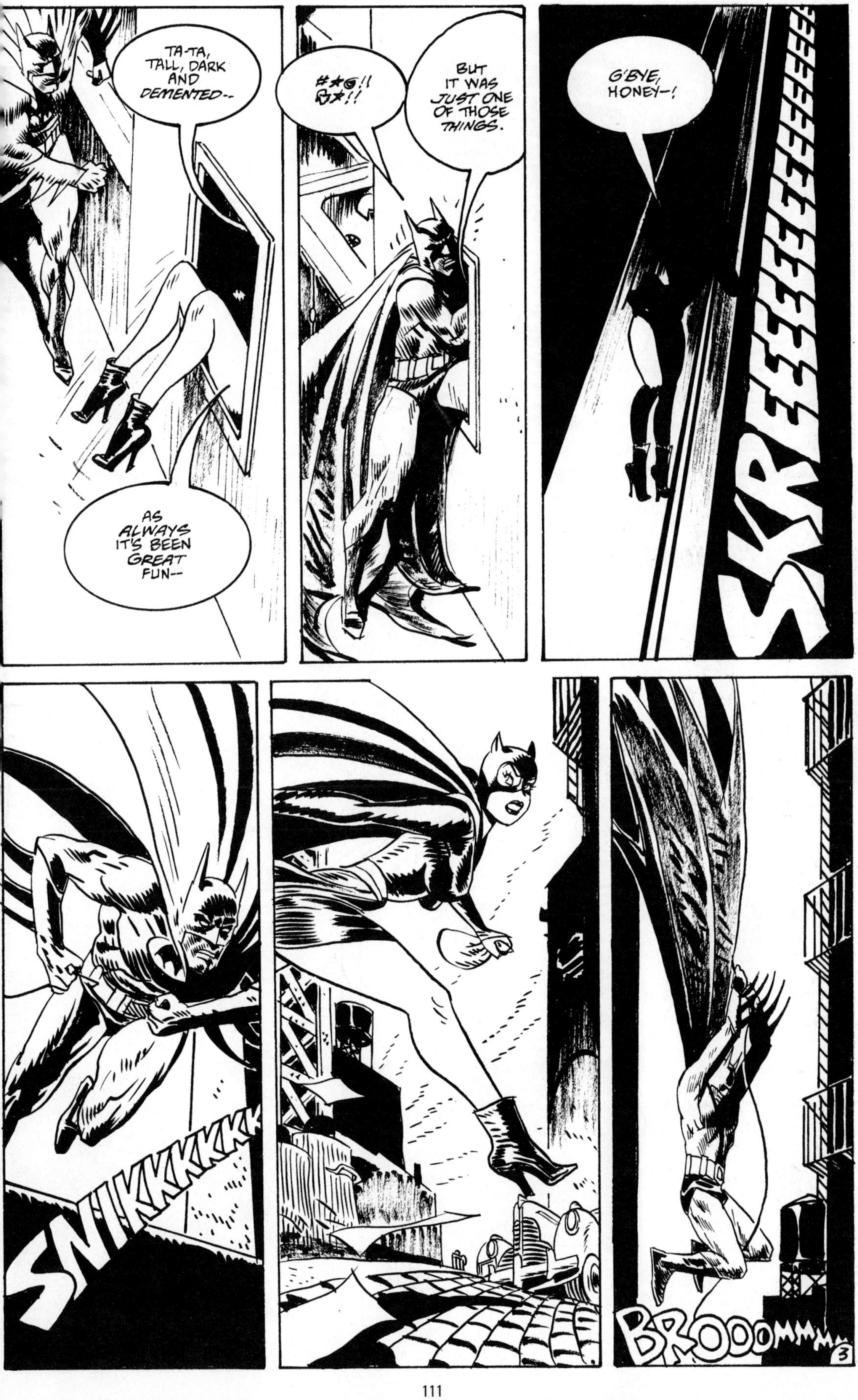

TA-TA, TALL, DARK AND DEMENTED--
AS ALWAYS IT'S BEEN GREAT FUN--
BUT IT WAS JUST ONE OF THOSE THINGS.
G'BYE, HONEY--!
SKREEEEEEEEEEEEEE
SNIKKKKKKK
BROOOMMMM
3

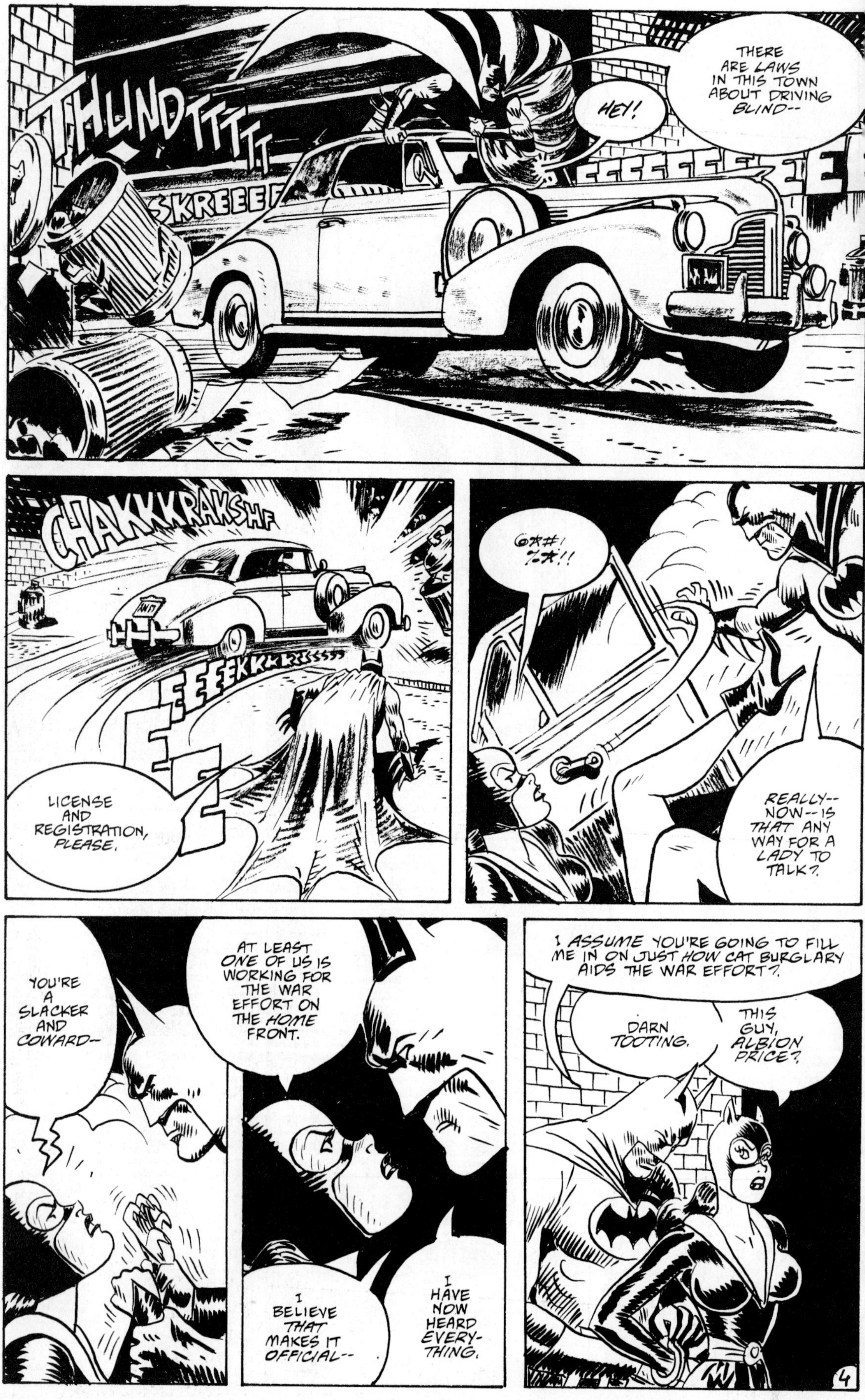
THUNDTTTTT
SKREEEE
EEEEEEE
HEY!
THERE ARE LAWS IN THIS TOWN ABOUT DRIVING BLIND--
CHAKKKRAKSHF
EEEEKK
LICENSE AND REGISTRATION, PLEASE.
REALLY-- NOW-- IS THAT ANY WAY FOR A LADY TO TALK?.
YOU'RE A SLACKER AND COWARD--
AT LEAST ONE OF US IS WORKING FOR THE WAR EFFORT ON THE HOME FRONT.
I BELIEVE THAT MAKES IT OFFICIAL--
I HAVE NOW HEARD EVERYTHING.
I ASSUME YOU'RE GOING TO FILL ME IN ON JUST HOW CAT BURGLARY AIDS THE WAR EFFORT?.
DARN TOOTING.
THIS GUY, ALBION PRICE?
4

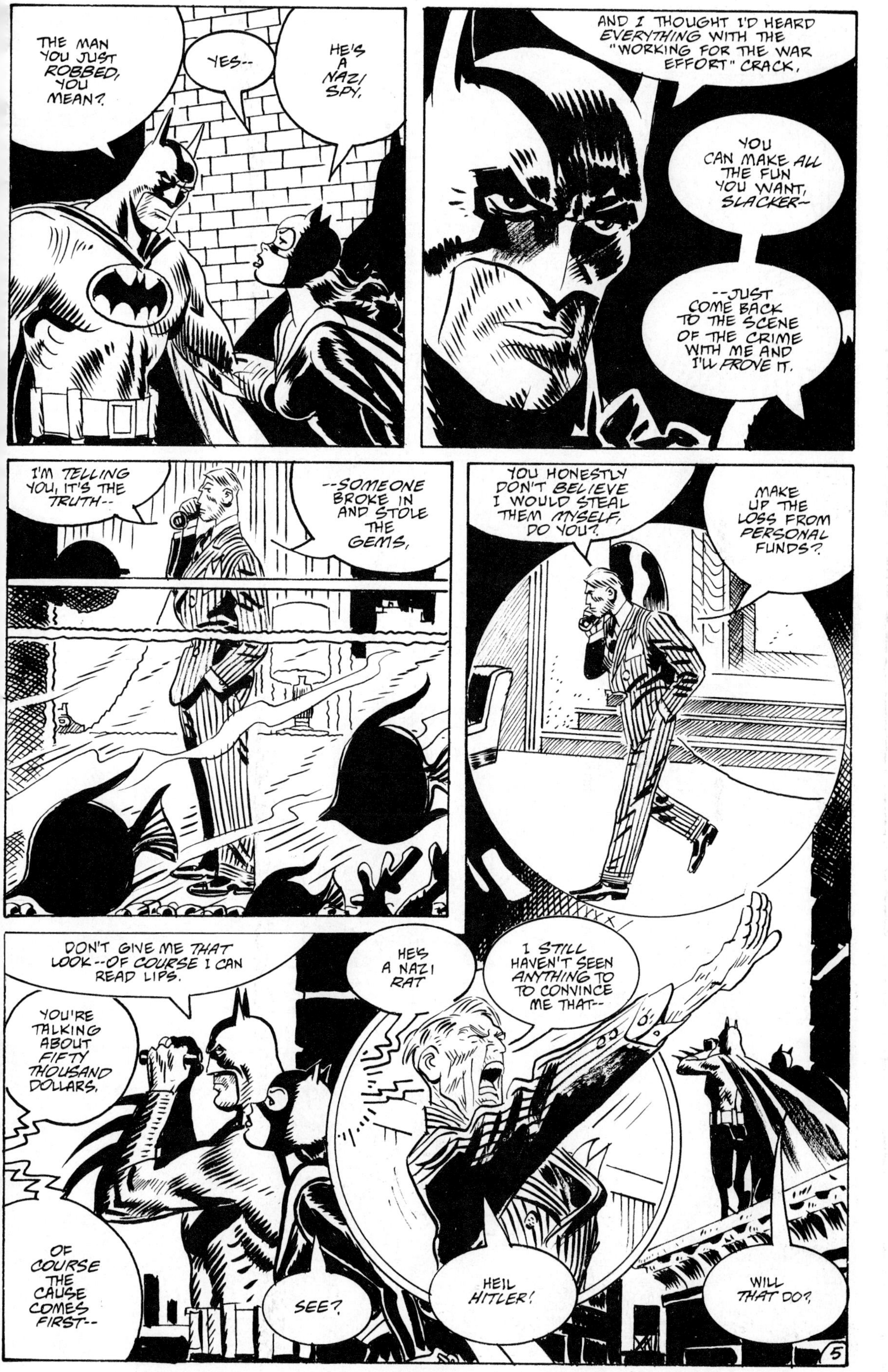
THE MAN YOU JUST ROBBED, YOU MEAN?
YES--
HE'S A NAZI SPY.
AND I THOUGHT I'D HEARD EVERYTHING WITH THE "WORKING FOR THE WAR EFFORT" CRACK.
YOU CAN MAKE ALL THE FUN YOU WANT, SLACKER--
--JUST COME BACK TO THE SCENE OF THE CRIME WITH ME AND I'LL PROVE IT.
I'M TELLING YOU, IT'S THE TRUTH--
--SOMEONE BROKE IN AND STOLE THE GEMS.
YOU HONESTLY DON'T BELIEVE I WOULD STEAL THEM MYSELF, DO YOU?
MAKE UP THE LOSS FROM PERSONAL FUNDS?
DON'T GIVE ME THAT LOOK--OF COURSE I CAN READ LIPS.
YOU'RE TALKING ABOUT FIFTY THOUSAND DOLLARS.
HE'S A NAZI RAT
I STILL HAVEN'T SEEN ANYTHING TO TO CONVINCE ME THAT--
OF COURSE THE CAUSE COMES FIRST--
SEE?
HEIL HITLER!
WILL THAT DO?
5

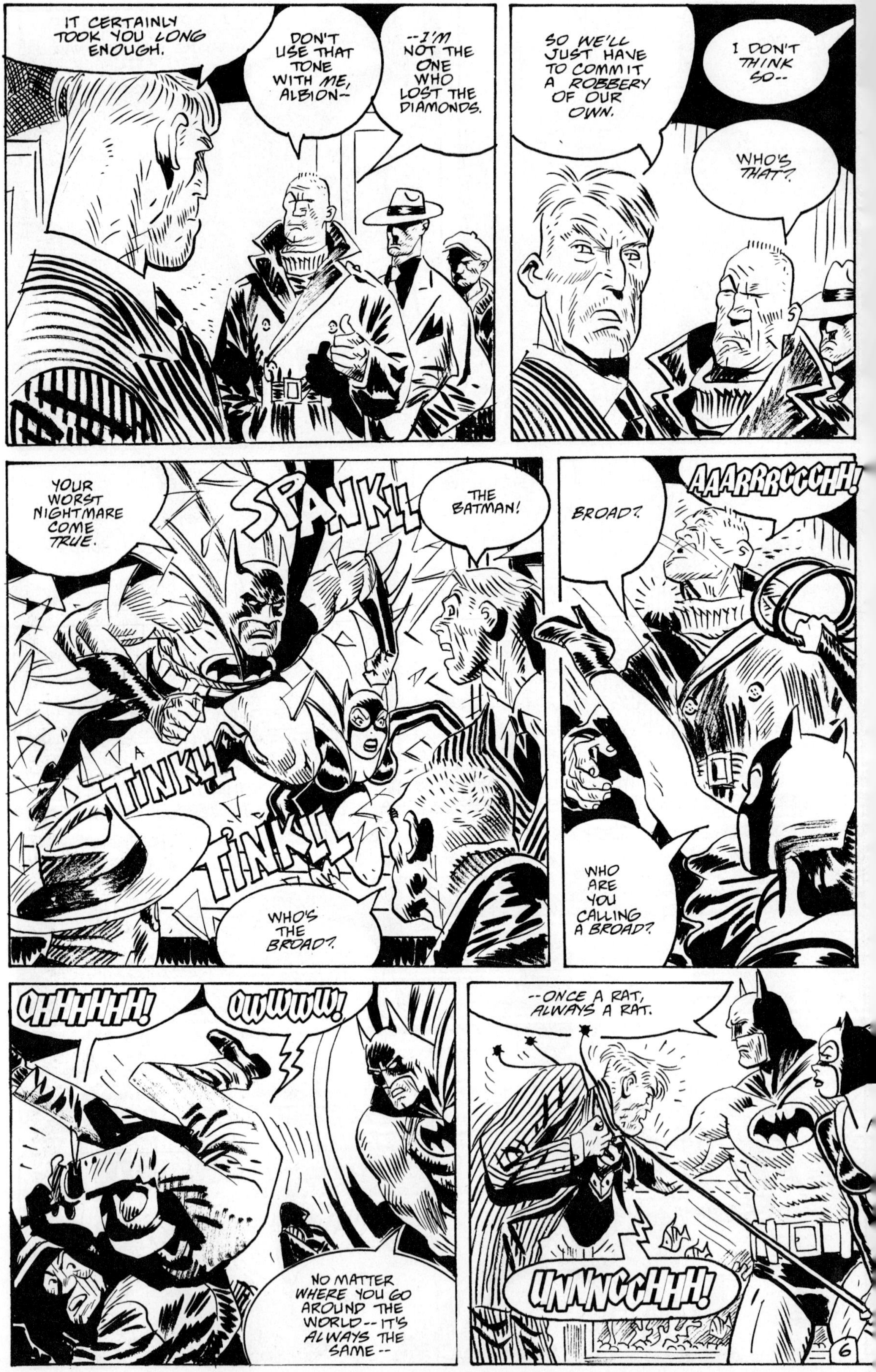
IT CERTAINLY TOOK YOU LONG ENOUGH.
DON'T USE THAT TONE WITH ME, ALBION--
--I'M NOT THE ONE WHO LOST THE DIAMONDS.
SO WE'LL JUST HAVE TO COMMIT A ROBBERY OF OUR OWN.
I DON'T THINK SO--
WHO'S THAT?
YOUR WORST NIGHTMARE COME TRUE.
SPANK!!
THE BATMAN!
TINK!!
TINK!!
WHO'S THE BROAD?
BROAD?
AAARRRGGGHH!
WHO ARE YOU CALLING A BROAD?
OHHHHHH!
OWWWW!
NO MATTER WHERE YOU GO AROUND THE WORLD-- IT'S ALWAYS THE SAME--
--ONCE A RAT, ALWAYS A RAT.
UNNNGCHHH!
6

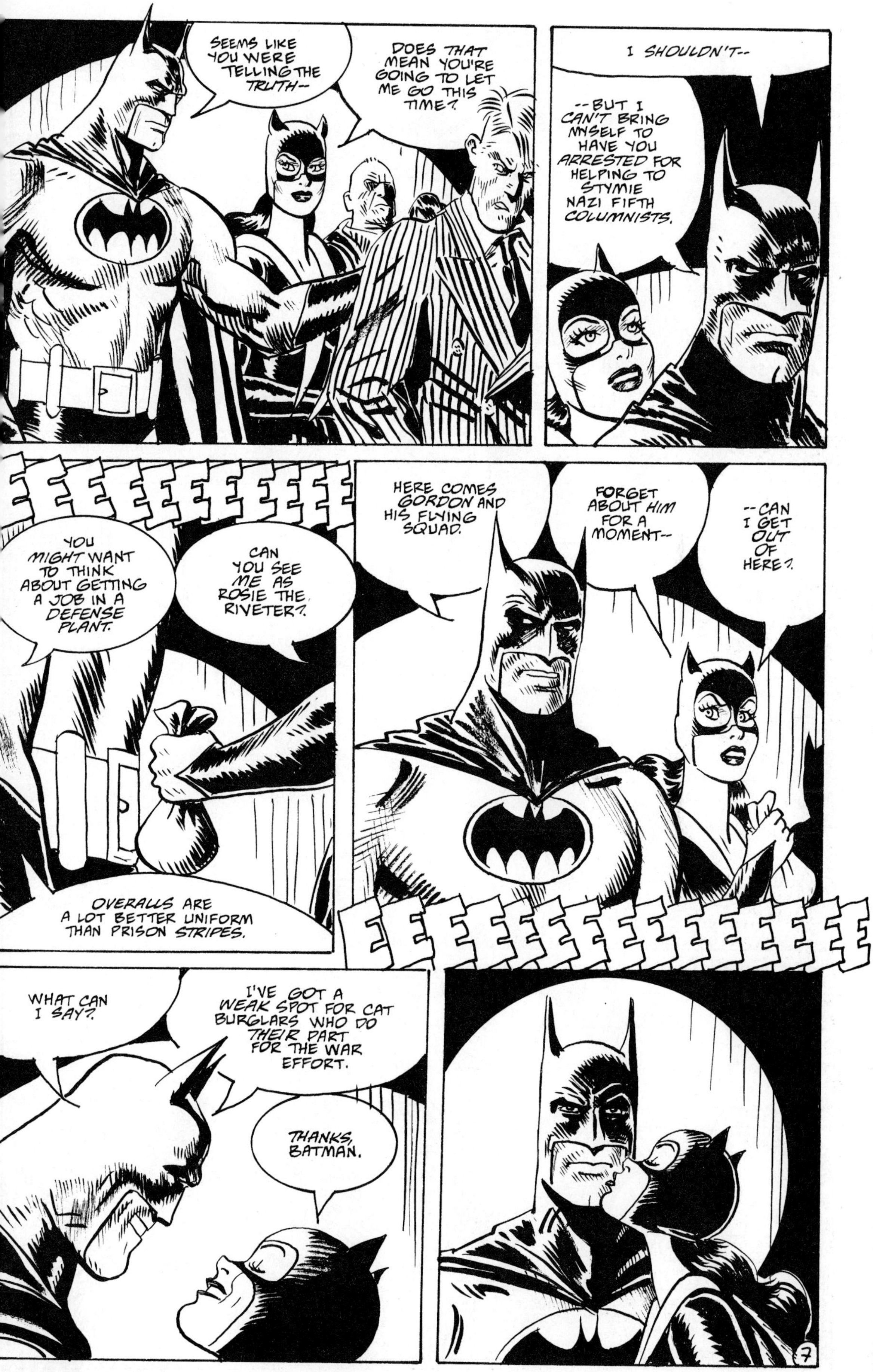

SEEMS LIKE YOU WERE TELLING THE TRUTH--
DOES THAT MEAN YOU'RE GOING TO LET ME GO THIS TIME?
I SHOULDN'T--
--BUT I CAN'T BRING MYSELF TO HAVE YOU ARRESTED FOR HELPING TO STYMIE NAZI FIFTH COLUMNISTS.
EEEEEEEEEEEE
YOU MIGHT WANT TO THINK ABOUT GETTING A JOB IN A DEFENSE PLANT.
CAN YOU SEE ME AS ROSIE THE RIVETER?
OVERALLS ARE A LOT BETTER UNIFORM THAN PRISON STRIPES.
HERE COMES GORDON AND HIS FLYING SQUAD.
FORGET ABOUT HIM FOR A MOMENT--
--CAN I GET OUT OF HERE?
EEEEEEEEEEEEEEEE
WHAT CAN I SAY?
I'VE GOT A WEAK SPOT FOR CAT BURGLARS WHO DO THEIR PART FOR THE WAR EFFORT.
THANKS, BATMAN.
7

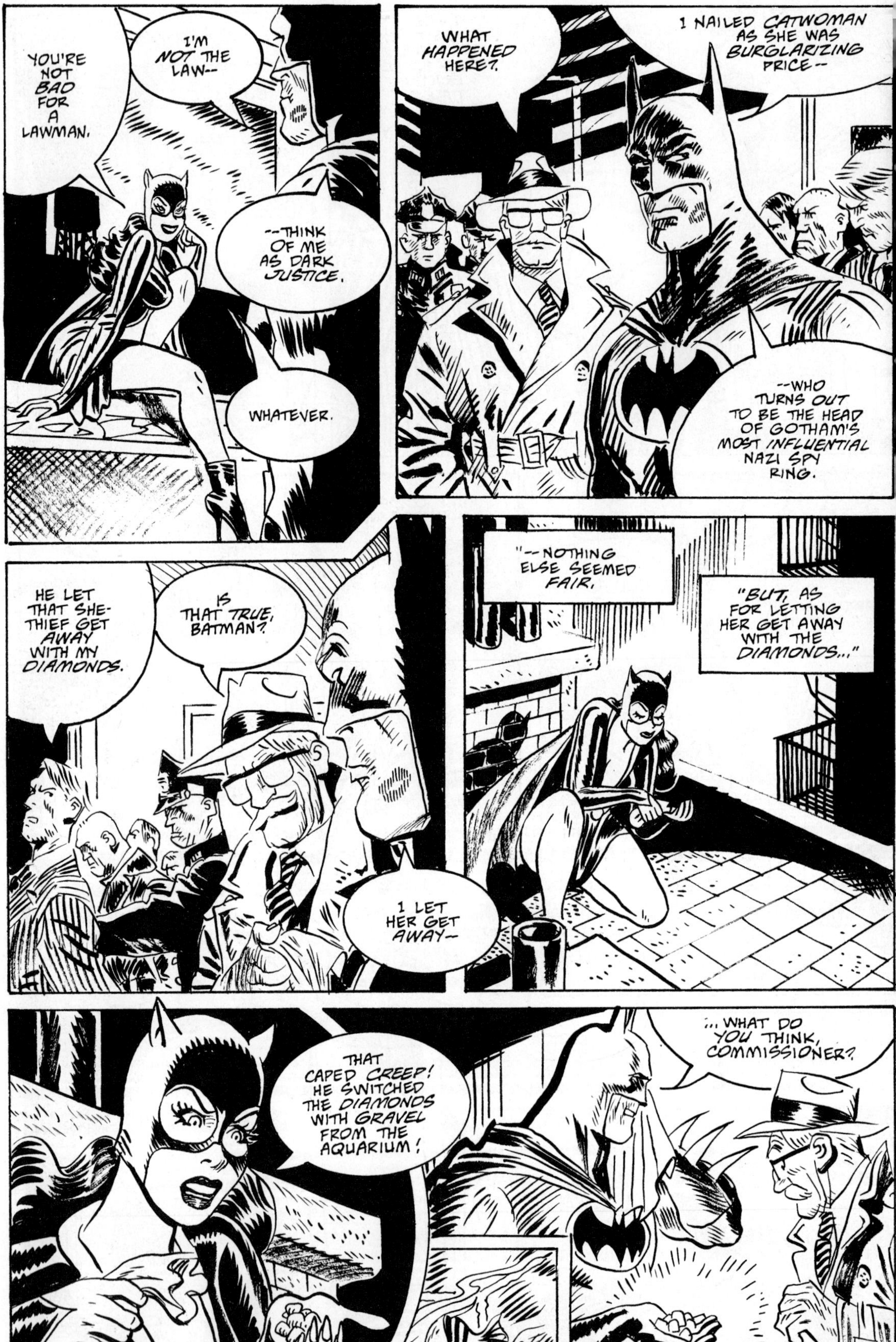
YOU'RE NOT BAD FOR A LAWMAN.
I'M NOT THE LAW--
--THINK OF ME AS DARK JUSTICE.
WHATEVER.
WHAT HAPPENED HERE?
I NAILED CATWOMAN AS SHE WAS BURGLARIZING PRICE--
--WHO TURNS OUT TO BE THE HEAD OF GOTHAM'S MOST INFLUENTIAL NAZI SPY RING.
HE LET THAT SHE-THIEF GET AWAY WITH MY DIAMONDS.
IS THAT TRUE, BATMAN?
I LET HER GET AWAY--
"--NOTHING ELSE SEEMED FAIR.
"BUT, AS FOR LETTING HER GET AWAY WITH THE DIAMONDS..."
THAT CAPED CREEP! HE SWITCHED THE DIAMONDS WITH GRAVEL FROM THE AQUARIUM!
...WHAT DO YOU THINK, COMMISSIONER?
"...THERE ARE DAYS WHEN I THINK I WOULD'VE MADE A PRETTY GOOD THIEF MYSELF..."
8

THE END

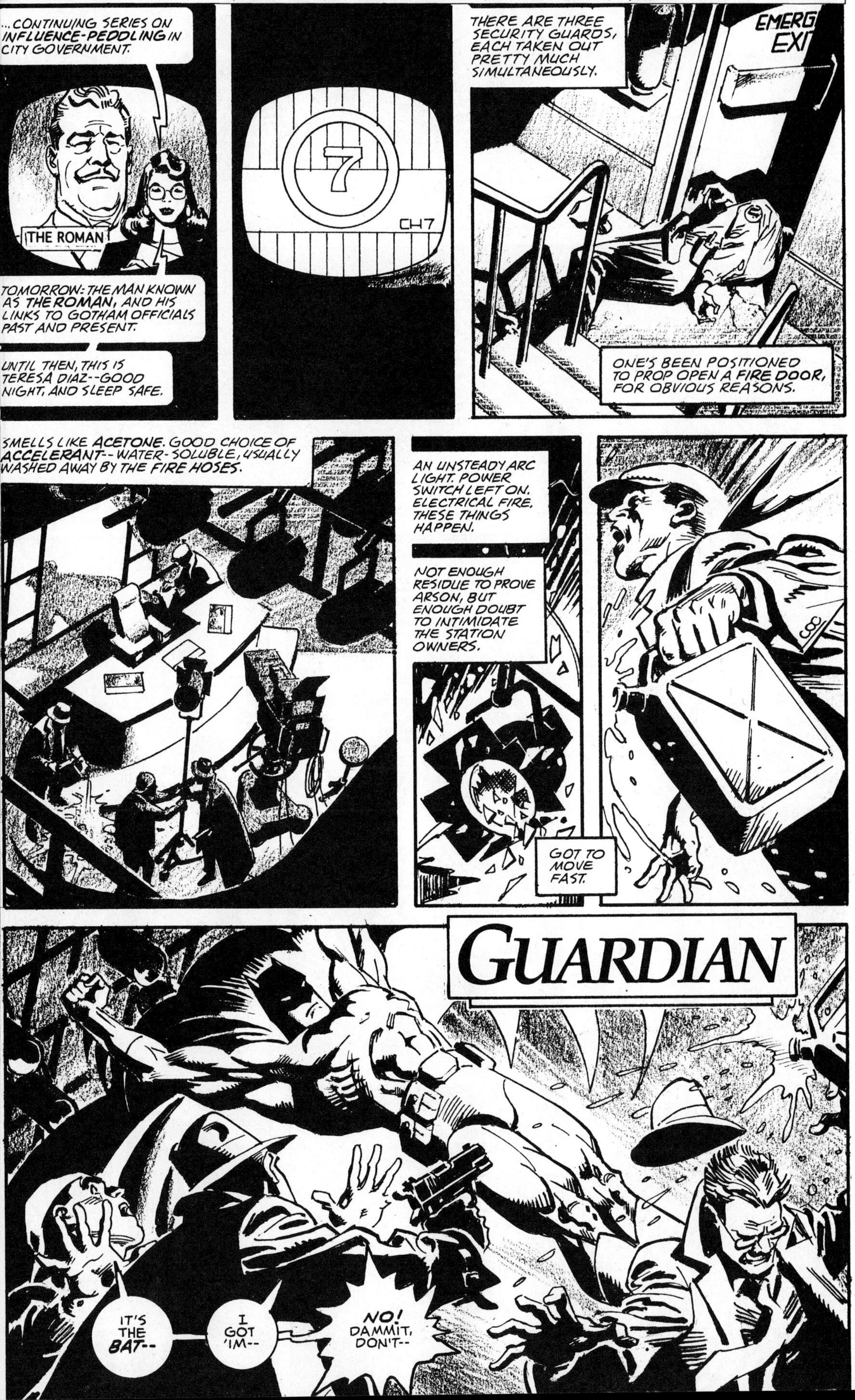
...CONTINUING SERIES ON INFLUENCE-PEDDLING IN CITY GOVERNMENT.
THE ROMAN
TOMORROW: THE MAN KNOWN AS THE ROMAN, AND HIS LINKS TO GOTHAM OFFICIALS PAST AND PRESENT.
UNTIL THEN, THIS IS TERESA DIAZ--GOOD NIGHT, AND SLEEP SAFE.
7
CH7
THERE ARE THREE SECURITY GUARDS, EACH TAKEN OUT PRETTY MUCH SIMULTANEOUSLY.
EMERG
EXI
ONE'S BEEN POSITIONED TO PROP OPEN A FIRE DOOR, FOR OBVIOUS REASONS.
SMELLS LIKE ACETONE. GOOD CHOICE OF ACCELERANT--WATER-SOLUBLE, USUALLY WASHED AWAY BY THE FIRE HOSES.
AN UNSTEADY ARC LIGHT. POWER SWITCH LEFT ON. ELECTRICAL FIRE. THESE THINGS HAPPEN.
NOT ENOUGH RESIDUE TO PROVE ARSON, BUT ENOUGH DOUBT TO INTIMIDATE THE STATION OWNERS.
GOT TO MOVE FAST.
GUARDIAN
IT'S THE BAT--
I GOT 'IM--
NO! DAMMIT, DON'T--

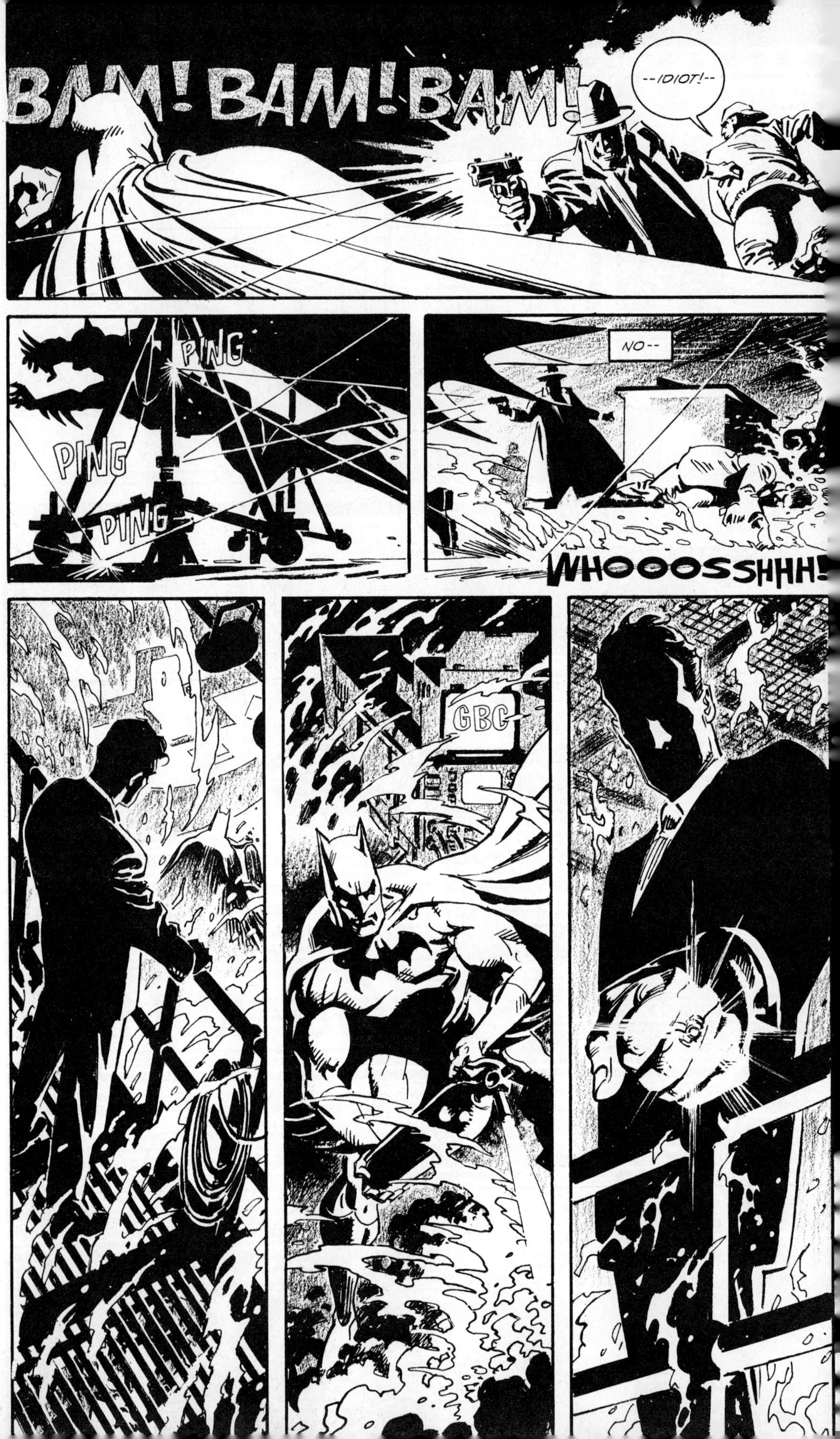
BAM! BAM! BAM!
--IDIOT!--
PING
PING
PING
NO--
WHOOOSSHHH!
GBC

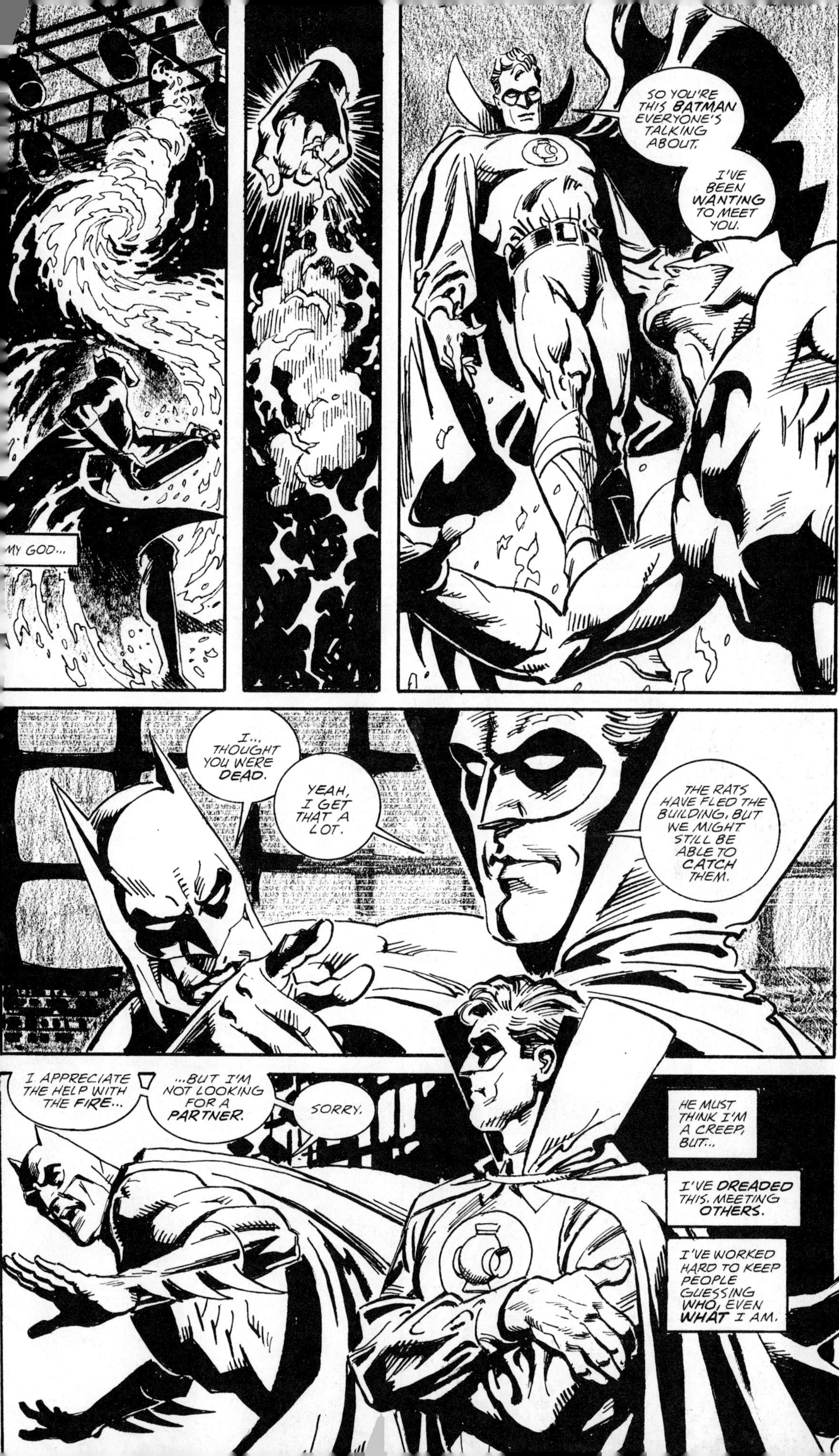
MY GOD...
SO YOU'RE THIS BATMAN EVERYONE'S TALKING ABOUT.
I'VE BEEN WANTING TO MEET YOU.
I... THOUGHT YOU WERE DEAD.
YEAH, I GET THAT A LOT.
THE RATS HAVE FLED THE BUILDING, BUT WE MIGHT STILL BE ABLE TO CATCH THEM.
I APPRECIATE THE HELP WITH THE FIRE...
...BUT I'M NOT LOOKING FOR A PARTNER.
SORRY.
HE MUST THINK I'M A CREEP, BUT...
I'VE DREADED THIS. MEETING OTHERS.
I'VE WORKED HARD TO KEEP PEOPLE GUESSING WHO, EVEN WHAT I AM.

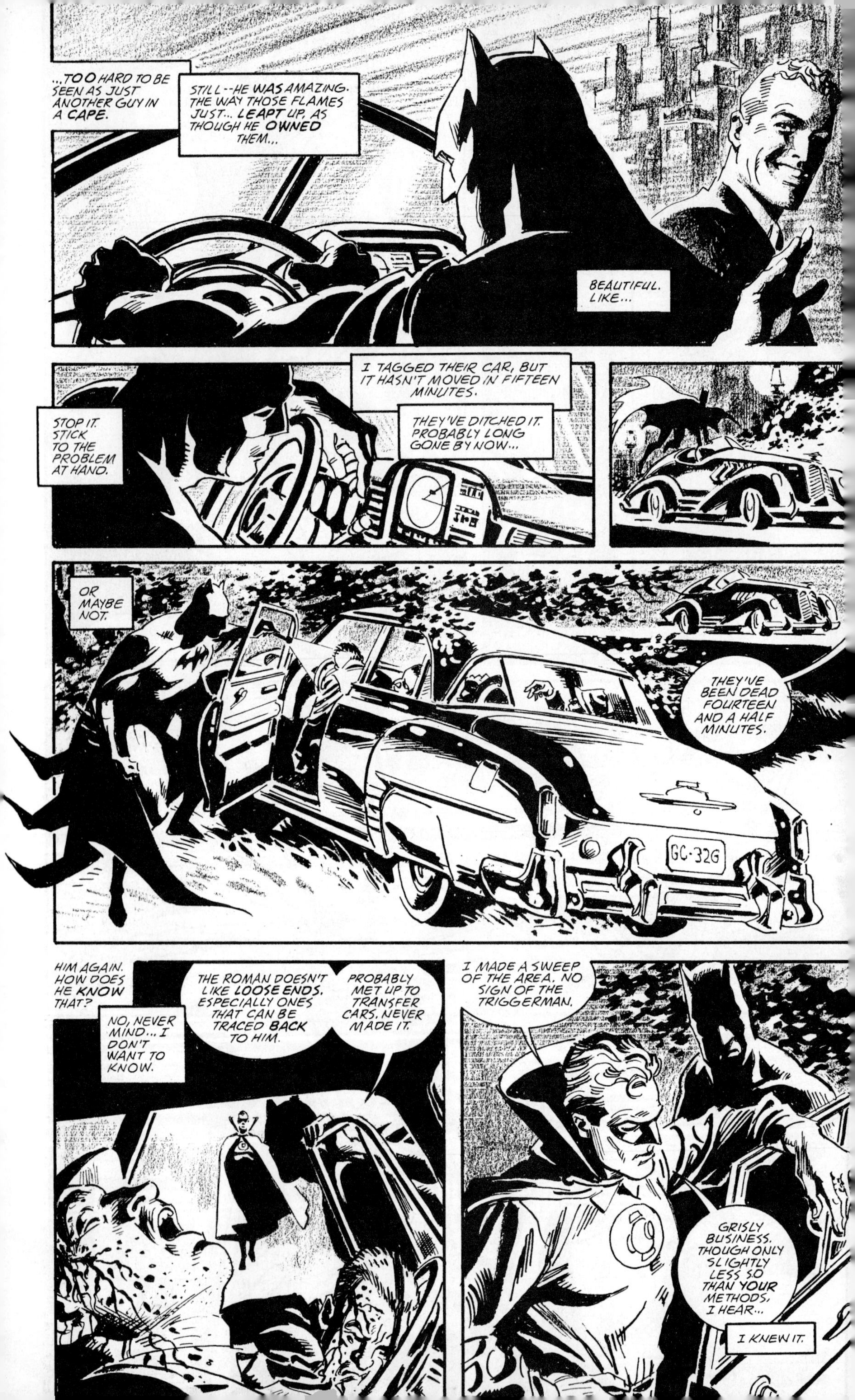

...TOO HARD TO BE SEEN AS JUST ANOTHER GUY IN A CAPE.
STILL--HE WAS AMAZING. THE WAY THOSE FLAMES JUST... LEAPT UP, AS THOUGH HE OWNED THEM...
BEAUTIFUL. LIKE...
STOP IT. STICK TO THE PROBLEM AT HAND.
I TAGGED THEIR CAR, BUT IT HASN'T MOVED IN FIFTEEN MINUTES.
THEY'VE DITCHED IT. PROBABLY LONG GONE BY NOW...
OR MAYBE NOT.
THEY'VE BEEN DEAD FOURTEEN AND A HALF MINUTES.
GC-32G
HIM AGAIN. HOW DOES HE KNOW THAT?
NO, NEVER MIND... I DON'T WANT TO KNOW.
THE ROMAN DOESN'T LIKE LOOSE ENDS. ESPECIALLY ONES THAT CAN BE TRACED BACK TO HIM.
PROBABLY MET UP TO TRANSFER CARS. NEVER MADE IT.
I MADE A SWEEP OF THE AREA. NO SIGN OF THE TRIGGERMAN.
GRISLY BUSINESS. THOUGH ONLY SLIGHTLY LESS SO THAN YOUR METHODS, I HEAR...
I KNEW IT.

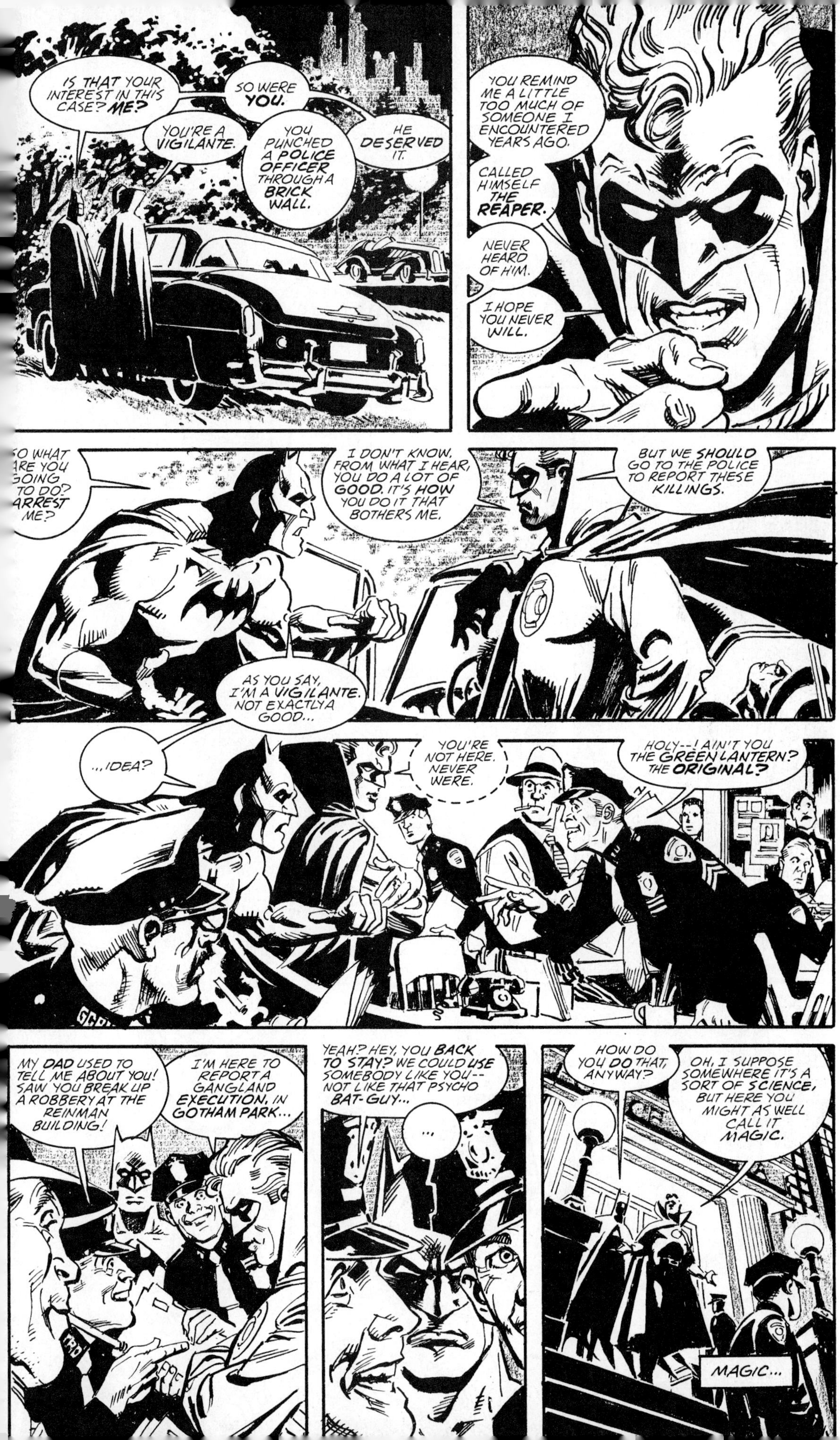
IS THAT YOUR INTEREST IN THIS CASE? ME?
SO WERE YOU.
YOU'RE A VIGILANTE.
YOU PUNCHED A POLICE OFFICER THROUGH A BRICK WALL.
HE DESERVED IT.
YOU REMIND ME A LITTLE TOO MUCH OF SOMEONE I ENCOUNTERED YEARS AGO.
CALLED HIMSELF THE REAPER.
NEVER HEARD OF HIM.
I HOPE YOU NEVER WILL.
SO WHAT ARE YOU GOING TO DO? ARREST ME?
I DON'T KNOW. FROM WHAT I HEAR, YOU DO A LOT OF GOOD. IT'S HOW YOU DO IT THAT BOTHERS ME.
BUT WE SHOULD GO TO THE POLICE TO REPORT THESE KILLINGS.
AS YOU SAY, I'M A VIGILANTE. NOT EXACTLY A GOOD...
...IDEA?
YOU'RE NOT HERE. NEVER WERE.
HOLY--! AIN'T YOU THE GREEN LANTERN? THE ORIGINAL?
MY DAD USED TO TELL ME ABOUT YOU! SAW YOU BREAK UP A ROBBERY AT THE REINMAN BUILDING!
I'M HERE TO REPORT A GANGLAND EXECUTION, IN GOTHAM PARK...
YEAH? HEY, YOU BACK TO STAY? WE COULD USE SOMEBODY LIKE YOU-- NOT LIKE THAT PSYCHO BAT-GUY...
...
HOW DO YOU DO THAT, ANYWAY?
OH, I SUPPOSE SOMEWHERE IT'S A SORT OF SCIENCE, BUT HERE YOU MIGHT AS WELL CALL IT MAGIC.
MAGIC...

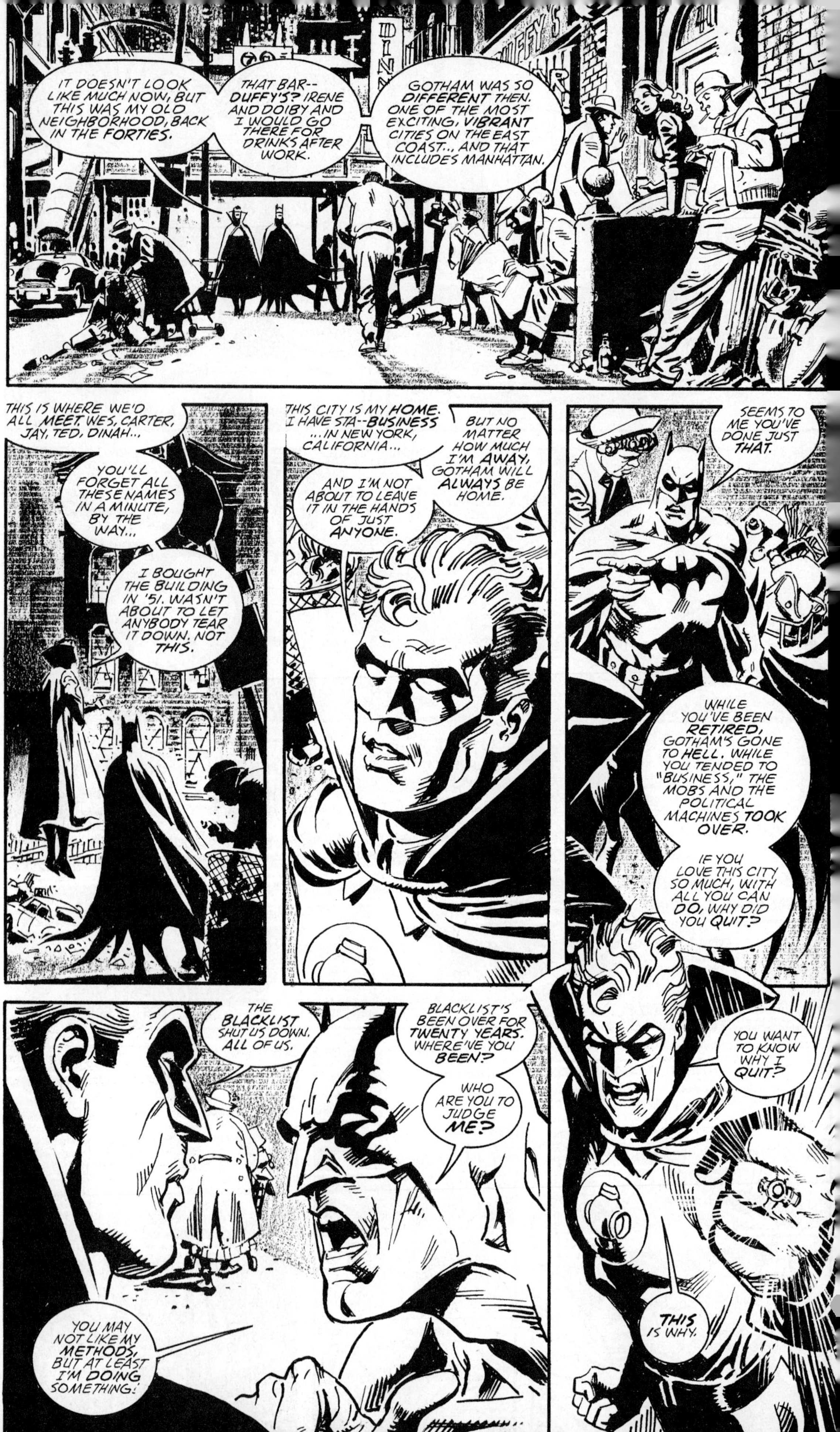
IT DOESN'T LOOK LIKE MUCH NOW, BUT THIS WAS MY OLD NEIGHBORHOOD, BACK IN THE FORTIES.
THAT BAR-- DUFFY'S? IRENE AND DOIBY AND I WOULD GO THERE FOR DRINKS AFTER WORK.
GOTHAM WAS SO DIFFERENT THEN. ONE OF THE MOST EXCITING, VIBRANT CITIES ON THE EAST COAST... AND THAT INCLUDES MANHATTAN.
THIS IS WHERE WE'D ALL MEET. WES, CARTER, JAY, TED, DINAH...
YOU'LL FORGET ALL THESE NAMES IN A MINUTE, BY THE WAY...
I BOUGHT THE BUILDING IN '51. WASN'T ABOUT TO LET ANYBODY TEAR IT DOWN. NOT THIS.
THIS CITY IS MY HOME. I HAVE STA--BUSINESS ...IN NEW YORK, CALIFORNIA...
BUT NO MATTER HOW MUCH I'M AWAY, GOTHAM WILL ALWAYS BE HOME.
AND I'M NOT ABOUT TO LEAVE IT IN THE HANDS OF JUST ANYONE.
SEEMS TO ME YOU'VE DONE JUST THAT.
WHILE YOU'VE BEEN RETIRED, GOTHAM'S GONE TO HELL. WHILE YOU TENDED TO "BUSINESS," THE MOBS AND THE POLITICAL MACHINES TOOK OVER.
IF YOU LOVE THIS CITY SO MUCH, WITH ALL YOU CAN DO, WHY DID YOU QUIT?
THE BLACKLIST SHUT US DOWN. ALL OF US.
BLACKLIST'S BEEN OVER FOR TWENTY YEARS. WHERE'VE YOU BEEN?
WHO ARE YOU TO JUDGE ME?
YOU MAY NOT LIKE MY METHODS, BUT AT LEAST I'M DOING SOMETHING!
YOU WANT TO KNOW WHY I QUIT?
THIS IS WHY.

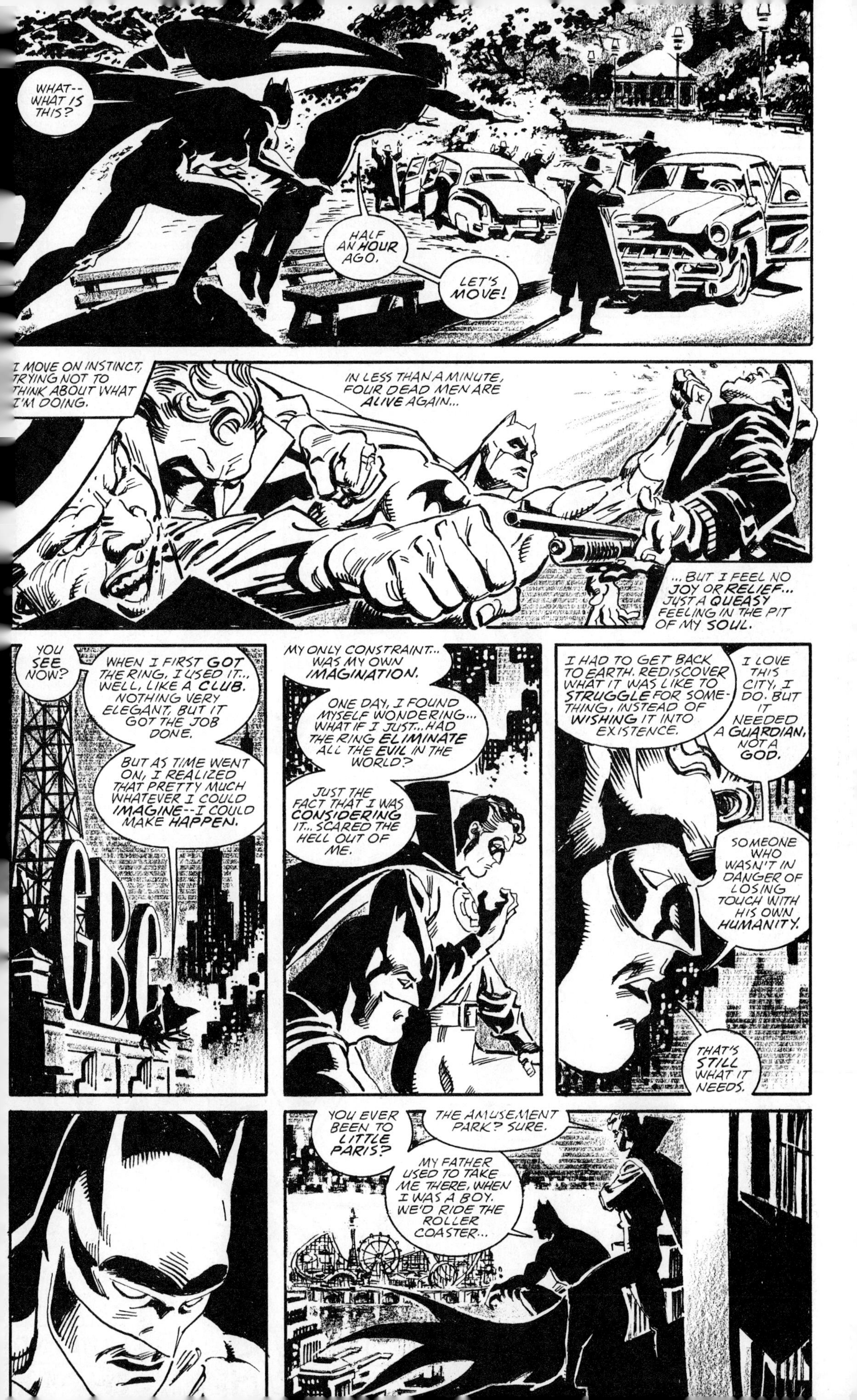

WHAT-- WHAT IS THIS?
HALF AN HOUR AGO.
LET'S MOVE!
I MOVE ON INSTINCT, TRYING NOT TO THINK ABOUT WHAT I'M DOING.
IN LESS THAN A MINUTE, FOUR DEAD MEN ARE ALIVE AGAIN...
...BUT I FEEL NO JOY OR RELIEF... JUST A QUEASY FEELING IN THE PIT OF MY SOUL.
YOU SEE NOW?
WHEN I FIRST GOT THE RING, I USED IT... WELL, LIKE A CLUB. NOTHING VERY ELEGANT, BUT IT GOT THE JOB DONE.
BUT AS TIME WENT ON, I REALIZED THAT PRETTY MUCH WHATEVER I COULD IMAGINE--I COULD MAKE HAPPEN.
GBC
MY ONLY CONSTRAINT... WAS MY OWN IMAGINATION.
ONE DAY, I FOUND MYSELF WONDERING... WHAT IF I JUST...HAD THE RING ELIMINATE ALL THE EVIL IN THE WORLD?
JUST THE FACT THAT I WAS CONSIDERING IT... SCARED THE HELL OUT OF ME.
I HAD TO GET BACK TO EARTH. REDISCOVER WHAT IT WAS LIKE TO STRUGGLE FOR SOMETHING, INSTEAD OF WISHING IT INTO EXISTENCE.
I LOVE THIS CITY, I DO. BUT IT NEEDED A GUARDIAN, NOT A GOD.
SOMEONE WHO WASN'T IN DANGER OF LOSING TOUCH WITH HIS OWN HUMANITY.
THAT'S STILL WHAT IT NEEDS.
YOU EVER BEEN TO LITTLE PARIS?
THE AMUSEMENT PARK? SURE.
MY FATHER USED TO TAKE ME THERE, WHEN I WAS A BOY. WE'D RIDE THE ROLLER COASTER...

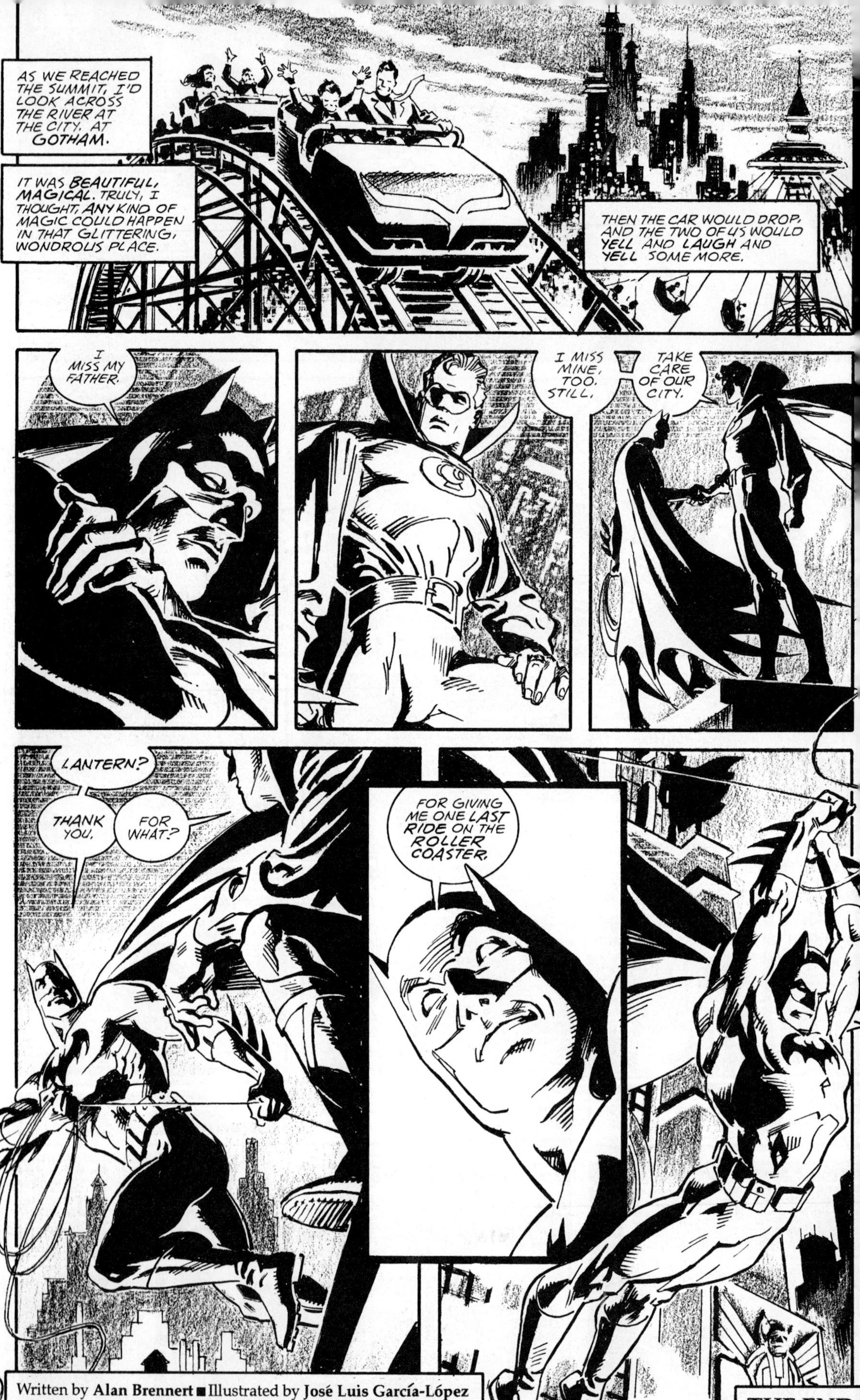
AS WE REACHED THE SUMMIT, I'D LOOK ACROSS THE RIVER AT THE CITY. AT GOTHAM.
IT WAS BEAUTIFUL, MAGICAL. TRULY, I THOUGHT, ANY KIND OF MAGIC COULD HAPPEN IN THAT GLITTERING, WONDROUS PLACE.
THEN THE CAR WOULD DROP, AND THE TWO OF US WOULD YELL AND LAUGH AND YELL SOME MORE.
I MISS MY FATHER.
I MISS MINE, TOO. STILL,
TAKE CARE OF OUR CITY.
LANTERN?
THANK YOU.
FOR WHAT?
FOR GIVING ME ONE LAST RIDE ON THE ROLLER COASTER.
THE END

Written by **Alan Brennert** ■ Illustrated by **José Luis García-López**
Lettered by **John E. Workman, Jr.** ■ Edited by **Mark Chiarello**

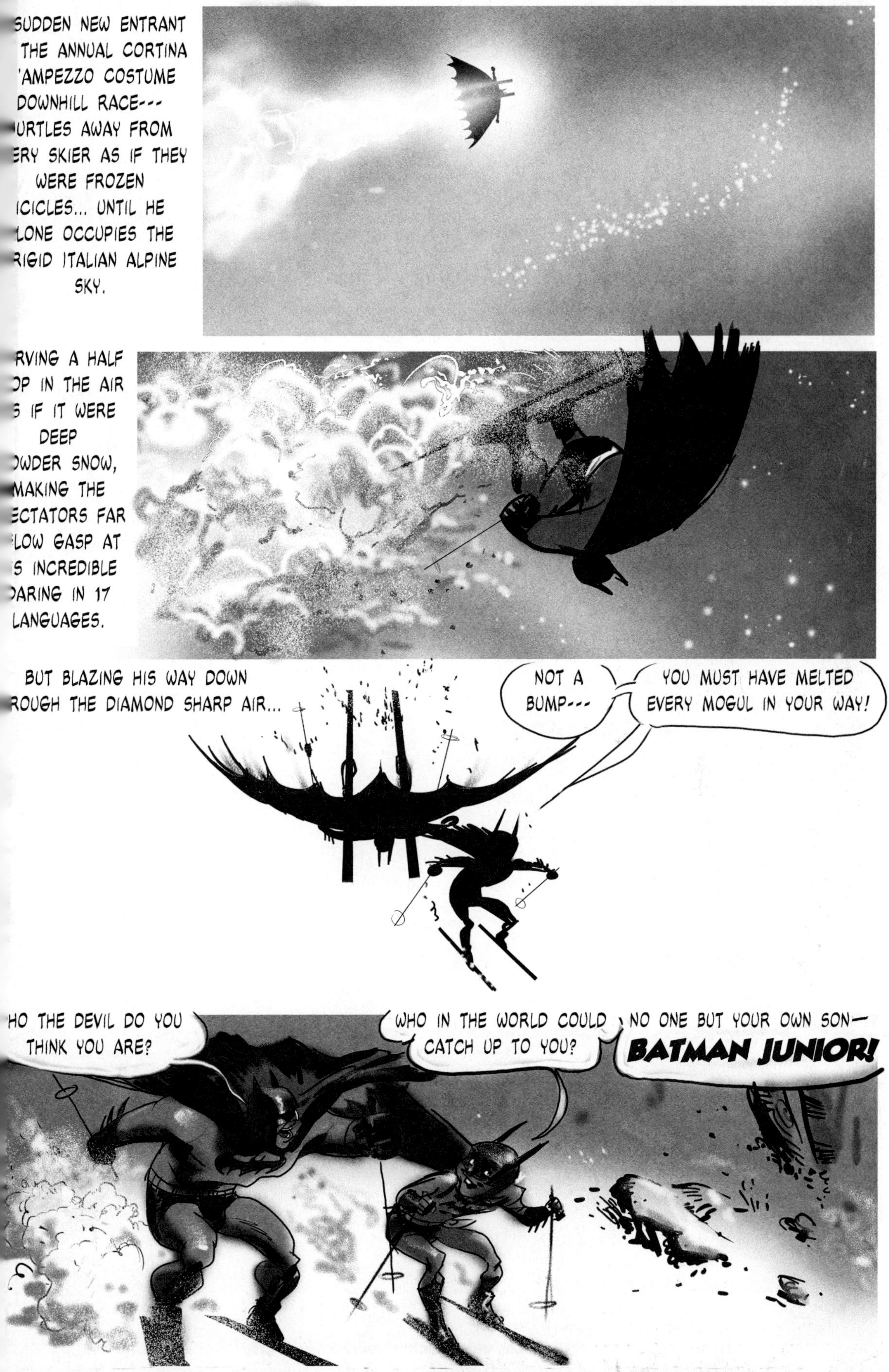
SUDDEN NEW ENTRANT THE ANNUAL CORTINA 'AMPEZZO COSTUME DOWNHILL RACE--- URTLES AWAY FROM ERY SKIER AS IF THEY WERE FROZEN ICICLES... UNTIL HE LONE OCCUPIES THE RIGID ITALIAN ALPINE SKY.
RVING A HALF OP IN THE AIR S IF IT WERE DEEP OWDER SNOW, MAKING THE ECTATORS FAR LOW GASP AT S INCREDIBLE DARING IN 17 LANGUAGES.
BUT BLAZING HIS WAY DOWN ROUGH THE DIAMOND SHARP AIR...
NOT A BUMP---
YOU MUST HAVE MELTED EVERY MOGUL IN YOUR WAY!
HO THE DEVIL DO YOU THINK YOU ARE?
WHO IN THE WORLD COULD CATCH UP TO YOU?
NO ONE BUT YOUR OWN SON—
BATMAN JUNIOR!

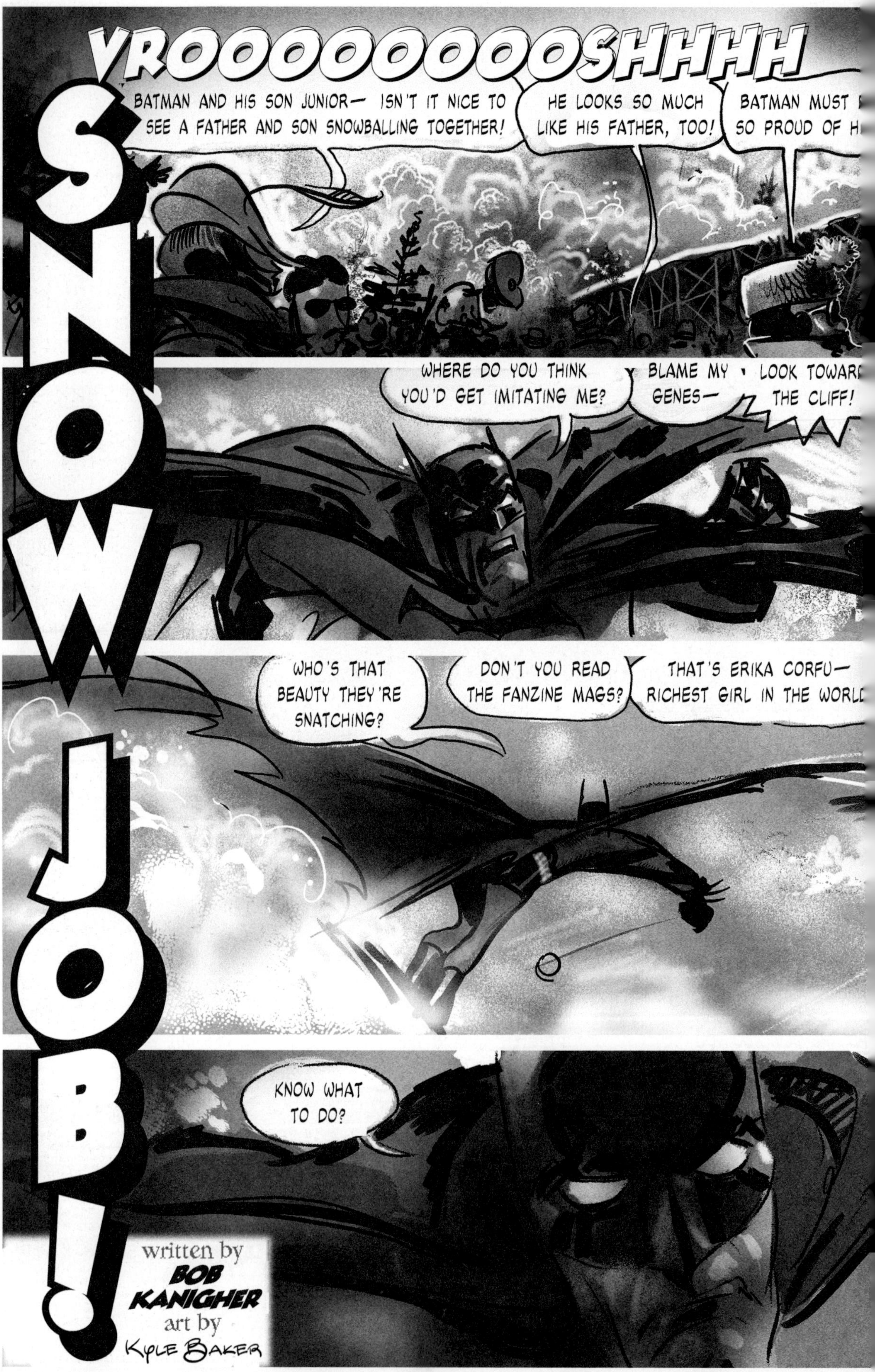
VROOOOOOOOOSHHHH
SNOW JOB!
BATMAN AND HIS SON JUNIOR— ISN'T IT NICE TO SEE A FATHER AND SON SNOWBALLING TOGETHER!
HE LOOKS SO MUCH LIKE HIS FATHER, TOO!
BATMAN MUST SO PROUD OF
WHERE DO YOU THINK YOU'D GET IMITATING ME?
BLAME MY GENES—
LOOK TOWAR THE CLIFF!
WHO'S THAT BEAUTY THEY'RE SNATCHING?
DON'T YOU READ THE FANZINE MAGS?
THAT'S ERIKA CORFU— RICHEST GIRL IN THE WORL
KNOW WHAT TO DO?
written by BOB KANIGHER
art by KYLE BAKER

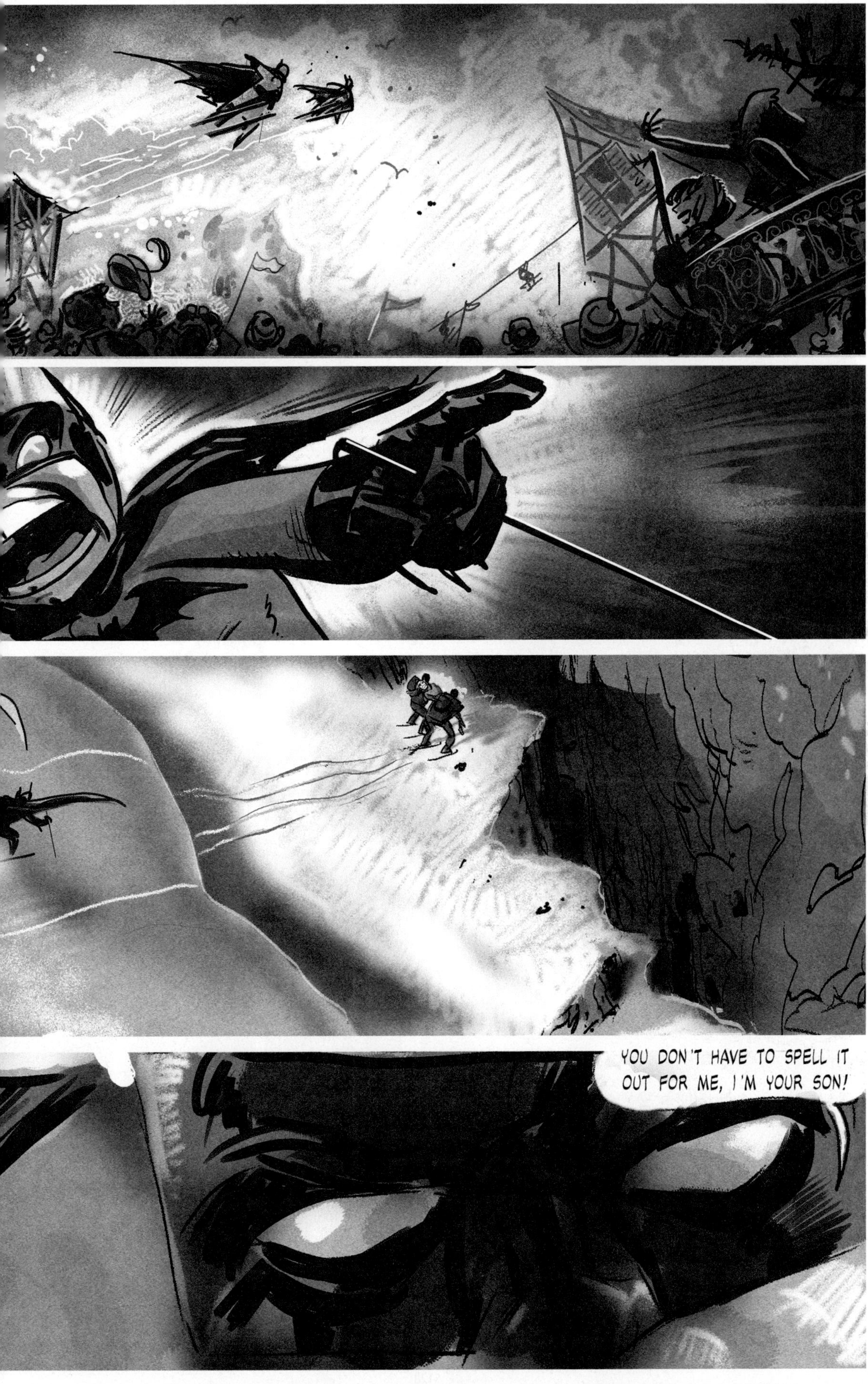
YOU DON'T HAVE TO SPELL IT OUT FOR ME, I'M YOUR SON!

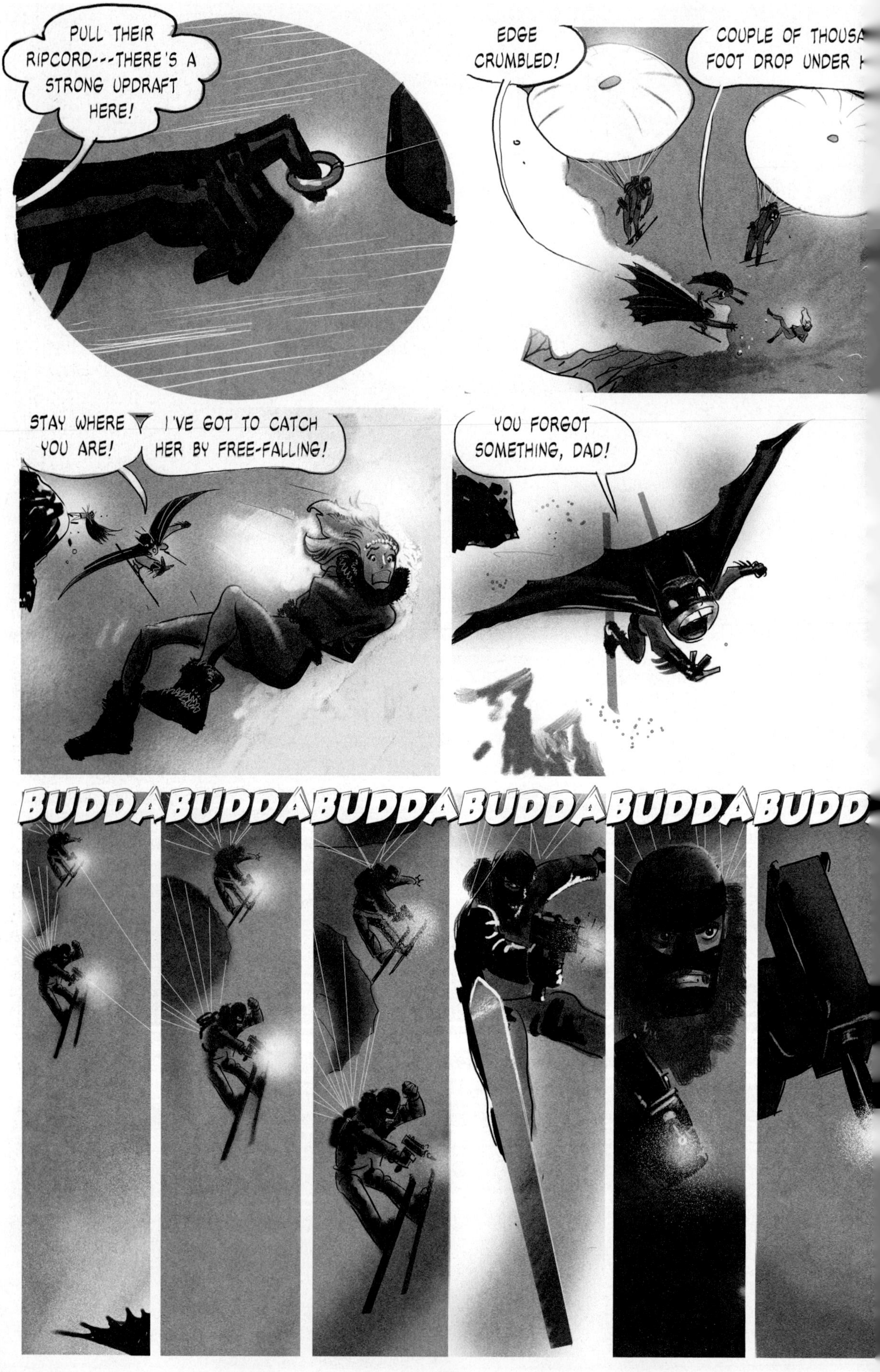
PULL THEIR RIPCORD---THERE'S A STRONG UPDRAFT HERE!
EDGE CRUMBLED!
COUPLE OF THOUSA
FOOT DROP UNDER
STAY WHERE YOU ARE!
I'VE GOT TO CATCH HER BY FREE-FALLING!
YOU FORGOT SOMETHING, DAD!
BUDDABUDDABUDDABUDDABUDDABUDD

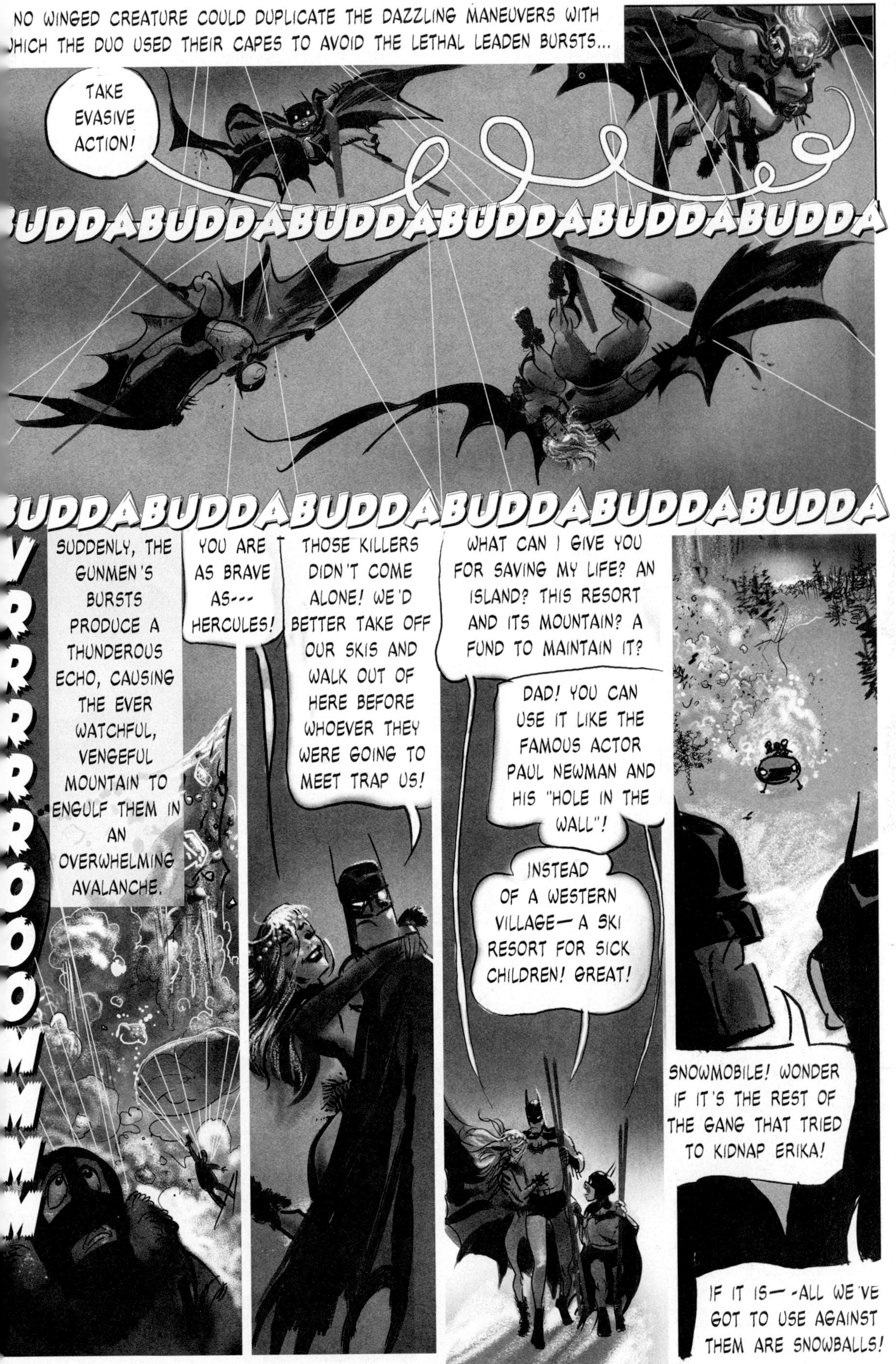
NO WINGED CREATURE COULD DUPLICATE THE DAZZLING MANEUVERS WITH WHICH THE DUO USED THEIR CAPES TO AVOID THE LETHAL LEADEN BURSTS...
TAKE EVASIVE ACTION!
BUDDABUDDABUDDABUDDABUDDABUDDA
BUDDABUDDABUDDABUDDABUDDABUDDA
VRRRRROOOOOMMMMMM
SUDDENLY, THE GUNMEN'S BURSTS PRODUCE A THUNDEROUS ECHO, CAUSING THE EVER WATCHFUL, VENGEFUL MOUNTAIN TO ENGULF THEM IN AN OVERWHELMING AVALANCHE.
YOU ARE AS BRAVE AS--- HERCULES!
THOSE KILLERS DIDN'T COME ALONE! WE'D BETTER TAKE OFF OUR SKIS AND WALK OUT OF HERE BEFORE WHOEVER THEY WERE GOING TO MEET TRAP US!
WHAT CAN I GIVE YOU FOR SAVING MY LIFE? AN ISLAND? THIS RESORT AND ITS MOUNTAIN? A FUND TO MAINTAIN IT?
DAD! YOU CAN USE IT LIKE THE FAMOUS ACTOR PAUL NEWMAN AND HIS "HOLE IN THE WALL"!
INSTEAD OF A WESTERN VILLAGE— A SKI RESORT FOR SICK CHILDREN! GREAT!
SNOWMOBILE! WONDER IF IT'S THE REST OF THE GANG THAT TRIED TO KIDNAP ERIKA!
IF IT IS— -ALL WE'VE GOT TO USE AGAINST THEM ARE SNOWBALLS!

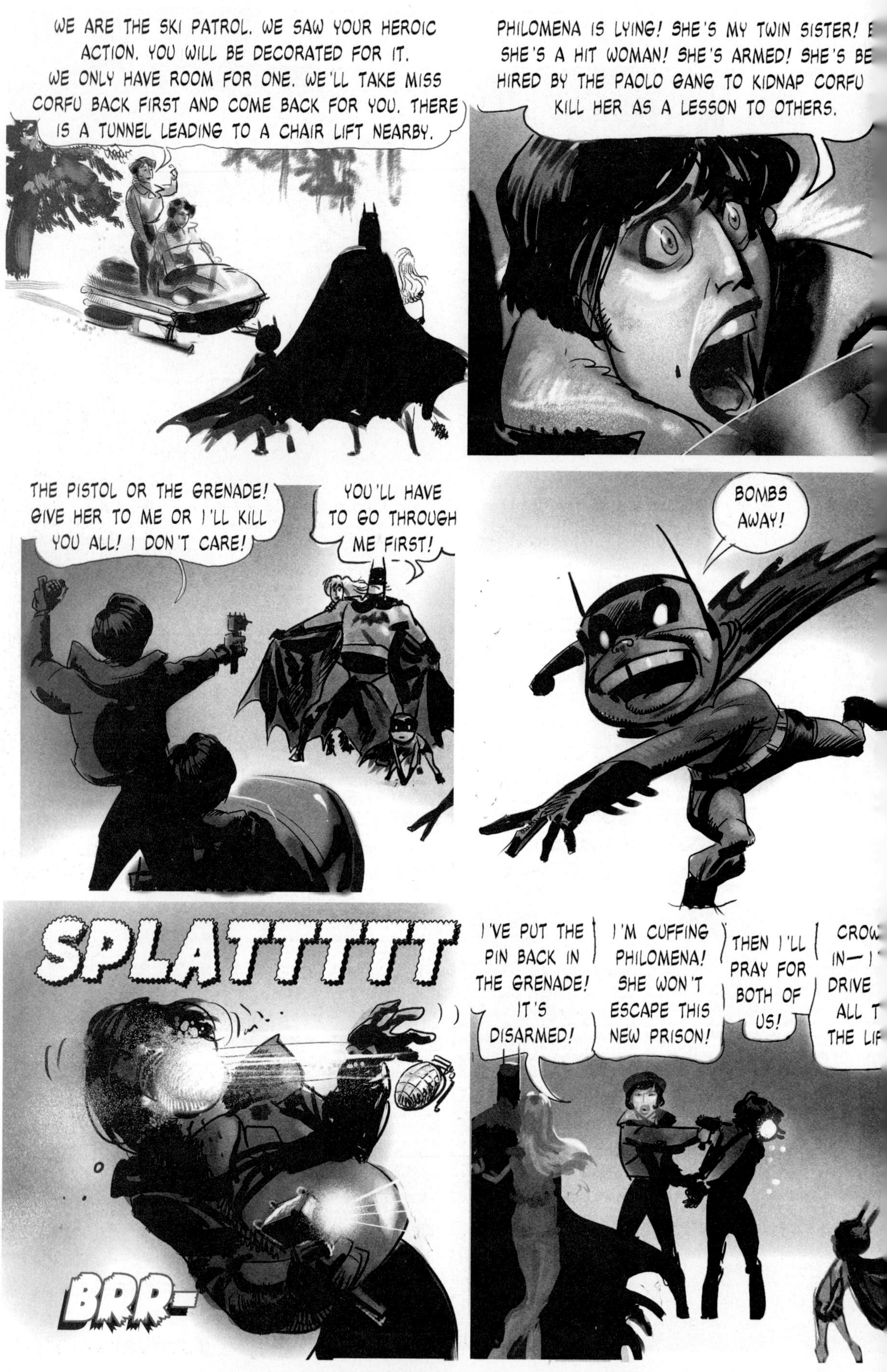
WE ARE THE SKI PATROL. WE SAW YOUR HEROIC ACTION. YOU WILL BE DECORATED FOR IT. WE ONLY HAVE ROOM FOR ONE. WE'LL TAKE MISS CORFU BACK FIRST AND COME BACK FOR YOU. THERE IS A TUNNEL LEADING TO A CHAIR LIFT NEARBY.
PHILOMENA IS LYING! SHE'S MY TWIN SISTER! E
SHE'S A HIT WOMAN! SHE'S ARMED! SHE'S BE
HIRED BY THE PAOLO GANG TO KIDNAP CORFU
KILL HER AS A LESSON TO OTHERS.
THE PISTOL OR THE GRENADE! GIVE HER TO ME OR I'LL KILL YOU ALL! I DON'T CARE!
YOU'LL HAVE TO GO THROUGH ME FIRST!
BOMBS AWAY!
SPLATTTTT
BRR-
I'VE PUT THE PIN BACK IN THE GRENADE! IT'S DISARMED!
I'M CUFFING PHILOMENA! SHE WON'T ESCAPE THIS NEW PRISON!
THEN I'LL PRAY FOR BOTH OF US!
CROW
IN— I
DRIVE
ALL T
THE LIF

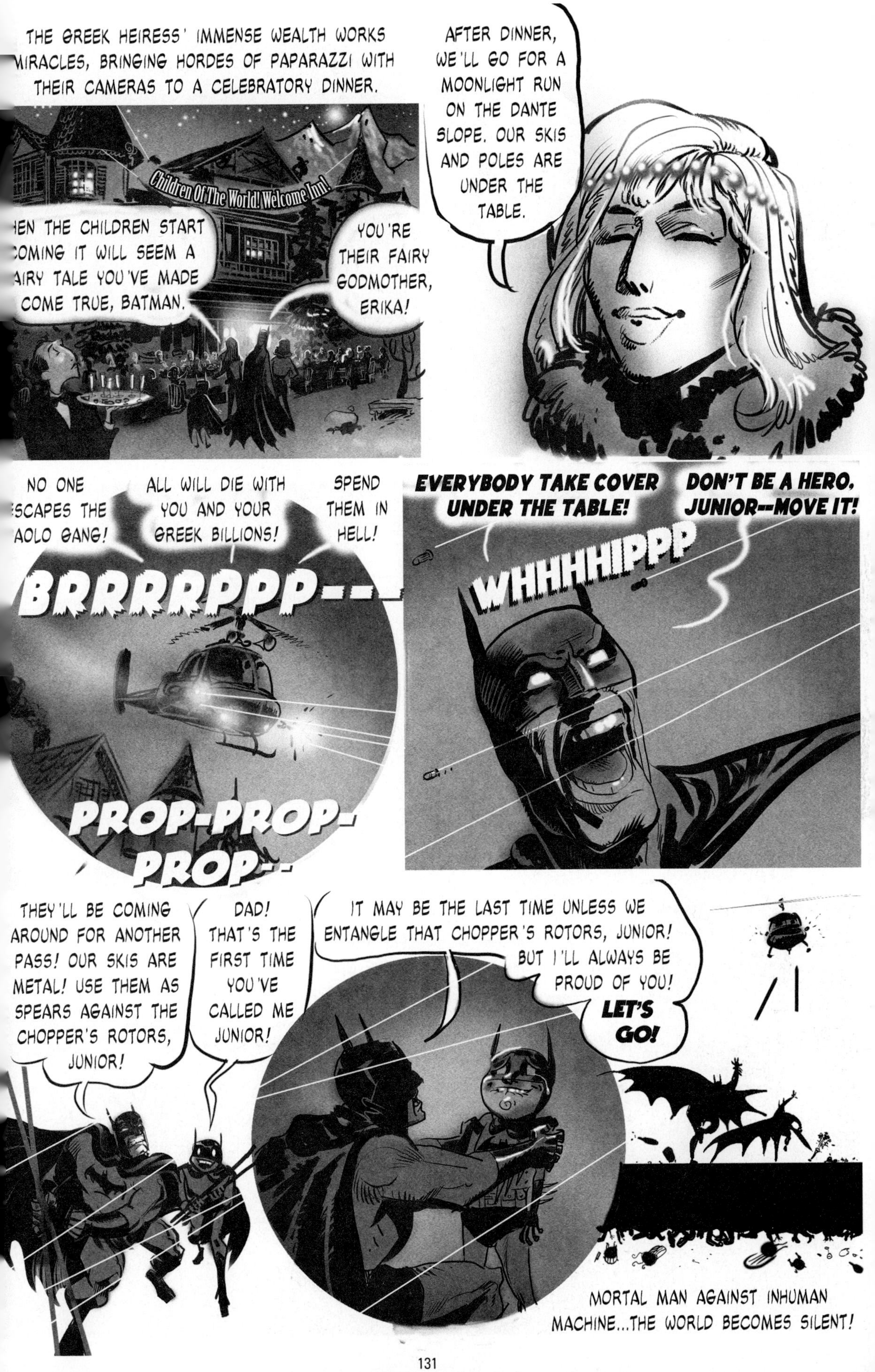
THE GREEK HEIRESS' IMMENSE WEALTH WORKS MIRACLES, BRINGING HORDES OF PAPARAZZI WITH THEIR CAMERAS TO A CELEBRATORY DINNER.
Children Of The World! Welcome Inn!
HEN THE CHILDREN START COMING IT WILL SEEM A AIRY TALE YOU'VE MADE COME TRUE, BATMAN.
YOU'RE THEIR FAIRY GODMOTHER, ERIKA!
AFTER DINNER, WE'LL GO FOR A MOONLIGHT RUN ON THE DANTE SLOPE. OUR SKIS AND POLES ARE UNDER THE TABLE.
NO ONE SCAPES THE AOLO GANG!
ALL WILL DIE WITH YOU AND YOUR GREEK BILLIONS!
SPEND THEM IN HELL!
BRRRRPPP---
PROP-PROP-PROP--
EVERYBODY TAKE COVER UNDER THE TABLE!
DON'T BE A HERO, JUNIOR--MOVE IT!
WHHHHIPPP
THEY'LL BE COMING AROUND FOR ANOTHER PASS! OUR SKIS ARE METAL! USE THEM AS SPEARS AGAINST THE CHOPPER'S ROTORS, JUNIOR!
DAD! THAT'S THE FIRST TIME YOU'VE CALLED ME JUNIOR!
IT MAY BE THE LAST TIME UNLESS WE ENTANGLE THAT CHOPPER'S ROTORS, JUNIOR!
BUT I'LL ALWAYS BE PROUD OF YOU!
LET'S GO!
MORTAL MAN AGAINST INHUMAN MACHINE...THE WORLD BECOMES SILENT!

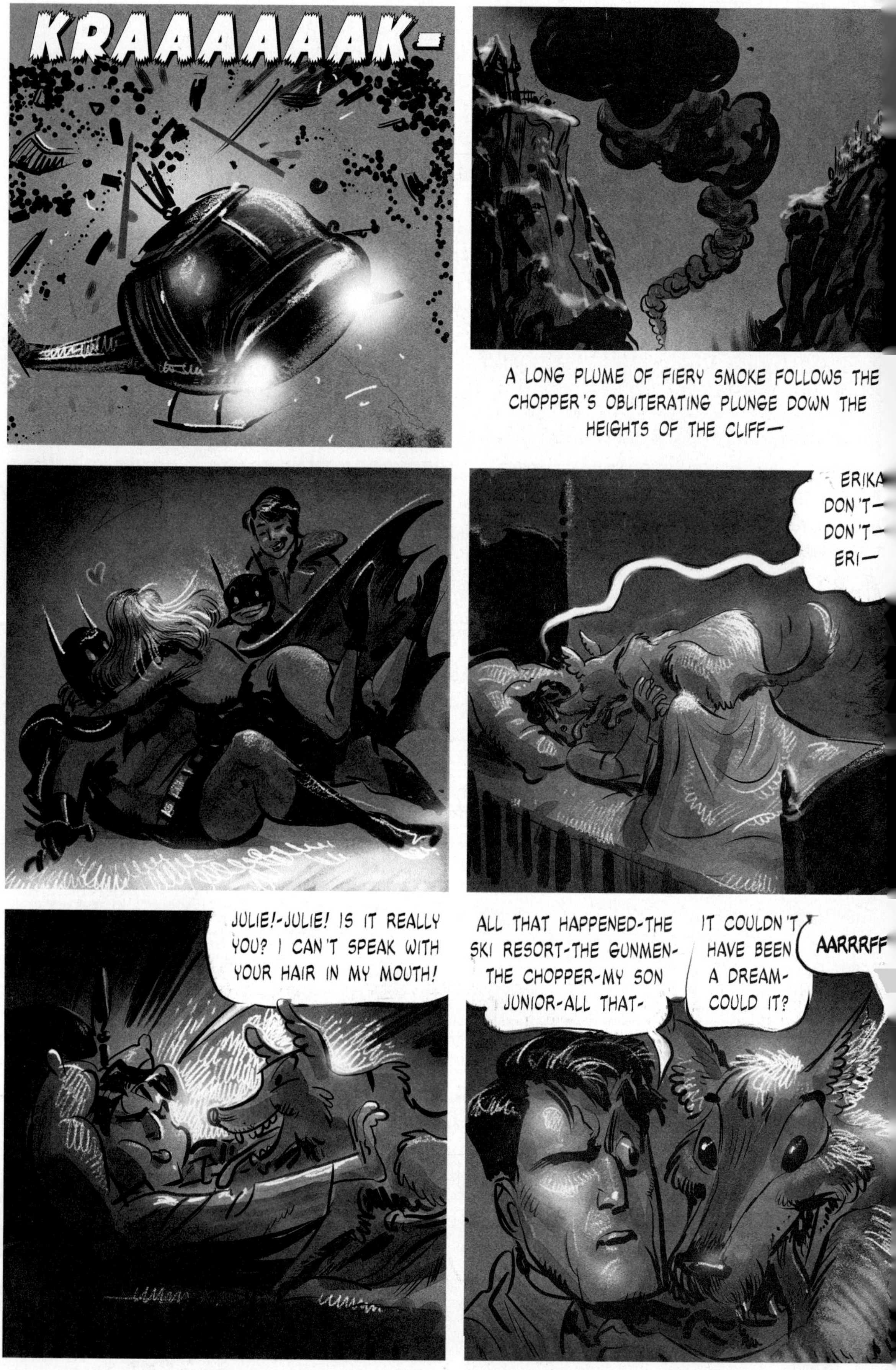
KRAAAAAAK-
A LONG PLUME OF FIERY SMOKE FOLLOWS THE CHOPPER'S OBLITERATING PLUNGE DOWN THE HEIGHTS OF THE CLIFF—
ERIKA DON'T— DON'T— ERI—
JULIE!-JULIE! IS IT REALLY YOU? I CAN'T SPEAK WITH YOUR HAIR IN MY MOUTH!
ALL THAT HAPPENED-THE SKI RESORT-THE GUNMEN-THE CHOPPER-MY SON JUNIOR-ALL THAT-
IT COULDN'T HAVE BEEN A DREAM-COULD IT?
AARRRFF

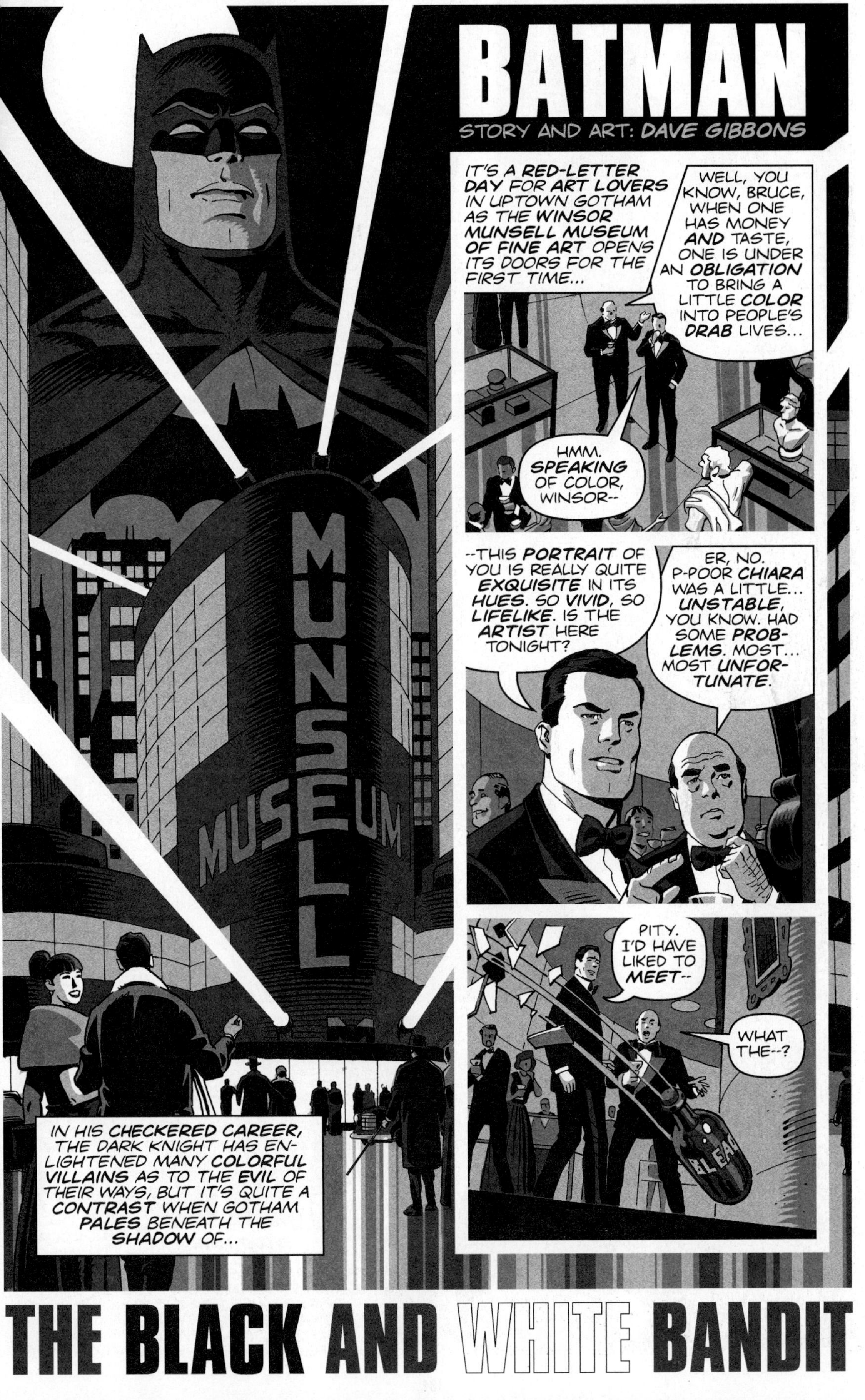
BATMAN
STORY AND ART: DAVE GIBBONS
MUNSELL
MUSEUM
IN HIS CHECKERED CAREER, THE DARK KNIGHT HAS ENLIGHTENED MANY COLORFUL VILLAINS AS TO THE EVIL OF THEIR WAYS, BUT IT'S QUITE A CONTRAST WHEN GOTHAM PALES BENEATH THE SHADOW OF...
THE BLACK AND WHITE BANDIT
IT'S A RED-LETTER DAY FOR ART LOVERS IN UPTOWN GOTHAM AS THE WINSOR MUNSELL MUSEUM OF FINE ART OPENS ITS DOORS FOR THE FIRST TIME...
WELL, YOU KNOW, BRUCE, WHEN ONE HAS MONEY AND TASTE, ONE IS UNDER AN OBLIGATION TO BRING A LITTLE COLOR INTO PEOPLE'S DRAB LIVES...
HMM. SPEAKING OF COLOR, WINSOR--
--THIS PORTRAIT OF YOU IS REALLY QUITE EXQUISITE IN ITS HUES. SO VIVID, SO LIFELIKE. IS THE ARTIST HERE TONIGHT?
ER, NO. P-POOR CHIARA WAS A LITTLE... UNSTABLE, YOU KNOW. HAD SOME PROBLEMS. MOST... MOST UNFORTUNATE.
PITY. I'D HAVE LIKED TO MEET--
WHAT THE--?

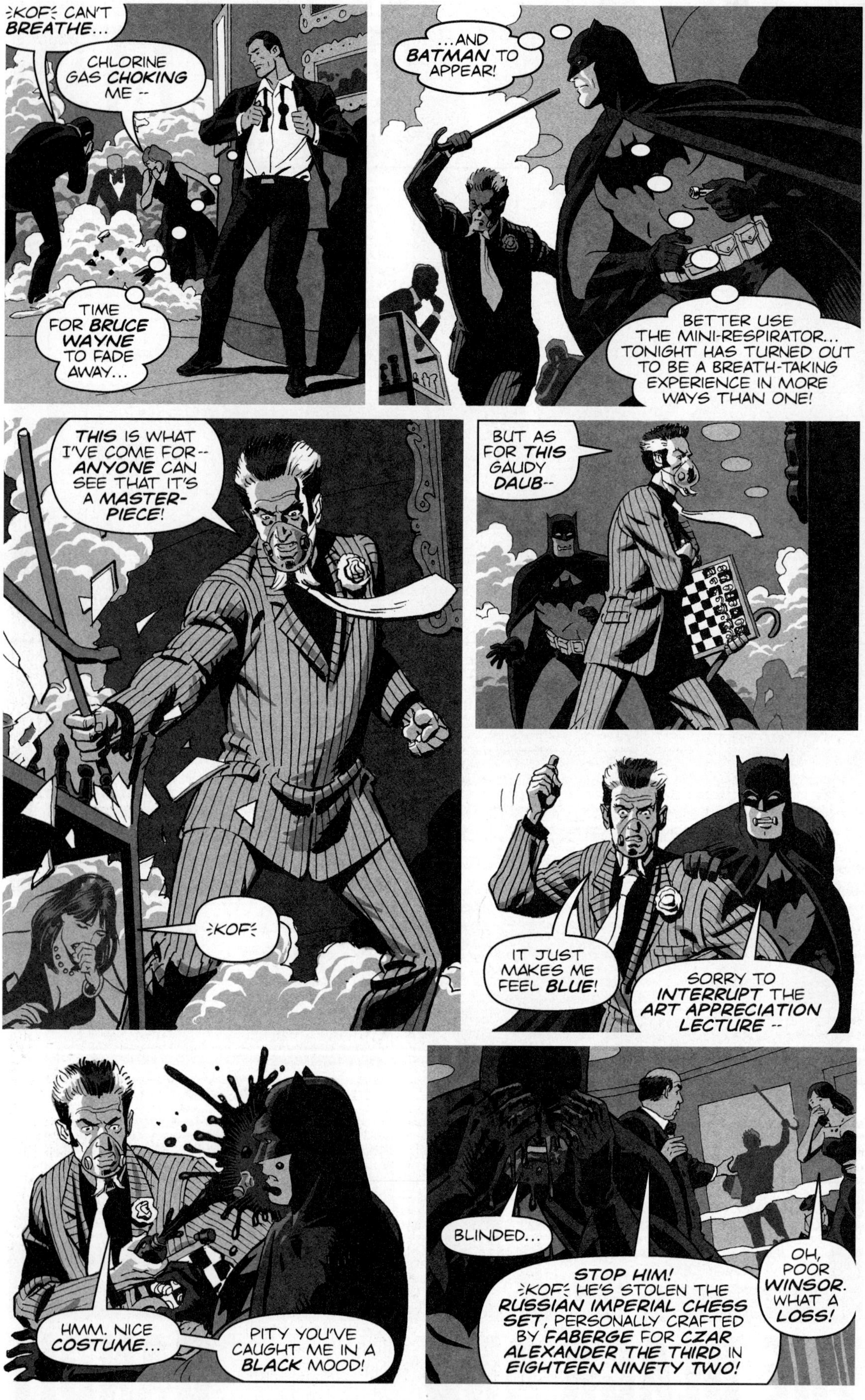

KOF CAN'T BREATHE...
CHLORINE GAS CHOKING ME --
TIME FOR BRUCE WAYNE TO FADE AWAY...
...AND BATMAN TO APPEAR!
BETTER USE THE MINI-RESPIRATOR... TONIGHT HAS TURNED OUT TO BE A BREATH-TAKING EXPERIENCE IN MORE WAYS THAN ONE!
THIS IS WHAT I'VE COME FOR-- ANYONE CAN SEE THAT IT'S A MASTER-PIECE!
KOF
BUT AS FOR THIS GAUDY DAUB--
IT JUST MAKES ME FEEL BLUE!
SORRY TO INTERRUPT THE ART APPRECIATION LECTURE --
HMM. NICE COSTUME...
PITY YOU'VE CAUGHT ME IN A BLACK MOOD!
BLINDED...
STOP HIM! KOF HE'S STOLEN THE RUSSIAN IMPERIAL CHESS SET, PERSONALLY CRAFTED BY FABERGE FOR CZAR ALEXANDER THE THIRD IN EIGHTEEN NINETY TWO!
OH, POOR WINSOR. WHAT A LOSS!

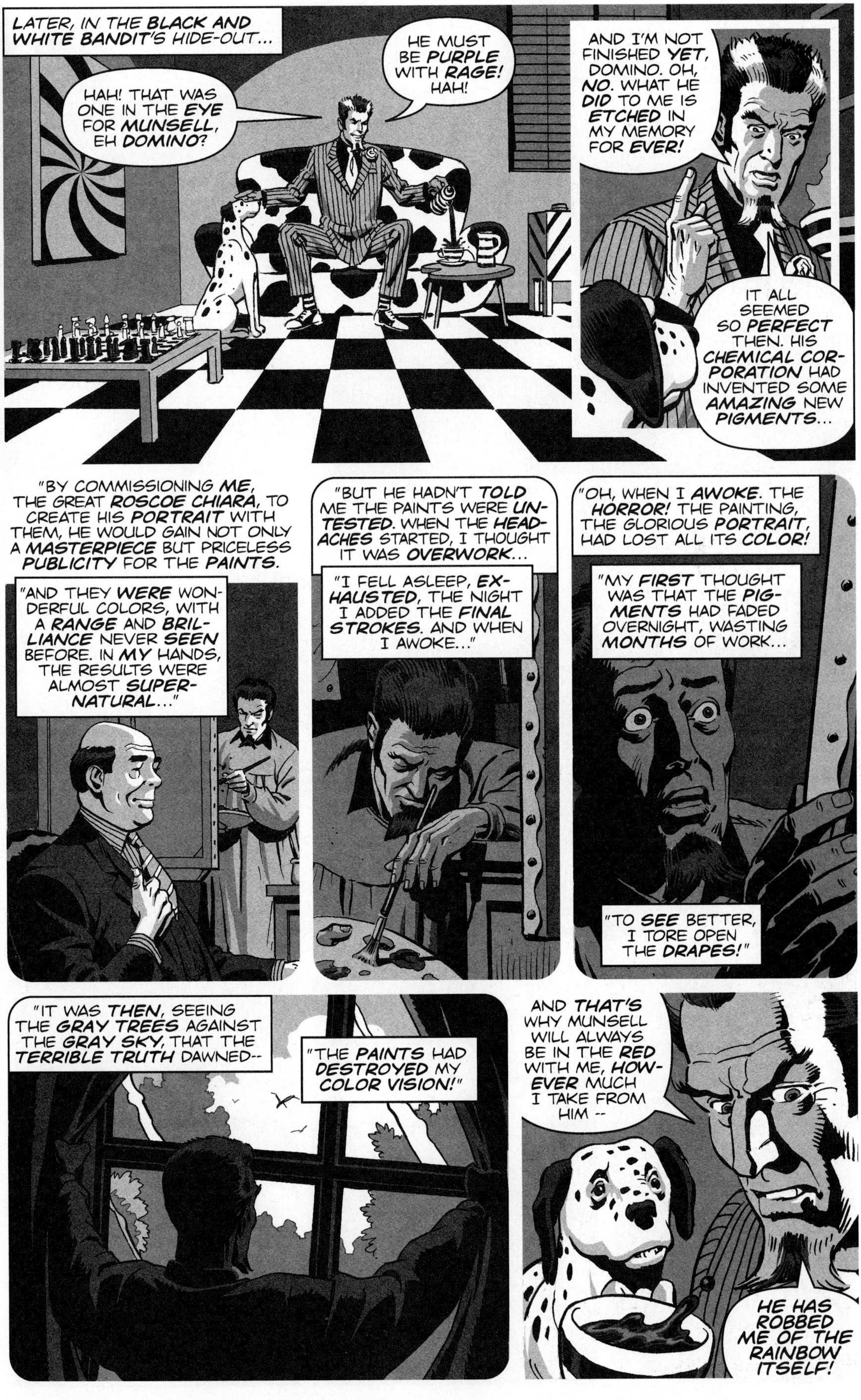

LATER, IN THE BLACK AND WHITE BANDIT'S HIDE-OUT...
HAH! THAT WAS ONE IN THE EYE FOR MUNSELL, EH DOMINO?
HE MUST BE PURPLE WITH RAGE! HAH!
AND I'M NOT FINISHED YET, DOMINO. OH, NO. WHAT HE DID TO ME IS ETCHED IN MY MEMORY FOR EVER!
IT ALL SEEMED SO PERFECT THEN. HIS CHEMICAL CORPORATION HAD INVENTED SOME AMAZING NEW PIGMENTS...
"BY COMMISSIONING ME, THE GREAT ROSCOE CHIARA, TO CREATE HIS PORTRAIT WITH THEM, HE WOULD GAIN NOT ONLY A MASTERPIECE BUT PRICELESS PUBLICITY FOR THE PAINTS.
"AND THEY WERE WONDERFUL COLORS, WITH A RANGE AND BRILLIANCE NEVER SEEN BEFORE. IN MY HANDS, THE RESULTS WERE ALMOST SUPERNATURAL..."
"BUT HE HADN'T TOLD ME THE PAINTS WERE UNTESTED. WHEN THE HEADACHES STARTED, I THOUGHT IT WAS OVERWORK...
"I FELL ASLEEP, EXHAUSTED, THE NIGHT I ADDED THE FINAL STROKES. AND WHEN I AWOKE..."
"OH, WHEN I AWOKE. THE HORROR! THE PAINTING, THE GLORIOUS PORTRAIT, HAD LOST ALL ITS COLOR!
"MY FIRST THOUGHT WAS THAT THE PIGMENTS HAD FADED OVERNIGHT, WASTING MONTHS OF WORK...
"TO SEE BETTER, I TORE OPEN THE DRAPES!"
"IT WAS THEN, SEEING THE GRAY TREES AGAINST THE GRAY SKY, THAT THE TERRIBLE TRUTH DAWNED--
"THE PAINTS HAD DESTROYED MY COLOR VISION!"
AND THAT'S WHY MUNSELL WILL ALWAYS BE IN THE RED WITH ME, HOWEVER MUCH I TAKE FROM HIM --
HE HAS ROBBED ME OF THE RAINBOW ITSELF!

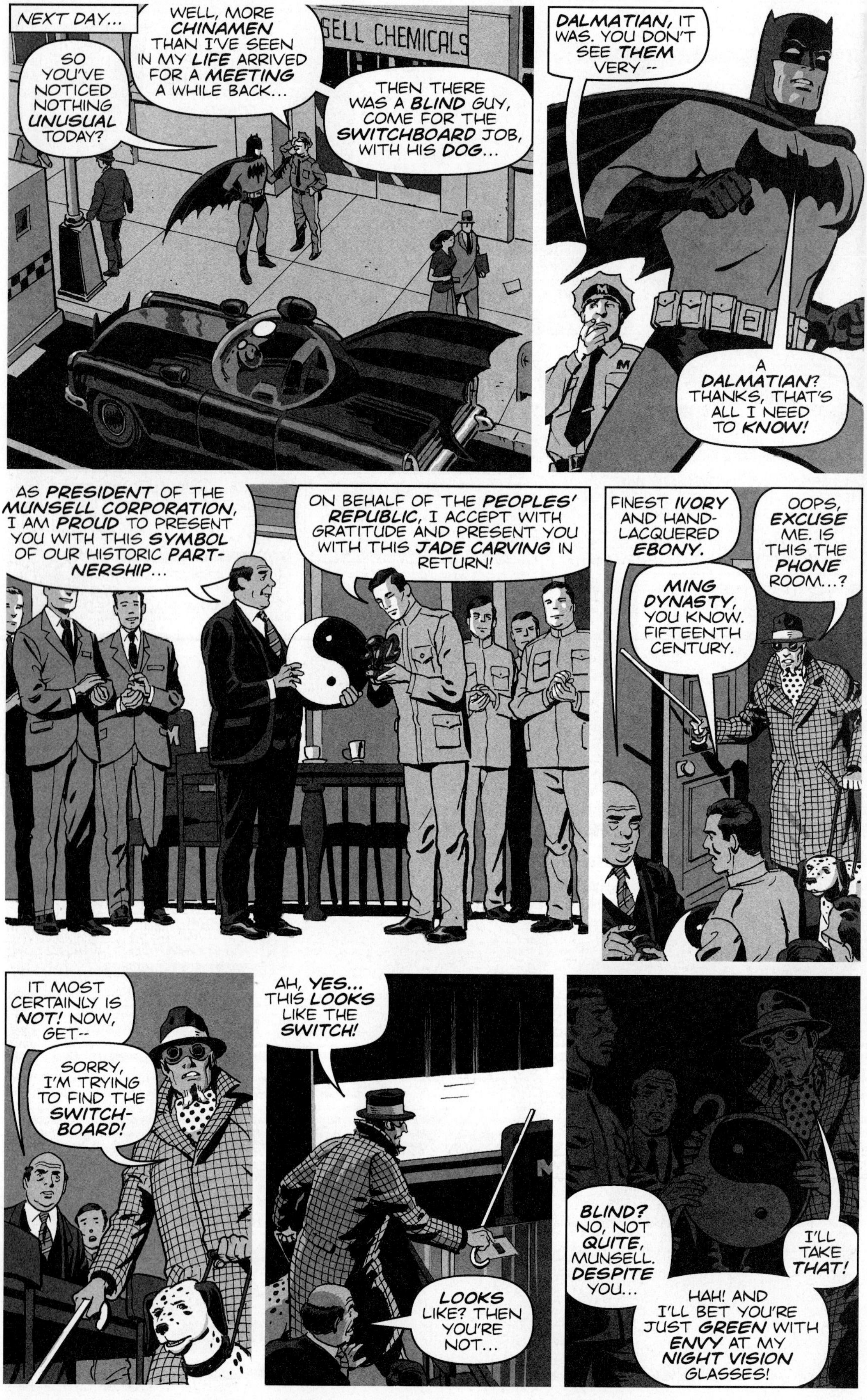
NEXT DAY...
SO YOU'VE NOTICED NOTHING UNUSUAL TODAY?
WELL, MORE CHINAMEN THAN I'VE SEEN IN MY LIFE ARRIVED FOR A MEETING A WHILE BACK...
THEN THERE WAS A BLIND GUY, COME FOR THE SWITCHBOARD JOB, WITH HIS DOG...
SELL CHEMICALS
DALMATIAN, IT WAS. YOU DON'T SEE THEM VERY --
A DALMATIAN? THANKS, THAT'S ALL I NEED TO KNOW!
AS PRESIDENT OF THE MUNSELL CORPORATION, I AM PROUD TO PRESENT YOU WITH THIS SYMBOL OF OUR HISTORIC PART-NERSHIP...
ON BEHALF OF THE PEOPLES' REPUBLIC, I ACCEPT WITH GRATITUDE AND PRESENT YOU WITH THIS JADE CARVING IN RETURN!
FINEST IVORY AND HAND-LACQUERED EBONY.
MING DYNASTY, YOU KNOW. FIFTEENTH CENTURY.
OOPS, EXCUSE ME. IS THIS THE PHONE ROOM...?
IT MOST CERTAINLY IS NOT! NOW, GET--
SORRY, I'M TRYING TO FIND THE SWITCH-BOARD!
AH, YES... THIS LOOKS LIKE THE SWITCH!
LOOKS LIKE? THEN YOU'RE NOT...
BLIND? NO, NOT QUITE, MUNSELL. DESPITE YOU...
I'LL TAKE THAT!
HAH! AND I'LL BET YOU'RE JUST GREEN WITH ENVY AT MY NIGHT VISION GLASSES!

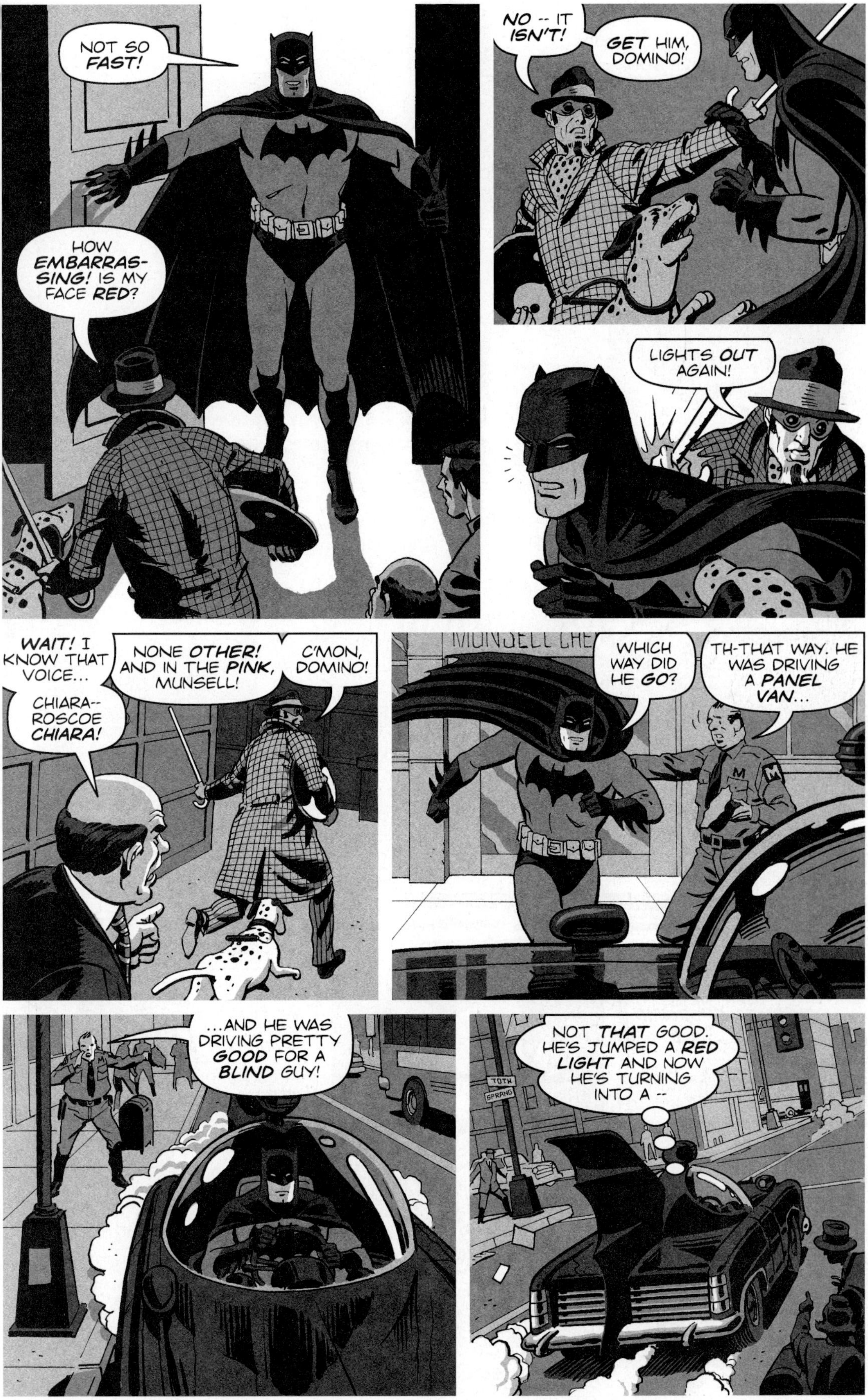
NOT SO FAST!
HOW EMBARRAS-SING! IS MY FACE RED?
NO -- IT ISN'T!
GET HIM, DOMINO!
LIGHTS OUT AGAIN!
WAIT! I KNOW THAT VOICE...
CHIARA-- ROSCOE CHIARA!
NONE OTHER! AND IN THE PINK, MUNSELL!
C'MON, DOMINO!
MUNSELL CHE
WHICH WAY DID HE GO?
TH-THAT WAY. HE WAS DRIVING A PANEL VAN...
...AND HE WAS DRIVING PRETTY GOOD FOR A BLIND GUY!
TOTH
SPRANG
NOT THAT GOOD. HE'S JUMPED A RED LIGHT AND NOW HE'S TURNING INTO A --

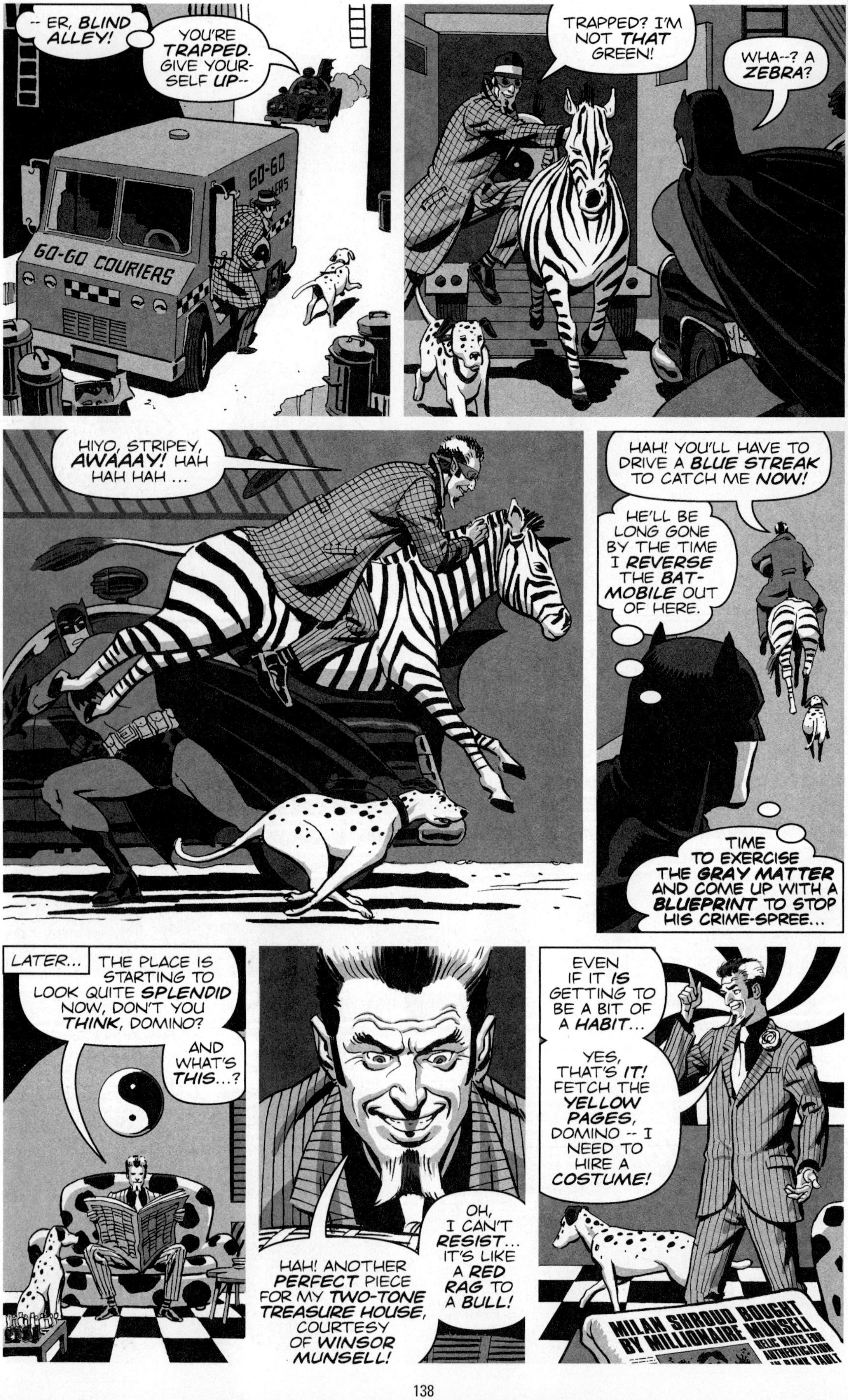
-- ER, BLIND ALLEY!
YOU'RE TRAPPED. GIVE YOURSELF UP--
GO-GO COURIERS
GO-GO COURIERS
TRAPPED? I'M NOT THAT GREEN!
WHA--? A ZEBRA?
HIYO, STRIPEY, AWAAAY! HAH HAH HAH ...
HAH! YOU'LL HAVE TO DRIVE A BLUE STREAK TO CATCH ME NOW!
HE'LL BE LONG GONE BY THE TIME I REVERSE THE BATMOBILE OUT OF HERE.
TIME TO EXERCISE THE GRAY MATTER AND COME UP WITH A BLUEPRINT TO STOP HIS CRIME-SPREE...
LATER...
THE PLACE IS STARTING TO LOOK QUITE SPLENDID NOW, DON'T YOU THINK, DOMINO?
AND WHAT'S THIS...?
HAH! ANOTHER PERFECT PIECE FOR MY TWO-TONE TREASURE HOUSE, COURTESY OF WINSOR MUNSELL!
OH, I CAN'T RESIST... IT'S LIKE A RED RAG TO A BULL!
EVEN IF IT IS GETTING TO BE A BIT OF A HABIT...
YES, THAT'S IT! FETCH THE YELLOW PAGES, DOMINO -- I NEED TO HIRE A COSTUME!
MILAN SHROUD BOUGHT BY MILLIONAIRE MUNSELL

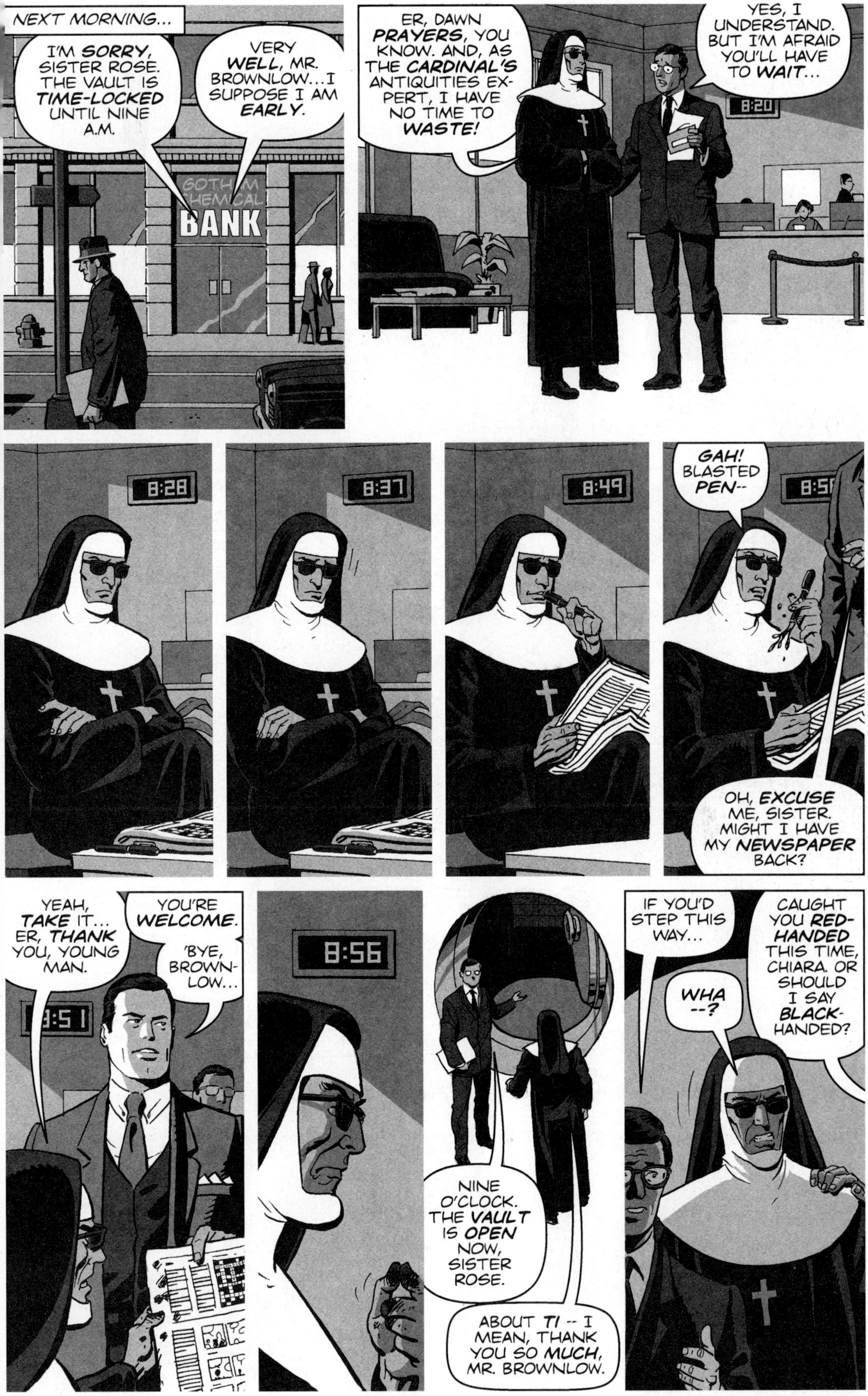
NEXT MORNING...
I'M SORRY, SISTER ROSE. THE VAULT IS TIME-LOCKED UNTIL NINE A.M.
VERY WELL, MR. BROWNLOW...I SUPPOSE I AM EARLY.
GOTHAM CHEMICAL BANK
ER, DAWN PRAYERS, YOU KNOW. AND, AS THE CARDINAL'S ANTIQUITIES EXPERT, I HAVE NO TIME TO WASTE!
YES, I UNDERSTAND. BUT I'M AFRAID YOU'LL HAVE TO WAIT...
8:20
8:28
8:37
8:49
GAH! BLASTED PEN--
OH, EXCUSE ME, SISTER. MIGHT I HAVE MY NEWSPAPER BACK?
YEAH, TAKE IT... ER, THANK YOU, YOUNG MAN.
YOU'RE WELCOME.
'BYE, BROWNLOW...
8:56
NINE O'CLOCK. THE VAULT IS OPEN NOW, SISTER ROSE.
ABOUT TI -- I MEAN, THANK YOU SO MUCH, MR. BROWNLOW.
IF YOU'D STEP THIS WAY...
CAUGHT YOU RED-HANDED THIS TIME, CHIARA. OR SHOULD I SAY BLACK-HANDED?
WHA --?

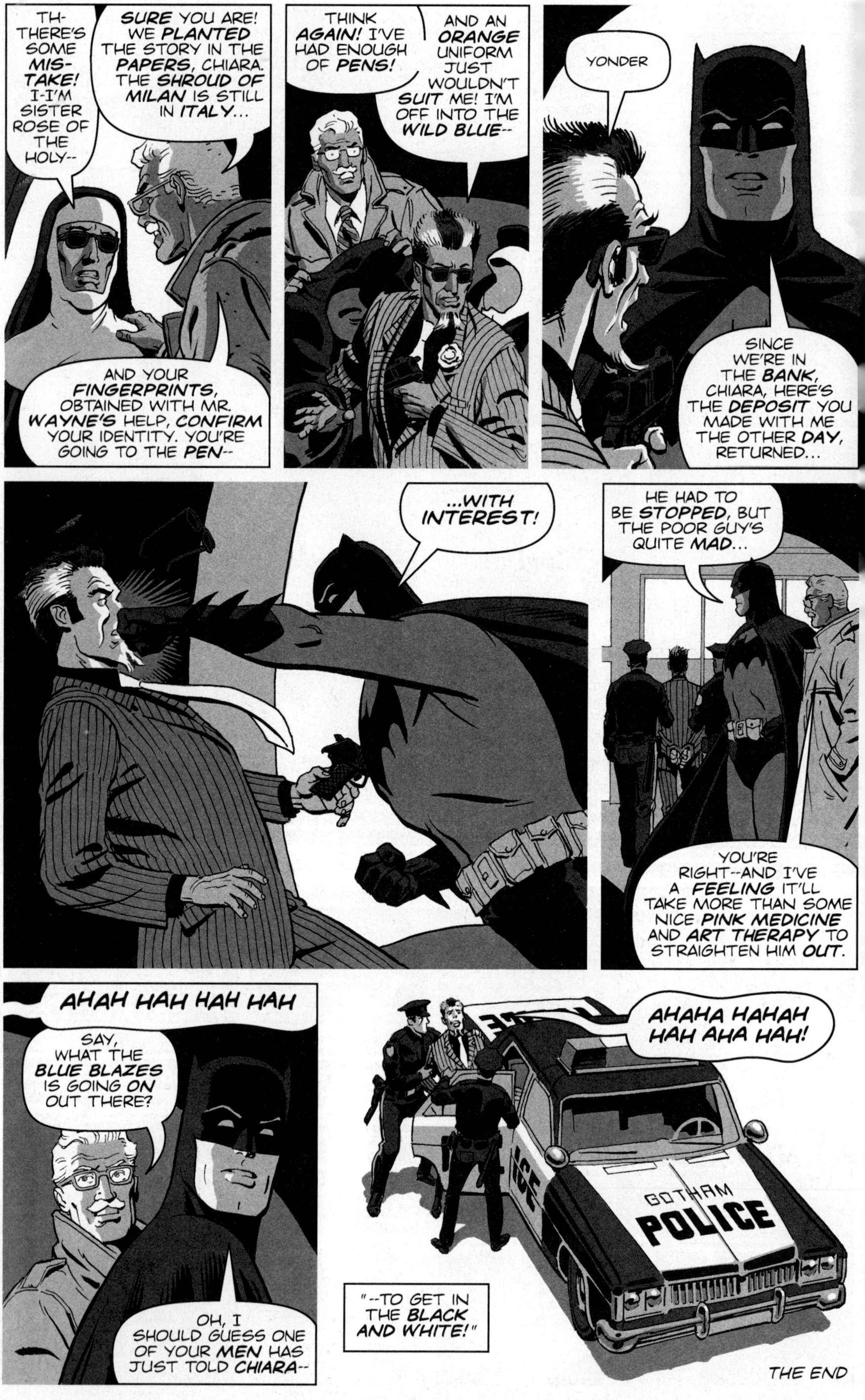
TH- THERE'S SOME MIS- TAKE! I-I'M SISTER ROSE OF THE HOLY--
SURE YOU ARE! WE PLANTED THE STORY IN THE PAPERS, CHIARA. THE SHROUD OF MILAN IS STILL IN ITALY...
AND YOUR FINGERPRINTS, OBTAINED WITH MR. WAYNE'S HELP, CONFIRM YOUR IDENTITY. YOU'RE GOING TO THE PEN--
THINK AGAIN! I'VE HAD ENOUGH OF PENS!
AND AN ORANGE UNIFORM JUST WOULDN'T SUIT ME! I'M OFF INTO THE WILD BLUE--
YONDER
SINCE WE'RE IN THE BANK, CHIARA, HERE'S THE DEPOSIT YOU MADE WITH ME THE OTHER DAY, RETURNED...
...WITH INTEREST!
HE HAD TO BE STOPPED, BUT THE POOR GUY'S QUITE MAD...
YOU'RE RIGHT--AND I'VE A FEELING IT'LL TAKE MORE THAN SOME NICE PINK MEDICINE AND ART THERAPY TO STRAIGHTEN HIM OUT.
AHAH HAH HAH HAH
SAY, WHAT THE BLUE BLAZES IS GOING ON OUT THERE?
OH, I SHOULD GUESS ONE OF YOUR MEN HAS JUST TOLD CHIARA--
"--TO GET IN THE BLACK AND WHITE!"
AHAHA HAHAH HAH AHA HAH!
GOTHAM POLICE
THE END

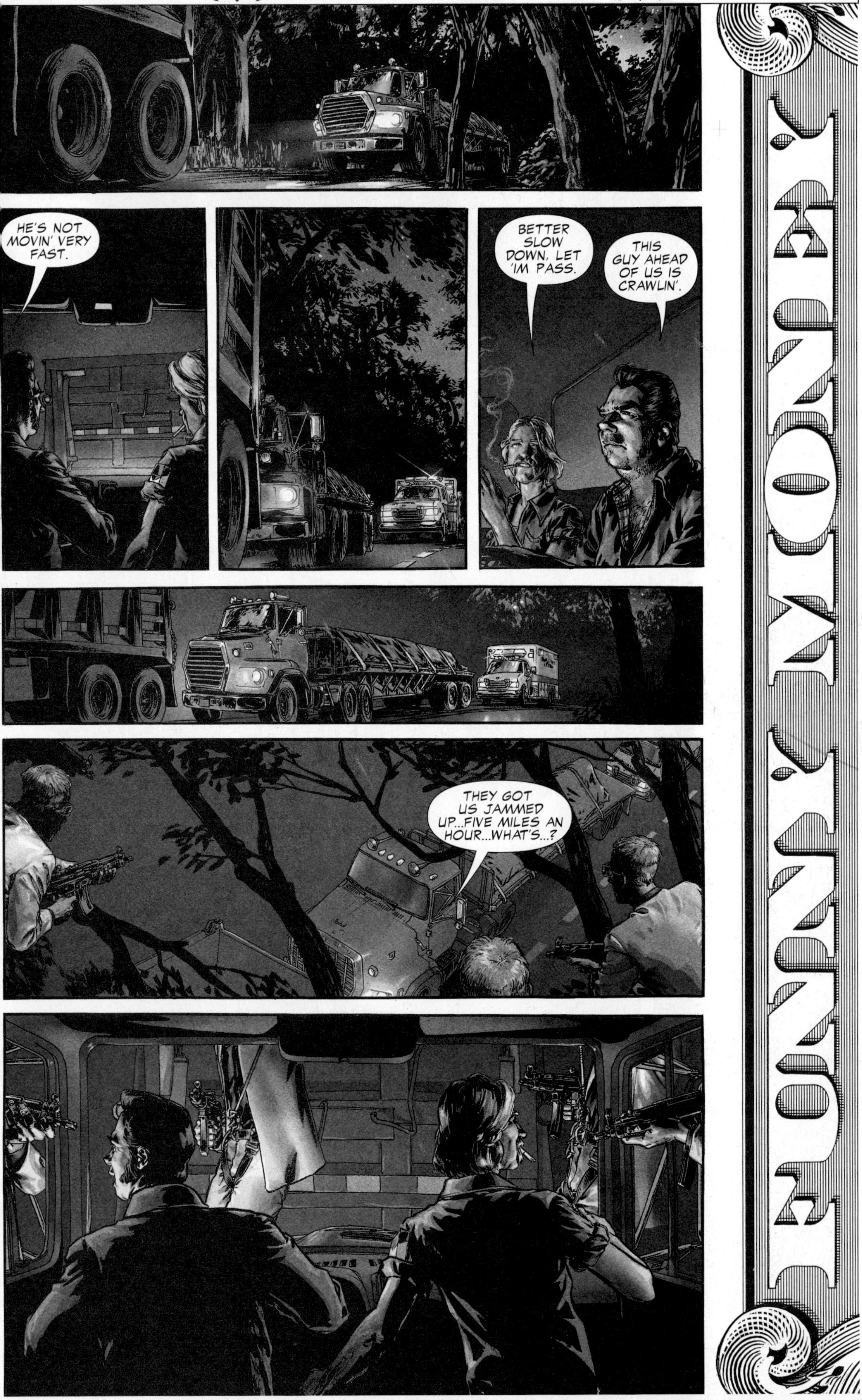
HE'S NOT MOVIN' VERY FAST.
BETTER SLOW DOWN, LET 'IM PASS.
THIS GUY AHEAD OF US IS CRAWLIN'.
THEY GOT US JAMMED UP...FIVE MILES AN HOUR...WHAT'S...?

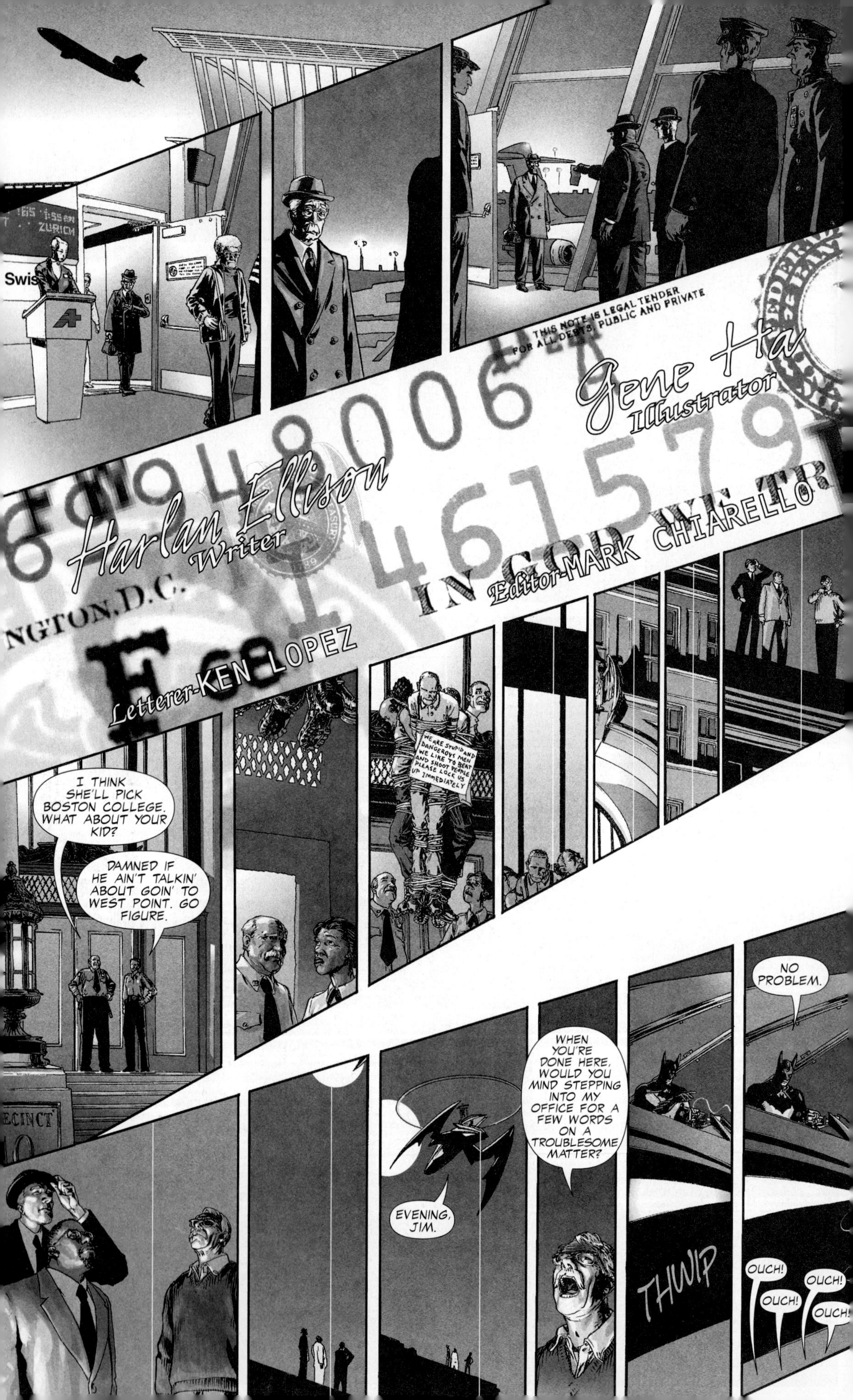

THIS NOTE IS LEGAL TENDER FOR ALL DEBTS, PUBLIC AND PRIVATE
Harlan Ellison Writer
Gene Ha Illustrator
Editor-MARK CHIARELLO
Letterer-KEN LOPEZ
WE ARE STUPID AND DANGEROUS MEN WE LIKE TO BEAT AND SHOOT PEOPLE PLEASE LOCK US UP IMMEDIATELY
I THINK SHE'LL PICK BOSTON COLLEGE. WHAT ABOUT YOUR KID?
DAMNED IF HE AIN'T TALKIN' ABOUT GOIN' TO WEST POINT. GO FIGURE.
EVENING, JIM.
WHEN YOU'RE DONE HERE, WOULD YOU MIND STEPPING INTO MY OFFICE FOR A FEW WORDS ON A TROUBLESOME MATTER?
NO PROBLEM.
THWIP
OUCH!
OUCH!
OUCH!
OUCH!

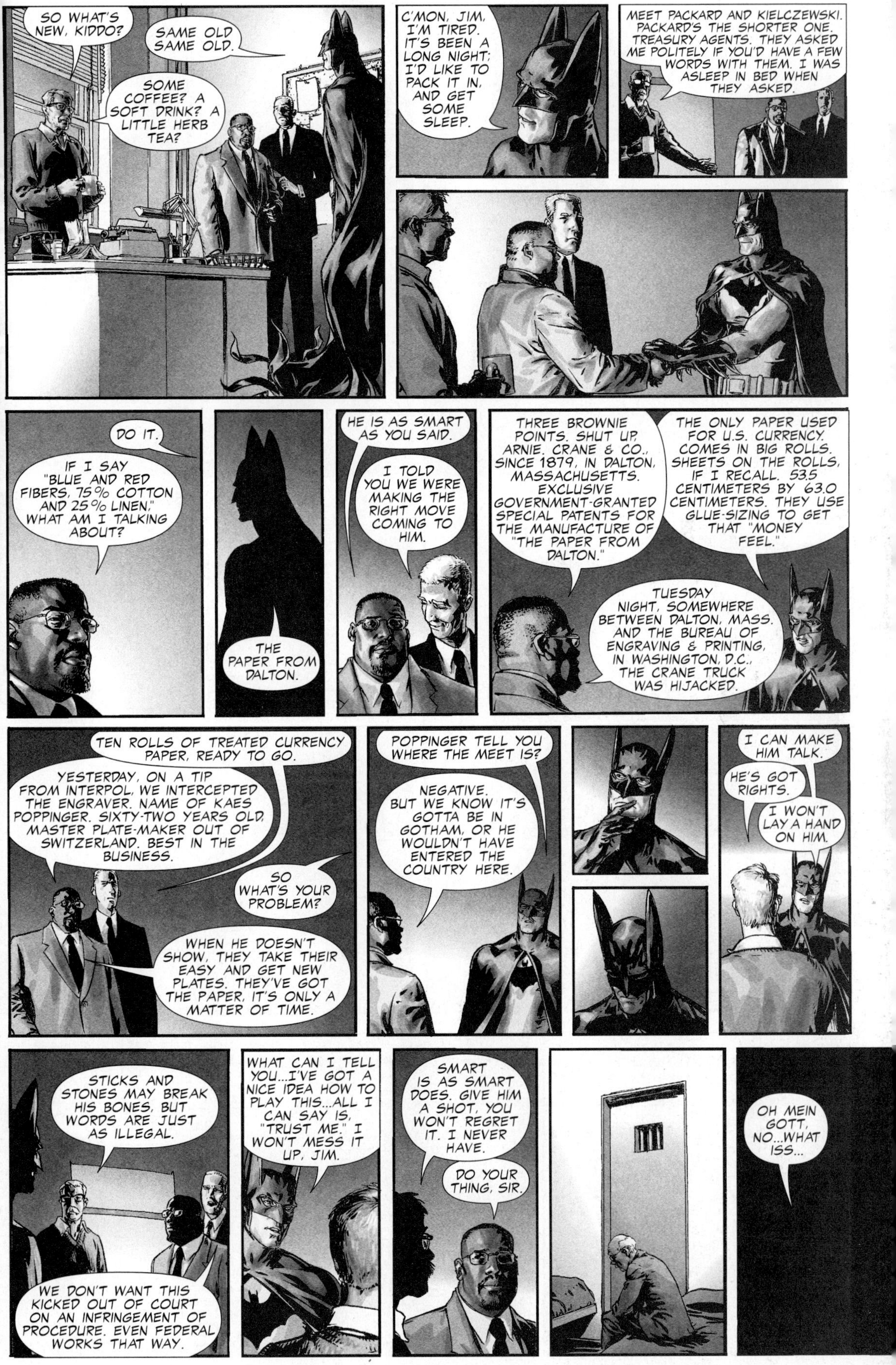
SO WHAT'S NEW, KIDDO?
SAME OLD SAME OLD.
SOME COFFEE? A SOFT DRINK? A LITTLE HERB TEA?
C'MON, JIM, I'M TIRED. IT'S BEEN A LONG NIGHT; I'D LIKE TO PACK IT IN, AND GET SOME SLEEP.
MEET PACKARD AND KIELCZEWSKI. PACKARD'S THE SHORTER ONE. TREASURY AGENTS. THEY ASKED ME POLITELY IF YOU'D HAVE A FEW WORDS WITH THEM. I WAS ASLEEP IN BED WHEN THEY ASKED.
DO IT.
IF I SAY "BLUE AND RED FIBERS, 75% COTTON AND 25% LINEN," WHAT AM I TALKING ABOUT?
THE PAPER FROM DALTON.
HE IS AS SMART AS YOU SAID.
I TOLD YOU WE WERE MAKING THE RIGHT MOVE COMING TO HIM.
THREE BROWNIE POINTS. SHUT UP, ARNIE. CRANE & CO., SINCE 1879, IN DALTON, MASSACHUSETTS. EXCLUSIVE GOVERNMENT-GRANTED SPECIAL PATENTS FOR THE MANUFACTURE OF "THE PAPER FROM DALTON."
THE ONLY PAPER USED FOR U.S. CURRENCY. COMES IN BIG ROLLS. SHEETS ON THE ROLLS, IF I RECALL. 53.5 CENTIMETERS BY 63.0 CENTIMETERS. THEY USE GLUE-SIZING TO GET THAT "MONEY FEEL."
TUESDAY NIGHT, SOMEWHERE BETWEEN DALTON, MASS. AND THE BUREAU OF ENGRAVING & PRINTING, IN WASHINGTON, D.C., THE CRANE TRUCK WAS HIJACKED.
TEN ROLLS OF TREATED CURRENCY PAPER, READY TO GO.
YESTERDAY, ON A TIP FROM INTERPOL, WE INTERCEPTED THE ENGRAVER. NAME OF KAES POPPINGER. SIXTY-TWO YEARS OLD, MASTER PLATE-MAKER OUT OF SWITZERLAND. BEST IN THE BUSINESS.
SO WHAT'S YOUR PROBLEM?
WHEN HE DOESN'T SHOW, THEY TAKE THEIR EASY AND GET NEW PLATES. THEY'VE GOT THE PAPER, IT'S ONLY A MATTER OF TIME.
POPPINGER TELL YOU WHERE THE MEET IS?
NEGATIVE. BUT WE KNOW IT'S GOTTA BE IN GOTHAM, OR HE WOULDN'T HAVE ENTERED THE COUNTRY HERE.
I CAN MAKE HIM TALK.
HE'S GOT RIGHTS.
I WON'T LAY A HAND ON HIM.
STICKS AND STONES MAY BREAK HIS BONES, BUT WORDS ARE JUST AS ILLEGAL.
WE DON'T WANT THIS KICKED OUT OF COURT ON AN INFRINGEMENT OF PROCEDURE. EVEN FEDERAL WORKS THAT WAY.
WHAT CAN I TELL YOU...I'VE GOT A NICE IDEA HOW TO PLAY THIS...ALL I CAN SAY IS, "TRUST ME." I WON'T MESS IT UP, JIM.
SMART IS AS SMART DOES. GIVE HIM A SHOT, YOU WON'T REGRET IT. I NEVER HAVE.
DO YOUR THING, SIR.
OH MEIN GOTT, NO...WHAT ISS...

WHO...ARE YOU...WHAT DO YOU WANT...?

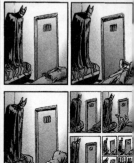

PLEASE... GOTT IN HIMMEL... SPEAK...SAY A THING...ANY THING...

YOU HAVE THE PLATES?

YES... PLEASE...YOU FRIGHTEN ME...

YOU HAVE NOTHING TO FEAR FROM ME, KAES POPPINGER. IF YOU ELECT TO ASSIST US.

WHAT IS IT YOU WANT FROM ME?

THE PLATES, WHERE ARE THEY NOW?

IN A PLAIN EXPRESS PACKAGE AT GENERAL PICKUP, GOTHAM POST OFFICE, IN MY NAME.

AND YOU CAN TAKE ME TO YOUR ASSIGNED MEETINGPLACE?

YES.

AND IF I TAKE YOU TO A PLACE OF SECRET WORK, WILL YOU DO AS I ASK?

YES.

THEN KNOW THIS, KAES POPPINGER: WHEN OUR WORK IS DONE, YOU WILL BE PUT ON THE FIRST PLANE TO ZURICH, AND YOU WILL FIND A NEW WAY TO USE YOUR GREAT TALENT, AND YOU WILL NEVER SET FOOT IN AMERICA AGAIN. IS IT AGREED?

YES. YES, I WILL DO ALL THAT.

THEN COME WITH ME NOW, LITTLE MAN OF GREAT ABILITY. COME WITH ME NOW...AND BEGIN THE SECOND CHANCE FOR YOUR LIFE.

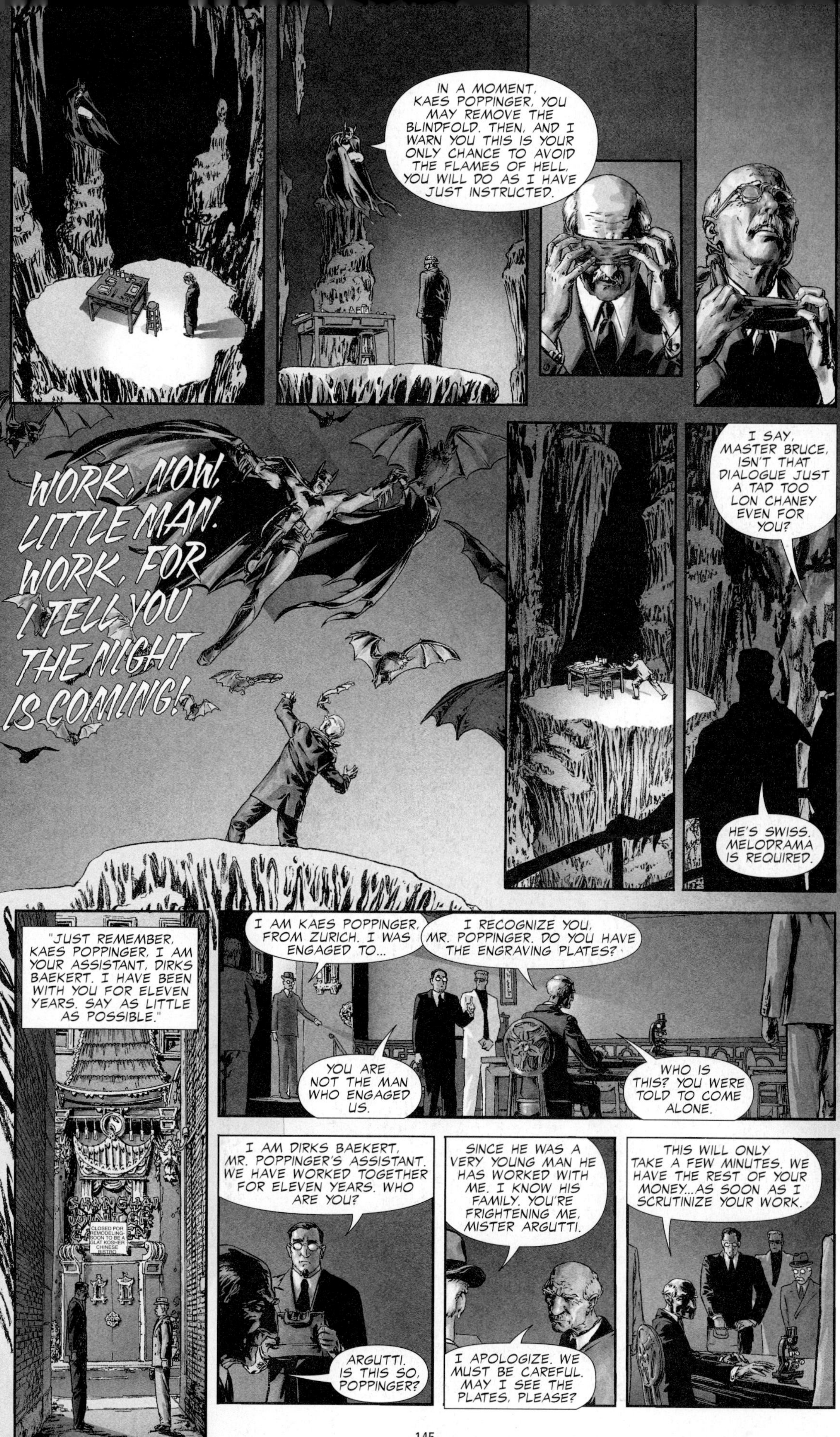
IN A MOMENT, KAES POPPINGER, YOU MAY REMOVE THE BLINDFOLD. THEN, AND I WARN YOU THIS IS YOUR ONLY CHANCE TO AVOID THE FLAMES OF HELL, YOU WILL DO AS I HAVE JUST INSTRUCTED.
WORK, NOW, LITTLE MAN. WORK, FOR I TELL YOU THE NIGHT IS COMING!
I SAY, MASTER BRUCE, ISN'T THAT DIALOGUE JUST A TAD TOO LON CHANEY EVEN FOR YOU?
HE'S SWISS. MELODRAMA IS REQUIRED.
"JUST REMEMBER, KAES POPPINGER, I AM YOUR ASSISTANT, DIRKS BAEKERT. I HAVE BEEN WITH YOU FOR ELEVEN YEARS. SAY AS LITTLE AS POSSIBLE."
SHANGHAI
CLOSED POR REMODELING- SOON TO BE A GLAT KOSHER CHINESE BISTRO
I AM KAES POPPINGER, FROM ZURICH. I WAS ENGAGED TO...
I RECOGNIZE YOU, MR. POPPINGER. DO YOU HAVE THE ENGRAVING PLATES?
YOU ARE NOT THE MAN WHO ENGAGED US.
WHO IS THIS? YOU WERE TOLD TO COME ALONE.
I AM DIRKS BAEKERT, MR. POPPINGER'S ASSISTANT. WE HAVE WORKED TOGETHER FOR ELEVEN YEARS. WHO ARE YOU?
ARGUTTI. IS THIS SO, POPPINGER?
SINCE HE WAS A VERY YOUNG MAN HE HAS WORKED WITH ME. I KNOW HIS FAMILY. YOU'RE FRIGHTENING ME, MISTER ARGUTTI.
I APOLOGIZE. WE MUST BE CAREFUL. MAY I SEE THE PLATES, PLEASE?
THIS WILL ONLY TAKE A FEW MINUTES. WE HAVE THE REST OF YOUR MONEY...AS SOON AS I SCRUTINIZE YOUR WORK.

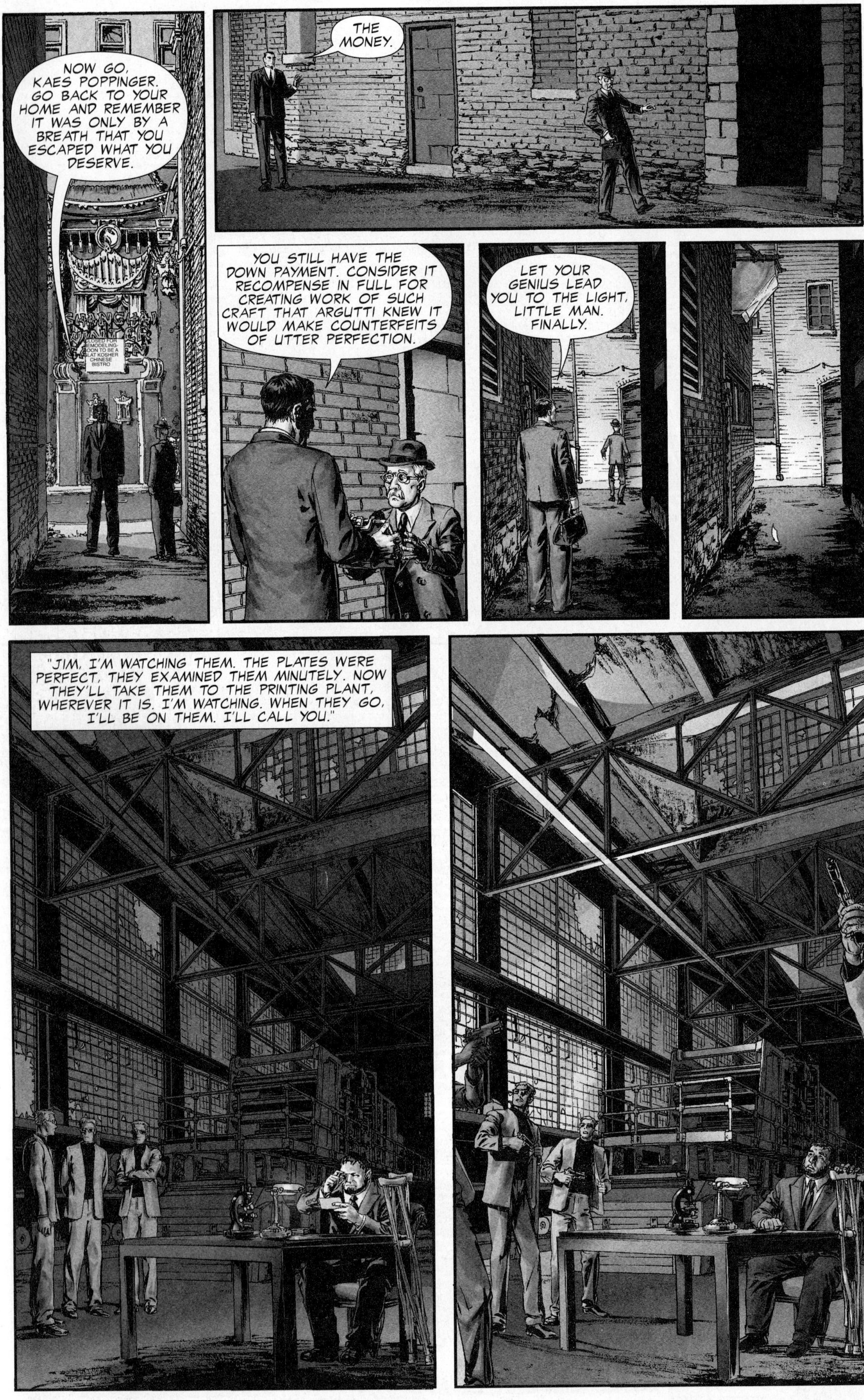
NOW GO, KAES POPPINGER. GO BACK TO YOUR HOME AND REMEMBER IT WAS ONLY BY A BREATH THAT YOU ESCAPED WHAT YOU DESERVE.
SHANGHAI
CLOSED FOR REMODELING- SOON TO BE A GLAT KOSHER CHINESE BISTRO
THE MONEY.
YOU STILL HAVE THE DOWN PAYMENT. CONSIDER IT RECOMPENSE IN FULL FOR CREATING WORK OF SUCH CRAFT THAT ARGUTTI KNEW IT WOULD MAKE COUNTERFEITS OF UTTER PERFECTION.
LET YOUR GENIUS LEAD YOU TO THE LIGHT, LITTLE MAN. FINALLY.
"JIM, I'M WATCHING THEM. THE PLATES WERE PERFECT, THEY EXAMINED THEM MINUTELY. NOW THEY'LL TAKE THEM TO THE PRINTING PLANT, WHEREVER IT IS. I'M WATCHING. WHEN THEY GO, I'LL BE ON THEM. I'LL CALL YOU."

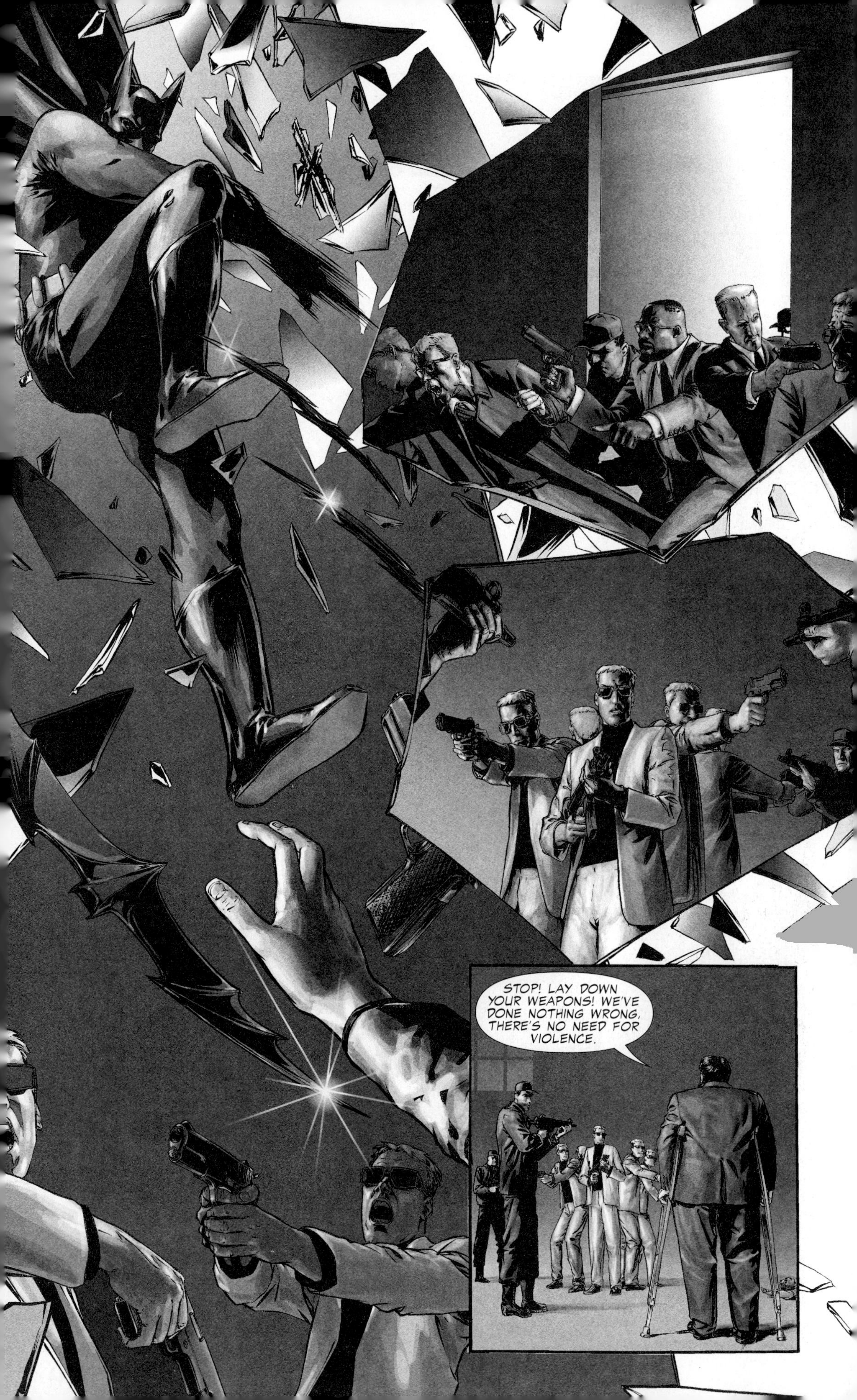
STOP! LAY DOWN YOUR WEAPONS! WE'VE DONE NOTHING WRONG, THERE'S NO NEED FOR VIOLENCE.

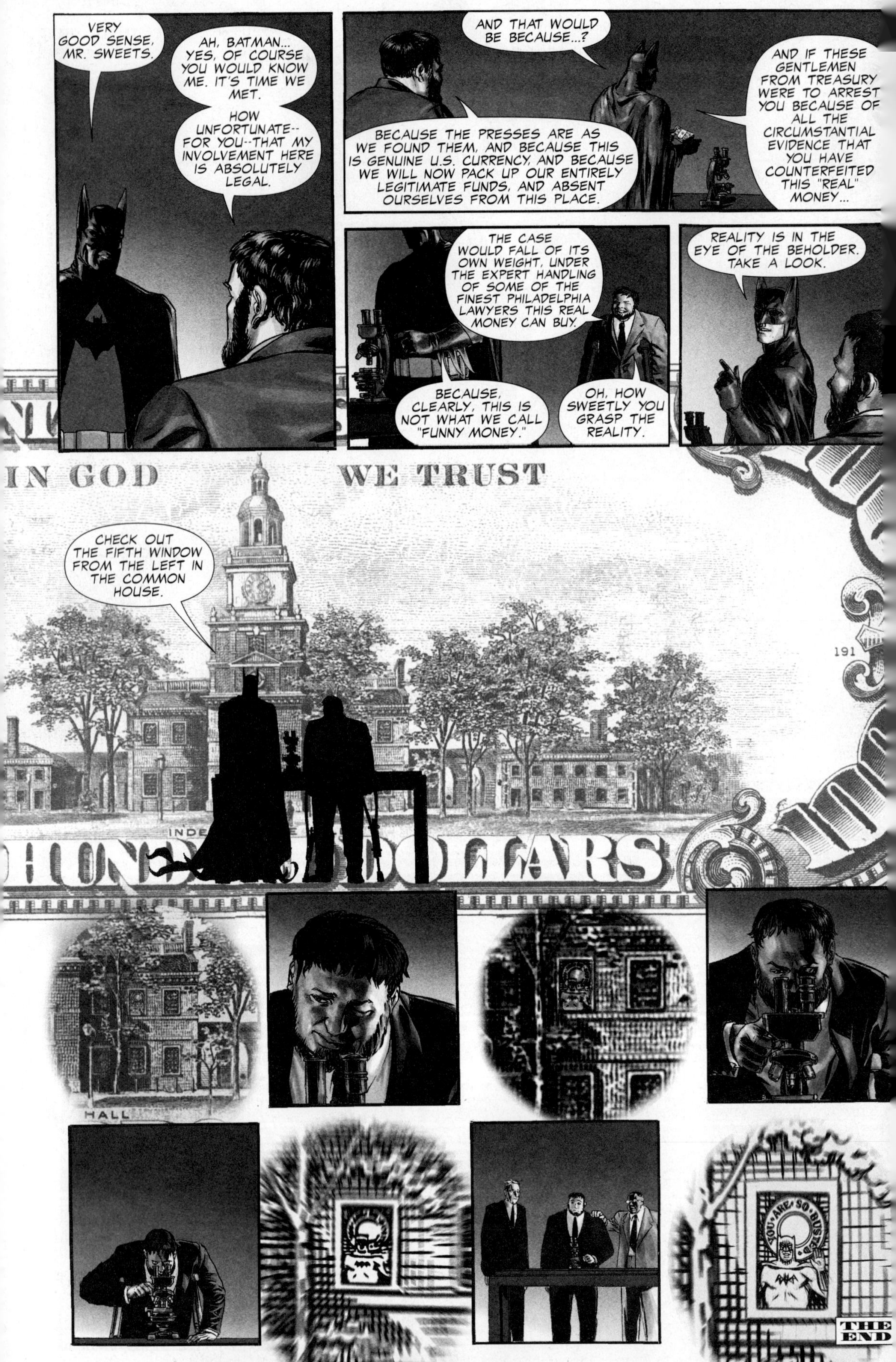
VERY GOOD SENSE, MR. SWEETS.
AH, BATMAN... YES, OF COURSE YOU WOULD KNOW ME. IT'S TIME WE MET.
HOW UNFORTUNATE-- FOR YOU--THAT MY INVOLVEMENT HERE IS ABSOLUTELY LEGAL.
AND THAT WOULD BE BECAUSE...?
BECAUSE THE PRESSES ARE AS WE FOUND THEM, AND BECAUSE THIS IS GENUINE U.S. CURRENCY, AND BECAUSE WE WILL NOW PACK UP OUR ENTIRELY LEGITIMATE FUNDS, AND ABSENT OURSELVES FROM THIS PLACE.
AND IF THESE GENTLEMEN FROM TREASURY WERE TO ARREST YOU BECAUSE OF ALL THE CIRCUMSTANTIAL EVIDENCE THAT YOU HAVE COUNTERFEITED THIS "REAL" MONEY...
THE CASE WOULD FALL OF ITS OWN WEIGHT, UNDER THE EXPERT HANDLING OF SOME OF THE FINEST PHILADELPHIA LAWYERS THIS REAL MONEY CAN BUY.
BECAUSE, CLEARLY, THIS IS NOT WHAT WE CALL "FUNNY MONEY."
OH, HOW SWEETLY YOU GRASP THE REALITY.
REALITY IS IN THE EYE OF THE BEHOLDER. TAKE A LOOK.
IN GOD WE TRUST
CHECK OUT THE FIFTH WINDOW FROM THE LEFT IN THE COMMON HOUSE.
191
DOLLARS
HALL
YOU·ARE·SO·BUSTED·
THE END

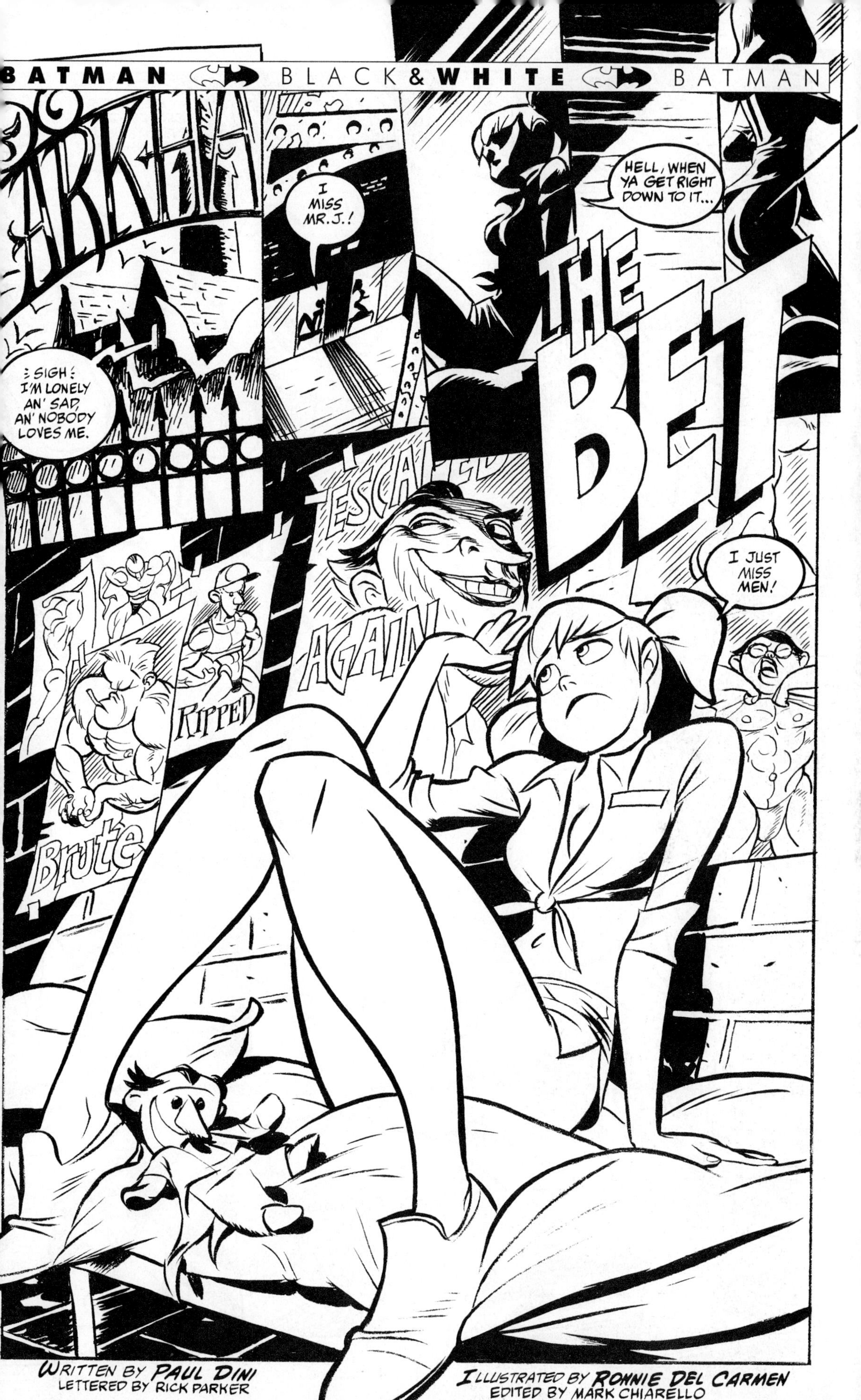
ARKHAM
SIGH I'M LONELY AN' SAD, AN' NOBODY LOVES ME.
I MISS MR. J.!
HELL, WHEN YA GET RIGHT DOWN TO IT...
THE BET
ESCAPED AGAIN
RIPPED
Brute
I JUST MISS MEN!

WRITTEN BY PAUL DINI
LETTERED BY RICK PARKER
ILLUSTRATED BY RONNIE DEL CARMEN
EDITED BY MARK CHIARELLO

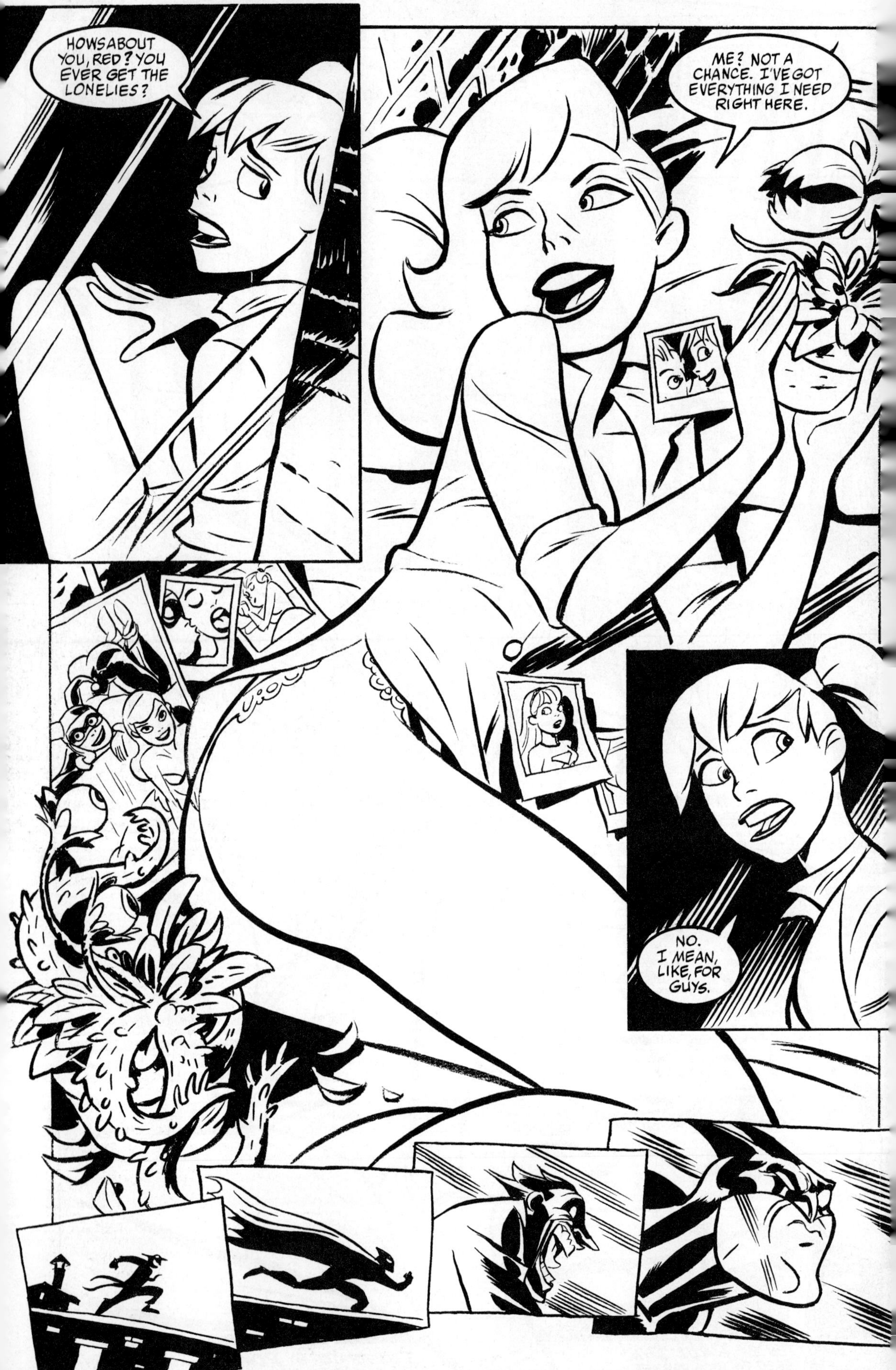
HOWSABOUT YOU, RED? YOU EVER GET THE LONELIES?
ME? NOT A CHANCE. I'VE GOT EVERYTHING I NEED RIGHT HERE.
NO. I MEAN, LIKE, FOR GUYS.

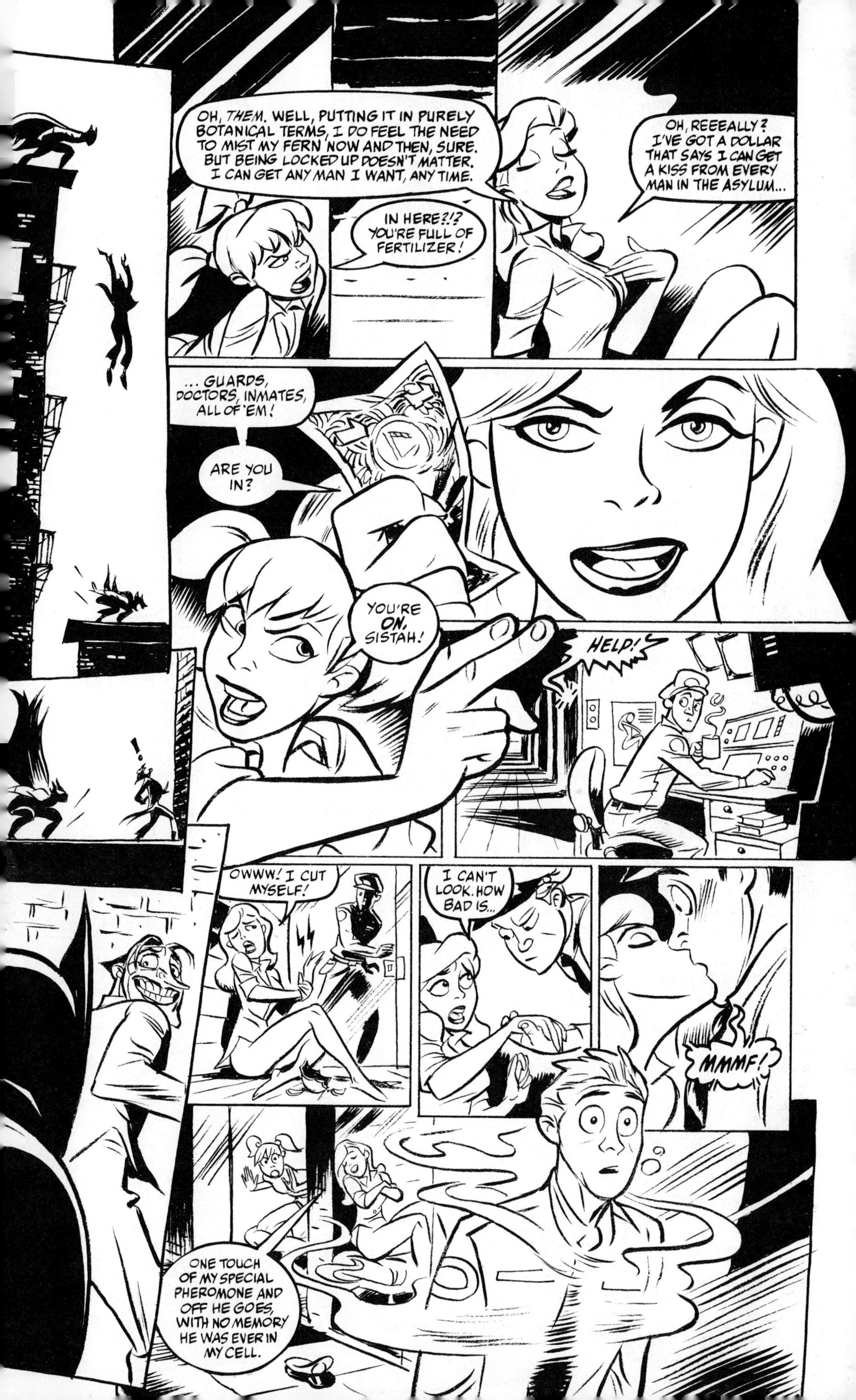
OH, THEM. WELL, PUTTING IT IN PURELY BOTANICAL TERMS, I DO FEEL THE NEED TO MIST MY FERN NOW AND THEN, SURE. BUT BEING LOCKED UP DOESN'T MATTER. I CAN GET ANY MAN I WANT, ANY TIME.
IN HERE?!? YOU'RE FULL OF FERTILIZER!
OH, REEEALLY? I'VE GOT A DOLLAR THAT SAYS I CAN GET A KISS FROM EVERY MAN IN THE ASYLUM...
... GUARDS, DOCTORS, INMATES, ALL OF 'EM!
ARE YOU IN?
YOU'RE ON, SISTAH!
HELP!
OWWW! I CUT MYSELF!
I CAN'T LOOK. HOW BAD IS...
MMMF!
ONE TOUCH OF MY SPECIAL PHEROMONE AND OFF HE GOES, WITH NO MEMORY HE WAS EVER IN MY CELL.

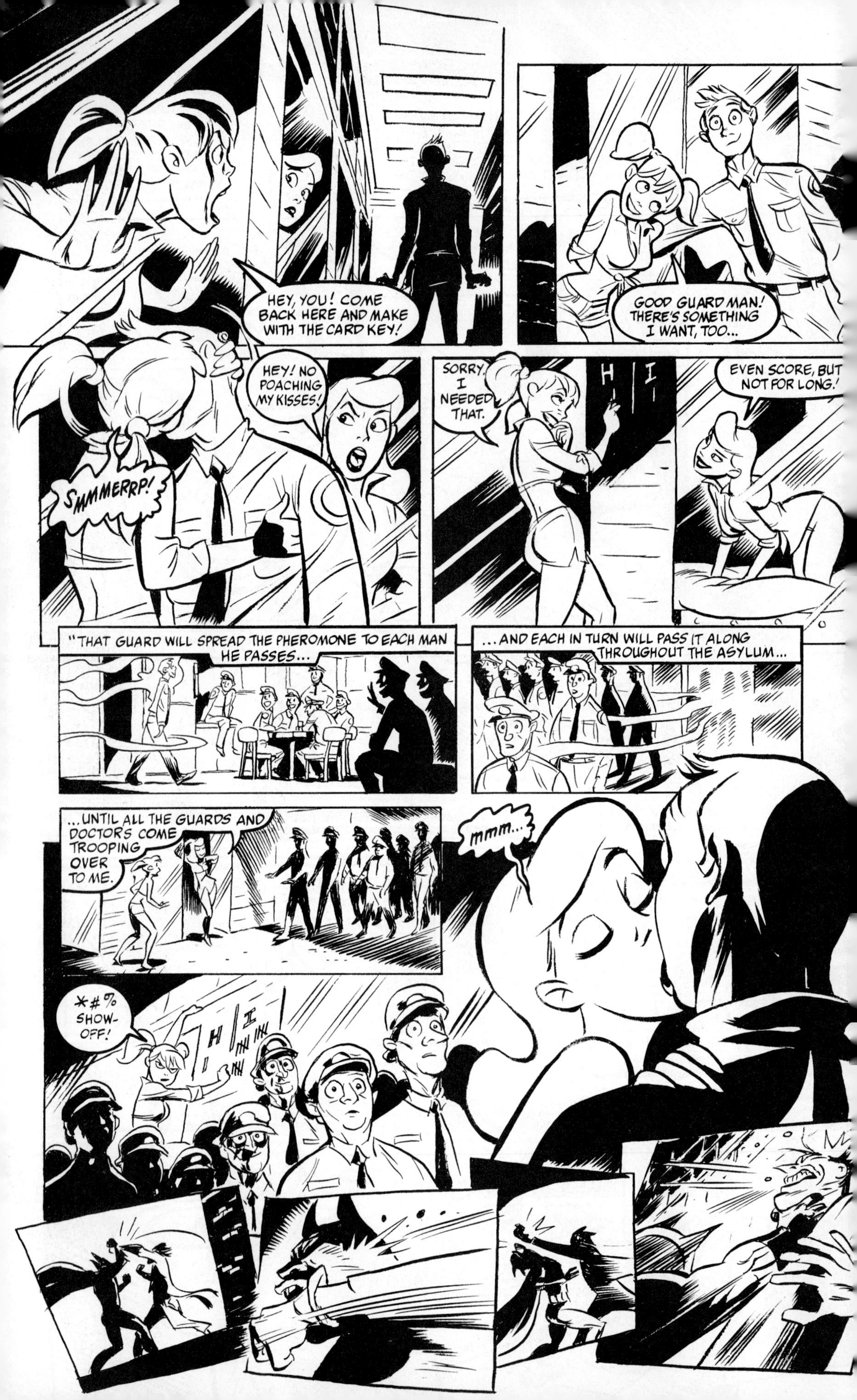
HEY, YOU! COME BACK HERE AND MAKE WITH THE CARD KEY!
GOOD GUARD MAN! THERE'S SOMETHING I WANT, TOO...
SMMMERRP!
HEY! NO POACHING MY KISSES!
SORRY. I NEEDED THAT.
EVEN SCORE, BUT NOT FOR LONG!
"THAT GUARD WILL SPREAD THE PHEROMONE TO EACH MAN HE PASSES...
...AND EACH IN TURN WILL PASS IT ALONG THROUGHOUT THE ASYLUM...
...UNTIL ALL THE GUARDS AND DOCTORS COME TROOPING OVER TO ME.
mmm...
*#% SHOW-OFF!

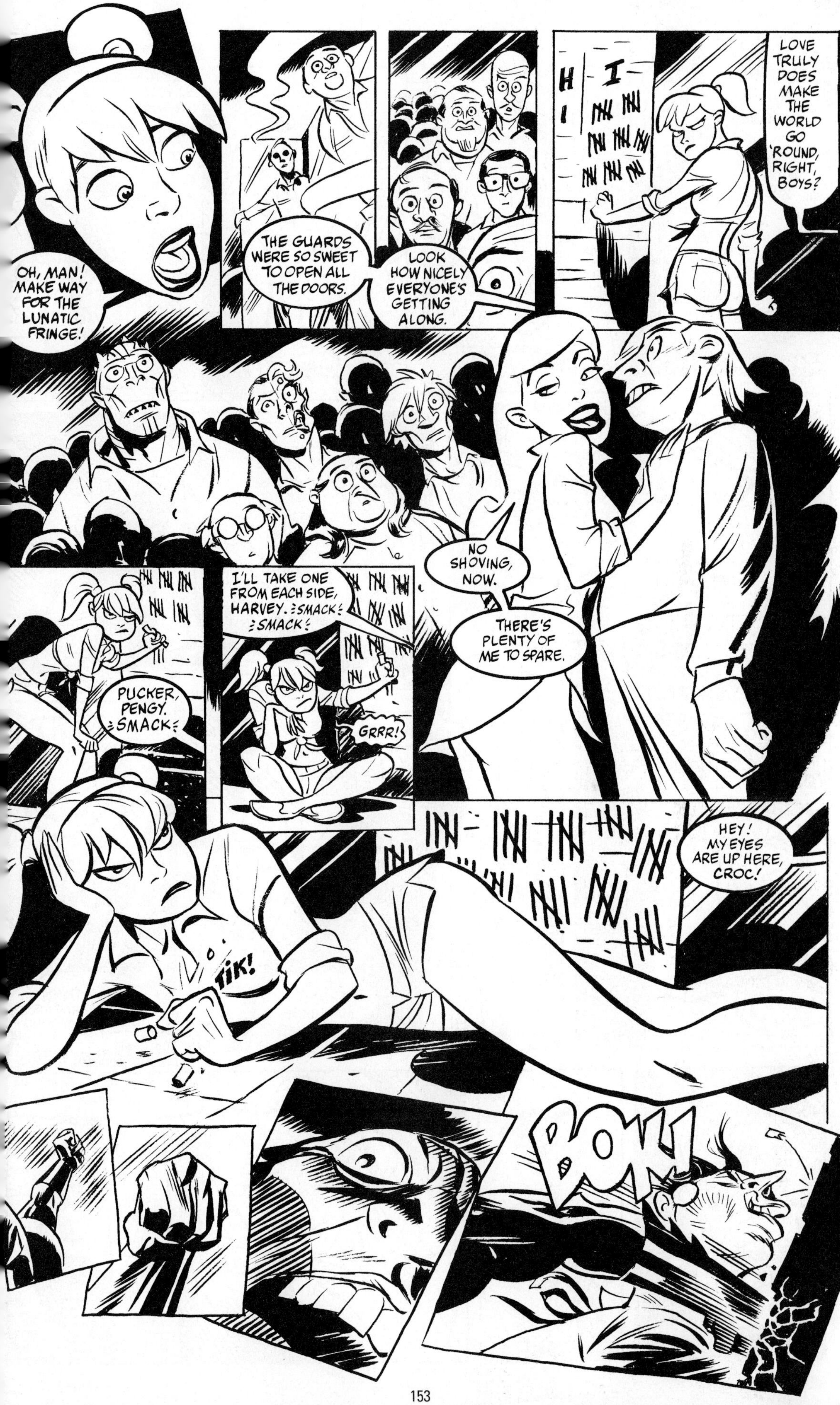
OH, MAN! MAKE WAY FOR THE LUNATIC FRINGE!
THE GUARDS WERE SO SWEET TO OPEN ALL THE DOORS.
LOOK HOW NICELY EVERYONE'S GETTING ALONG.
HI
LOVE TRULY DOES MAKE THE WORLD GO 'ROUND, RIGHT, BOYS?
NO SHOVING, NOW.
THERE'S PLENTY OF ME TO SPARE.
PUCKER, PENGY. SMACK
I'LL TAKE ONE FROM EACH SIDE, HARVEY. SMACK SMACK
GRRR!
HEY! MY EYES ARE UP HERE, CROC!
TIK!
BOK!

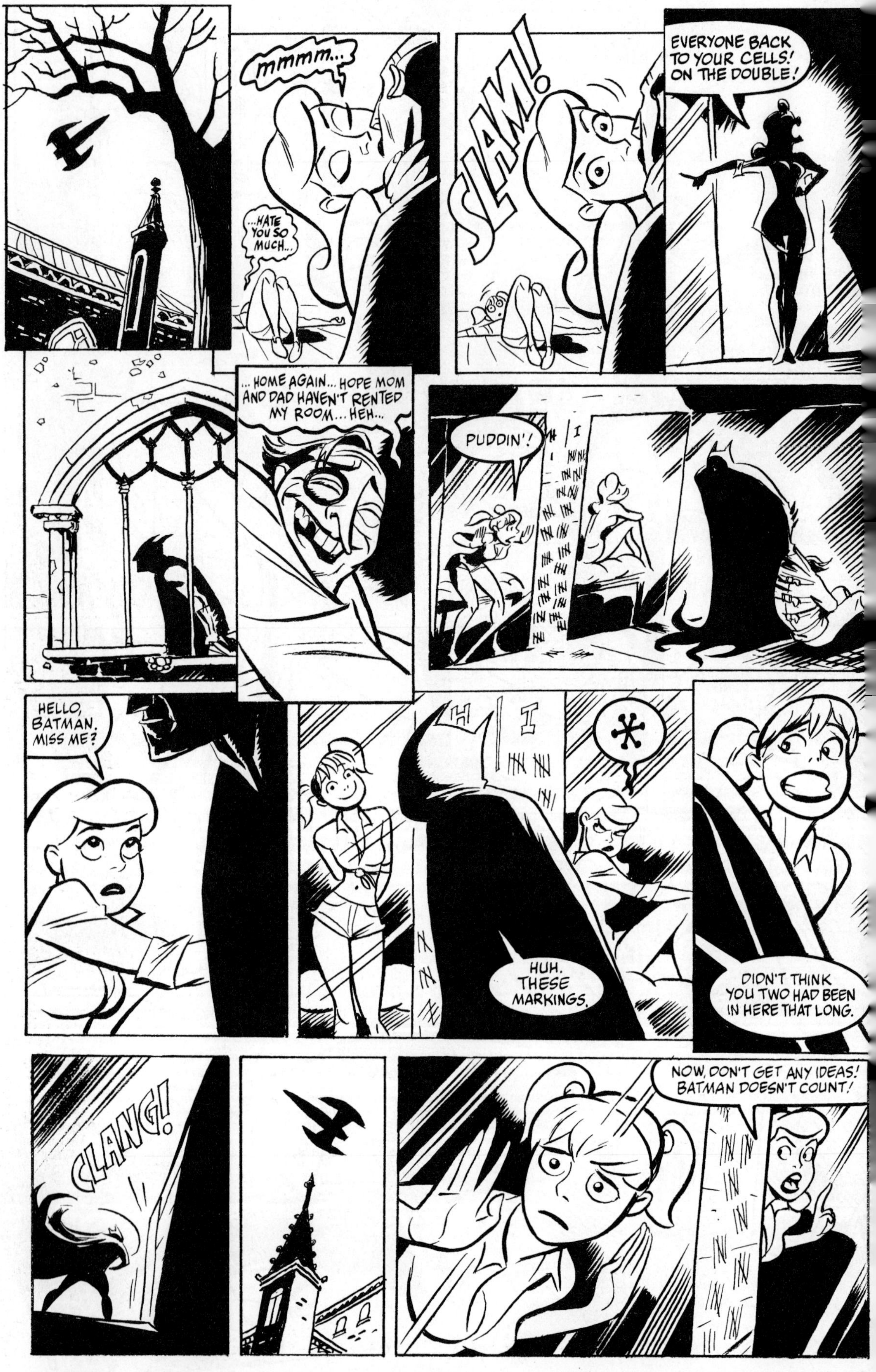
mmmm...
...HATE YOU SO MUCH...
SLAM!
EVERYONE BACK TO YOUR CELLS! ON THE DOUBLE!
...HOME AGAIN... HOPE MOM AND DAD HAVEN'T RENTED MY ROOM... HEH...
PUDDIN'!
HELLO, BATMAN. MISS ME?
HUH. THESE MARKINGS.
DIDN'T THINK YOU TWO HAD BEEN IN HERE THAT LONG.
CLANG!
NOW, DON'T GET ANY IDEAS! BATMAN DOESN'T COUNT!

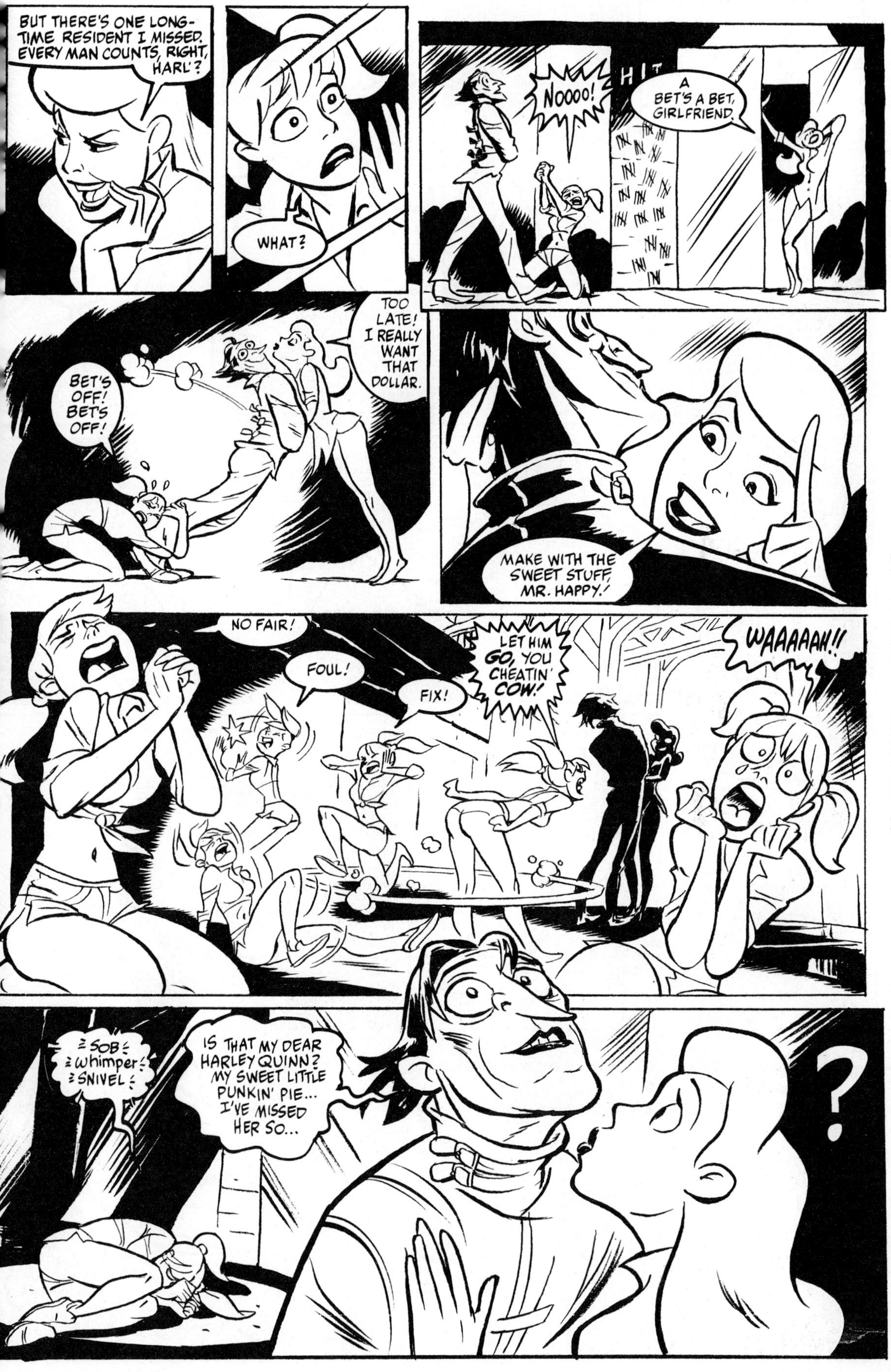

BUT THERE'S ONE LONG-TIME RESIDENT I MISSED. EVERY MAN COUNTS, RIGHT, HARL'?
WHAT?
NOOOO!
A BET'S A BET, GIRLFRIEND.
BET'S OFF! BET'S OFF!
TOO LATE! I REALLY WANT THAT DOLLAR.
MAKE WITH THE SWEET STUFF, MR. HAPPY!
NO FAIR!
FOUL!
FIX!
LET HIM GO, YOU CHEATIN' COW!
WAAAAAH!!
SOB whimper SNIVEL
IS THAT MY DEAR HARLEY QUINN? MY SWEET LITTLE PUNKIN' PIE... I'VE MISSED HER SO...
?

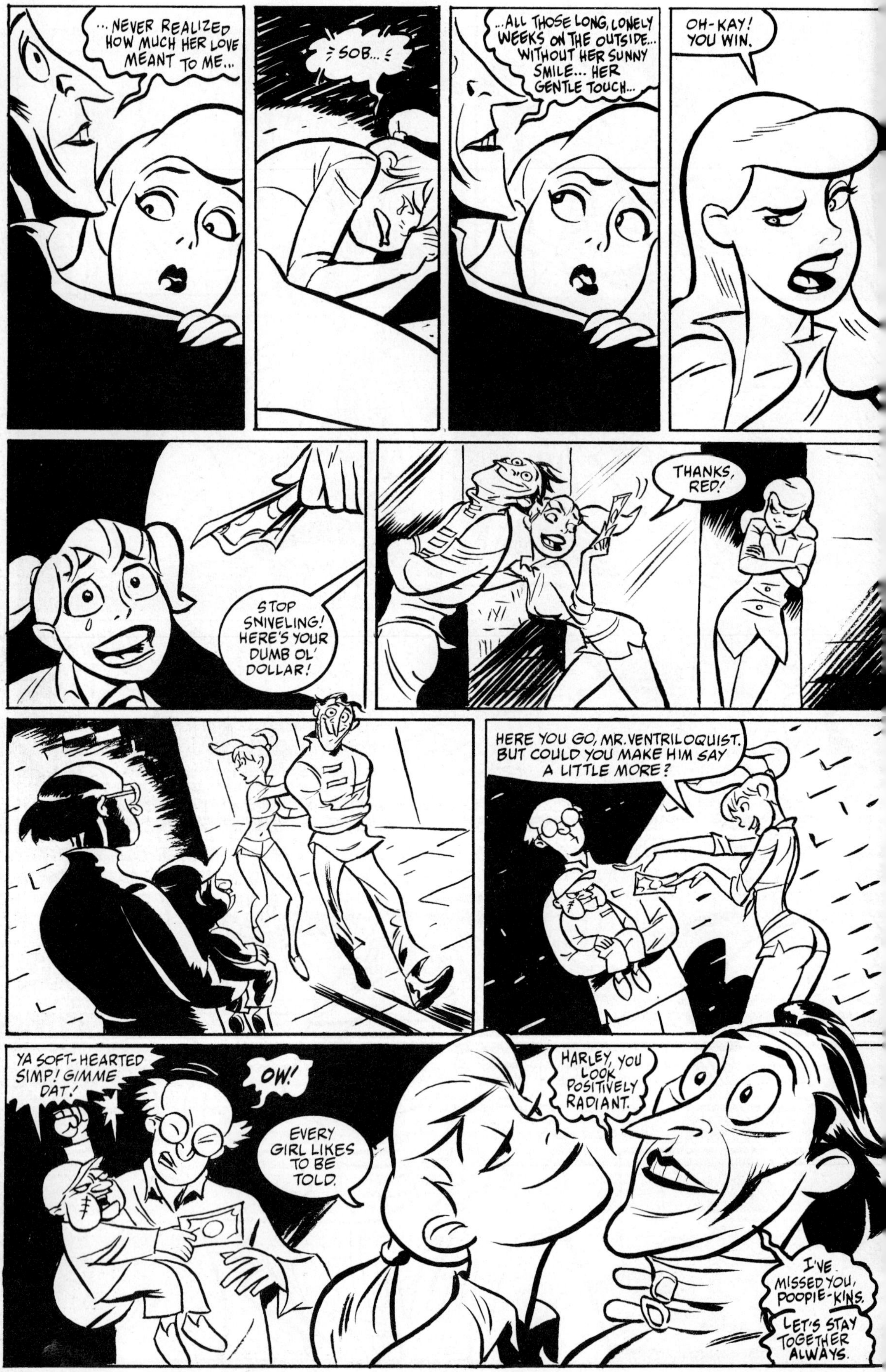
...NEVER REALIZED HOW MUCH HER LOVE MEANT TO ME...
SOB...
...ALL THOSE LONG, LONELY WEEKS ON THE OUTSIDE... WITHOUT HER SUNNY SMILE... HER GENTLE TOUCH...
OH-KAY! YOU WIN.
STOP SNIVELING! HERE'S YOUR DUMB OL' DOLLAR!
THANKS, RED!
HERE YOU GO, MR. VENTRILOQUIST. BUT COULD YOU MAKE HIM SAY A LITTLE MORE?
YA SOFT-HEARTED SIMP! GIMME DAT!
OW!
EVERY GIRL LIKES TO BE TOLD.
HARLEY, YOU LOOK POSITIVELY RADIANT.
I'VE MISSED YOU, POOPIE-KINS.
LET'S STAY TOGETHER ALWAYS.

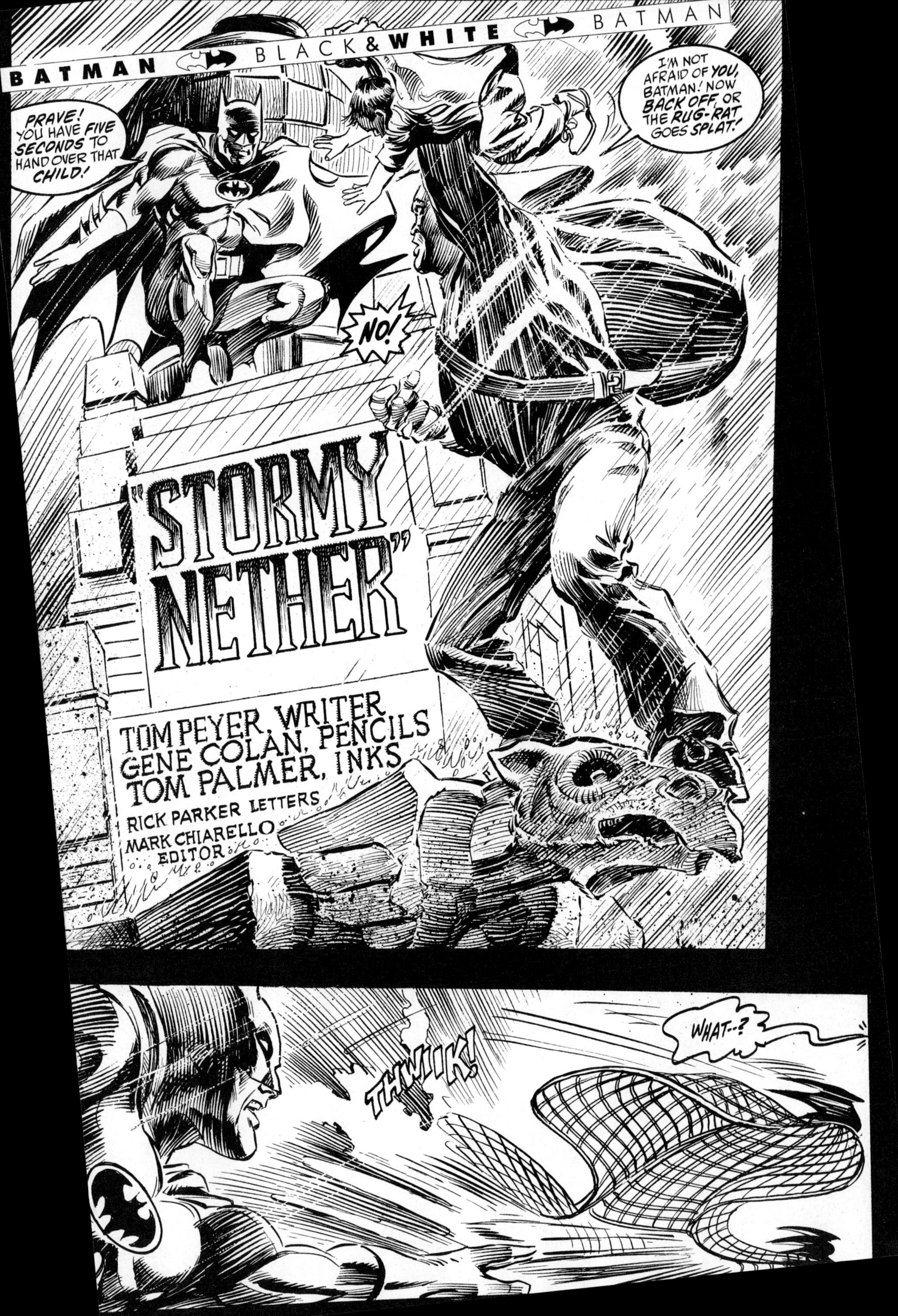

BATMAN BLACK & WHITE BATMAN
PRAVE! YOU HAVE FIVE SECONDS TO HAND OVER THAT CHILD!
I'M NOT AFRAID OF YOU, BATMAN! NOW BACK OFF, OR THE RUG-RAT GOES SPLAT!
NO!
"STORMY NETHER"
TOM PEYER, WRITER
GENE COLAN, PENCILS
TOM PALMER, INKS
RICK PARKER LETTERS
MARK CHIARELLO EDITOR
THWIIK!
WHAT--?

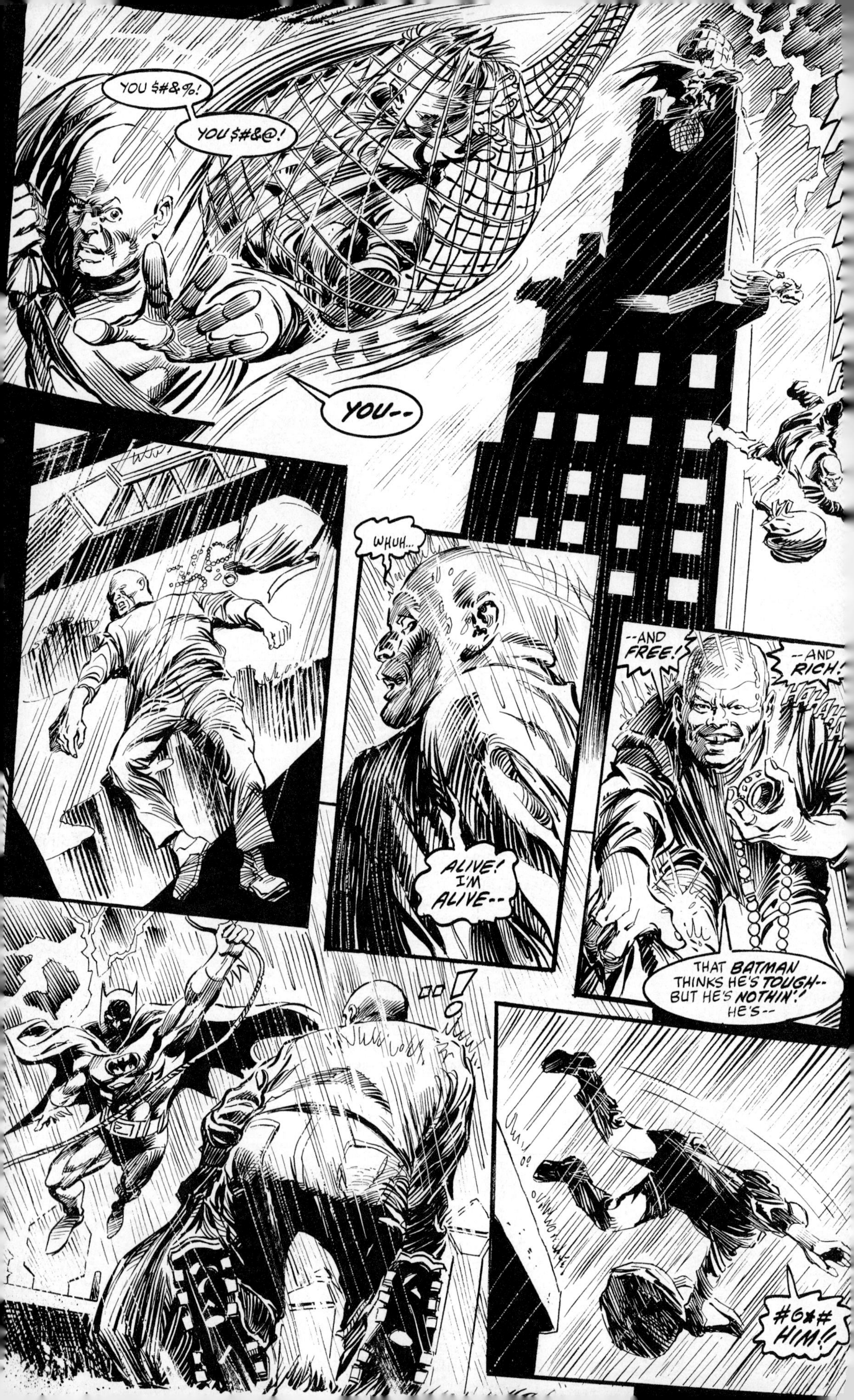
YOU $#&%!
YOU $#&@!
YOU--
WHUH...
ALIVE! I'M ALIVE--
--AND FREE!
--AND RICH!
THAT BATMAN THINKS HE'S TOUGH-- BUT HE'S NOTHIN'! HE'S--
#@*# HIM!!

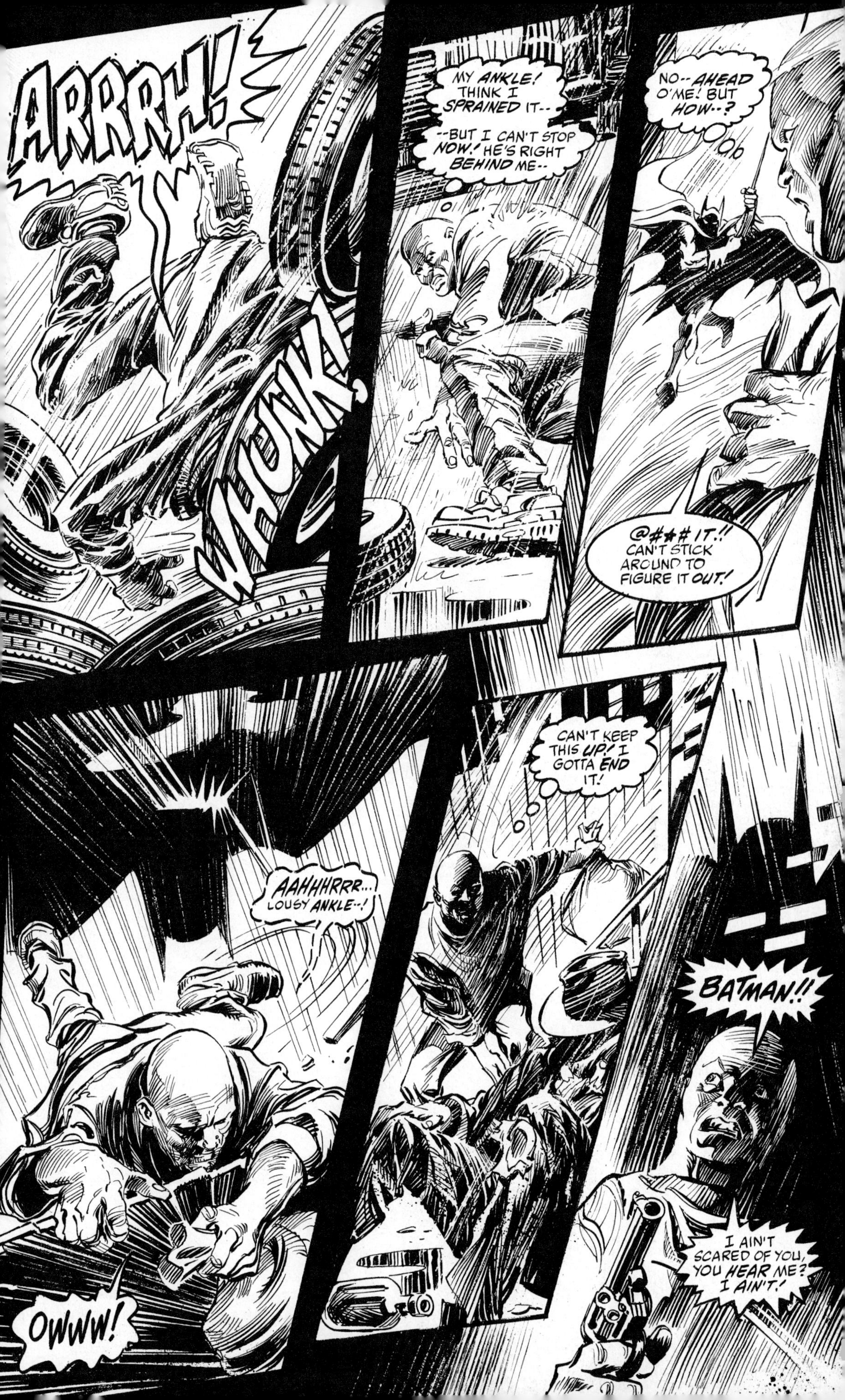

ARRRH!
WHUNK!
MY ANKLE! THINK I SPRAINED IT--
--BUT I CAN'T STOP NOW! HE'S RIGHT BEHIND ME--
NO-- AHEAD O'ME! BUT HOW--?
@#*# IT!! CAN'T STICK AROUND TO FIGURE IT OUT!
AAHHHRRR... LOUSY ANKLE--!
OWWW!
CAN'T KEEP THIS UP! I GOTTA END IT!
BATMAN!!
I AIN'T SCARED OF YOU, YOU HEAR ME? I AIN'T!

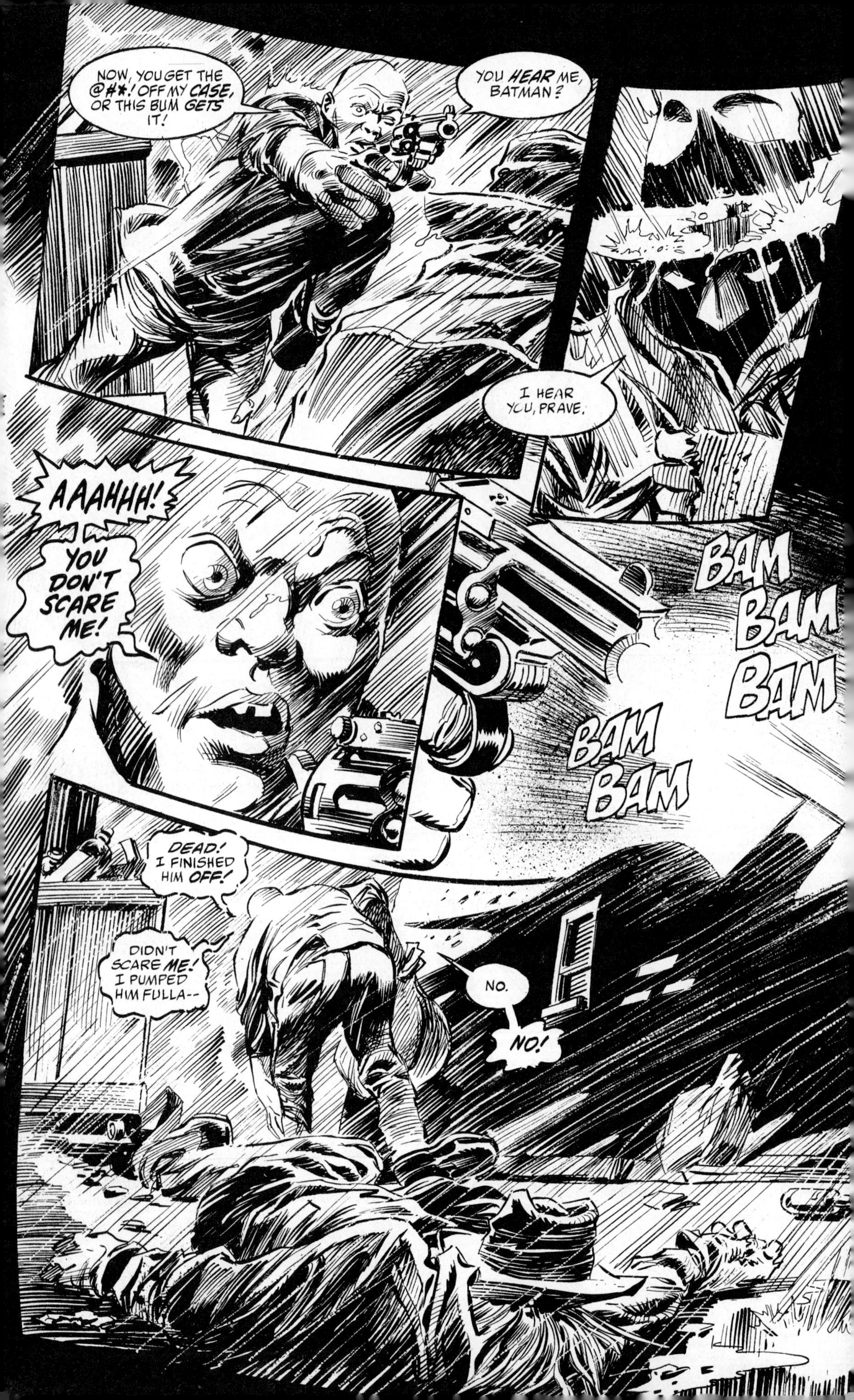
NOW, YOU GET THE @#*! OFF MY CASE, OR THIS BUM GETS IT!
YOU HEAR ME, BATMAN?
I HEAR YOU, PRAVE.
AAAHHH!
YOU DON'T SCARE ME!
BAM BAM BAM
BAM BAM
DEAD! I FINISHED HIM OFF!
DIDN'T SCARE ME! I PUMPED HIM FULLA--
NO.
NO!

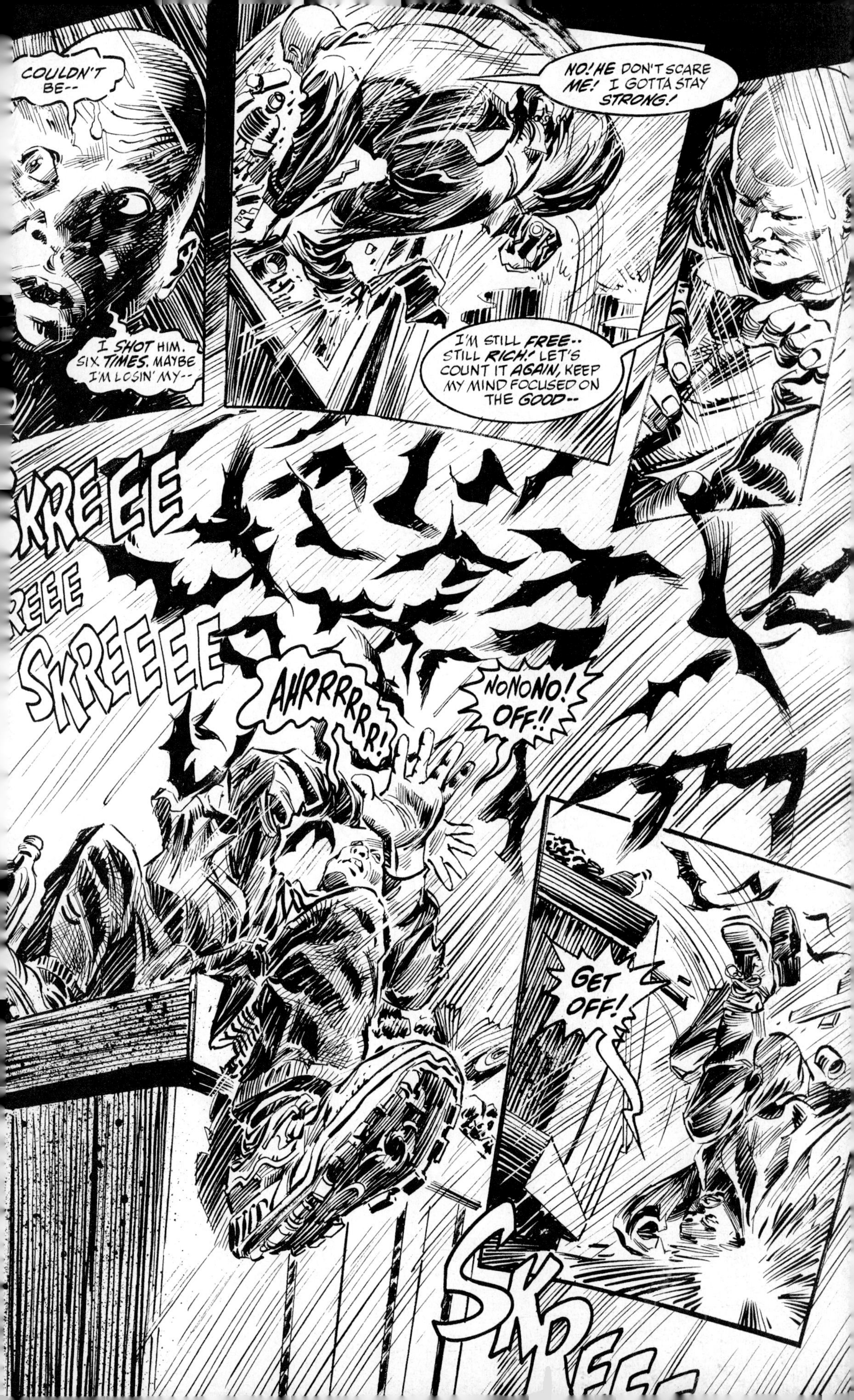
COULDN'T BE--
I SHOT HIM. SIX TIMES. MAYBE I'M LOSIN' MY--
NO! HE DON'T SCARE ME! I GOTTA STAY STRONG!
I'M STILL FREE-- STILL RICH! LET'S COUNT IT AGAIN, KEEP MY MIND FOCUSED ON THE GOOD--
SKREEE
REEE
SKREEEE
AHRRRRRRR!
NONONO! OFF!!
GET OFF!

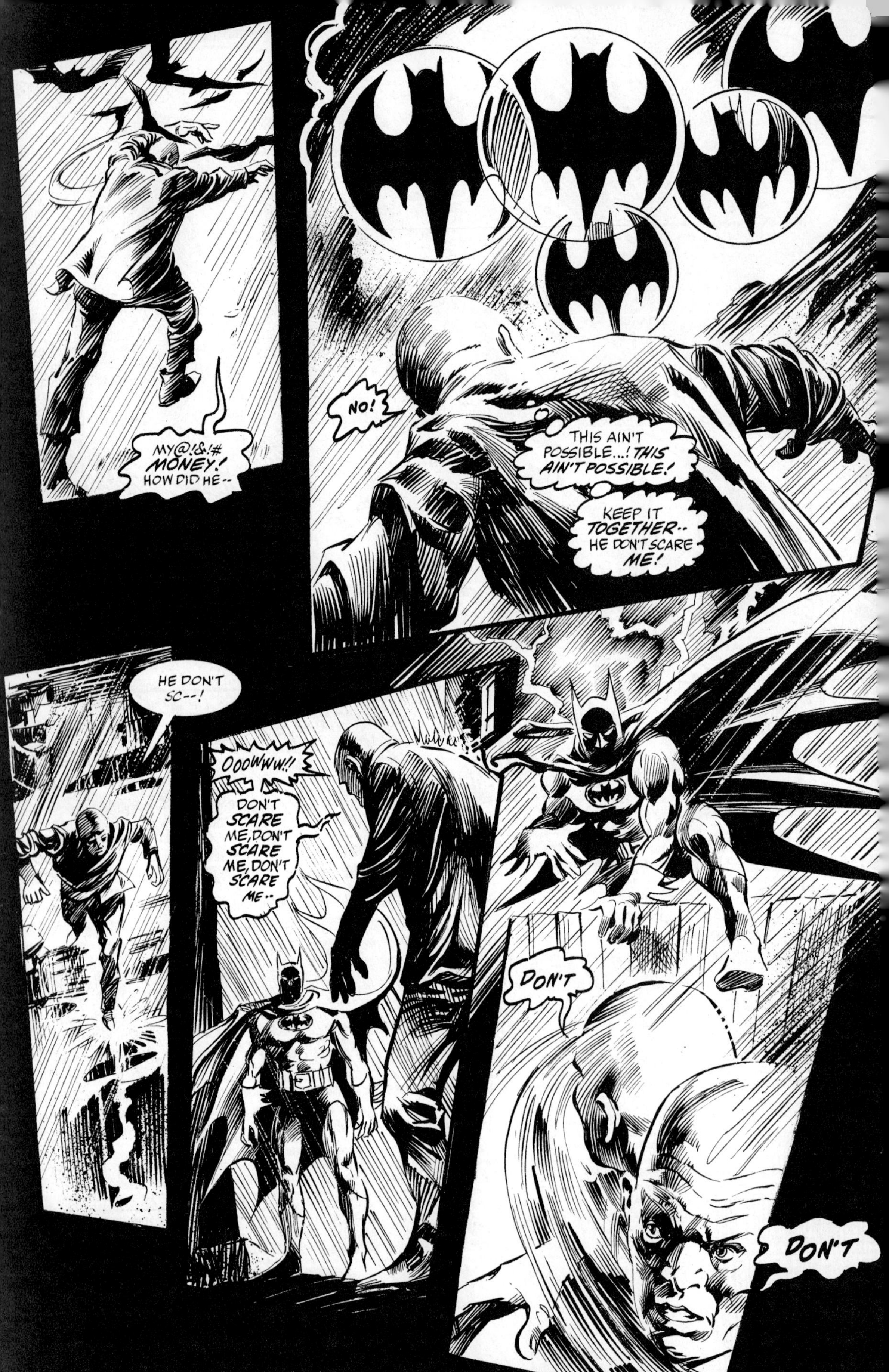
MY@!&!# MONEY! HOW DID HE--
NO!
THIS AIN'T POSSIBLE...! THIS AIN'T POSSIBLE!
KEEP IT TOGETHER.. HE DON'T SCARE ME!
HE DON'T SC--!
OOOWWW!!
DON'T SCARE ME, DON'T SCARE ME, DON'T SCARE ME..
DON'T
DON'T

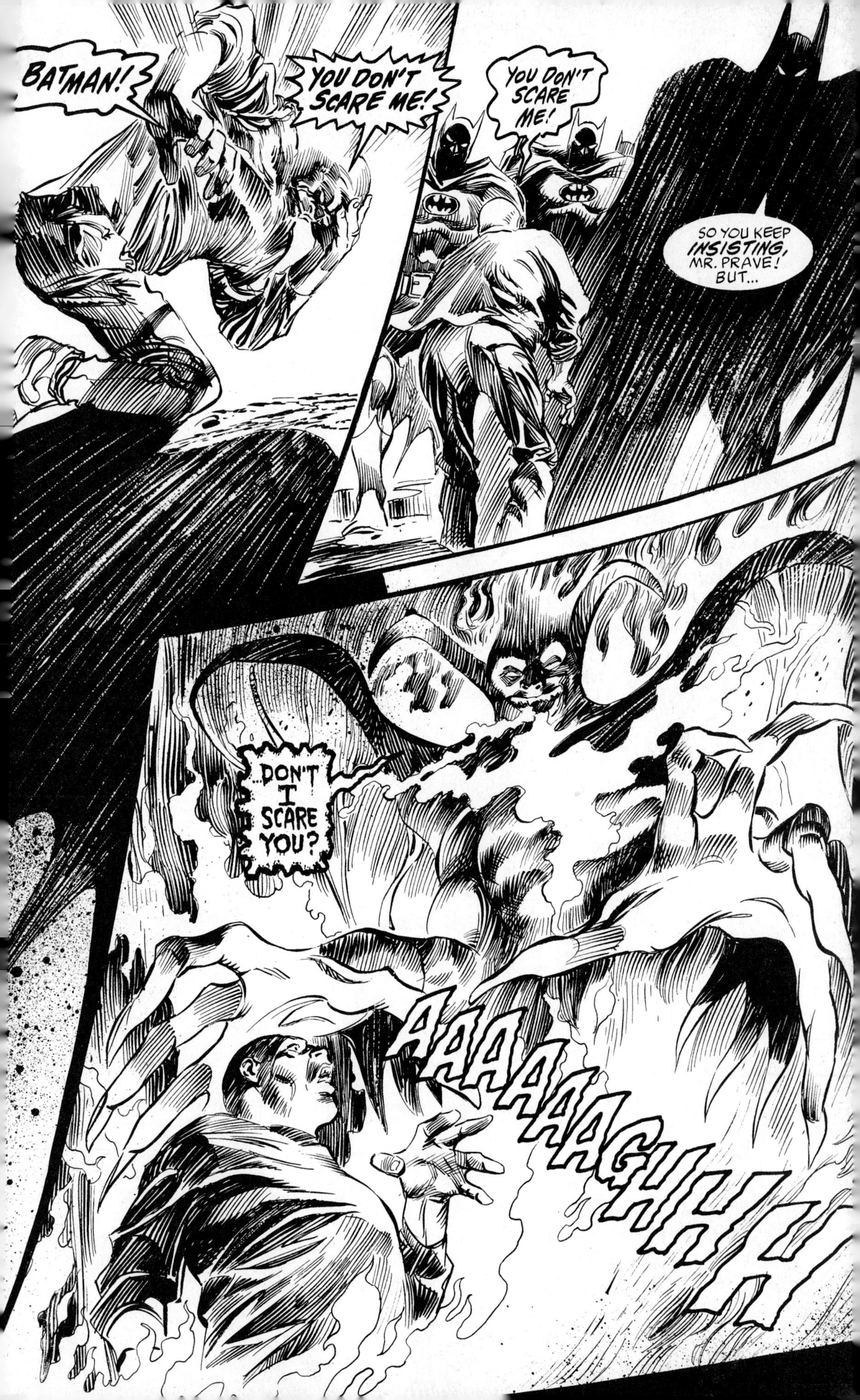
BATMAN!
YOU DON'T SCARE ME!
YOU DON'T SCARE ME!
SO YOU KEEP INSISTING, MR. PRAVE! BUT...
DON'T I SCARE YOU?
AAAAAAGHHH!

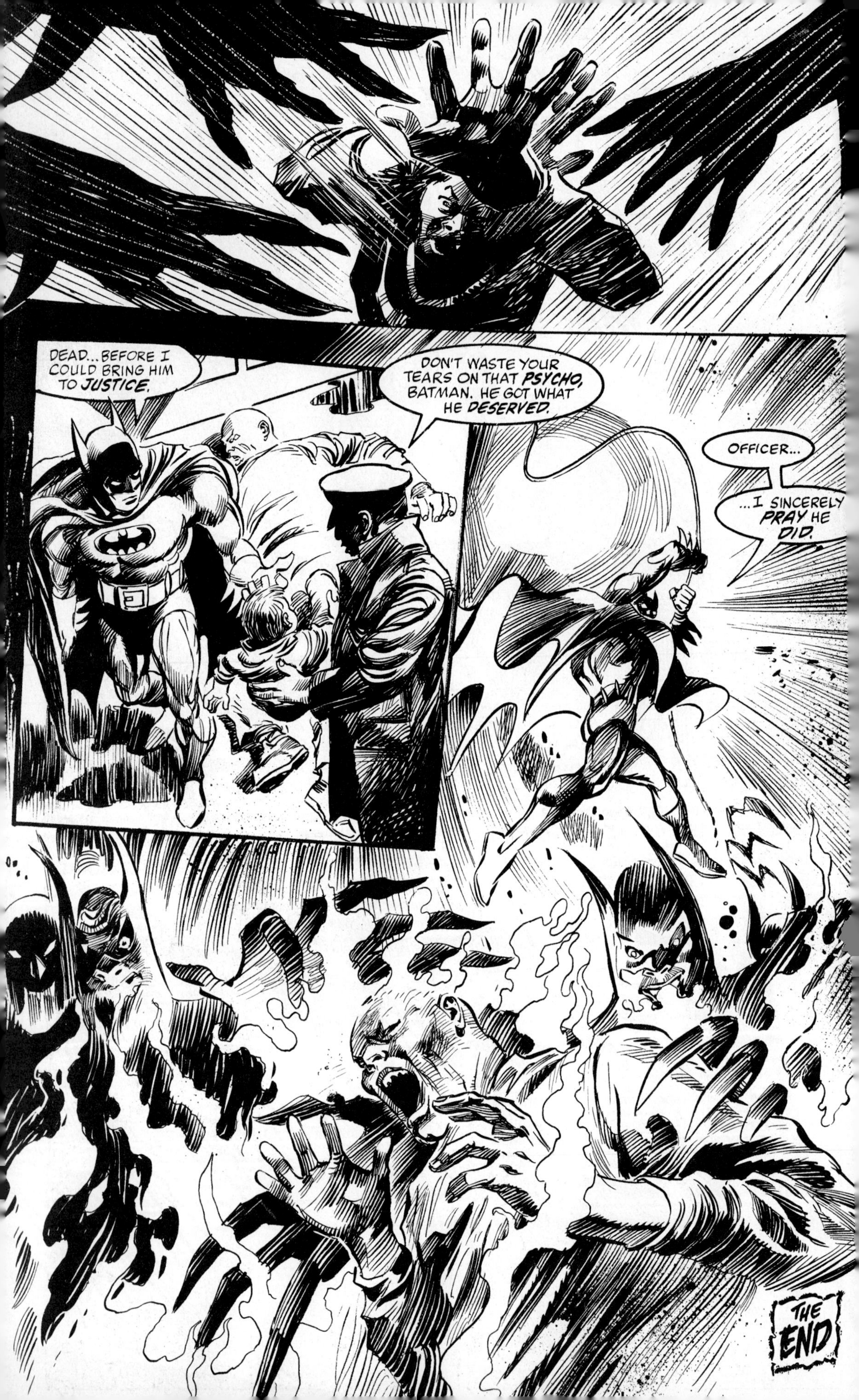

DEAD...BEFORE I COULD BRING HIM TO JUSTICE.
DON'T WASTE YOUR TEARS ON THAT PSYCHO, BATMAN. HE GOT WHAT HE DESERVED.
OFFICER...
...I SINCERELY PRAY HE DID.
THE END

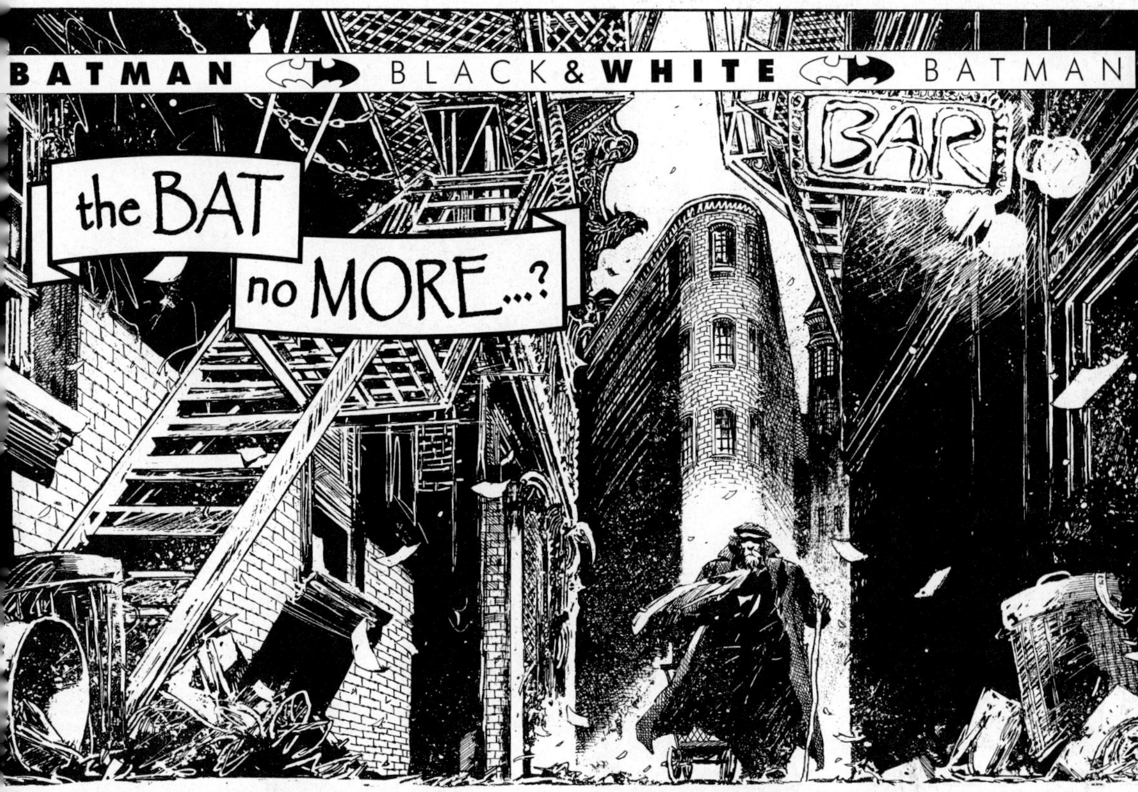
BATMAN BLACK & WHITE BATMAN
BAR
the BAT no MORE...?

script: Alan Grant / artist: Enrique Breccia / letters: Jack Morelli / editor: Mark Chiarello / Batman created by Bob Kane

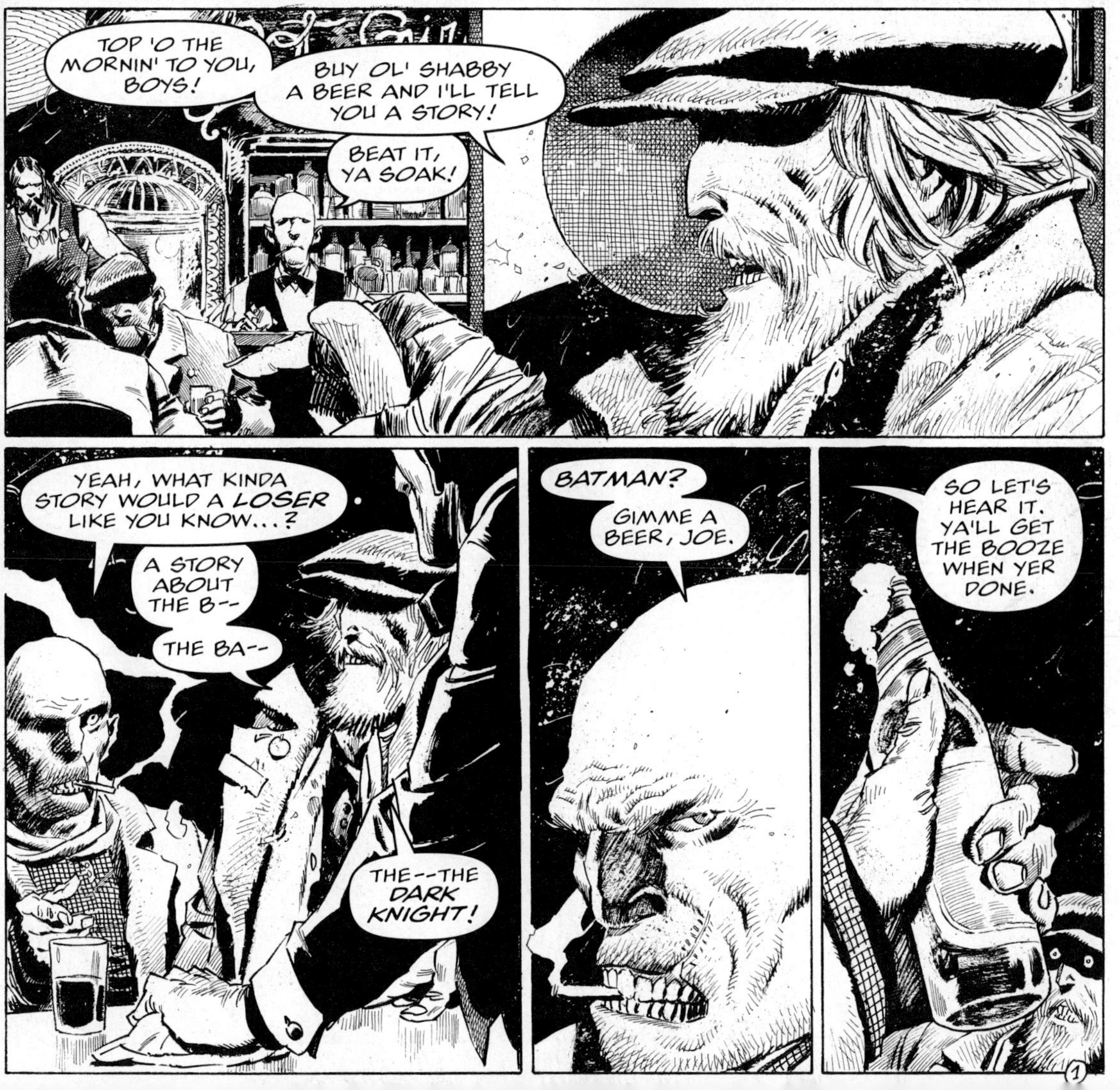
TOP 'O THE MORNIN' TO YOU, BOYS!
BUY OL' SHABBY A BEER AND I'LL TELL YOU A STORY!
BEAT IT, YA SOAK!
YEAH, WHAT KINDA STORY WOULD A *LOSER* LIKE YOU KNOW...?
A STORY ABOUT THE B--
THE BA--
THE--THE *DARK KNIGHT*!
BATMAN?
GIMME A BEER, JOE.
SO LET'S HEAR IT. YA'LL GET THE BOOZE WHEN YER DONE.
1

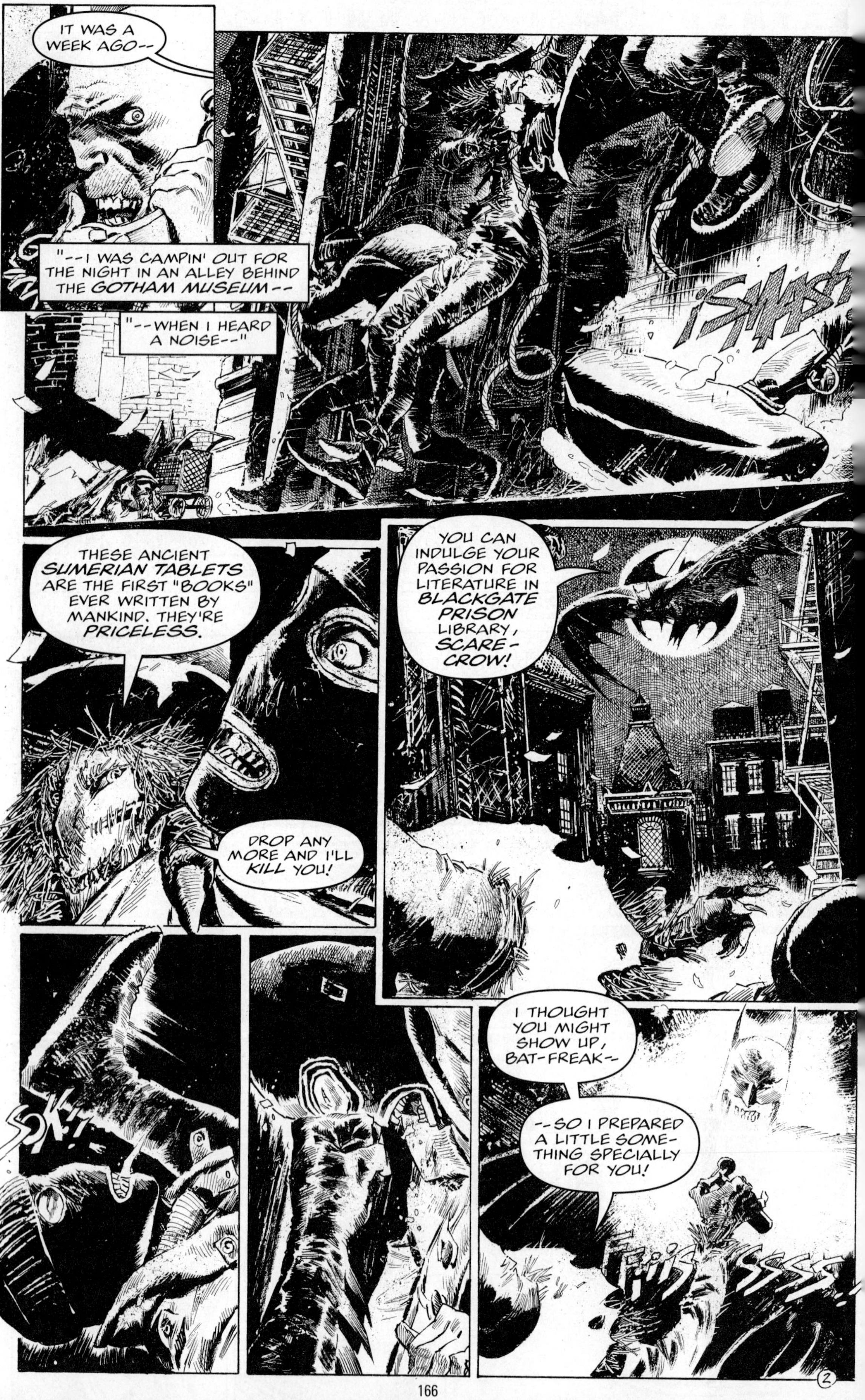
IT WAS A WEEK AGO--
"--I WAS CAMPIN' OUT FOR THE NIGHT IN AN ALLEY BEHIND THE GOTHAM MUSEUM--
"--WHEN I HEARD A NOISE--"
SMASH
THESE ANCIENT SUMERIAN TABLETS ARE THE FIRST "BOOKS" EVER WRITTEN BY MANKIND. THEY'RE PRICELESS.
DROP ANY MORE AND I'LL KILL YOU!
YOU CAN INDULGE YOUR PASSION FOR LITERATURE IN BLACKGATE PRISON LIBRARY, SCARE-CROW!
SOK!!
I THOUGHT YOU MIGHT SHOW UP, BAT-FREAK--
--SO I PREPARED A LITTLE SOME-THING SPECIALLY FOR YOU!
HISSSSS!!
2

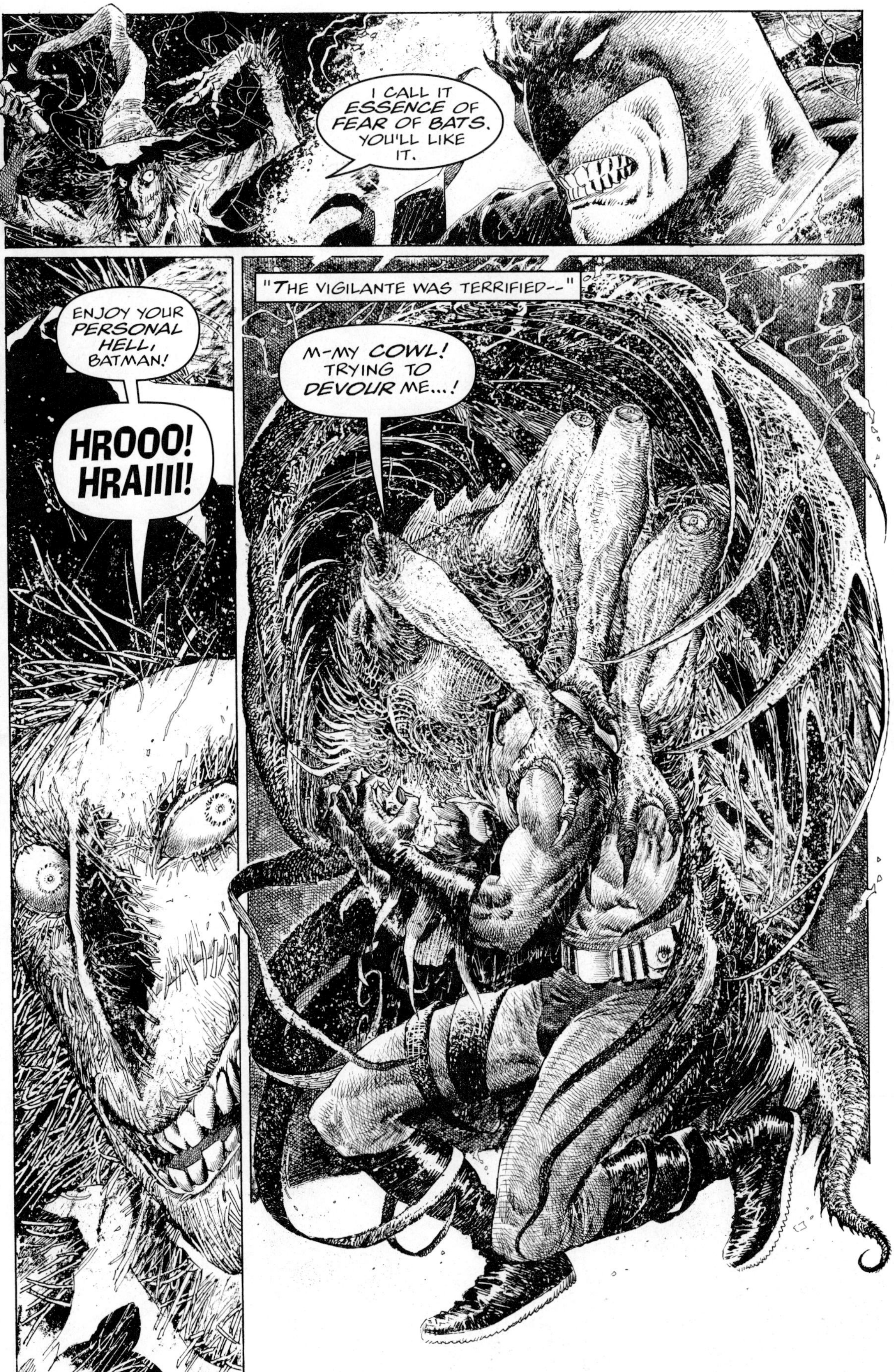
I CALL IT ESSENCE OF FEAR OF BATS. YOU'LL LIKE IT.
ENJOY YOUR PERSONAL HELL, BATMAN!
HROOO! HRAIIIII!
"THE VIGILANTE WAS TERRIFIED--"
M-MY COWL! TRYING TO DEVOUR ME...!

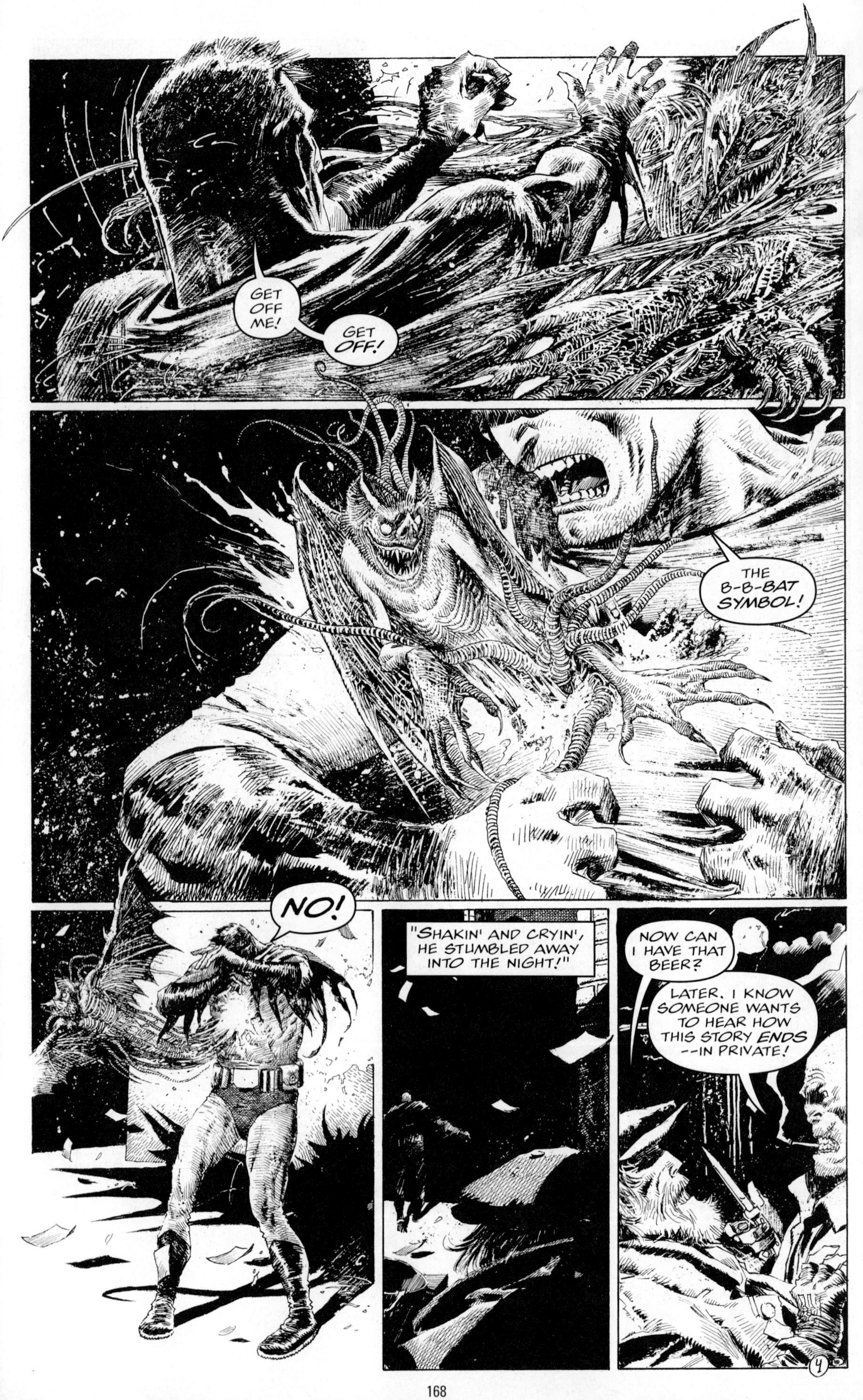
GET OFF ME!
GET OFF!
THE B-B-BAT SYMBOL!
NO!
"SHAKIN' AND CRYIN', HE STUMBLED AWAY INTO THE NIGHT!"
NOW CAN I HAVE THAT BEER?
LATER. I KNOW SOMEONE WANTS TO HEAR HOW THIS STORY ENDS --IN PRIVATE!
4

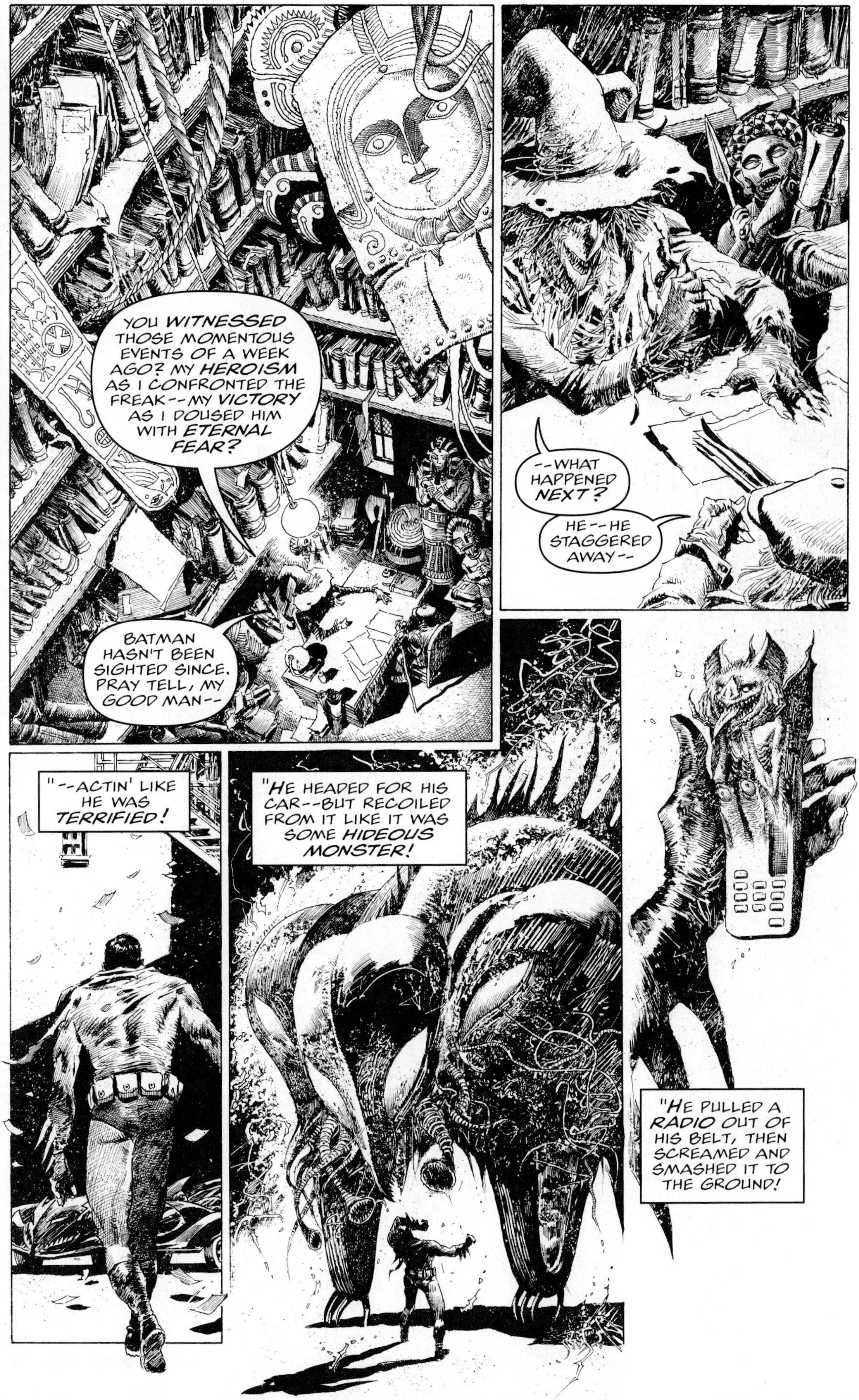
YOU WITNESSED THOSE MOMENTOUS EVENTS OF A WEEK AGO? MY HEROISM AS I CONFRONTED THE FREAK--MY VICTORY AS I DOUSED HIM WITH ETERNAL FEAR?
BATMAN HASN'T BEEN SIGHTED SINCE. PRAY TELL, MY GOOD MAN--
--WHAT HAPPENED NEXT?
HE--HE STAGGERED AWAY--
"--ACTIN' LIKE HE WAS TERRIFIED!
"HE HEADED FOR HIS CAR--BUT RECOILED FROM IT LIKE IT WAS SOME HIDEOUS MONSTER!
"HE PULLED A RADIO OUT OF HIS BELT, THEN SCREAMED AND SMASHED IT TO THE GROUND!

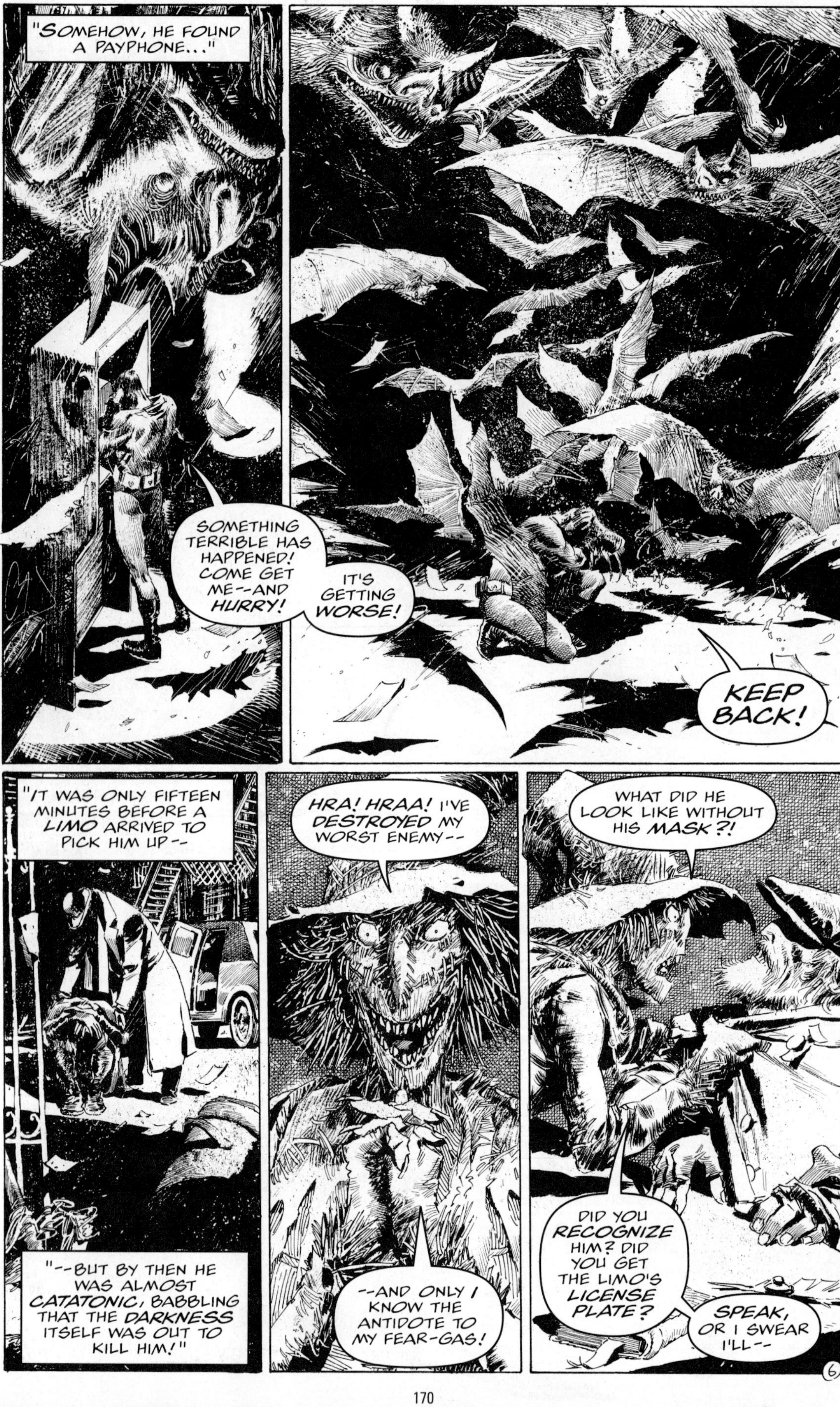
"SOMEHOW, HE FOUND A PAYPHONE..."
SOMETHING TERRIBLE HAS HAPPENED! COME GET ME--AND HURRY!
IT'S GETTING WORSE!
KEEP BACK!
"IT WAS ONLY FIFTEEN MINUTES BEFORE A LIMO ARRIVED TO PICK HIM UP--
"--BUT BY THEN HE WAS ALMOST CATATONIC, BABBLING THAT THE DARKNESS ITSELF WAS OUT TO KILL HIM!"
HRA! HRAA! I'VE DESTROYED MY WORST ENEMY--
--AND ONLY I KNOW THE ANTIDOTE TO MY FEAR-GAS!
WHAT DID HE LOOK LIKE WITHOUT HIS MASK?!
DID YOU RECOGNIZE HIM? DID YOU GET THE LIMO'S LICENSE PLATE?
SPEAK, OR I SWEAR I'LL--
6

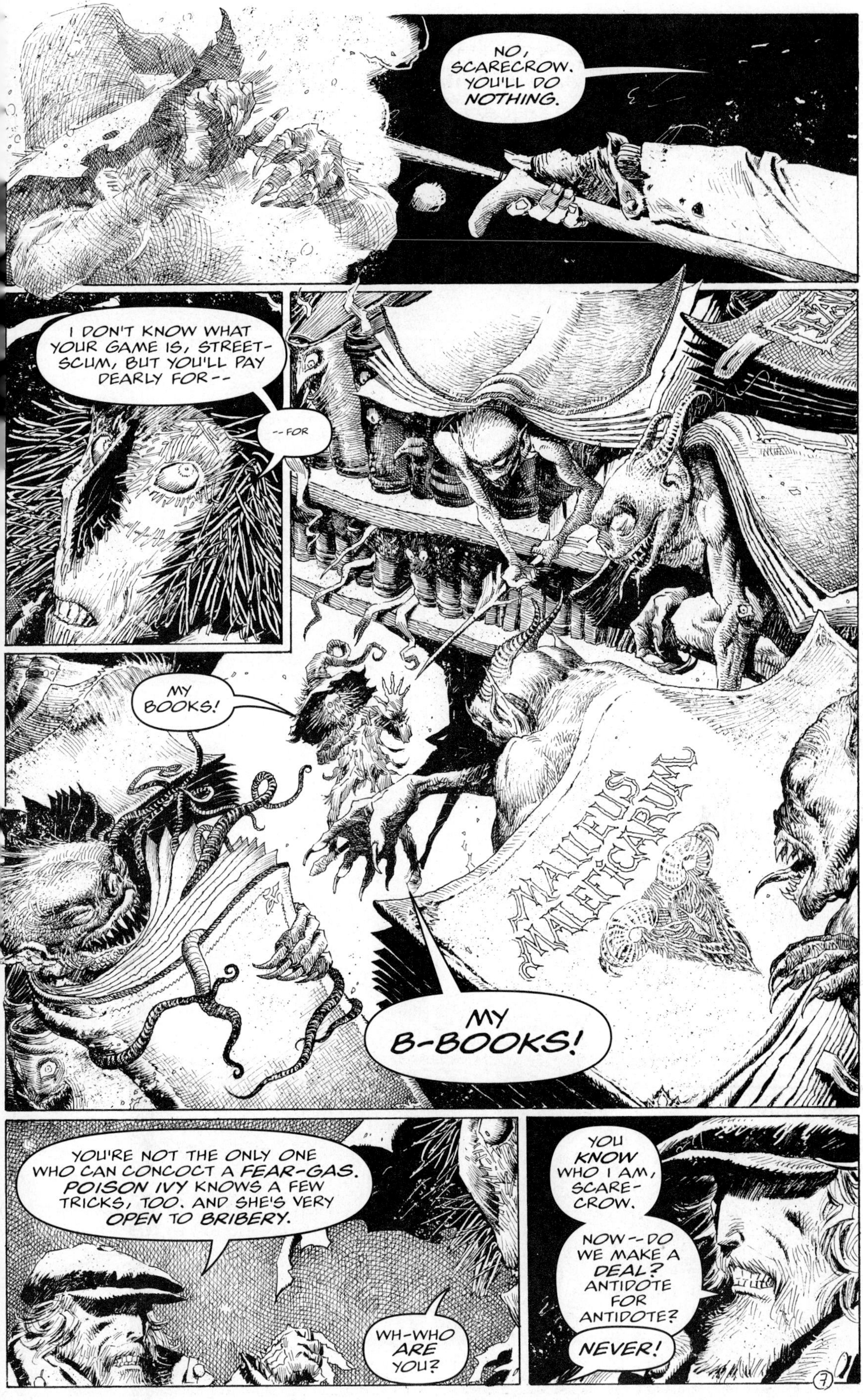
NO, SCARECROW. YOU'LL DO NOTHING.
I DON'T KNOW WHAT YOUR GAME IS, STREET-SCUM, BUT YOU'LL PAY DEARLY FOR--
--FOR
MY BOOKS!
MALLEUS MALEFICARUM
MY B-BOOKS!
YOU'RE NOT THE ONLY ONE WHO CAN CONCOCT A FEAR-GAS. POISON IVY KNOWS A FEW TRICKS, TOO. AND SHE'S VERY OPEN TO BRIBERY.
WH-WHO ARE YOU?
YOU KNOW WHO I AM, SCARE-CROW.
NOW--DO WE MAKE A DEAL? ANTIDOTE FOR ANTIDOTE?
NEVER!
7

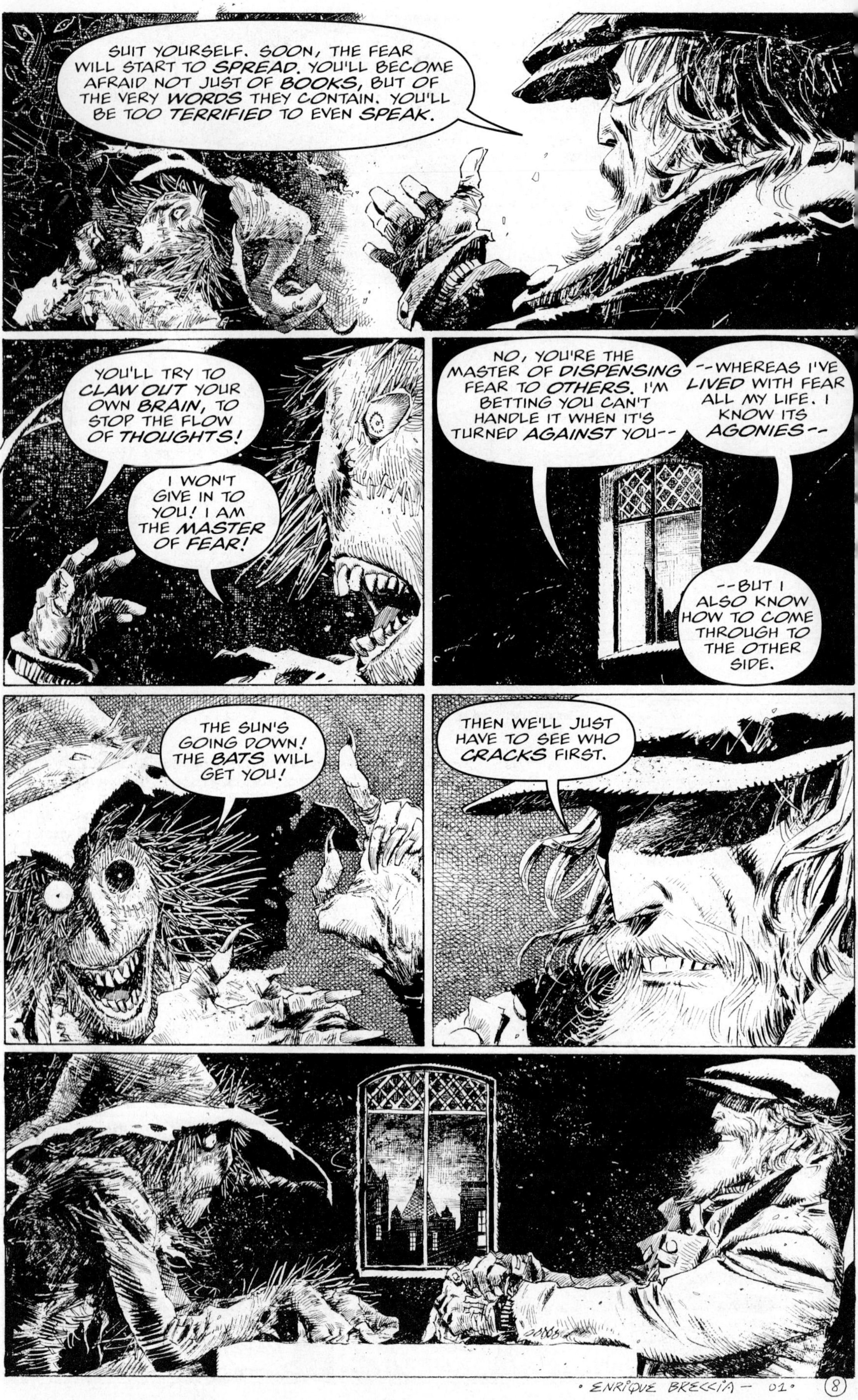
SUIT YOURSELF. SOON, THE FEAR WILL START TO SPREAD. YOU'LL BECOME AFRAID NOT JUST OF BOOKS, BUT OF THE VERY WORDS THEY CONTAIN. YOU'LL BE TOO TERRIFIED TO EVEN SPEAK.
YOU'LL TRY TO CLAW OUT YOUR OWN BRAIN, TO STOP THE FLOW OF THOUGHTS!
I WON'T GIVE IN TO YOU! I AM THE MASTER OF FEAR!
NO, YOU'RE THE MASTER OF DISPENSING FEAR TO OTHERS. I'M BETTING YOU CAN'T HANDLE IT WHEN IT'S TURNED AGAINST YOU--
--WHEREAS I'VE LIVED WITH FEAR ALL MY LIFE. I KNOW ITS AGONIES--
--BUT I ALSO KNOW HOW TO COME THROUGH TO THE OTHER SIDE.
THE SUN'S GOING DOWN! THE BATS WILL GET YOU!
THEN WE'LL JUST HAVE TO SEE WHO CRACKS FIRST.

• ENRIQUE BRECCIA — 01 •

John Arcudi applied his unique storytelling blend of action, humor, and wicked social commentary to the fan-favorite MAJOR BUMMER. He has also written notable work for GEN13 and the critically acclaimed new DOOM PATROL.

Brian Azzarello revitalized the hard-boiled crime comic book genre with his gritty 100 BULLETS, the Eisner Award-winning series that he co-created. His other DC credits include HELLBLAZER, JONNY DOUBLE, and EL DIABLO.

Kyle Baker is the Eisner Award-winning creator of such graphic novels as WHY I HATE SATURN, YOU ARE HERE, THE COWBOY WALLY SHOW, and KING DAVID. His madcap blend of kinetic art and wicked humor makes him a truly one-of-a-kind comic book genius.

Jordi Bernet made a splash on the international comics scene when he took over *Torpedo* from Alex Toth in 1982. He has been professionally illustrating comics since the age of 15, and his expressive style can be found in such books as *Tex*, *Custer*, and *Andrax*.

Enrique Breccia has been dazzling audiences on three continents for over thirty years with his gorgeous, ultra-detailed illustration on works such as the internationally popular Alvar Mayor series. His most recent effort is the fully painted LOVECRAFT graphic novel for Vertigo.

Alan Brennert won an Emmy in 1991 for the acclaimed television program *LA Law* and has written for many other TV series including *China Beach*, the '80s *Twilight Zone*, and the '90s *Outer Limits*. His prolific fiction output includes the Nebula-winning short story "Ma Qui" and the DC graphic novel BATMAN: HOLY TERROR.

Ken Bruzenak won a Harvey in 1988 for his innovative lettering work on *American Flagg!* He has lettered runs on BATMAN, *Alpha Flight*, AMERICAN CENTURY, *Fantastic Four*, AZRAEL, and many, many more.

Mark Buckingham helped define the Vertigo "look" with his atmospheric inking work on titles such as HELLBLAZER, SANDMAN, SHADE THE CHANGING MAN, and DEATH: THE HIGH COST OF LIVING. He is also a very talented penciller with runs on HELLBLAZER, BATMAN: SHADOW OF THE BAT, and *Peter Parker: Spider-Man* among his credits.

John Buscema is, quite simply, one of the legends of comic book art. John's powerful and exuberant work on such books as *Silver Surfer*, *Conan the Barbarian*, *The Avengers* and *Thor* has made an indelible impact on more than one generation of budding artists. John Buscema passed away on January 10, 2002.

John Byrne has, at one time or another, worked on virtually every character owned by Marvel and DC, including notable runs on WONDER WOMAN, *Fantastic Four*, and *The Uncanny X-Men*. His hugely successful revamp of Superman in the MAN OF STEEL miniseries launched a revival of the character whose success continues to this day.

Howard Chaykin turned the comics world on its head with such innovative and visually striking books as *American Flagg!*, *Black Kiss*, and BLACKHAWK. A pioneer of the graphic novel, Howard continues to push the boundaries of entertainment as producer/screenwriter for Hollywood projects. His most recent comic book work includes AMERICAN CENTURY for Vertigo.

Chris Claremont is one of the best-selling comics authors in the world. In addition to his stellar 17-year run on *The Uncanny X-Men*, Chris is the co-creator of several top-selling series, including *Excalibur*, *Wolverine*, and *New Mutants*. He is now writing GEN13 for WildStorm.

Gene Colan is a master of light and shadow with his cinematic renderings of such characters as Daredevil, Batman, Dracula, and Wonder Woman. Gene pioneered the use of "finished pencils" as artwork, and his 50-plus years of comic book work have left an indelible impression on the industry.

Ronnie Del Carmen is one of the most sought-after talents in animation and has worked for Warner Bros., DreamWorks SKG, and, most recently, Pixar. Ronnie's dynamic yet streamlined approach triumphs both on the printed page as well as the television and movie screen.

Paul Dini is an Emmy Award-winning writer/producer for the Batman and Superman animated television series. He is also the creator of the character Harley Quinn and has won multiple Eisners for his work on BATMAN ADVENTURES: MAD LOVE.

Warren Ellis is the award-winning creator of such cutting-edge titles as TRANSMETROPOLITAN and THE AUTHORITY. The appeal of Warren's books reaches beyond the traditional comic book readership, and both *Rolling Stone* and *Entertainment Weekly* have lauded his innovative work.

Harlan Ellison has been called "one of the greatest living American short story writers" by the *Washington Post*. In a writing career spanning more than 40 years, he has won more awards for his 62 books, 1400+ stories, essays, articles and newspaper columns, two dozen teleplays and a dozen motion pictures than any other living fantasist.

José Luis García-López helped shape the image of the super-hero in the '70s and '80s with his extensive work for DC's comics and its licensing department. His simultaneously stylish and realistic illustration can be found in hundreds of DC comics, including SUPERMAN, LEGENDS OF THE DARK KNIGHT, and the acclaimed miniseries TWILIGHT.

Dave Gibbons won the prestigious Hugo Award for his collaboration with Alan Moore on the revolutionary miniseries WATCHMEN. His distinctive art style has graced the pages of GREEN LANTERN, *2000 A.D.*, and *Give Me Liberty*. His writing credits include *Batman vs. Predator* and the 1990 SUPERMAN/BATMAN WORLD'S FINEST Prestige Format miniseries (illustrated by Steve Rude).

Alan Grant is the internationally acclaimed author of comics featuring such characters as Judge Dredd, Batman, Lobo, Robocop and Terminator. He is also the co-author of *The Bogie Man*, Scotland's best-selling independent comic, and one of the founders of Bad Press.

Gene Ha combines the meticulous, draftsmanlike quality of commercial art with the sense of wonder and drama of the comic book. His work displays a virtuosity that makes books like TOP TEN and BATMAN: FORTUNATE SON extraordinary.

Bob Kanigher is the creator of many beloved and enduring DC characters such as Sgt. Rock, The Metal Men, and Enemy Ace. The writer/editor is best known for his successful tenure on WONDER WOMAN, his revamp of the Silver Age Flash, and his powerful war stories in such comics as OUR ARMY AT WAR and SHOWCASE. He passed away on May 6, 2002.

Jim Lee debuted in the comic book world in 1986 when his art graced the pages of *Alpha Flight,* but he is most acknowledged for his trend-setting work on *Uncanny X-Men*, which was soon followed by the epic launch of the million-copy-selling issue of *X-Men* #1 in 1991. Jim is the creator of such popular comic book titles as WILDC.A.T.S and GEN 13, and is the editorial director of the groundbreaking company he founded, WildStorm Productions.

John Paul Leon has lent his frenetic and powerful artistic style to the acclaimed Milestone founding title STATIC as well as the Marvel series *Earth X*. He has also done work for books featuring Superman, Robocop, and The X-Men.

Paul Levitz distinguished himself as a comic book writer with his memorable and much-beloved run on THE LEGION OF SUPER-HEROES and his creation of The Huntress. He has been on the DC staff for almost three decades, currently as its president and publisher.

Ken Lopez entered comics in 1980 as a high school intern and has gone on to letter countless books for both Marvel and DC. His credits include JLA, JSA, HARLEY QUINN, YOUNG JUSTICE, and SUPERMAN: THE MAN OF STEEL.

Jack Morelli has had his lettering, at one time or another, appear in every modern Marvel Comics title. He is also a talented writer and is the author of the *Stars of the Negro League* trading card set.

Bill Oakley was one of our field's best and most sought-after lettering talents. His work can be found in THE LEAGUE OF EXTRAORDI-NARY GENTLEMEN, THE SPECTRE, and HAWKMAN. Bill Oakley passed away on February 16, 2004.

Tom Palmer burst onto the comics scene in the late 1960s with a fresh, illustrative inking style that perfectly complemented artists like Neal Adams, Gene Colan, and John Buscema. Tom remains an inking legend, his work adding polish to countless comics over the years. Tom is presently adding his masterly hand to the pages of *The Incredible Hulk*.

Rick Parker has had his wacky artwork appear in *The New York Times*, *The Chicago Tribune*, on *60 Minutes*, and on CNN. He has done art and lettering for too many DC and Marvel comics to list here in this humble biography.

Tom Peyer is a master of breathing new life into old characters with his quirky and highly entertaining work on such books as HOUR-MAN, TOTEMS, and L.E.G.I.O.N. His most recent work includes a run on DC/WildStorm's edgy THE AUTHORITY and Marvel's *Punisher*.

Paul Pope has gained the respect of critics in both the comic book and mainstream media with such books as *Sin Titulo*, *THB*, *Escapo*, and HEAVY LIQUID. His organic, high-energy linework has earned him the title "the Jim Morrison of comics."

Kelley Puckett received raves for his kinetic and emotionally intense scripting on BATGIRL. He is the author of BATMAN/NIGHTWING: BLOODBORNE and has also penned many memorable stories for BATMAN ADVENTURES.

Paul Rivoche has a magnificent graphic style which demonstrates a mastery of light and shadow and shows through in his work on *Mister X* and DC's Vertigo Comics miniseries BRAVE OLD WORLD.

Eduardo Risso is a masterly illustrator whose fluid, hard-hitting art style is the comic book equivalent of '40s film noir. Eduardo's work, including the award-winning 100 BULLETS which he co-created, has a loyal following in the U.S. as well as Europe and South America.

Alex Ross has helped broaden the medium of comic books with his multiple award-winning painting in such blockbusters as *Marvels* and KINGDOM COME. His bold, emblematic renderings of DC's greatest super-heroes can be found in the graphic novels BATMAN: WAR ON CRIME, SUPERMAN: PEACE ON EARTH, and WONDER WOMAN: THE SPIRIT OF TRUTH.

Steve Rude combines the classic storytelling of Kirby and Ditko with a retro/futurist vision that is all his own. Steve illustrated such books as WORLD'S FINEST and *X-Men: Children of the Atom* and also co-created the popular *Nexus* with Mike Baron in 1981.

Tim Sale is the artist of such critically and commercially successful series as SUPERMAN FOR ALL SEASONS, *Daredevil: Yellow*, BATMAN: THE LONG HALLOWEEN, and BATMAN: DARK VICTORY. His art has also graced the pages of *Billi 99*, *The Amazon*, and CHALLENGERS OF THE UNKNOWN. Tim is presently illustrating *Spider-Man: Blue* for Marvel Comics.

Tony Salmons is an artist's artist: his work on books like VIGILANTE and *Dakota North*, BATMAN: LEGENDS OF THE DARK KNIGHT and GANGLAND has earned him recognition within the professional comic artist community.

Steven T. Seagle has applied his writing talents to such acclaimed books as SANDMAN MYSTERY THEATRE, *Kafka*, HOUSE OF SECRETS, *Uncanny X-Men*, and THE CRUSADES. In addition to his comics work he has written for film, television, and animation.

Marie Severin is a brilliant cartoonist and colorist whose work graced the EC Comics of the 1950s and the Marvel comics of the 1960s. Marie's protean style can just as easily render powerful images of heroes such as The Sub-Mariner and the Hulk as it can the hilarious caricatures of *Not Brand Ecch*.

Walter Simonson first captivated the comic book community by teaming with writer Archie Goodwin on the critically acclaimed miniseries MANHUNTER. His incredible run on *Thor* revolutionized the character, and he continues to lend his epic storytelling ability to such characters as Orion.

Richard Starkings is known primarily as a purveyor of fine lettering but has worked in the comic book industry as a cartoonist, writer, colorist, production manager, and publisher. He founded the Comicraft Design and Lettering studio with John "JG" Roshell in 1992.

Ty Templeton captured the essence of the animated Caped Crusader's charm with his run on BATMAN: GOTHAM ADVENTURES as cover artist and writer. Ty's art and clever writing style is suffused with a bouncy sense of humor that has made him one of the industry's top comedic talents.

Daniel Torres came to the attention of European and American comic book audiences with his successful series of books based on his character Rocco Vargas. His clean, distinct linework has graced the pages of such books as *Opium*, *El Octavo Dia* and *Aphrodite*.

John G. Workman has worn many hats during his 30+ years in the comics industry: editor, writer, designer, art director, penciller, inker, colorist, and production director. His lettering has graced the pages of countless DC titles.

BATMAN BLACK and WHITE

DON'T MISS THESE OTHER

BATMAN BLACK AND WHITE COLLECTIONS!

BATMAN
BLACK and WHITE

BATMAN
BLACK & WHITE
VOLUME THREE

FEATURING THE TALENTS OF:

NEAL **ADAMS** CHRISTIAN **ALAMY** DOUG **ALEXANDER** MICHAEL **ALLRED** BRENT **ANDERSON** MARK **ASKWITH** TERRY **AUSTIN** BRIAN **AZZARELLO** CHRIS **BACHALO** MIKE W. **BARR** HILARY **BARTA** **BATT** SIMON **BISLEY** BRIAN **BOLLAND** JOHN **BOLTON** PHILIP **BOND** ED **BRUBAKER** MIKE **CAREY** MIKE **CARLIN** CLAUDIO **CASTELLINI** TOMMY **CASTILLO** HOWARD **CHAYKIN** ERIC **CHERRY** DARWYN **COOKE** RICHARD **CORBEN** DENYS **COWAN** ALAN **DAVIS** DAN **DECARLO** TODD **DEZAGO** CHUCK **DIXON** DANIELLE **DWYER** MARK **FARMER** JOHN **FLOYD** NATHAN **FOX** NEIL **GAIMAN** ALEX **GARLAND** GARY **GIANNI** DAVE **GIBBONS** DICK **GIORDANO** MICHAEL **GOLDEN** ARCHIE **GOODWIN** PAUL **GRIST** ROB **HAYNES** ANDREW **HELFER** KLAUS **JANSON** GEOFF **JOHNS** MICHAEL WILLIAM **KALUTA** JOE **KELLY** TEDDY **KRISTIANSEN** JOE **KUBERT** PAUL **KUPPERBERG** JIM **LEE** **LIBERATORE** JIM **MAHFOOD** STEVE **MANNION** DWAYNE **MCDUFFIE** DON **MCGREGOR** TED **MCKEEVER** MICK **MCMAHON** MIKE **MIGNOLA** FRANK **MILLER** **MOEBIUS** SCOTT **MORSE** DEAN **MOTTER** JOSÉ **MUÑOZ** TROY **NIXEY** ANN **NOCENTI** KEVIN **NOWLAN** DENNIS **O'NEIL** JOHN **OSTRANDER** KATSUHIRO **OTOMO** JASON **PEARSON** SCOTT **PETERSON** WILL **PFEIFER** SEAN **PHILLIPS** WHILCE **PORTACIO** JON **PROCTOR** RODNEY **RAMOS** DAN **RASPLER** SAL **REGLA** ROBERT **RODI** P. CRAIG **RUSSELL** TONY **SALMONS** MARK **SCHULTZ** JULIUS **SCHWARTZ** BILL **SIENKIEWICZ** MARC **SILVESTRI** WALTER **SIMONSON** RYAN **SOOK** BRIAN **STELFREEZE** KARL **STORY** JAN **STRNAD** KIMO **TEMPERANCE** BRUCE **TIMM** JILL **THOMPSON** ALEX **TOTH** CYRUS **VORIS** MATT **WAGNER** JOHN **WATKISS** AARON **WEISENFELD** MIKE **WIERINGO** KENT **WILLIAMS** SCOTT **WILLIAMS** BARRY **WINDSOR-SMITH** JUDD **WINICK** BILL **WRAY** JORGE **ZAFFINO** DANIJEL **ZEZELJ**

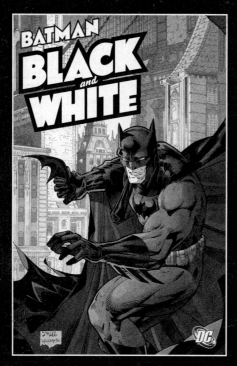

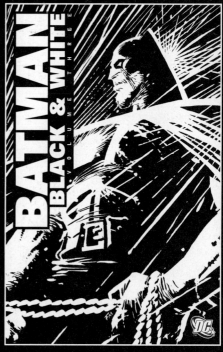